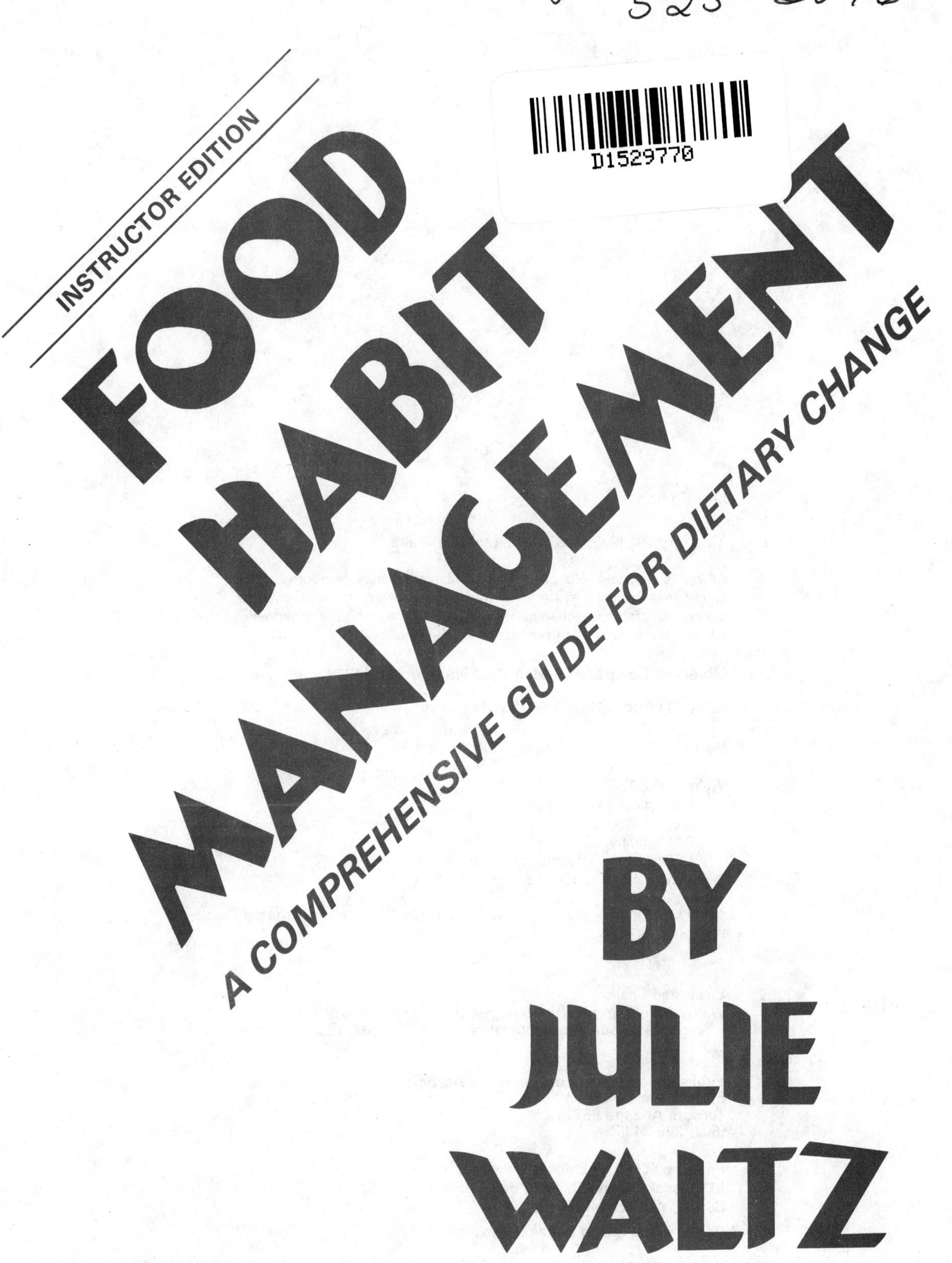
INSTRUCTOR EDITION
FOOD
HABIT
MANAGEMENT
A COMPREHENSIVE GUIDE FOR DIETARY CHANGE
BY
JULIE
WALTZ

1987 Edition

Library of Congress Catalog Card Number: 82-14338

ISBN: 0-931836-01-8-17.95

Library of Congress Cataloging in Publication Data

Waltz, Julie, 1942-
Food Habit Management

Bibliography: p.
1. Reducing—Psychological aspects.
2. Behavior modification. 3. Food habits.
I. Title.
RM222.2.W265 613.2'5'019 82-14338
ISBN 0-931836-00-X

Suggested Citation:
Waltz, Julie. *Food Habit Management.* Tucson, Arizona: Northwest Learning Associates Inc., 1978, 1982, 1987

Published by Northwest Learning Associates Inc.
5728 N. Via Umbrosa
Tucson, Arizona 85715
(602) 299-8435

Printed by Outdoor Empire Publishing, Inc.
511 Eastlake Avenue E., P.O. Box C-19000
Seattle, Washington 98109

Printed in the United States of America.

To all of you
whose goal is to help others
reach their goals.

INTRODUCTION

This book provides the essentials necessary for proper implementation of **Food Habit Management** techniques. Behavior modification, applied learning theory, and self-management training are combined to teach people how to develop functional eating habits and patterns. The purpose of this book is to teach people the **process** of developing and establishing good food habits, assessing current eating patterns and food intake, isolating problem areas and specific needs, developing control strategies related to specific problems and needs, experimenting with strategies, evaluating the results, and when necessary, redesigning the strategies and once again experimenting with and evaluating them until the desired results are obtained. When the above techniques and exercises are practiced thoroughly, they will produce the desired results—proper food habit management.

Diagrammatically, the process looks like this:

Once learned, this process can be applied repeatedly whenever eating patterns need to be changed. As people's life situations change, their eating patterns may change, and this process will help them to adjust. In short, people learn a process which carries them from awareness of the need for changes in eating patterns to establishment of those changes.

Although this book is aimed at habits relevant to weight loss and maintenance, it can also be used, with appropriate modification, to effect changes in other dietary needs, such as reduced sodium, fat or carbohydrate diets. Appropriate modifications would have to be made in some of the assignments and in some of the suggestions, but the over-all process of assessment, isolation of problems and needs, development of strategies, experimentation and evaluation remains the same. Consequently, this book may be used in conjunction with dietary instructions for heart disease, hypertension, diabetes, and other medical or dental problems, as well as in the programs for the elderly, and athletic and fitness programs.

This book is appropriate for any person who is sincere about wanting to change his or her eating habits, and who is willing to put forth the time and effort necessary to accomplish those changes. It is not appropriate for anyone who is looking for a quick and easy way to lose weight. The responsibility for learning the material clearly belongs to the student. Each person who studies the book will be gathering information and conducting a series of personal experiments, represented formally by the end-of-the-chapter assignments. These assignments are the means through which the book is individualized for each person. Therefore, it is essential that people not only do the assignments, but also that they both want to do them and allow sufficient time in their schedules to do them regularly.

Instructors who use this book need not have professional training in medicine, nutrition or related fields to teach it as it is written. What is required is an honest desire to work with people who have weight or dietary problems, and the ability to work effectively with people in an individual or classroom situation. Specific nutritional guidance beyond the information written in Chapter 16, "Nutritional Considerations in Weight Loss and Control," should be given only by a dietitian, physician, or someone specifically trained to provide nutritional consultation.

Everything in color is for the instructor's use. This material is a guide to help you, the instructor, develop your own course in **Food Habit Management.** There are suggestions for organizing and teaching the course and some thoughts about ways of supporting desired change. Objectives and supplementary instructions are included for each of the first fourteen lessons, along with instructions for supplementary lessons 15 through 17, and for the recording forms and reference tools. **These instructions have been overlaid in color onto the student text so that your format and pagination are identical with that of your students.** Consequently, existing blank pages were used for your instructions and where some inconsistency in their location occurs, an editor's note at the beginning of each new section will direct you to the appropriate pages. Beginning with Chapter 6, the number of pages of recording forms following each chapter has been reduced to accustom students to refer to the back of the book for extra forms. There are sufficient forms for continued daily recording after completion of the course.

Food Habit Management may be modified to fit specific needs. Additions, omissions, condensations, combinations, and sequential changes of lessons are totally appropriate. The basis for **Food Habit Management** is provided in this book. Now the task is to personalize it in your own way and teach the course.

TABLE OF CONTENTS

LESSON OUTLINES AND INSTRUCTIONS

Instructor Notes begin on pages shown below.

SUPPLEMENTARY LESSONS—OUTLINES AND INSTRUCTIONS

INSTRUCTION OUTLINES FOR RECORDING FORMS AND REFERENCE TOOLS

TEACHING IN A THERAPEUTIC SETTING

Teaching in a therapeutic setting is no different than teaching in any other kind of setting except for the tendencies to: **(1)** follow up on emotional issues which are not directly related to the class discussion, and **(2)** become less attentive toward applying the basic rules of learning theory. The following outline includes many of the basic issues involved in effective teaching but it is not an all-inclusive list. The purpose of presenting this outline is to raise instructors' levels of consciousness regarding their teaching techniques.

A. Basic Objectives

1. To transfer mastery of old skills to mastery of new skills.
2. To teach **the process** of working with oneself within the context of class material.
3. To teach students how things work—the framework upon which the theories and techniques are built. The specific techniques become "end points" and not used as tools to accomplish the task unless the framework is built. Simply teaching weight loss exercises is far less effective for long-term use than would be true if the framework of human behavior was taught and the weight loss techniques were placed on and within the context of that framework. **People tend to remember the principles and overlying methodology longer and more effectively than they remember most of the specific little tasks.**
4. To give students the experience of trying things out, of seeing what is effective.

B. Developing an Effective Class

1. Appropriate goals. (For the instructor)

   a. Mastery cannot be accomplished within the time limit of most classes. Can you become a proficient skier in a six-lesson course? You can learn enough to be able to follow through with practice between the lessons and when the lessons are completed. The real learning is most often a solitary occurance—it happens between the student and the skiis, between the student and the piano, etc. **The instructional lessons prepare the student to accomplish that learning and they guide the learning tasks in sequential levels so that they are within the student's capabilities.**

   b. Realize that much of the class time may be used by a student to change attitudes and "mind sets"; to see things in terms of "How can I?" instead of "Why can't I?"; to learn how to proceed independently.

   c. Teach the students to work for improvement, rather than perfection. Improvement is a stimulus for continued effort, but perfection is often a stimulus for frustration and a sense of failure.

2. Effective learning climate.

   a. Individualizing the course for each person.

   (1). Have the students select their own tasks for practice within each lesson's assignment.

   (2). Base suggested homework tasks upon the results of the previous week's performance.

   (3). Ask students to relate principles from class discussion to their own experiences and situations.

   b. Graduating the difficulty of the learning tasks.

   (1). Make sure each week's assignments are flexible enough to allow students to select their tasks according to capability. Example: selection of specific techniques, adjustment of frequency or duration, etc.

   (2). Again, stress improvement, not perfection. Few humans attain sainthood anyway and when people strive only for perfection it perpetuates the "all or nothing approach": I do it all perfectly or I do none of it at all. Thus, they set themselves up to do nothing rather than something. (I mentioned this point earlier and have repeated it again because the perfection goal is so common among students, and creates a tremendous obstacle in the learning process.)

   (3). If a student consistently avoids a given task or follows through poorly in the practice of it, assume it is too difficult and swap it for a different task. It would be easier to assume that lack of motivation or poor student compliance is the problem but more often than not, the real problem is that the student either does not know how to do the task or finds the task too difficult to do.

   c. Providing a low risk atmosphere for learning.

   (1). Teach the concept of **experimentation.** If the experiment fails, it represents a strategy or technique error rather than a personal failure. Then, it's "back to the drawing board" to design a new strategy or try a different technique.

(2). Teach your students that the purpose of trying different tasks and strategies is for them to discover **how they respond** when using them. If the tasks/strategies produce a desirable response from them, they can then consider building them into habitual patterns. If they don't like their response or find the task useless, they can discard it or swap it for a different one, again for the purpose of discovering the gamut and variety of things which are effective with them.

(3). Transmit the attitude that your students don't ever have to do the specific tasks or assignments again, if they don't want to, when the class is over. The job during class is to simply try new ideas, approaches and procedures on for size to see how or whether they fit. When they get through investigating, they can select which, if any, tasks they want to maintain. This notion gets many students past the resistance to trying new things and to the feeling of being overwhelmed by the discovery that there is so much they could, or should do. It puts the choice about future commitment into the students' hands, and delays consideration of that choice until the end of the class (course). Thus, students are freer to experiment during the class without feeling that they have to continue doing every single task they find effective.

d. Teaching the importance of risk-taking and mistake-making.

(1). Trying something new involves taking risks; taking risks implies making mistakes. Mistakes, though, are human, normal, natural and part of the learning process. In trying to get this concept across to my students, I often use the following example. "You couldn't learn to do figure eights on ice skates without leaning over on the edge of your skates. To lean over means you run the risk of falling down. If you never fall down you don't learn how far you can lean in one direction, and how far you need to lean to accomplish the turn. In other words, risk is part of the learning process for anything and so are mistakes." I tell all of my students that I hope they fail at least once during the class—that way I'll know they were trying new things and not just playing around with what they already had experience with.

(2). "So you made a mistake—what did you learn?" Teach students how to handle the mistakes they make. Teach them to manually shift their heads through the processes of reevaluation and establishment of a new plan to offset the emotional browbeating they might customarily do when they make a mistake (why didn't I, couldn't I, won't I; what's the matter with me; I'm no good, stupid; etc.)

(3). Teach students to record information about their mistakes for future learning. Ex.: I have students record everything they eat when on a binge (without counting calories!) as well as some of the circumstances which preceeded the binge, like mood or feeling, prior activity, etc. The reasons for this are: **(a)** it gives them a chance, later on, to go over all their binge records to determine any possible patterns of emotional response, food selection or anything that might help them plan ahead effectively to reduce the food consumption or off-set future binges; **(b)** it turns a negative occurance into something of at least some positive value; and **(c)** by approaching it in a matter-of-fact manner it takes away some of the negative pay off for having a binge and reduces some of the fear and anxiety associated with binges.

e. Teaching students to accept their "humanness".

(1). Flexibility: learning how to let up without letting go of the control plan. People frequently load extra tasks upon themselves when under stress or when fatigued. When they can't do everything they expect themselves to do, but insist upon doing everything anyway, they create a situation in which they set up and promote their own failure. **The task is to teach them how to make a "stress plan" of limited, sequentially difficult tasks.**

(2). Re-starting the control plan. No matter how proficient people are in using their new habits, periodically they simply "blow the whole routine". Getting back to the control plan sometimes presents a formidable psychological hurdle, especially if immediate return to full and perfect control is the goal. **Teach the concept of "reconditioning".** When a runner breaks training and doesn't run for a few days, he knows that on the first day he returns to running he can't run the same distance with the same speed as he did prior to stopping. He therefore establishes a retraining or reconditioning plan of shorter time periods and shorter distances and incrementally lengthens them until, as speed and endurance are increased, he has returned to the full distance in the desired time. This notion applies well to what happens when a student breaks behavioral training and has to establish a reconditioning plan for return to previous levels of performance. The step from full to zero control is relatively easy; the step from zero to full control is too large and **requires a specific plan of smaller steps to make return to full control achievable without excess stress or time expenditure.**

(3). Taking a night off. Periodically students resist using their control plans because they simply want to wallow in their old behavior. Sometimes lack of compliance or poor attendance are signs of the need for a sanctioned night off. In the Food Habit Management program this is interpreted as the need for a binge. By recognizing this very human need and planning around it you can teach students how to recognize and cope with that need themselves. For example, I teach students how to have a planned "food holiday" which is a sanctioned, time-limited, planned period of free eating with a previously established plan of what to do and what to eat on the first and second days following the holiday. All foods for those two days are prepared and prepackaged for consumption in advance.

People tend to eat what they prepared because that's easiest and thus, people slide back into a pattern which makes return to the original control plan much easier on the third day. For people with an established frequency of binges, the holidays are planned just prior to each anticipated binge. Those who only have occasional binges plan their holidays accordingly. Others simply develop a holiday menu of all the foods they've been choosing not to eat and carry the list around in the eventuality that they may someday want to have a holiday. For them the knowledge that they can have a holiday is all they need to break their resistance to long-term control.

C. Maximizing Learning

1. Let students relate their learning experiences since the last class session before starting on new class material. Discuss what went well, what didn't work so well, problem-solve and evolve new plans for the mistakes or failures. If people can clear their minds of old business and questions first, they are freer to concentrate on new information. By starting with the discussion first, it warms the group up, establishes cohesion and allows the latecomers to hear the new material without your having to repeat yourself. This way you can get the class started on time, thus reinforcing those students who were punctual. Also, giving students the opportunity to talk about their "experiments" encourages them to do the homework assignments.

2. In teaching the lesson use terms and language that **all** of your students can understand. Complex terminology is nice for professionals but if your students feel devalued because they can't understand what you've said, you reduce their opportunities for successful and enthusiastic learning.

3. Use stories and illustrative examples wherever possible. People love stories and it helps to hold their attention. Encourage your students to contribute experiential stories of their own.

4. Use a multi-sensory approach. Straight lecture is known to be the least effective avenue for teaching. Vary the routine by use of the chalkboard, having the students write something, having students verbally apply the principles to their own situations, or use role play or "action" exercises.

5. Repeat the important information at least once. If you aren't sure your message got through to the students, ask someone to rephrase or paraphrase it.

6. Encourage study at home through the use of related, useful homework assignments. If students see the value of the assignments and if they are taught how to learn from doing them, they will be likelier to do them consistently. It is helpful to view recording forms as instruments for discovering information and measuring progress, and if students look upon them in these ways and are taught to use them accordingly, follow-through is much better. Also teach them that partial completion of homework is far better than no completion; that logging data in retrospect is far better than logging nothing. If they don't remember to record until 3:00 p.m. it is better to record for the remainder of the day and to try to recall what happened prior to that time so that they **(a)** don't have a handy excuse for not doing the recording and **(b)** are not encouraged to do nothing because they couldn't do it all perfectly.

7. Ask your students to go home and teach each lesson to someone they live, work or socialize with. By having to make sense out of each lesson in order to explain it to someone else, they are forced to think about and internalize the information, and questions or gaps in understanding are made obvious so that they can consult with you about them at the next class session. Teaching each lesson has two additional benefits: it encourages people to follow through on the assignments because they've publicly disclosed their intent, and it teaches another person what's going on so that that person can be more appropriately supportive.

8. Have your students list ways they are likely to sabotage their chances of success in the course and sign an agreement to purposely put off using them until after the course is over.

9. Have your students list ways they could support their progress and to purposely follow through with at least one of them during the course.

10. Support your students' successes, no matter how small. When you hear reports of "Well, I only did it a couple of times—it should have been more," turn it around by reinforcing that the couple of times they did do it is what is important, and how could they set themselves up to do it a couple of more times during the coming week?

11. If your students didn't do the assigned work, don't make a big deal out of it. Ask them how they could help themselves follow through better during the coming week and go on to something else. It is often helpful to ask them to specify what they could do to ensure better follow through, like telling someone else what their tasks will be, putting up reminder notes, blocking a specific and appropriate hour out of each day's schedule for study, etc. Some students won't complete their recording forms, even though they will do some behavior change experiments. When this happens it may be helpful to remember that some students have to "audit" the course before they can "take" the course; they have to try it out before they can commit themselves to studying it. Some people get into a swimming pool by just jumping into the water; others put their toes in first, then both feet, then wade in up to their knees, shiver and complain, then wade in a little farther until, at long last, they are fully submerged.

The responsibility for learning clearly belongs to the student. The instructor's job is to provide the best climate possible for learning to take place, and to prepare the content and assignments in such a way that the student is able to utilize the learning tools to teach himself. And when problems arise in the course of learning, the instructor's job is to help the student recognize what the problems and needs are, and to teach him how to determine a new course of action.

DESIGNING THE COURSE

The **Food Habit Management** book may be used exactly as it is written. The basic information, illustrative stories and examples, recording forms and instructions for their use, and supplementary lessons on nutrition and exercise are all provided. The sequence of lessons may be used without modification. Many instructors, however, prefer to alter the course in some way. The purpose of this chapter is to present a variety of suggestions for ways to adapt the course to your particular needs and wishes. Some considerations for determining the course content, the length of the course, the frequency and length of each session, class size, classroom setting, additional materials, fees and payment, teaching assistants, follow-up sessions, and some guidelines for selecting students are presented throughout this chapter.

COURSE CONTENT

There are fourteen distinct Food Habit Management lessons in the student's book. Whether your course is aimed at men, women, working or nonworking people, adolescents or retired people, some lessons will be more important, will require more emphasis, or be less relevant than other lessons. Except for the first and last ones, the remaining lessons may be used in any sequence, combined, or omitted, as circumstances dictate. For example, you may adjust the timing of the lesson on Vacations and Holidays to coincide with the dates of specific holidays. Or the nutrition and exercise lessons may be added separately, combined with other lessons, exchanged for lessons of your own on the same subjects, or left to the students to read and practice on their own. It goes without saying that additional information of your own on related subjects may be inserted wherever you choose. Only the first and last lessons need to remain unchanged in content and sequence. The first lesson and its homework provide the foundation from which the entire course is built; and the last lesson represents the bridge between the course and independent maintenance of progress.

Though the Food Habit Management course is not a diet program itself, specific diets may be used in conjunction with it **as long as concentration upon food habit change** is not lost. Stringent diets of less than 1,000 calories per day, or very rigid weight-reducing diets which require strict adherence to lists of acceptable and unacceptable foods are not recommended for use with this course. Diets of these types prevent the students from experimenting with many of the suggested assignments. Unless students have the freedom to learn to develop control with problem foods and have some freedom to select foods based upon their needs at the time, they will not learn long-term control. The issue is not to teach people to avoid particular foods, when there is no medical reason for their restriction, but rather how to have them in limited quantities. Most of the students I work with find that the freedom to have desirable foods is also the freedom not to **have** to have them. In other words, forbidding consumption of particular foods often has the effect of making these foods even more desirable. When one bite is taken of such a food, effective control of how much is eaten may be lost. For these reasons the use of a daily calorie count or a dietary exchange plan is preferred. Both of them allow people to make their own food choices while providing them with guidelines to follow.

People on long-term, permanent, or special diets (such as those which require reduction of salt, sugar, fat, gluten or other food substances because of medical needs) can use them in conjunction with the course. The habit changes need to be made in light of the requirements of the diet, and modifications in the homework can be made as needed. Some concepts like the food holiday, discussed in lesson thirteen, may have to be modified or eliminated based upon the particular person's dietary plan. The lesson on food substitutions for snack control may also require modification.

The use of appetite suppressants is not recommended for this course, because of the importance of teaching students to apply behavioral control techniques for the regulation of food intake. If you intend to use appetite suppressants, begin using them after the first lesson and terminate them before the midpoint of the course is reached. The entire second half of the course should be taught without the aid of any temporary control measure. Then, when the course is completed, the students will have the conviction that their progress was the result of their own efforts and not because of the appetite suppressants.

For students who have had intestinal by-pass surgery, or gastroplasty or who have been on a medically-supervised fasting program, this course is both appropriate and necessary for long-term weight control. Ideally, students who are preparing for either surgery or a supervised fast should do the first lesson **before** the surgery or the start of the supervised fast. During recovery they apply the environmental control techniques and study the lessons on mealtime patterns, snack control, social eating, nutrition and exercise. They could also learn how to use the food data records and to measure food portions accurately. Time delay and social eating strategies could be planned in advance. As students resume regular food consumption, they are likely to be intellectually and psychologically prepared to apply behavioral control techniques. Moreover, they are more likely to do so if they have previously invested a lot of time and effort in studying and planning. If, however, you do not have contact with these students until after recovery from surgery or completion of the fasting program, begin the course with the very first lesson. Don't encourage them to eat everything they want. Rather, encourage them to record their urges for food, as explained in the instructions for that lesson. It will be essential for these students to record their food intake daily and to have definite techniques to use for regulating and pacing their food consumption. The environmental control lessons should be taught next, and the rest of the lessons can be given in whatever sequence seems most appropriate.

LENGTH OF THE COURSE

The course can be adjusted to almost any length by combining some lessons, eliminating those that aren't relevant, and adding your own lessons. The course can be taught in as short a time as six weeks, or it can be taught over a period of several months. Here are some examples of ways to combine the lessons in the book to shorten or lengthen the course.

Six-Session Course

1	Before You Begin and Environmental Impact and Food Cues
2	Controlling Your Home Environment PLUS Controlling Your Work Environment or Daily Food Management
3	Controlling Your Mealtime Environment and Eating Slowly: Reducing Efficiency Extra Assignment: Control Meals
4	Snack Control: Delayed Eating Response and Snack Control: Food Substitutions
5	Social Eating: Restaurants and Social Eating: Buffets, Cafeterias, Entertaining at Home Extra Assignment: Restart/Stress Plan
6	Maintaining Control

Assign the lesson on Vacations and Holidays and the supplementary lessons on support, nutrition and exercise for study and practice after the course is completed. A lot of information is crowded into a six-session format. There are, however, some specific ways a six-session course could be useful.

1. To provide a study and training structure for people who feel that if they just knew how to set up a program for themselves, they could follow through with it on their own. This is for people who are newly overweight or who basically have a management problem with respect to food selection and placement.
2. To offer people who are not committed to making change an opportunity to "audit" the course, to experiment with the techniques and approach in order to determine their readiness for change or the applicability of the course to their needs. Students do pay tuition, but the short course format allows skeptical people a slightly less expensive, less extensive opportunity to determine whether or not the approach suits their particular learning style.
3. To provide a review course for people who have previously taken this or a similar course and feel the need for a "booster shot" to reinforce what they are doing; to get some new ideas; to update their daily plans to fit new life circumstances; or to simply get them back into the rhythm of active study and change.

Eight-Session Course

1	Before You Begin and Environmental Impact and Food Cues
2	Controlling Your Home Environment and Controlling Your Work Environment
3	Controlling Your Mealtime Environment and Eating Slowly: Reducing Efficiency
4	Daily Food Management and Control Meals
5	Snack Control: Delayed Eating Response Snack Control: Food Substitutions
6	Social Eating: Restaurants Social Eating: Buffets, Cafeterias, Entertaining at Home
7	Restart/Stress Plan Vacations and Holidays
8	Maintaining Control and Developing a Support Network

The information on nutrition could be added to each of the lessons; it could be added as a separate lesson to make a nine-session course; or it could replace one of the lessons in the sequence. The information on exercise could be inserted to create a ten-session course, it could be blended into several lessons, it could replace an existing lesson, or be assigned for independent study after completion of the course.

Twelve-Session Course

1	Before You Begin and Environmental Impact and Food Cues
2	Controlling Your Home Environment
3	Controlling Your Work Environment and Daily Food Management

4 Controlling Your Mealtime Environment
Eating Slowly: Reducing Efficiency

5 Nutritional Considerations in Weight Loss and Control

6 Snack Control: Delayed Eating Response
Snack Control: Food Substitutions

7 Social Eating: Restaurants
Social Eating: Buffets, Cafeterias, Entertaining at Home

8 Developing Your Personal Exercise Program

9 Control Meals
Restart/Stress Plan

10 Vacations and Holidays
(Reinforce Application of Control Meals)

11 Developing A Support Network

12 Maintaining Control

This format allows you to pair related lessons together. The reason for combining the lessons on controlling the work environment and daily food management is to allow students who are employed and those who work at home to select the lesson most appropriate for them. Women who work outside of the home may need to focus on both lessons, emphasizing the lesson which meets their greatest need. The Control Meals lesson pairs well with the Restart /Stress Plan lesson since each provides a separate dimension of restart planning. The Control Meals lesson also pairs well with the Vacations and Holidays lesson since both lessons emphasize techniques for building flexibility. Carrying over the Control Meals lesson from one week to the next allows you to spend a greater proportion of time on the Restart/Stress Plan, while being able to introduce the Control Meals concept. Then, in the following lesson, you could pick up on the Control Meals chapter and tie it in to vacation and holiday meal planning.

There is no limit to the ways the chapters in this book can be sequenced, blended, substituted, replaced, or expanded. Additional information of your own can be inserted into weekly lessons, substituted for one or more chapters in the book, or inserted to expand the length of the course. Specific chapters may be singled out and taught separately as periodic reinforcement or follow-up lessons for former students. For example, teach the Suggestions for Holiday Weight Control from Chapter 13 as a pre-Christmas planning workshop. You could even open that up to the public as advertising for your longer course, which you could schedule for the following January. The Restart/Stress Plan chapter could be developed into a single session post-holiday restart planning workshop, following the Christmas season, and used for follow-up or as a public introduction to you and your course. Except for the first and last lessons (Chapters 1 and 14) there is no mandatory sequence to where each lesson is placed. All chapters not directly assigned for study during the course are, of course, available to your students for study when the course is completed.

Another alternative is to provide two Food Habit Management courses: a basic skills course and an advanced course. Here is an example for Food Habit Management Part I and Part II.

Part I

1 Before You Begin and
Environmental Impact and Food Cues

2 Controlling Your Home Environment PLUS
Controlling Your Work Environment or
Daily Food Management

3 Controlling Your Mealtime Environment and
Eating Slowly: Reducing Efficiency

4 Snack Control: Delayed Eating Response
Snack Control: Food Substitutions

5 Social Eating: Restaurants
Social Eating: Buffets, Cafeterias, Entertaining at Home

6 Maintaining Control

Blend in the material from Nutritional Considerations in Weight Loss and Control, beginning with the third week.

Part II

1 Restart Planning:
Control Meals
Restart/Stress Plan

2 Exercise:
Developing Your Personal Exercise Program

3 Building Flexibility:
Vacations and Holidays
Control Meals

4 Support:
Developing a Support Network

The advantage of a two-part course is that it allows students to feel they can advance to a higher level of training. Part II provides a "fresh" start for people whose enthusiasm is sagging. The two-part system allows former students who want periodic reinforcement or retraining to enroll in whichever part of the course they need the most.

FREQUENCY AND LENGTH OF CLASS SESSIONS

The Food Habit Management course is designed for presentation of only one lesson each week to provide a sufficient amount of time for experimentation and practice. As in lessons of any type, the hours of practice between instruction periods are the essential ingredient for success. The once-a-week format also discourages people from becoming too dependent upon the group or instructor.

One-and-a-half to two hours should be allowed for each class session, depending upon your comfort and preference. Classes of longer than two hours become tiresome for everyone; one-hour sessions may not give you enough time for group discussion, presentation of new material and explanation of homework. One-hour session work best for individualized instruction.

Occasionally people will miss a session for one reason or another. Establish a policy for make-up lessons and let your students know what it is at the first class or individual session. If people know they will have to miss two or more sessions at the time of registration, encourage them to take the course later on when they will be able to attend all of the sessions.

CLASS SIZE

Determine the size of your classes by the capacity of the classroom and the number of students you feel comfortable working with. Generally, enrollments of eight to twelve people appear to be optimal for both instructors and students. Classes of fewer than four students are too small to offer a satisfactory group experience, particularly if someone misses a session. Classes of more than fifteen students may be too large to allow you to give each student some individual attention during each class. My experience, and the experience of other instructors, is that people achieve better progress in a group situation than they do when taking the course in an individual one-to-one arrangement. People learn a great deal from each other's experiences, and group sessions tend to be less tedious and more fun. Remember, however, that it is the individual attention you give to each student which keeps them active, personally invested and feeling good about the course. So be careful not to short-change that time by having too many students in your class.

CLASSROOM SETTING

As implied earlier in the chapter, this course may be taught in a wide variety of settings. It is equally appropriate in a clinical environment, such as a hospital or physician's or dentist's office, a neighborhood recreational center, an exercise facility, a church meeting room, a business conference room, and a community college or adult education classroom. Reasonably comfortable chairs and good lighting are important. Tables and a blackboard are not essential but they do make the teaching and note-taking processes much easier.

ADDITIONAL MATERIALS

Resource materials for determining the calories or exchanges of foods and beverages, or printed guides for special diets may be required in addition to those provided in the **Food Habit Management** book. Depending upon the orientation of your course, you may also want to have some reference books on behavior modification, nutrition and exercise for your own and your students' use. There are several books listed in the bibliography which are particularly good for these purposes. All of them can be easily ordered through any bookstore. Your county extension agent or Department of Agriculture representative can suggest a number of interesting pamphlets and posters which make good instructional supplements.

Some instructors like to have their students graph their progress with particular skills. If these graphs are put on a bulletin board or taped to a wall where they can be seen each week, they can be a source of motivation and reinforcement.

Students need to have some visible signs of progress other than their weight changes, and these graphs will not only help them see their progress, they will give other people opportunities to notice and support their efforts. These graphs, if begun in class, can be taken home at the end of the course and maintained by the students on their own. The students could be encouraged to bring their graphs in for follow-up consultations or group sessions.

I strongly recommend that you do not keep weight record graphs visible for others to see. This can be very discouraging and upsetting for some students and will only reinforce them to focus on the scale more than on their food habit changes.

Some things that really help students focus intently on what they are actually doing are: (1) graphing the frequency of recording food intake; (2) staying within calorie or exchange levels; (3) recording the number of times each technique or exercise was done; (4) recording the number of times a plan for a specific meal or snack was made in advance; or (5) recording when a strategy was made for some problem area or event. If they graph a number of different things, progress can go down in one or two areas without causing them to be overly discouraged. The graphs will give you a ready way to reinforce their efforts and perhaps offer suggestions for the areas of slower progress. Here is a sample graph.

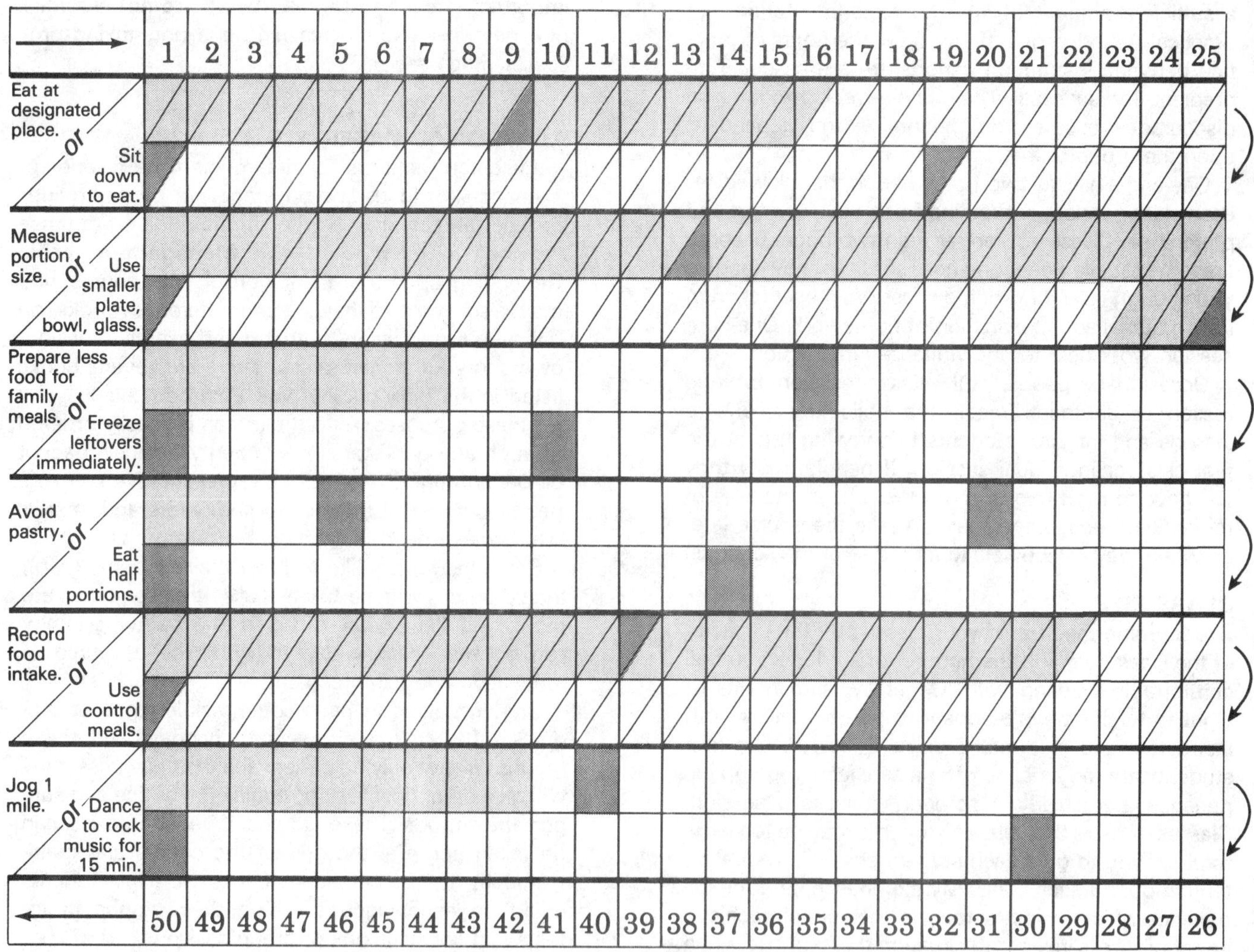

More information about this graph appears on pages 225 and 226.

FEES AND PAYMENT

My recommendation is that you set two fees for the course: one for tuition, and one for books and materials. The purchase of books reinforces the educational concept and conveys the expectation of active participation. It is most efficient if the students purchase their books and materials directly from you at the time of the first meeting, or at an orientation session prior to the first meeting. One way students can sabotage their progess is by not getting to the store to purchase their books until several weeks have passed. By dispensing the books yourself, at or before the first session, you know that every student has the necessary materials to complete that very essential first week of data collection.

Payment for tuition and materials should be made in advance of the first class session or at the time of the first session, unless you have a mechanism for billing people on an extended basis. Early payment will relieve you of having to worry about money matters throughout the course, and advance payment reinforces many students' commitment to attend all sessions.

TEACHING ASSISTANT (T. A.)

Although a teaching assistant is not essential to effective teaching of this course, a T. A. can be a highly valuable asset. Class registration, administrative details, weight recording (if it is to be done during the class), assistance in explaining and illustrating how to do the homework, teaching make-up lessons, or even teaching the class when the instructor is ill are all tasks which can be effectively done by T. A.'s. Most of the teaching assistants in my classes are former students who have taken the course earlier, who have been successful in establishing new food habits, who have lost a significant amount of weight in relation to their weight goals, and who feel positive about their experiences. These people volunteer their time to work as teaching assistants in exchange either for participation in classes as a refresher and for fun, or because they want to learn to teach the material. New students in the classes frequently report that having talked with someone who has been successful, but is still working on habit change projects, is an added source of encouragement to them.

FOLLOW-UP SESSIONS

No matter how long a course is, many students feel that it is over too quickly, and express apprehension at being "on their own." They have learned a method for setting up experiments and for working with themselves. They have learned techniques to enable them to change their habits successfully. What they need next is time for practice, experience, and the development of proficiency.

Follow-up sessions are not mandatory but they are recommended. Many people seem to benefit greatly from periodic opportunities to share their experiences, obtain new ideas for managing problems, and to reinforce their commitment. Where possible, a specified number of follow-up sessions of approximately one hour length and spaced approximately three to six weeks apart may be arranged. An additional fee can be charged for these sessions.

Many students prefer not to commit themselves to regularly scheduled follow-up sessions. They would rather set up appointments whenever they need them. My students seem to prefer this method of follow-up. Consequently, each week I set aside a block of time for half-hour follow-up consultations and let my students know the procedure for making appointments with me.

From the instructor's viewpoint, follow-up sessions offer an excellent opportunity for determining the effectiveness of the course and for learning which techniques, concepts and projects were most effective. This feedback will enable you to develop the course further on the basis of the experience of the students who took it. Most of all, it's fun to see everyone again!

SELECTION OF STUDENTS

There are no easy formulas for predicting who will or will not succeed in this course. There are, however, some guidelines which can be used to help you select your students. People who are not committed to changing their eating habits and patterns for their **own** reasons do not expend consistent effort in accomplishing change. People who are undergoing significant stress or emotional strain have other priorities which must claim their time and attention. These people would increase their chances for success in the course by taking it at another time. People who are in the process of changing residences or jobs, or who are significantly pressured to complete other tasks would increase their chances for success in the course by waiting until those particular pressures abate and they are reasonably able to focus on changing their eating habits.

People who don't show enthusiasm for taking the course, who have lots of reasons for why they can't take it now, or who just feel that the approach of the course doesn't fit them comfortably should not be persuaded to take it. Whatever the circumstances, people who begin the course with discomfort are not likely to enjoy it or be successful in it.

Correct timing and readiness for learning play important roles in any successful learning experience. Children do not learn to read successfully until they are developmentally and maturationally ready to do so. People do not successfully change their eating habits until they are psychologically ready to do so. Commitment is one good indicator of that psychological readiness. If people want to take the course for their very own reasons, are willing to make the time and expend the effort required to study and complete the assignments, and are in agreement that this course must be treated as a high priority in their lives until they have established their desired changes, then those people are likely to be very successful in the course. Whenever I'm uncertain about a potential student's level of readiness, I ask him or her, "After all of the other approaches you've tried for weight control, what makes you think this approach will work for you?" Then I settle back and let the person talk me into accepting her into the course, or else talk herself out of enrolling in the course.

Some people may be sincere in their desire to change their eating habits and be equally sincere that one or more persons close to them are not in support of those changes. This is more common for problems of weight control than for other dietary considerations. There are some people who have a vested interest in keeping other people overweight. What this means for the people who want to take the course is that they first have to decide that they want to change their eating habits in spite of the wishes of the other people. A simultaneous course in assertiveness training or some extra coaching or rehearsing sessions to develop and practice different ways of relating to these people over weight-related matters might be very helpful. Sometimes seemingly nonsupportive people don't intend to be nonsupportive at all. Others may become quite supportive, if invited to attend a session with you to learn about the approach of the course.

Marital partners may want to take the course together. A parent may want to take the course with a son or daughter. Other family members, close friends or roommates may want to take the course together. That should not present a problem, unless one member is likely to try to take charge of what the other member is doing. If this is the case, each member should take the course separately. If this is not the case, going through the course with a friend or relative can be much more fun and more reinforcing than taking the course alone.

No matter what guidelines you use, your intuition will probably be the best indicator of whether a student is likely to benefit from the course. It will be equally important for your students to have a clear picture of what your course is all about so they can decide whether it is right for them. All of this can be done by individual appointment, group orientation session or telephone conversation. By taking the time to talk with your students beforehand, you will reduce the number of drop-outs from the course, and the prior contact will make the first session more comfortable for you and your students.

TEACHING THE COURSE

"It is not enough to teach your students to understand; you must also convince them of their ability to use what they understand." One of my advisors in college said this to me when I was a fledgling teacher and I've never forgotten it. To me, nothing quite equals the fun of listening to my students discussing new ideas, to someone's triumphant report of one small victory, to someone else's ideas for problem-solving an unsuccessful venture. Some of their questions and challenges may send me scurrying to my resources to gather more information. But it is their ideas, their unique problems and the results of their experiments which contribute to the wealth of information from which I benefit daily. For me, there is no bigger payoff than when a student quietly says, "I can do it."

Once the course is designed, the materials are selected and the students are seated before you, there remains the biggest task of all: teaching the course effectively. People have many ideas about what makes a good learning experience, and there are lots of conflicting opinions over which elements of style and method are required to teach effectively. If you have had previous teaching experience, you most likely have your own list of essential elements. If you have not taught before, some of the ideas presented in this chapter may be particularly helpful. In either case, the ideas and suggestions in this chapter reflect my own orientation and experience. They are presented as food for your own thoughts and not as absolute requirements in order to teach effectively. My objective in writing this chapter is simply to share my experience with you in the hope that it will be helpful as you begin your course in food habit management. Short discussions of lesson format and teaching style will be followed by some general comments about teaching the course to individuals and in the classroom, and teaching the course to adolescents. Ideas about teaching methods are included throughout this chapter.

LESSON FORMAT AND TEACHING STYLE

Whether teaching the course to one individual or to a class, the recommended format follows this progression: general discussion of the previous week's experiences; presentation of the new lesson; and explanation of the coming week's assignment, which includes any modifications of calorie or dietary recommendations.

Spend the first portion of each session "touching base" with your students. Ask them to report their experiences and encourage them to ask or answer questions. In a group setting, encourage every member to contribute something. When something successful is reported, reinforce or reward it. When something unsuccessful is reported, look for a positive element and reinforce it. Then "problem-solve" a way for handling that same situation more successfully in the future.

Here is an example. "While you didn't refuse the dessert as planned, you didn't eat the appetizers and took only one helping of each item served at dinner. I think you did very well. If you are faced with a similar situation again and do not want to eat all or any of the dessert, based on what you found out from last Saturday's experience, what could you do about it? Would you prefer to refuse the dessert? If so, what could you say? Would you prefer to take it and leave it uneaten? If so, what could you do to make sure that it is left uneaten? Would you prefer to share it with someone? If so, how could you arrange for that in advance? Would you prefer to eat the dessert and leave other items uneaten instead? If so, which items could you leave uneaten and specifically what could you do to help yourself stick to your plan?"

Beginning each class session with a discussion of the previous week's experiences serves three purposes. First, it allows the students to get their questions and problems out of the way, thereby clearing their minds for concentration on new material. Second, it gets people actively involved; and in a group situation, the sharing of information fosters a sense of group cohesion. And third, it allows the late arrivers in a group situation to join the class without having missed essential information, and alleviates your need to back-track to repeat what had previously been discussed.

The largest proportion of class time should be allotted to your presentation of the new lesson. As you explain the new material, relate stories or anecdotes to demonstrate how the concepts apply to real people, and also to keep the students' attention. People seem to love stories. Use a chalkboard or large sheets of paper to illustrate diagrams or to list the major points you are making. The combination of verbal and visual modes of presentation are more effective than one mode alone, and writing as you talk will capture people's attention.

Ask for, and answer, questions about the new information. Ask questions of each student, such as, "How does this concept apply to you?", or, "What techniques might you find useful in this type of situation?" If you do this periodically as you present the new material, it will help to keep your students awake, alert and thinking. It also gives people a chance to talk, and it gives you a chance to encourage the quiet ones to contribute something.

Explain the homework assignment carefully. If you are using forms that have not been used previously, illustrate how to fill them out on the chalkboard or refer to the completed examples in their books. If you are using forms which are not in their books, pass out samples and ask the students to refer to them as you talk. Whenever possible, have the students fill out a little of the information on their blank forms. On the Weight Record, for example, ask the students to write in the date and their current weight, and perhaps the date for the next "weigh-in." For the Weekly Progress Record, have the students write down the specific techniques they will focus on for the coming week.

When you are using forms with which the students are already familiar, answer any questions concerning their use, and, if relevant, show them how to make any necessary changes specific to the new assignment. This is often the best time to discuss any recommended changes in calorie levels or dietary guidelines. Before they leave the class session, you may wish to have the students list the specific techniques for practice and experimentation on their Weekly Progress Records. My experience has been that students seem to follow through on their assignments much more effectively when they have done a little work on them during the class session. It is also helpful to have them refer to their records during the initial discussion of the previous week's experiences. This reinforces the importance and usefulness of doing the homework and gives the students some positive input for having done the work.

If you prefer that your students use their own scales, ask that they weigh themselves before coming to class, **and** that they bring their completed Weight Records with them. If you prefer that they use your scale, they should weigh themselves before the class session and bring their Weight Records up to date at that time. Thus, they will have the necessary information on hand when you discuss any changes in the calorie or dietary recommendations.

All people learn at different rates of speed. It is very important that your students understand and expect this. Emphasize that they should not interpret it as a sign of their personal failure. Continual encouragement and repetition of information will be necessary throughout the course.

One way to help students reinforce their own understanding of the material is to have them explain thoroughly each lesson to someone with whom they frequently eat. This allows them to share what they are doing in the program and increases the probability of understanding, support and encouragement from those people. Explaining how to design, implement and evaluate behavior change experiments to others usually has the effect of increasing the students' interest and commitment toward doing their assignments. People are eager to prove that their experiments will work. Besides, it all makes interesting conversation.

TEACHING INDIVIDUALS

The advantage of individual instruction is that the instructor can mold the entire design, organization and instruction of the course around the specific needs of one student. Whereas this allows a maximum degree of flexibility, it is terribly important to have a definite course structure so that both you and your student can build appropriate expectations for what will be covered during each session. That structure will help you avoid the pitfalls of loosely defined, general sessions which can become focused on counseling rather than on active teaching. Many students want to pass the responsibility for making a change to the instructor, and it is easy to fall into the role of providing suggestions, showing understanding when assignments aren't done, and offering sympathy for all the problems the student encountered during the past week. It is critical to the success of this approach that the student adopts the responsibility for achieving success in the course. This is likely to happen when you, as the instructor, are the facilitator and the student is cast in the role of active participant and principal researcher in the task of developing good eating habits.

It is important to set immediately the format pattern of the individual sessions. Decide in advance how you want to begin each session, when and where you want the student to weigh, and how you want to end the session. If you want to use a previously determined sequence of lessons, give a copy of that sequence to the student at the first lesson. However, you may prefer to wait until the student has completed a week of investigation before you determine the sequence of lessons. In this way you can tailor-make the lesson based upon his or her needs and problems. You may work the sequence out with the student, or work it out on your own and present a copy to the student at the next lesson.

The number of lessons in the course should be established so that you and the student know when the course will be completed. You may want to determine the number of lessons according to the specific material you want to cover, and by the severity of the student's eating problems. When the number of lessons is established, it helps the student utilize the time more effectively. It also establishes the fact that your help and guidance are temporary and available only for the purpose of teaching the student how to proceed on his or her own. Additional sessions, as needed, may be arranged after completion of the course.

As suggested in the section on lesson format, ask

questions of your student, give illustrative stories and examples, and encourage your student to problem-solve unsuccessful experiments. Insist on the student's participation in the review and modification of the calorie level or dietary plan. Find reasons for your student to refer to his or her homework records during the session, and make sure that some entries are made on the forms to be used for the coming week. This emphasizes an active student role and encourages the student to see the homework as an integral part of the whole learning experience.

There is a tendency for some students to try to use individualized instruction as a form of therapeutic counseling. They may raise issues or problems which are not appropriate or directly related to the lesson. When this happens, it may be easy for an instructor to become sidetracked. If you adopt a strong instructional format and consistently defer discussion of the unrelated issues until the formal lesson is completed, it will be fairly easy to train your students to concentrate on the course material. If a student has many other problems which interfere with his or her ability to focus on the course during or outside of the lesson, perhaps a referral to an appropriate agency or person for guidance would be helpful. Your diligence in maintaining an instructor-student relationship will enable your student to develop the necessary autonomy and skill to carry what is learned from the course into a long-term pattern for effective food habit management.

CLASSROOM TEACHING

The advantages of classroom teaching are many. You can reach more students at one time, thus minimizing your time and energy expenditure. The sense of group cohesion, the peer pressure to participate, and the sheer variety of questions and problems make classroom instruction enjoyable for instructors and students alike. Many of the suggestions made earlier in this chapter apply directly to classroom teaching. If you haven't read the section on lesson format on pages (19) - (20), please read it carefully before continuing with this section.

One of the challenges in classroom teaching is holding the group's attention. One way to accomplish that is to get the students actively involved as quickly as possible. Beginning each class with the sharing of the week's progress is one way to achieve this goal. Questions like, "How can I do that?" directed to you can be turned back to the student with a counter-question like, "What ideas do you have?" Or you can direct the question to other students by asking, "Does anyone have an idea that might be helpful?" Some of the quieter students can be asked whether they experienced similar results with their experiments. This flow of involvement between you and the students takes some of the initial teaching pressure off of you and allows all of you to get warmed up.

Holding the group's attention during presentation of the lesson can be accomplished by alternating lengthy explanations with stories and examples of what other students have done. The use of the chalkboard to list or underscore the points you are making also breaks up the presentation. Ask the students for examples of how they might apply the concepts. When you answer their questions, be precise and to the point. You may lose the group's attention by answering questions which require lengthy answers or detailed planning. Too much time spent with one individual can cause others to become restless or bored.

Keep yourself and the group centered on the subject material. Students may ask questions or want to share information unrelated to the focus of the class. Invite them to ask or share the information with you after class and turn the group's attention back to what was previously being discussed.

Some students may want to bring up emotional problems or interpersonal relationship problems which are loosely associated with eating control. It is very easy, in a weight control class, to get sidetracked on emotional problems, because many people lose control of their food intake when emotionally upset or stressed. It is also easy for other class members to be sympathetic and want to help. Unless you quickly and firmly defer these problems until after the class has been dismissed, a shift in orientation from a classroom to a group therapy format could result. Once this happens, it is often difficult to work the group back into the classroom orientation.

It is very important to end the class on a positive note. If a number of students have had problems or failures during the week, the mood of the group may be down. If the homework assignment seemed difficult or overwhelming when explained, some of the group's enthusiasm may be tarnished. This is when I usually tell a story about some of the awful experiences I had when learning to ski, and get the students to laugh. Then I both review what it's like to learn anything in the beginning, and remind them how far they have all progressed since the first day of class. I also remind them that the goal is for improvement, not perfection, and that the objective of the class is to experiment with new ideas to see what happens. This is usually sufficient to restore the students' optimism.

TEACHING ADOLESCENTS

Teaching the Food Habit Management course to adolescents provides a unique challenge because the adolescent years represent a time of great physical and emotional change. This is the time when teen-agers are learning new social behaviors, their bodies and body images are changing, and their relationships with their parents may be strained over a variety of issues. The desire for more independence, but not necessarily the desire to take responsibility for it, and the strong need to do whatever the peer group is doing will be felt in the classroom and in the responses to the homework assignments. In addition, the adolescents' parents may have questions or concerns about the course and the assignments, and some may even present periodic obstacles to their teen-agers' progress. What is required, then, is a blend of information and training for both the adolescents and their interested parents.

The course for adolescents is best designed with a group approach and a classroom format. It is also helpful to have an orientation session at the beginning and at least one follow-up session at the end of the course for the teen-agers to attend with their parents. While the parents do not attend the class sessions, their participation in the orientation and follow-up sessions should be encouraged.

Beginning the course with an orientation session for adolescents and their parents is an excellent way to (1) present the objectives and approach of the course, (2) give examples of assignments, and (3) answer questions. This is also a good time to discuss how changes in habit patterns made by one member of a family can affect other members of the family. For example, a teen-ager who begins taking responsibility for making his or her own snacks may instigate other concerns, such as the purchase of appropriate foods, keeping other family members from eating those foods, cleaning up the kitchen after making the snacks, and so on. The issues of who pays for those snack foods and who shops for them must also be dealt with. Other frequent sources of concern are the storage of tempting foods, the snacking habits of other family members and what is eaten at mealtime. Changes in the adolescents' patterns may create some discomfort for others, especially for the mothers whose routines are the most significantly affected.

You must help parents understand the reasons for the various assignments and enlist their active support. This can be accomplished in a variety of ways, one of the most effective of which is to open an avenue of sharing between the adolescent and the parent. Instructing the adolescent to teach each week's lesson to one or both parents, and asking the parents to set time aside for the weekly lesson accomplishes three things: it puts the responsibility for information sharing on the adolescent; it supplies a specific way for the parent to give support; and it keeps the parent tuned in to what the teen-ager will be doing and why. Parents need to understand why their son or daughter may eat some high-calorie foods, and why it is important to do the specific experiments. This enables them to shift more successfully from the concept of a diet to the concept of experimenting and changing habits. If this is all explained and outlined at the orientation session, the avenue for discussion and sharing between the adolescents and their parents has been opened, and it will be easier for both to continue the pattern.

Another matter for discussion during the orientation session is the issue of sabotage and how it could affect the teen-agers as well as their parents. One way to open the discussion is to talk about how people build habit patterns which involve other people as well. When one persons makes a change, the other person may still respond in the old pattern, thus making it more difficult for the first person to maintain the change. For example, a mother who wants to do something nice for her daughter may automatically purchase a favorite high-calorie food item or suggest taking her out for a special food treat. The daughter may refuse and without fully realizing the difficulty this creates for her daughter, the mother may say, "You can have a treat once in a while, can't you?" The daughter may interpret this as a deliberate attempt to sabotage her progress; the mother may simply need to have the problem explained to her.

Adolescents need to look at how they could sabotage their own progress, and how they could get their parents to help them do it. An example for a girl might be to ask to have a slumber party and then plan a lot of high-calorie treats for everyone to eat. Then, if the parent points this out, the daughter might become angry and go on a food binge to punish the parent.

After giving a few examples, it is helpful to allow five minutes or so for each adolescent and his or her parents to discuss their sabotage techniques with each other, and to write them down. Then ask each person to let the other one know how he or she can be approached when it looks like a sabotage technique is being used. For example, if the teen-ager notices that tempting snack foods are being purchased—because it isn't fair to deprive the others of treats—and then stored in visible places—because it is convenient to keep them there—he or she needs to have a way of bringing this to the parent's attention in a way that won't result in an argument. If the parent has given the teen-ager some ideas about how to bring up issues like that with him or her, it is more likely that the parent will hear what is being said and be more receptive to working out an alternate, mutually satisfactory, arrangement.

In brief, then, the orientation session is an important

part of the course. It brings the adolescents and their parents together to learn about the course, to have their questions answered, to set the stage for the adolescents to take responsibility for their own participation and progress, and to begin a process of communication between the adolescents and their parents over issues related to the course. The parents will not be attending any of the class sessions unless the adolescents decide as a group that they would like to invite them to hear a particular lesson. It is important to remind the parents of this and invite them to contact you if they have questions or problems as the course progresses. Then turn your attention to the adolescents for a few minutes. You may want to share some stories or anecdotes with them. You may want to give them their course materials or some supplementary information to read. Or you may want to give them some questionnaires or data sheets to fill out at home. In doing this, you reinforce the concept that the course belongs to them, and also transmit the expectation that they will be active participants in their course.

Once you have decided upon the specific lessons and their progression, look for ways to make each one particularly relevant to adolescents. Many teen-agers aren't as aware as adults are of the number or variety of food cues in the environment. A few photographs or slides showing average grocery stores, neighborhood streets, shopping centers and even school corridors can help you get your message across. So can some samples of newspapers and teenage magazines. One good warm-up exercise is to ask the students to give you slogans for food and beverage commercials like, "Bet you can't eat just one" (Frito-Lay potato chips), or, "It's the real thing" (Coca-Cola), or, "We do it all for you" (McDonald's).

Some discussion topics will have greater impact if they are combined with appropriate examples and demonstrations. When you talk about the use of smaller plates, bowls and glasses, bring in some samples. Measure out a specific portion of food and put it on a large plate and put the same amount on a smaller plate. Place one cup of pudding in a cereal bowl and one cup of pudding in a custard cup. Let the students decide which size container seems more satisfying to them. It is also very important to show them a one-ounce piece of cheese, a three-ounce piece of meat, and whole and half-cup amounts of various foods because many teen-agers underestimate the amount of their portions.

The lessons on snack control will be more effective if you have the students develop partial lists of alternate activities and potential food substitutions during the class session. This enables you to help them generate ideas and to make sure that their lists are realistic. Strategies for social eating should also be written out during the class and experimented with during the following week. Where possible, have the students plan around specific social events such as school dances, football games, movies, bowling, hiking, or just going out to eat with their friends. Have them role-play ways to say "no, thank you" and have them practice ordering food from a waitress. You can divide the group into pairs to practice with each other.

If you use the Weekly Progress Record, have the students fill them out for the coming week before leaving class. This will guide them toward a realistic number of exercises to try, and help prevent them from becoming overloaded. Also, have the students practice making some entries on their Food Data Records in class before using them for homework. They will do their homework more consistently if they understand clearly how to do it.

When you reach the last lesson, review the main items you covered during the course. Have the students complete a Restart/Stress Plan in class and demonstrate how to use the Reference Outline of Techniques and Exercises. Set the date for your follow-up lesson and ask them to bring their parents. Review what you specifically want them to do between the last class and the follow-up session. Have them make out a separate Weekly Progress Record for each week.

A follow-up session is not required, but it is highly recommended. A period of three to four weeks should be allowed between the last class and the follow-up session. This gives the students plenty of time to practice and to make mistakes. Spend the follow-up session discussing the progress and changes with the students and their parents and do as much problem-solving with them as time allows. Review the use of the Restart/Stress Plan and help them make any necessary modifications. Explore ways to continue recording and make necessary adjustments in calorie levels or dietary plans. Encourage the students to continue to share their projects and progress with their parents; encourage the parents to continue to support and reinforce their teen-agers' efforts. Set a date for the next follow-up session, if you are planning to have one. If you aren't planning another follow-up, let the students know how they can contact you if they are having problems.

There are certainly many more ideas, suggestions and techniques for working with adolescents than were presented here. Much of what applies to adults also applies to teen-agers. There are many ideas to draw from throughout the book.

In review, some important points to remember

when teaching to either adolescents or adults are:

1. Make your explanations and instructions simple and clear;
2. Use audio-visual aids and demonstrations whenever possible;
3. Encourage active participation in class;
4. Keep the class sessions focused on relevant material;
5. Teach the students how to handle mistakes and problem-solve new strategies;
6. Keep them from trying to do too many things at one time;
7. Have them do a little work on each week's homework forms in class;
8. Have them role-play how to say things that are difficult for them;
9. Encourage them to take responsibility for their progress and projects;
10. Reward them for all of their efforts; and
11. End each session with positive comments.

If you can maintain a positive attitude, encourage problem-solving, and help your students feel good about themselves, the class sessions should be enjoyable and rewarding for everyone.

SUPPORTING AND MAINTAINING CHANGE

Author's note: Most of the information in this section appears in identical, similar or expanded form in the supplementary student lesson, Developing A Support Network, on pages 223-234. It has been condensed here for your review and implementation.

Once your students have progressed through the course a major challenge remains: supporting and maintaining their changes. You, as the instructor, and other students in a group situation, have represented a strong source of encouragement for each person's efforts to make and maintain change. The cessation of regular meetings means a reduction of overt, active support and reinforcement. The means for continuing that support and reinforcement must transfer to the student's own environment in the form of self, friends and relatives; and the mechanism for that must be initiated and established while the course is still in progress. Then, when the course is over, the students will have a support system which is established and running.

This chapter will focus on factors which discourage the maintenance of change as well as factors which encourage continuation of the changed habits and patterns. Subtopics in this chapter include: the tendency to think the course is over upon completion of the last session, disorganization or loss of routine, resistance to change, fear of losing control, sabotage techniques, solitary focus on scale weight, and establishment of an unrealistic goal weight. Other subtopics include: developing a new reputation, being supportive of oneself, obtaining support from others, and maintaining visible signs of continuing effort.

TENDENCY TO THINK THE COURSE IS OVER AT THE LAST SESSION

Many of my students have commented that when the course was over other people made comments such as, "You don't have to do that anymore, do you?" or, "The course is over so let's go out for pizza and celebrate!" or, "Are you **still recording?**" When the person reaches goal weight, others automatically assume that he or she can return to former overeating patterns. So familiar "food pushers" resume the practice of insisting that the person "take just a little more."

There is also a tendency, when the course is over, for the students to assume that they have completed the major part of their required work and to relax their control and support efforts. In some instances the books, reminder notes and other visual effects of the course are put away. Some people stop talking about their experiments and progress, assuming that other people are tired of hearing about them. Before long, tempting food items may return to their previous places of easy visibility and old eating habits may return. In short, the training regimen is broken and the carefully established network of support, which was built while the course was in progress, is eroded. For some people, this is a familiar pattern and follows the completion of any formal weight-reduction effort.

It is important for students to understand that although the course has a definite closing date in terms of the sessions with you, it has no closing date with regard to themselves. One way to help your students grasp this notion is to teach them to think of the course as having three stages: the beginning, the middle, and the end. The beginning is the formal instructional period. There they learn the concepts, process, methods and techniques. The middle stage is the independent establishment of habits and patterns. Students accomplish these on their own, **after** completion of the course. The end stage is represented by the students' incorporation, or internalization, of the changes as an integral part of themselves. This stage is easily identified because they feel very comfortable with their eating habits and their ability to maintain those habits.

A critical factor in the successful transition from the formal course to the independent establishment of new habits and patterns, or the transition from the beginning to the middle state, is the maintenance of the training regimen which was established during the course. Daily review of the Reference Outline or Weekly Progress Record, daily recording of food intake and accomplishment of specific techniques and exercises, weekly weighing and continual sharing of information and progress with other people must be maintained faithfully after completion of the course and continued throughout the second stage. Adherence to the training regimen provides a sense of continuity with the course, aids immeasurably in changing the old "I can't do it on my own" reputation, and reinforces the belief that establishing new eating habits is an ongoing process.

When the students reach their desired weight and are comfortable with their habits and ability to maintain changes, strict adherence to daily recording may not be necessary. However, other aspects of the training regimen, such as keeping tempting foods out of sight, leaving reminder notes in visible places, using strategy cards, keeping replacement activities and lower-calorie snack foods readily available, and weekly weighing may be vital to the maintenance of the habit changes.

LOSS OF ROUTINE

Sometimes students feel that after they have been

successful for a period of time they can relax their environmental control and preplanning efforts. Because they are no longer grazing randomly through the kitchen, for example, students may mistakenly assume that they are no longer susceptible to the visibility of tempting foods. If they haven't ordered too much food in a restaurant for a while, they may think that they no longer have to preplan their orders according to the usual strategies.

Encourage your students to adopt the attitude that whatever gave them trouble before will always give them trouble. They will always have the potential to respond to food cues in the old, uncontrollable way. By reducing the presence or frequency of cues, and by planning strategies in advance for hard-to-control situations, the opportunities for responding in the old, uncontrollable way are greatly reduced. And if such materials required for control as lower-calorie foods, smaller containers, soapy water for mixing bowls, prepackaged meals or snacks and specific Restart/Stress Plans are not available, they will not be used. The result is a return to the old habit patterns.

Remind your students that the objective of the course is not to produce more effective martyrs who can surround themselves with tempting food cues and insurmountable obstacles. **The objective is to teach people to appraise realistically their strengths, weaknesses and predictable responses, and then plan accordingly with the intent of reducing the opportunities for loss of control and increasing the opportunities for maintenance of control.** If people make it easier to do what they want to do and correspondingly harder to do what they don't want to do, they'll be able to live quite easily with that objective.

RESISTANCE TO CHANGE

Periodic resistance to change is normal and natural. Most of my students experience it at least once during the course and several times after completion of the course. Sometimes the resistance is caused by the need for a day or a night away from the usual control routine. A planned food holiday may be all that is necessary to reestablish positive feelings toward control techniques. At other times, the resistance may be ascribable to discomfort with the new, less familiar habits which customarily feel awkward and strange for a while. I usually explain this to my students by making an analogy to the difference between an old friend and a new acquaintance. You already know what to say to, and how to conduct yourself around the old friend. You can relax without being especially watchful of yourself. New acquaintances are not well known; so you have to tread more carefuly into topics of conversation, appropriate behaviors, and so on. In time, the new acquaintance feels like an established friend and a sense of comfort emerges. This will happen with the new habits too. They will become more comfortable as they become more familiar. Thus, the more the new habits are practiced, the sooner they become familiar and hence, more comfortable.

FEAR OF LOSING CONTROL

Sometimes people need to go out of control deliberately to break the tension created by long periods of good control. I tell students to expect this. Once they see that they can reestablish control again, there is a little less fear of losing control. When they lose and reestablish control again, their fear decreases a little more. Eventually they alter their old expectations that everything is fine until they lose control once, and then regain all their weight, and come to a realization that loss of control is temporary, that it is normal and natural, and that it is to be expected and planned for. By planning ahead for temporary losses of control, permission is given to feel okay about it, and the preestablished plan for return to control serves as insurance that control will be resumed.

The function of the Restart Plan, explained in lesson ten, is to provide a specific plan for the resumption of control following loss of the regular routine. You can teach the concept of a Restart Plan at any appropriate time during the course.

Particularly, if your course extends over a period of two months or more, the issue of reestablishing control will come up as students report they had a "bad week" or that they just "blew the whole routine." Teach the concept of a Restart Plan and have each student write one out to use for experimentation. Then, by the time the course is over, they are familiar with the procedure and may have reduced some of their worry about losing and regaining control. If you teach the Restart Plan concept toward the end of the course, have each student complete one before the last session is adjourned. In this way, they will have given some specific thought to what they will do to reestablish control. When the time comes to actually do it, they will be prepared. If you are having a follow-up session, be sure to ask the students about their Restart Plans and to report on their results.

SABOTAGE TECHNIQUES

There seems to be a perverse aspect to human nature which causes people, in the midst of achieving success, to do something deliberately to promote failure. I call this sabotage. The pattern of removing the mainstays of support—the recording forms, reminder notes and book, and of not sharing information regularly with other people—can be regarded as deliberate sabotage maneuvers and should be dealt with during, or in advance of, the concluding session. Because sabotage hinders progress, it is important that students recognize their methods and make specific plans for dealing with them. Ask them to look at the predictability of their behavior at the end of weight-reduction programs and to identify how they sabotage their continued progress. Ask them to list these sabotage mechanisms and then, alongside each one, write down one idea for either preventing themselves from doing it (sabotaging the sabotage, so to speak) or for supporting themselves through it.

Examples:

sabotage technique	prevention/support idea
Forget to record.	Leave recording forms and pencil taped to visible, accessible place.
Buy the treats my children have been deprived of.	Periodically give each child money to go to the store and purchase a small amount of the treat and consume it before returning home.
Assume people are bored by my reports of progress and projects and stop talking about them.	Vary the people with whom I talk: offer to exchange favors with the one person who listens to me regularly.

This list should be prepared during the session with you and not be assigned as homework, because many students will sabotage themselves by not making the list at all. Once the list is made there is a greater likelihood that it will be used.

SOLITARY FOCUS ON SCALE WEIGHT

Students who base their success solely upon the scale find it easier to let their habits slide than do students who focus primarily upon their habits. When the old habits return, so does the weight. Additionally, the inevitable small rises in scale weight due to menstrual cycles, higher salt intake and water retention can set off a chain reaction of discouragement, helplessness, guilt, depression and overeating. No one needs that. Therefore, stress the practice of weighing only once a week. Encourage students to keep charts or graphs of their progress with habits and controlled food intake. If they succeed in those areas, the weight will come down.

UNREALISTIC WEIGHT GOAL

One particularly discouraging aspect of weight reduction is the struggle to attain an unrealistic or inappropriate weight goal. This can result in an "I can't do it, so why bother?" attitude and lead to weight regain. To help my students avoid this pitfall, I suggest that they concentrate on weight reduction in increments of ten pounds. When they have lost the first ten pounds, they can set a new goal of up to ten pounds more. At the end of the second ten-pound loss they can strike a new bargain with themselves for up to an additional ten pounds. With each ten-pound loss the students have the opportunity to evaluate their progress and make a decision about whether to lose more weight or to maintain their current weight for a short evaluation period. If, at the end of the evaluation period, the person decides to lose more weight, a new weight increment can be established; if the weight is acceptable, a decision to maintain it can be made. The underlying issue is one of providing frequent opportunities to decide upon a course of action and to make those decisions realistically. Besides, a weight loss of five pounds out of ten is a far more rewarding comparison than five pounds out of fifty. And fifty pounds seems so far away. It is very reinforcing for students to be able to meet their goals. Having smaller goals means that they reach them more frequently.

DEVELOPING A NEW REPUTATION

Many of my students complain that their old, overeating reputations get in the way of establishing their new habit changes. Other people continue to respond to them as overeaters, and they find it easier to fall back into the old patterns. In addition, some students continue to regard themselves as overeaters who are temporarily controlling their food intake. These people expect, according to the old reputation, that they will eventually regain the weight. The overeating responses have been predictable, and people have learned how to elicit them either from themselves or from others.

When habits change the support mechanisms have to change too, in order to fit the new habits. If this doesn't happen, the old habits return. A person's own reputation can be a very powerful support mechanism. Thus, it becomes necessary to modify or change the reputation to fit the new habits.

The first task in changing a reputation is to isolate the specific habits which are associated with that reputation. For example, a person with the reputation of being a hearty eater might eat large portions, take two or more servings of each food item, never refuse offers of food or never leave a scrap of food behind on the plate. Other people will expect a hearty eater to behave accordingly. Thus, comments such as, "George is such a hearty eater; I know he'll have another helping" only serve to lure people into their old predictable patterns.

The next task is to select the new habits which fit the desired reputation. If the new reputation is one of being a moderate eater, for example, habits such as taking single servings, choosing fewer food items, declining offers of extra food, or leaving some food left over on the plate, are appropriate.

The third, and hardest, task in changing a reputation is to perform the habit changes regularly and consistently. When other people notice the changes, their frequent response may be to try hard to push the person back into the old, overeating habits. The real task, then, is to patiently retrain others to expect the new habits. Comments such as, "I know I always used to eat in front of the TV, but now I prefer to sit at a table and pay attention to my food," teach others what to expect. It takes time to get used to new habits and to begin to feel comfortable with them. If the new habits are performed consistently, everyone eventually learns to expect them and then they don't feel strange anymore. I still remember one man's comment in class one day. "We went to my mother's for dinner last week and I was extremely hungry. I had decided to have a second helping of meat and, as I was taking it, my mother said, 'I haven't seen you take a second helping for such a long time. Are you sure you really want it?' That made me realize that I had changed."

As in all habit changes, improvement, rather than perfection, is the goal. It is difficult to be regular and consistent with newly developing habits, particularly when there are other people involved. There are too many opportunities to slide back into the old habits or even to forget to do the new ones. Encourage your students to expect that changing reputations takes time and to be patient with themselves and others during the retraining process.

BEING SUPPORTIVE OF ONESELF

Probably the most common way my students undermine their progress is to demand that they accomplish too many changes too fast and without error. This "all or nothing" approach sets them up to feel dissatisfied with themselves whenever they aren't doing everything perfectly. Because perfect performance never occurs, students tend to be unhappy with themselves much of the time. Moreover, when students do achieve desired progress in one or two areas, they frequently discount, or devalue, their success by stating that they usually don't do that well or by pointing out all the other areas of poor progress. Familiar phrases are: "Yes, I did well then, but you don't know how many times I didn't do it at all!" and "That doesn't count, because it's easy for me to do."

People continually tend to strive to meet their ultimate performance goals. Often those goals remain unchanged, despite how much progress is made. If students only look ahead toward their goals and not backward to measure their progress, it may appear to them that very little success has been achieved. It is similar to what happens when a person faces a long journey. If the traveler concentrates solely upon reaching the destination, he or she may become impatient and lose sight of the distance already traveled. By periodically stopping along the way and tracing progress on a map, the traveler will be able to judge progress fairly and be likelier to pace his or her energies accordingly.

Teach your students to think of their success in terms of **improvement** and to measure their progress from the very first week of the course. Comparison of the first week's data sheets with the recording forms from each successive week will provide the information necessary to measure progress. Teaching the students to think in terms of improvement is a more complicated task and usually involves some training in how to interpret what they do in positive terms.

The method I find the easiest to use in teaching students to interpret their progress more positively is to pick up their negative statements and teach them how to reword them in more positive terms. The initial discussion period at the beginning of the class or individual session provides an excellent opportunity to hear self-discounting statements. When a student makes a comment such as, "Oh, I only did that for one day," I usually rephrase the statement to, "I did that for one day, which is more than I was able to do it the previous week." With a comment such as, "I ruined everything because of my food binge," I usually ask if the person was able to get back into control within a day or two. If the answer is "yes," I rephrase the comment to, "I did have a binge, but I was able to get back into control afterward. And that's the important part." If the answer is "no," I rephrase it to, "I had a binge during the week, but I know a little more about my binge pattern. Now I can make a plan for getting back into control more quickly."

This kind of rephrasing is easy to do. The more your students hear you do it, the sooner they learn the difference between being self-supportive and being self-destructive as they interpret what they do. Within a few sessions my students are usually tuning in to one another's discounting statements and spontaneously saying something such as, "Hey, you just put yourself down. Say it another way." After a while, they'll begin to rephrase their own statements. I remember one woman's self-satisfied remark: "I'm not perfect but I certainly am better!"

Statements students make to themselves also play an integral role in the maintenance of habit changes. A comment such as, "I only put food items away because I'll get fatter if I don't," puts the change only in the context of weight reduction. Thus it is relegated to temporary status. The implication is that when the weight is lost the food can be brought out again. If the statement is rephrased to "I put all food items away because I don't want a messy kitchen," or simply, "I just don't like to have food sitting around," it allows the habit changes to be interpreted in a broader and more integrated context. Thus, if weight isn't lost for a week or two, the food is still kept out of sight, because putting food away is simply part of the daily routine.

Most of my students are prone to pay more attention to their mistakes than to their successes. As one student commented, "Why give myself credit for what I was supposed to do? If I do something extra or better, then I can give myself a pat on the back." When I asked this same student if he paid much attention to his mistakes he said, "Sure. I really give myself a bad time and it takes me a while to stop thinking about it."

I make a suggestion to my students that for every mistake or failure they think about, they also give thought to one expected, or more-than-expected, success, and give themselves a mental pat on the back. The objective is to train them to give equal thought time to positives and negatives. If most of the thought time is spent on negative results, people can't help but feel depressed. If at least equal thought time is given to positive results, even if they are routine, and therefore expected, people will feel much more encouraged and optimistic.

OBTAINING SUPPORT FROM OTHERS

In the very beginning of the course the students were asked to explain their lessons and homework projects to at least one friend, relative or co-worker. One of the reasons given for that assignment was to reinforce their own knowledge by presenting the information logically to someone else. A second reason was to reinforce the students' commitment to doing their homework assignments by talking about them and sharing the results of their experiments.

Another reason for asking the students to explain their lessons to someone else was to share exactly what they are and are not doing. **And why?** When a person is trying to lose weight, the two most logical points of focus by other people are how much is being eaten and how much weight has been lost. What does a person say to someone who is trying to lose weight? "You look thinner." And what is said when that same person has a food item on the plate which is high in calories? "You shouldn't be eating that, should you?" For many people who have been trying to keep extra weight off for years, either point of focus may be more harmful than helpful. In sharing specific information with others, the students are able to initiate more appropriate discussion topics, and thus begin the process of teaching others what to ask or talk about.

In similar fashion, if students are able to share information about the progress being made on specific habits, and even some of the problems encountered in developing effective strategies, other people will be able to respond in more supportive and appropriate ways.

Teach your students to make **specific** requests of others, when their assistance is needed. Generalized requests for help only leave other people confused and uncertain about what to do. A good example of this was provided by one of my students. Cocktail parties were particularly difficult for her, and she frequently felt the need for some help in maintaining control of her food intake. When she had asked her husband for help in the past, he usually responded by taking the plate of food away from her or whispering to her that she shouldn't be eating. This angered her and she deliberately ate more, which only made her feel more frustrated. Further, her anger made her husband angry because he had, in his own way, answered her request for help. After talking about it in class, she realized that she needed to tell him specifically what to do. She made a plan for the next cocktail party, which was scheduled for the following weekend. She explained her control plan to him and said that whenever her control became shaky she would like to be able to restate her plan to him, right then, and would like him to praise her for maintaining control up to that time. He agreed and they worked out the signals together. Whenever she needed support, she tapped her husband on the arm; he excused himself from the conversation; they sat together while she restated her plan; and he praised her control efforts. By request, he said nothing about what she ate and did not take her plate away from her. Their subsequent evaluation was that they both felt much more comfortable than usual. The husband did not feel that he had to watch over his wife and he was free to enjoy himself. The student was able to take responsibility for her own food intake and for getting some encouragement when it was needed.

Many of my students complain that other people are always bringing them gifts of food, despite the fact that they have told these people how difficult it is for them to receive food gifts. Sometimes this represents a deliberate sabotage maneuver on the part of the other people, but often it is simply because the people want to give a gift of some kind and can't think of what else to give. Here again, specific information is important. For example, one husband was fond of bringing his wife candy and baked goods which she had always appreciated. She had made several requests that he stop bringing them to her. However, it wasn't until she presented him with a list of alternative small gift items that he was able to change his pattern. He had not known what to give her and, because he liked to bring her gifts, the idea list was very helpful.

Encourage your students to take responsibility for asking for praise or attention when they need it. People can't readily tune into other people's needs for support. When your students complain that no one ever seems to care about what they're doing, suggest that they practice making requests or statements which will elicit support from others. A comment such as "You never pay any attention to what I'm doing" is much less helpful than "I would like to tell you about what I'm doing. Will you listen to me for a few minutes?" By saying something such as: "Look. I've kept my food records complete for two weeks. Isn't that neat?" others will eventually learn to ask questions or to make comments about progress.

Remind your students to show appreciation to others for their interest, questions, help, and support. Everyone likes to be appreciated. When thoughtful gestures, attention, praise, or encouragement are offered and then rewarded by a word or two of thanks, they will occur more often.

MAINTAINING VISIBLE SIGNS OF CONTINUING EFFORT

When students can see visible evidence of their efforts toward making and maintaining change, they are encouraged to continue them. Reminder notes, recording forms, the book, the Reference Outline, graphs or charts of progress, opaque containers, alternate activity materials, shopping lists, strategy cards, and smaller plates are all reinforcers of change and represent continuation of progress. Not only does their visibility serve as a reminder to use them, but also their availability assures that they **will** be used. Even more importantly, their visibility becomes a statement of the student's intent to make these practices an integral part of the daily routine and reinforces the student's conviction that new daily food habits are being established. Stress the importance of this throughout the course and praise your students whenever they tell you they are keeping things visible.

Students who invest in themselves and in the maintenance of their habit changes find that the investment reinforces and supports their commitment to reach for and maintain their goals. Each time a person purchases something or does something specific and visible in support of the desired change, this very powerful statement is made: "I am very determined to reach my goals and I want everyone to see the progress I'm making." Changing physical appearance is one way to do that.

Many of your students, particularly those who have lost and regained weight repeatedly, may tend to put off making changes in their physical appearance until after their goal weight is reached. They may be reluctant to purchase new clothes, try on new clothing styles, or even experiment with a new hair style. They may prefer to wait until later when the investment of time and money seems more appropriate. If they do this, when they look in the mirror they become discouraged at the lack of visible change in their appearance. This is counterproductive to establishing good feelings about themselves and the habit changes they have made.

Many of your students will have clothes in their closets ranging from the smallest they've ever worn to the largest. Others will wear the same ones no matter how loose they become. As they lose weight and their current clothes become too baggy, some students will begin altering them to make them smaller. This is not only helpful but also it is preferred to the sloppy appearance of the larger clothes.

Many of my students discover that after they've altered their clothes they think they look just as overweight as before, even though the actual clothing size is smaller. It is often very difficult for the eye to distinguish the quantitative change in appearance, that the actual body size is smaller, when the same clothing items are worn at each size. A qualitative change, or actual difference in the appearance of the clothing items, is far more readily recognizable. For this reason, I suggest that my students either restyle clothes that they are reducing in size—so that they look different—or that they exchange their larger clothing for completely different clothes of a smaller size. In both instances, the actual change in appearance will be far more uplifting than the change in size alone. This is as important for men as it is for women.

For those students whose closets are filled with

clothes of many sizes, the following suggestions will be helpful. First, ask them to group their clothes according to size, from largest to smallest. Then ask them to put all the clothing items which are too small in a different closet. "Out of sight, out of mind" is the idea. It may be very disheartening to be reminded continually of all those clothes they used to wear when they weren't so heavy. Besides, many people become so tired of seeing those clothes in the closet that when they are at last able to wear them, a lot of the fun of having something new or different to wear is diminished.

Once the smaller clothes have been removed, the items which are too big have to be moved out of the main closet. I encourage my students to get rid of all the clothes which are too large. They can give or throw them away, sell them, or exchange them for clothes of a smaller size. The point is that if those clothes are kept in the house "just in case they will be needed again," the expectation of weight regain has been reinforced. If, on a particular day or night, a student needs to put something on which is a little larger in order to be comfortable, it means that some weight has been regained. If he or she has a bigger clothing item to wear and uses it, the tendency is to rely on the bigger, more comfortable clothes more often until those clothes eventually fit. The result is that the person made it easier to regain the weight by keeping those clothes around. If, on the other hand, there were no larger clothing items available, a couple of days of discomfort may follow, but there likely will be strong motivation to resume the weight-reduction efforts.

A number of my students express dismay at the thought of parting with their old clothes. I recommend that these students package the old clothes, wrap them for mailing, and send them to a friend or relative who lives in another city for storage. In this way, the clothes are available, but not readily accessible. By the time the clothes are returned through the mail, the weight-reduction efforts will likely be reestablished. The "make it easier to do what you want to do and harder to do what you don't want to do" adage applies well to this situation.

Encourage your students to experiment with their appearance during the time they are losing weight. Suggest that they try on different clothing styles and colors. When they reach a new size, or as body proportions change, different styles may be more appropriate or attractive. People who tend to wear bulky clothing, such as heavy sweaters, boxy jackets, and loosely fitting shirts or blouses, will appear to be heavier than they actually are because the clothing adds bulk to their body size. Tucking blouses or shirts into skirts or pants, removing jackets or coats whenever possible, and using lightweight sweaters, sweater vests or jersey shirts will reduce the bulk, and consequently the physical space the person takes up. The overall result is a smaller appearance.

Encourage your students to buy a few little things for themselves when they reach a new size, or when they have achieved a desired performance level. This helps them feel good about themselves while they are making changes. A small item of clothing, a bottle of cologne or after-shave lotion, a book or game, tickets to a play or sporting event, a record or tape, a piece of sheet music, or some item related to a hobby or recreational activity provides a psychological lift. And the incentive to continue to make changes is reinforced. The purchase of even a few items represents an investment in themselves. The greater a student's investment, the more likely he or she will maintain control of eating habits.

One way to incorporate some of the ideas in this chapter is to spend a few minutes on support and reinforcement techniques in each lesson. Another way is to add a separate lesson to teach the concepts and assign some of the techniques for homework. Perhaps the easiest way to incorporate the ideas is to keep them in mind and add them to your class discussions whenever they are relevant. The initial discussion at the beginning of each lesson provides an excellent opportunity to pick up some of your students' needs for encouragement or for support and maintenance ideas. Whatever method you choose, a little extra time spent on ways to support and reinforce change will help your students learn to handle the inevitable periods of frustration and discouragement. They will emerge with the conviction that they really can maintain their new habits and patterns.

CONCLUSION

This instructor's material was written as a resource tool. It is not intended to be an absolute guide which must be followed in all situations. Its purpose is to assist you in the use of the student's book and in the development of your own food habit management course.

Perhaps the best way to use the instructor's material is to refer to it when specific needs arise as, for example, when designing the course, interviewing prospective students, selecting teaching techniques, and looking for reinforcement ideas. When planning specific lessons, the outlines and supplementary instructions may be particularly helpful, and the lesson outlines are useful as a reference while teaching.

A lot of information has been presented so that you will be able to select the specific ideas which apply to your instructional situation. Make modifications in the suggestions and add ideas of your own to make this a complete and useful reference. A carefully selected list of additional resource books is included in the bibliography. Most of them are available in paperback editions and may be ordered through any bookstore.

I hope this material will be helpful to you as you design and teach your course. I wish you as much fun and satisfaction from teaching your course as I derive from teaching mine. Good luck!

INSTRUCTOR NOTE

The text that appears in color is important to you. Special instructions and highlighted passages have been overlaid in color onto the student pages, so that the format and pagination of your instructor guide are identical.

FOOD HABIT MANAGEMENT

A COMPREHENSIVE GUIDE FOR DIETARY CHANGE

BY JULIE WALTZ

1987 Edition

Library of Congress Catalog Card Number: 82-14338

ISBN: 0-931836-01-8-17.95

Library of Congress Cataloging in Publication Data

Waltz, Julie, 1942-
Food Habit Management

Bibliography: p.
1. Reducing—Psychological aspects.
2. Behavior modification. 3. Food habits.
I. Title.
RM222.2.W265 613.2'5'019 82-14338
ISBN 0-931836-00-X

Suggested Citation:
Waltz, Julie. *Food Habit Management.* Tucson, Arizona: Northwest Learning Associates Inc., 1978, 1982, 1987

Published by Northwest Learning Associates Inc.
5728 N. Via Umbrosa
Tucson, Arizona 85715
(602) 299-8435

Printed by Outdoor Empire Publishing, Inc.
511 Eastlake Avenue E., P.O. Box C-19000
Seattle, Washington 98109
Printed in the United States of America.

TO MY STUDENTS

from whom I have
learned so much

Foreword

"In the present state of civilized society, with the provocatives of the culinary art, and the incentives of highly seasoned food, brandy and wine, the temptation to excess in the indulgences of the table are rather too strong to be resisted by poor human nature" (William Beaumont, 1833). Although almost 150 years have passed since Dr. Beaumont's elegant and accurate assessment of human nature, the statement remains extremely relevant to twentieth century Americans.

Today in America there is a high prevalence of obesity and it is estimated that 35 percent of all middle aged Americans are obese. Statistics also reveal that the average body weight of Americans has steadily increased over the past fifty years. This steady rise in spite of our increased concern for obesity is a major factor contributing to many diseases. And everyday millions of Americans go on diets and millions of Americans go off diets. Too often, the goal of these diets has been compliance with a planned, rigid diet. Such diets do not fit easily into the everyday routine of most patients and it is not surprising that approximately 95 percent of people who lose weight will regain the lost weight within a year after stopping the diet.

In physiological terms, the cure for obesity has been known for centuries. Just consume fewer calories than your body uses in a day. No magic, no mystery, just plain well-established fact. Nearly all diets are designed to reduce caloric intake, nearly all can produce successful results. So why do they fail?

This dismal outcome of dieting results from the failure of most diets and treatment programs to take into account the uniqueness of each person who is struggling to control body weight. In our current understanding, it is apparent that obesity is neither caused nor maintained by any single factor. Obesity can be the result of numerous biological, psychological, cultural, and environmental determinants. These influences vary greatly from one individual to another, and lead to important differences in overeating and underactivity. Since a variety of etiological factors can lead to the same result (excessive weight), it is essential that treatment be carefully individualized if long-term success is to be realized. Furthermore, most diets simply demand too much of normal human self-control. Sometimes they almost perversely take away the very food for which people yearn, despite the fact that these foods are often far from being the most fattening foods.

Fortunately, about fifteen years ago reports of treatment directed at helping people manage their food habits began to appear in scientific literature. Over the years these methods have been tested and refined, and the complexities of the new form of treatment became evident. It became increasingly apparent that it was not enough to change only basic habits; changes in attitudes, lifestyle and physical activity were also required.

Food Habit Management presents the latest and most innovative elements of these many years of research and clinical experience. Any program for dietary management must take into account individual variation in behavior, attitudes and lifestyle; diet alone is not enough.

The lessons in this manual cover the topics of awareness, how different environments affect behavior, basic eating style, food selection, physical activity and maintenance. In each lesson special attention is given to attitudes, assertiveness and planning. The sections dealing with getting back in control after lapses are excellent and present important and innovative techniques to handle one of the most difficult areas necessary for permanent weight control.

As a psychiatrist with a deep concern for the psychological suffering often experienced by the overweight individual, I am grateful to Julie Waltz for providing such a totally comprehensive and individualized habit management program. I am most delighted by the friendly, warm, honest and non-judgmental way in which she has presented her ideas. In the face of the overwhelming failure of most traditional approaches, it is time that we stop blaming the overweight person for lack of motivation, will power or what-have-you. It's time for a new attitude, a new approach and a totally new method of weight control.

This manual promises no miracles and no magic but it does provide new methods and attitudes. It provides the necessary framework for self-learning and self-control and each student will find the journey toward slimness vastly easier, more fun, and in the final analysis successful.

Henry A. Jordan, M.D.
Director
Institute for Behavioral Education
King of Prussia, PA
June, 1982

Acknowledgements

No author can claim originality for all of the concepts and ideas presented in his or her book and that is certainly true for me. The research and writings of Albert Stunkard, Richard Stuart, Stanley Schachter, Michael Mahoney, Henry Jordan, Leonard Levitz and James Ferguson have provided me with the fundamental background on which the ideas and methods in this book are based. I owe a great deal to my students and to the dietitians, physicians and social workers with whom I work for their numerous questions, ideas and observations. I particularly want to acknowledge Henry Jordan, whose interest and suggestions were instrumental in the design of this book. I also wish to thank Luanne Anderson, Denis Skog, and Naomi Urata for their contributions.

I am indebted to Peter Rettman, Charles D'Ambrosio, Kathy Heilbrunn, Robert Carter, Susan Sommerman, Irene Kinderis and the staff of the Adult Development Program for their help, support and encouragement. To Bob Kembel, a sincere thank you for hours of effort on behalf of this book and its home.

And, finally, I want to particularly acknowledge my daughters, Lori and Robin, and my friend and mentor, Fay Ainsworth, whose special caring and encouragement supported me through seemingly endless periods of frustration when I thought the work would never be done.

To all of these people, and to the others I have not specifically named, THANKS!

People often ask me if I have ever been overweight . . .

Preface

Hello,

Welcome to your course in Food Habit Management. I hope this book will help you gain the understanding and skills necessary for making controlled food intake part of your usual daily routine.

I would like to introduce myself and my book to you.

People often ask me if I have ever been overweight and how I became involved in weight control since my professional training is in special education. Yes, I have been overweight, from my early teens until fifteen years ago when I began working at the ADP. I am fascinated by how people learn. Realizing that I had learned to eat in ways that kept me overweight, I began experimenting to see if I could teach myself to eat differently. Some of my experiments were glorious successes and some were dismal flops! But over a period of eight months, I lost 42 pounds and more importantly, I learned to handle myself successfully in everyday circumstances, with problem foods, in difficult social situations, and when upset or depressed. That knowledge is still a working part of my life, and, while I still make mistakes and still have temporary lapses of control, I have maintained my weight loss comfortably. My enthusiasm prompted me to develop a class at the ADP using the process of learning that I had experienced. After thirteen-and-a-half years I am still teaching that same class, although the material has now been refined by information learned from researchers in the field of weight control and enriched by the experiences and reactions of my students.

The first edition of this book was written to answer my students' requests for a workbook to accompany the information given to them in class. The second edition was written to provide a basic workbook which instructors in the fields of medicine, social work, psychology, education, physical fitness, and weight control could use with their own students. That edition was used in private industry, hospitals, clinics, colleges and universities, large health care organizations, fitness centers, private offices, weight loss programs, and summer camps for weight reduction.

This is the third edition of **Food Habit Mangement** and it has been expanded to cover more information on the learning process and on techniques for restarting and maintaining control. Like the second edition, this one includes some of the experiences and stories my students have shared with me. I hope that in sharing them with you, you will see my students as people like yourself with many of the same feelings and worries that you are experiencing. Ninety-four percent of my students have lost weight with the approach used in this book and the majority of them have not regained what they lost. You can have the same success if

---

Ninety-four percent of my students have lost weight...

---

you recognize that changing your eating habits involves a step-by-step training process, like learning to play a musical instrument, and requires experimentation, time and patience. It's also a lot of fun. You don't have to be miserable to lose weight. The more fun you have and the more you laugh at the goofy things you do, the easier it will be to keep going. Your instructor will have lots of ideas to help you with the rough spots and to keep your sense of humor working.

As you look through your book, you will see that only the first and last lessons have been identified and no order has been given to the lessons in between. Your instructor will give you the sequence of the lessons according to the format used in your class or individualized program. This allows you to spend time with the areas which are relevant to your needs and to those of your classmates. Your instructor may give you information and assignments in addition to, or instead of, some of the lessons in the book. You can review those lessons not covered by your instructor on your own as supplementary information.

Effective long term weight control has three basic aspects: 1) a realistic daily control plan; 2) definite options to vary the basic plan to meet periodic needs as for vacations, holidays, special occasions; and 3) a plan for re-starting control when loss of control has occurred. Chapter 1 supplies the information necessary to begin an in-depth study of your current eating patterns and problems. The results of your study will form the basis upon which your entire control plan will be built. Chapters 2 through 6 and 8 through 9 provide the elements of a realistic, practical daily control plan. Flexibility and variations on the basic techniques are presented in Chapters 11 through 13 which deal with social eating, vacations, holidays and other variations of daily routine. Because loss of control is an area of constant worry and dread for many people, Chapters 7 and 10 are devoted to specific techniques for re-starting and re-establishing control of eating behaviors.

Chapter 14 marks the beginning of your independence. Study it carefully as you continue working with the techniques and methods you have learned in your course. Chapters 15, 16 and 17 are supplementary and deal with the topics of support, nutrition and exercise. If your instructor has expertise in these areas, he or she will probably add extra or similar information of their own selection.

A calorie counting system has been presented in the book, and the first lesson does require that you count the calories in what you eat and drink during the first week. Your instructor may teach you another system for recording food intake, most likely the "exchange" system. You may be using this book along with another treatment method where calorie counting is not required or a specific dietary plan is encouraged, such as one for heart disease or diabetes. Your instructor will teach you how to proceed and how to modify what is in the book and the accompanying record forms to meet your particular needs. The Reference Outline of Techniques and Exercises, located at the back of your book, is included for quick reference and is a functional part of your maintenance program. Directions for how and when to use it are in your book, and your instructor will explain it all to you at the appropriate time. The section called "Take Alongs" contains additional materials for reference. They are all on perforated pages so that you can remove them and take them along with you.

In taking this course you have shown a willingness to learn and an interest in yourself. I think that's great! You have a fascinating learning experience ahead of you. Good luck.

Sincerely,

Julie Waltz

January, 1987

Table of Contents

The initial spark of motivation must come from within.

Before You Begin

Almost daily we are confronted with the challenge of learning something: a concept, a task, a process, a point of view. We are concerned for how readily we grasp what is being taught, for how we will apply what we have learned, and for how long we will retain that knowledge. Effective dietary change involves many levels of learning. The process involved in accomplishing that learning is the subject of this introductory chapter.

My background is in the field of education with Bachelor and Master degrees in Special Education. Thus my concern has been in the area of handicapped learners, people who become bogged down in the learning process by physical, mental, educational or emotional handicaps. It is with this reference and personal history of overcoming my own weight problems that I have written this chapter. I do not view you or me as handicapped in the traditional sense, yet our ability to learn new eating behavior is indeed influenced by our past learning, our failures, our earned reputations for short-term change, and our feelings of fear and insecurity. Added to these and other emotional and psychological factors is the belief that as grown-up, reasonably intelligent and perhaps even well-read people in the field of nutrition or weight control we "ought" to be able to accomplish change in our eating behavior simply because we know better.

I strongly believe that the more people understand about the processes of learning and of changing behavior, the likelier they are to accomplish their goals. The purpose of this introduction is to help you understand more about the learning process and how it applies to the accomplishment of change in your life. Some information about motivation, psychological readiness for change and sabotage are included as well for these elements have great influence on the learning process. I will begin with motivation.

Many people come to me seeking motivation for controlling their food intake. I cannot help them for the initial spark of motivation must come from within the person seeking the change. That is true for you as well. Other people cannot truly motivate you. They can inspire you, push you, advise you and cheer for you, but they cannot create the drive necessary for you to achieve your goals. The effort expended in achieving a goal is voluntary. If you see no personal gain for reaching a particular goal, your efforts to make the necessary changes will be sporadic and of short duration. So the very first step in the change process is to determine that the changes you seek in yourself are ones that you personally want to create and for your very own personal reasons.

Do you recall hearing that young children do not learn to read until they are developmentally capable of the basic skills necessary to visually track, decode and encode words? The development of those skills is the function of reading readiness programs. In similar fashion, people do not seriously undertake an active program of long term behavior change until they are psychologically ready to do so. For example, you may not be committed and ready to accomplish change when you first seek help or enroll in a program to help you reach your goal. Spending money does not always imply commitment, nor does it necessarily reinforce shaky commitment.

Some people need to test the water before jumping in, so to speak. If you are a person who gets into a swimming pool by slowly putting in your toe, then your ankle, shin, knee, thigh, etc., you may find that you approach new weight reduction programs in the same careful, cautious manner. Many people need to "audit" a course before taking it for credit. In effect they go through the motions of attending the sessions without seriously doing the assigned tasks. It is a matter of trying the concepts and ideas on for size to see if they fit, if they feel OK before committing themselves to working with them. If this applies to you, give yourself room to listen and to play with the concepts, and perhaps take the course a second time. Many people have to go through this stage before they are receptive and ready for change.

If you are undergoing some other major life event while you are taking this course, you may not have the energy or concentration to make effective change in your eating behavior. Changing jobs, new marriage, divorce, moving to a new home, severe illness of someone important to you, are all examples of situations which may absorb a great deal of your available energy. If this is true for you, make arrangements to take the class at another time or simply audit the course as suggested above.

In addition you must be certain that the goals you set and the path you've chosen to take you to those goals are ones that you believe in and are willing to pay the price of hard, steady effort to achieve. Long-term change means long-term commitment, so the rewards of progress must be emotionally satisfying to you in the present as well as in the future.

To determine your own level of readiness for change read the steps listed at the top of the next page. If you can answer each statement in a clear and positive way, you are psychologically prepared to undertake a serious course of study in changing your eating behavior.

Signs of readiness for change.

1. **Clear statement of your own reasons for wanting to make change.**
2. **Clear statement of what you are willing to do to accomplish change.**
   a. Setting study time aside each week.
   b. Explaining each week's learning with someone for your reinforcement and their support of your progress.
   c. Willingness to experiment with the ideas.
   d. Attending scheduled appointments or class sessions regularly.
3. **Clear statement of a period of time** during which you will make consistent effort to study the material presented and do the assigned home study tasks.

If you are unable or unwilling to commit yourself to these steps at this time, discuss your situation with your instructor to determine the best plan for you. Perhaps auditing the course or taking it at another time would be the best approach. This may seem harsh to you but there is a related psychological element called resistance to change. While this is discussed more fully in Chapter 14, the resistance phenomenon emerges when a person attempts to corner, or trap, himself into something he is unwilling to do. Consider what happens when a fleeing animal is cornered and cannot escape. It lashes out, trying to strike down the opponent. In similar fashion, if you attempt to trap yourself into a series of commitments you don't want, the end result will be noncompliance and dropping out at one extreme, or lashing out and sabotaging your progress at the other extreme. If you recognize these tendencies in yourself, examine your motives. If they point to unwillingness to make change, wait until you feel differently before taking the course or plan to audit it as suggested earlier. If, however, you recognize the tendencies to drop out of weight control programs as being a result of frustration, or the tendency to sabotage your progress as a perverse quirk in your psychological make-up, continue reading. I will refer again to both of these tendencies toward the end of this chapter.

Assuming that you are motivated to study and to accomplish change, the next point of focus will be on the learning process itself, and a little later on, how that learning process applies to your behavior change program.

People accomplish their learning in many ways. Some people **learn by hindsight.** In fact, most of life's learning is by hindsight. An example is writing an English theme. You turn it in and then learn from the red marks the teacher puts on it. If you get an "A", you probably don't know specifically why you got that "A", if there were no comments alongside the grade, but if you got a "B" or "C", all those notes on the margins and the circled words will give you a concrete idea of why you earned whatever grade you were given. Similarly, when watching some young skaters train for world competition I noticed that the coaches were fairly quiet, not beginning their training "chatter" until the errors were made. It seems that when something is done well little time is spent analyzing why it went well. When errors occur a great deal of analysis typically takes place. The analysis provides the base for the learning.

Another method of learning is **by rote**. The first learning in any task is by conscious application of steps or rules. A good example is manually shifting a car. New drivers accelerate to 10 mph, shift; 20 mph, shift; 30 mph, shift. Veteran drivers know instinctively when to shift up or down from the feel or sound of the car's engine, and don't look at the speedometer for verification. Flexibility results from the continued practice of those steps or rules.

Learning by example is the method we as parents, teachers, supervisors, etc., employ when we share our wisdom and advice with others. Many people have little difficulty following the procedures established by others, and are careful to avoid the pitfalls others have experienced.

A great number of people have to learn from **personal experience**. An adolescent, for example, frequently rejects his parents' advice on a subject and goes through the very same learning and errors they went through in order to arrive at the very same conclusion. What is important is the experience gained in the process of trial and error.

You will see all four learning styles applied in your **Food Habit Management** course. Hindsight learning will be encouraged in the weekly discussions and problem solving sessions. Rote learning is reflected in the application of the basic techniques in Chapters 2 through 6. The early steps in any learning project, skiing, playing piano, speaking a foreign language, typing, are all by rote. Improvisation comes later. Learning by example will happen as you seek the advice of your instructor and fellow students. Experiential learning is the result of all your experiments in seeking effective change. This is the learning only you can accomplish and it is the learning style most necessary for effective, realistic long-term change.

There are four basic messages underlying the learning process. The first is that you need to do something before any learning can take place. Until you write and submit your English theme, as in the example used earlier, no learning can take place. Doing something involves the risk that it won't be done correctly. Risk involves courage because of the fear that others won't approve when something is done incorrectly. Continuous lack of error, on the other hand, could happen if you are not pushing yourself hard enough to try new things, if you are doing only what you already know how to do. If you never try anything new your skills will not increase.

The learning process is a bit complex but in its simplified form it follows a gradual progression; from simple to difficult; from concrete to abstract; and from rote to improvisation (on-the-spot flexibility). Many people are annoyed with themselves when they don't readily grasp the difficult or complex tasks, or the abstract concepts. They become impatient with their need to hear things repeated several times, and frustrated at the seemingly slow pace with which their competence advances. If you are one of these people, read again the opening sentence of this paragraph. The learning process is the same for every person and for every area of learning. Expect to begin this course with easy, concrete steps which will progress in difficulty and complexity. Some things will seem too easy for you, too simple. Do them anyway. It's fun to get off to an easy start. Some of the easiest steps have been the most effective for me simply because they were ones I could do readily and without a lot of planning or extra thought. What reinforces and excites most of us is being able to do the tasks. It's exhilarating to accomplish something!

Right now, at the very beginning of your Food Habit Management course, you already possess a set of eating and food managment skills which have been perfected and practiced to a fine, fluid, mastery level. They require little advance thought or preparation. When you use them they feel comfortable and secure, like an old shoe which has molded itself to the particular shape of your foot. What you are asking of yourself in changing your habits, is to accept the exchange of old, comfortable, familiar, secure patterns and procedures for a set of new patterns and procedures which, in the beginning, will feel awkward, inconsistent, unfamiliar and not very comfortable or secure. The old ways have satisfied very specific needs in your life and in replacing them you will learn new ways to meet the same needs. All new learning feels awkward and unsure. It is in the application of old adage, "practice makes perfect", that the familiarity is built, and that the blending and molding of the new approaches to fit your personality and life space takes place. In time your newly developing habits will feel secure and you will prefer them to your old routine. The challenge is to hang in there long enough for the change-over to take place. Here are some ideas to help you through the transition period.

1. **Set a weekly goal of experimenting with the ideas and tasks presented.** Open mindedness helps a lot. You may be surprised at the usefulness of some simple or seemingly silly technique.

2. **Make the first learning tasks so simple that it would be almost impossible not to be able to do them.** No matter how much practice you've had in dieting, begin with the easy steps first.

3. **Keep the assigned tasks within your skill level.** If you have difficulty with something, problem-solve the situation with your instructor after the first week. If you are still having difficulty with it in the second week, it is probably related to one of three things: it is too difficult a task for your skill level at this time, you don't like doing it so you avoid it, or it doesn't fit well into your lifestyle. Whichever is the case, move the task out of the way and go on to something else. Don't allow yourself to be hung up by any task or process for more than a week-and-a-half.

4. **Set the situation up in advance to help the desired behavior occur.** Reminder notes are helpful to jog your memory. For example, a note on my bathroom mirror reminds me to put an apple in my purse before going to bed. That way I won't forget it when I leave in the morning, since I always take my purse. Then I have something to eat on my way home from work which prevents me from stopping to buy a candy bar because I'm hungry.

5. **Select someone in your home environment and thoroughly explain each week's lesson to him or her.** If you live alone, choose someone you work with, a friend or a relative. By explaining your lessons and projects to someone else, you will have to make sense out of them. If you can't, it will show you what you aren't understanding and you can ask questions at the next class session. This also allows someone who cares about you to know what you're doing and why, and will enable that person to give you feedback and positive reinforcement. Children can be wonderful sources of encouragement; so if you have children above the age of four, let them know what you're doing. If you share all of this with others, you are less likely to give up during periods of discouragement or frustration. One very effective way to sabotage your success in losing weight is to tell no one what you're doing. Then when you have difficulty, you can give up, abandon your projects, and no one will know the difference.

6. **Focus on the process rather than on the end result.** If your eating behavior changes in the desired ways, the result you are looking for will occur. **Look daily at what you are doing** and if what you're doing is not bringing the desired changes in your eating behavior, change what you are doing, experimenting until you get the desired change. When you discover what works, practice it over and over and over again.

7. **Recognize the tendencies you may have toward sabotaging your progress and take action to avoid them.** There are many ways to sabotage your progress in this course. You could, for example, try to do too many things at one time and become overwhelmed, frustrated and discouraged. You might become too busy to do the homework assignments or too busy to come to the class sessions. You might plan elaborate dinners or parties. You might deliberately test yourself by walking into your favorite candy store on a day of shaky control to see if you can go in and not buy anything. You might even get someone else to sabotage your success by telling your favorite "food pushers" that you are trying to limit how much you eat and then let them talk you out of it by pushing your favorite foods at you. Incidentally, food pushers are not usually good reinforcers of controlled food intake, so when selecting people to share your progress with, don't include them.

8. **Talk about your successes and not your failures.** This is not an easy task since most of us are prone to notice our errors and failings, and equally quick to qualify all successes as being of minor importance or not of our own doing (i.e., "it was too hot to eat so that's why I lost weight"). If you only talk about the problems and failures, you and others will develop a negative attitude toward the whole project. If, instead, you chatter on about how nice it is to have the "junk" food out of the way, or about how delicious your "á la carte" lunch was at the restaurant, or about your progress with a particular task, like sitting down to eat;

you and others will enjoy what you have to say and all of you will develop positive attitudes toward you and your changes.

In concluding this introductory chapter, there is a personal message I would like to leave with you. The value of this course is not in the end result; it is in the learning and the growth which occur in the process of achieving the goals you set for yourself. If I could give you the dietary changes you seek as a gift, you would not be able to keep them, for the basis of knowledge required to keep and manage those changes comes from doing the work, making the mistakes, changing the procedures, understanding yourself, working within your own abilities and limitations. The joy of success comes from having made lots of mistakes earlier. And when you reach your goal, you will have earned it yourself. It will be your victory, not your mother's (who maybe nagged at you), or your teacher's (who showed you the way) or your friend's (who listened to you when you needed to talk). It will be your victory earned out of struggle at times, success at times, frustration, elation, and, most of all, faith—faith in yourself and in your ability to achieve your goals. You'll have that victory if you believe it will happen and if you believe in yourself. Go for it! And keep going for it!

Learning how to work with yourself can be one of the most exciting and challenging tasks in your life. All it requires is time, patience, commitment, and a darn good sense of humor! Are you ready? Good! Let's get started.

Chapter 1 - INSTRUCTOR NOTES (Text begins on page 17.)

Discussion Topics:

1. Influence of external factors upon eating response.

   a. Moods/feelings: depression, anxiety, loneliness, boredom, anger, frustration, happiness, fatigue. Depression, fatigue and boredom are the three most commonly cited factors which result in uncontrolled eating.

   b. Rationales: "I'd better eat now in case I won't have a chance to eat later," "It would only go to waste anyway," "It'll make her feel good if I eat it and I don't want to hurt her feelings," "I'll exercise it off later," "It's been an awful day and I need something to soothe me," "I need an energy boost," "I need a little something to settle my stomach."

   c. Advertising: radio/TV commercials, billboards, grocery ads in newspapers and on store windows, lighted signs for restaurants and food stores, pictures and recipes in magazines and papers, the scent of freshly baked bread or cookies drifting out of an open bakery window, the placement of "impulse foods" on store shelves.

   d. Celebrations: religious and cultural holidays (Hallowe'en, Thanksgiving, Christmas/Chanukah, New Year's Eve, Valentine's Day, Sweetest Day, Easter/Passover, Mother's Day, Father's Day, Memorial Day, Fourth of July, Labor Day), birthdays, anniversaries, graduations, weddings, achievement celebrations of all kinds (getting a desired job, leaving a disliked job, getting into college, passing a big test, finding a new house or apartment, getting the price you wanted for the sale of some item, waving goodbye to the relatives after a two-week stay at your house).

   e. Socialization: a vehicle to get together with others for social, business or family needs, and an accompaniment to other social activities (stopping for a bite to eat after a movie or sporting event). Another social influence is the effect of certain people upon eating response ("eating buddies" and "food pushers").

   f. Demonstration of caring: bringing food to those who are ill or grieving over the death of a loved one, "I love you" gifts from one person to another.

   g. Reputation: fabulous cook (therefore having to prepare high-calorie "specialties" for guests), big eater, dessert lover.

   h. Miscellaneous: to keep someone company, to avoid doing something unpleasant, to spite someone else, for self-punishment, to reward or pamper oneself, to relax, to wind up or wind down, to wake up or induce drowsiness, to think with, to take a break, to warm up or cool off.

(Continued on page 16.)

(Continued from page 15.)

2. Concept of stimulus response.
   a. Hunger response to the sight or smell of food, to the sound of someone eating, to an open bag of potato chips, to food that is offered by a host or hostess, to the sight of a clock if it is a normal meal time.
   b. Concept of paired associations (ie., the association made between two things, as food and a particular object).
      1. Discuss Pavlov's famous dog experiments in which he trained the dogs to salivate at the sound of a bell by always feeding them when he rang the bell. In time the dogs associated the sound of the bell with food, and the sound of the bell (without food being present) caused them to salivate in anticipation of eating. Paired associations can be broken, as Pavlov demonstrated by repeatedly ringing the bell without feeding the dogs. In time the dogs stopped salivating at the sound of the bell because they no longer expected to be fed.
      2. Relate this concept to what happens when people turn on the TV and find that they want to eat, or when they pick up a book or walk through a particular door and get an immediate urge to eat something.

Homework Assignments:

1. Food Data Record
   a. The instructions are on pages 20 and 21.
   b. If people have been dieting prior to enrolling in your class, it is not necessary that they deliberately increase their food intake in order to do this assignment effectively. Instruct them to write down **all food items they had urges to eat**, to record the amounts and calories they would have consumed, and to fill out all the rest of the information just as if those items had actually been eaten. The calories of the items in parentheses should **not** be added to the day's calorie total because they weren't eaten (if they were added in, the calorie intake would be inaccurate). The purpose of writing down the uneaten food items (the ones in parentheses) is for the students to gather a more accurate picture of their more typical, less controlled eating patterns.
   c. Encourage the students to record every day, even if they have to recall the information from memory. Ideally each person will bring in seven completed Food Data Records. Practically, many students will not record for several full days. Ask them to record for a **maximum** of three days: two weekdays and one weekend day. Stress that they will learn more from seven days of records than from three, but that even three days of data will give them some information on which to base the next lesson's experiments.
2. Data Analysis Form
   a. The instructions are on page 21.
   b. Inform your students that you will begin the next lesson with a general discussion of the information recorded on this form. It will encourage them to complete it and thereby provide additional incentive for doing the Food Data Records.
3. Weekly Weighing and the Weight Record
   a. Caution your students not to expect weight loss during the first week of data collection. Some students may gain weight, others may lose or maintain their weight. Whatever the result, they will have ample opportunities in the following weeks to lose weight.
   b. My recommendation for frequency of weighing is once a week. The scale is only an approximate measure of real weight loss, inasmuch as scale weight is also influenced by other factors such as change in water level (due to medication, menstrual cycle, increase/decrease in salt intake, perspiration, etc.), or in proportion of lean body (muscle) weight resulting from changes in exercise patterns. There is nothing more discouraging to many people than to jump on the scale after a day of good control and find that the scale weight is up. Others feel so elated to see the scale weight go down that they may indulge in an extra treat or two. In either case, daily weighing can create problems. **The task is to focus people away from the scale and onto their habits.** The scale is an "after the fact" measure. The only immediate measure of control effectiveness is either whether the food item/beverage was consumed or whether it was consumed in a planned amount.
   c. If you want to weigh your students yourself, instruct them accordingly. Because the students will rely on their home scales after the course is over, it is a good idea to have them weigh at home just before leaving for the class. This will provide them with a comparison between their scales and yours. If they do that weekly, they will see whether the changes on their scales are proportional to the changes on your scale. It is not important that the actual weight numbers be identical on the two scales; the important factor is consistency of the home scale with your scale. You may require them to record both weight numbers if they are not identical. In this way when the class is over, the students will be able to maintain their weight records without confusion.
   d. The instructions for the Weight Record are on pages 21 and 22.
   e. There are two Weight Records. One is the student's copy and one is for you. Ask the students to fill out both of

(Continued on page 23.)

1 (**INSTRUCTOR NOTES** for this chapter begin on page 15.)

Target: Data collection.
Objectives:
1. Develop awareness of eating habits, patterns and problems.
2. Isolate factors which influence a controlled eating response and factors which influence an uncontrolled eating response.
3. Determine average daily calorie consumption.

Motto:

Awareness is the first step toward change.

Environmental Impact and Food Cues

This lesson concentrates on the development of an awareness of external, or environmental, cue mechanisms and their impact on eating behavior. Many studies have demonstrated that overweight people are more likely to eat in response to a suggestion to eat than are thin people. Suggestions of this type include the following: the sight or smell of food, the sound of someone eating, a food advertisement on radio or TV, pictures of food, a newspaper grocery ad or recipe, or the request of someone else to have something to eat.

Another type of environmental cue is called a paired association. This term refers to the process of associating food, or eating, with a specific object or activity so that the sight of the object or engaging in the activity results in feelings of hunger. Even walking through the front door or the time of day may serve as effective hunger stimulants. If a person eats frequently while reading or watching TV, in time the process of settling down with something to read or turning on the TV set may result in a hunger response.

The above is an example of a cue response of the same type recognized by Pavlov in his famous experiment with the dogs. In his experiment the dogs had been taught that, immediately after the sound of a bell, they would be given food to eat. In time the sound of the bell caused the dogs to salivate in anticipation of the food, whether or not food was actually present. An expansion of that experiment involved only the sound of the bell; no food was given to the dogs. In time the sound of the bell no longer caused the dogs to salivate, because they stopped associating the bell with food. Similarly, environmental cues that are associated in people's minds with eating can be broken by separating the object or the activity from eating.

Social factors form another type of

environmental cue mechanism. Studies have illustrated that overweight people are much more responsive to social pressure to eat than are thin people. The role of host, hostess or guest may be strongly associated with the need to eat. Many overweight people talk about their inability to turn down a persuasive hostess because they don't want to hurt her feelings. People may also eat in order not to draw attention to themselves or to endure comments or questions like, "Are you on another diet?", or "You can have one night off, can't you?" One lady motivated herself to clean her house by inviting someone over for a cup of coffee and a piece of coffee cake, and then spent the hour or two before the person's arrival cleaning the house. She couldn't make her guest uncomfortable by not having a piece of cake herself, so she ate with her guest.

"Are you on another diet?" ..."You can have one night off, can't you?"

After the guest left she "evened up the edges of the cake" with a small slice every time she walked past the cake sitting in plain view on the kitchen counter.

When people get together with each other, food is often an accompaniment. Celebrations of all kinds include food. Consider the food customs associated with the following: Valentine's Day, Mother's Day, Father's Day, Memorial Day, Fourth of July, Labor Day, Halloween, Thanksgiving, Hanukkah, Christmas, Easter, birthdays, anniversaries, weddings and graduations. Family and social gatherings most often involve food. Frequently, business meetings include lunch, dinner or a drink as part of the meeting. Even illnesses and funerals involve food since preparing a meal is a tangible way for a person to demonstrate caring toward those who are ill or grieving. Food items, like candy, nuts or an ice cream cone, are frequently chosen for "I love you" gifts. Turning down such gifts because of concern about calories would be unthinkable for many people.

Eating is an acceptable activity in almost any social setting. Movie theatres, airplanes, study lounges, sporting events and the like are equipped with food for easy consumption. Eating is permissible during symphonies, operas, plays, meetings, conferences and even classrooms when the class convenes during normal eating hours. In short, a person may eat almost anywhere, including places where smoking or drinking may not be allowed. The message is that eating is always acceptable. Food processing and marketing represent a major industry, and there are few places a person can go where food items for sale are not in evidence. If their presence stimulates a desire to eat, if eating is acceptable behavior, and if others in the group are also eating, restricting food intake can be a formidable task.

Overweight people use many rationales for eating: they need ginger ale or milk to calm an upset stomach, a hard candy for

---

...if eating is acceptable behavior, restricting food intake can be a formidable task.

---

bad breath, a candy bar for energy, something hot to warm up with or something cold to cool off with. They eat to wind up or to wind down, to wake up or to induce drowsiness, to reduce tension, to alleviate boredom, to comfort themselves when depressed or lonely, to pamper or console themselves, and even to celebrate. For most people, the act of eating is sensually pleasurable. If a person feels better for having had something to eat, it is logical that the person will eat when in similar circumstances in the future. Eventually a lesson is learned: "If I have something to eat, I'll feel better." Moods or feeling states become active cue mechanisms which create a desire to eat.

People are often amazed at how much unaware eating they do in a day's time. Eating of this type is typified by reaching absentmindedly into a nearby bowl from which the person had been taking food, finding nothing left in the bowl, looking into the bowl, and exclaiming in amazement, "Did I eat all that?" Other examples are munching a couple of cookies from the cookie jar, eating a slice of bologna while making sandwiches, nibbling the leftovers on plates or in bowls, or taking two fingers full of peanut butter from an open jar when passing through the kitchen. Many men report that they consume a considerable number of calories while standing around the kitchen watching their wives prepare meals. A friend of mine coined the term "grazing" to refer to this type of random, frequent, unaware eating.

Not all unaware eating is random, however. Some is quite predictable. A woman in one of my classes related the following story. When buying her home the deciding factor was the existence of a large, walk-in pantry adjoining the laundry area. Over a period of a few months a pattern evolved. The woman would put a load of laundry in the washing machine, go into the pantry where she kept a chair and a book, shut the door and read and eat until the bell rang which signalled the end of the wash cycle. She would then put the clothes into the dryer, and return to the pantry to read and eat until the clothes were dry. This, to her amazement, was a daily pattern.

Another student discovered that when he entered his house through the door near the kitchen he went immediately to the refrigerator for something to eat. When he entered through the door near the living room, however, he would first change his clothes and then read the paper in the living room, seldom going into the kitchen until dinner was served.

Many people have more extensive random eating patterns at work than at home. Morning coffee breaks, food left in staff lounges, boxes of candy or doughnuts placed on counters or near coffee pots, vending machines, and nearby short-order restaurants provide opportunities for excess food consumption. Desk drawers are frequently storage places for snack foods. People who often eat at their desks may find they have a paired association between the desk and food. Others use the rationale that it is permissible to take a work break only to eat, and thus learn to eat in order to take a rest.

...when he entered his house through the door near the kitchen he went immediatly to the refrigerator for something to eat.

Explanation of Homework

Assignment for this week: observe what you eat, your eating behavior and patterns, and record the information faithfully.

The following exercises are intended to help you become very aware of your eating in terms of what, where, and when you eat, how hungry you are, what cues you to eat, how many calories you consume, and in which social situations you have good or poor control of your food intake. In short, at the end of this week you will have accumulated extensive data on your eating behavior. It is essential that you become aware of what you normally do before you begin making changes! Therefore **do not change anything this week.** Do what you usually do. These records are for your information and private use.

Food Data Record

There are seven Food Data Records on pages 25-37. Use one for each day of the week. These records are to be used for data collection on everything consumed except water. You may either weigh your food or use a volume measure to determine the amount. Any calorie book will help you in obtaining the calorie information. You will then need to record the time of day the food or beverage was consumed and whether it represented a meal or a snack. The next column asks you to rate how hungry you were *before* eating: 0 = no hunger, 1 = mild hunger, 2 = moderate hunger, and 3 = extreme hunger. Next, record what activity you were doing just before eating and then, where you ate.

The column for mood or feeling before eating may be the most difficult for you to complete. Terms which might be helpful in recording are: depressed, bored, nervous, angry, irritable, left-out, happy, tired or even "blah." If you can't identify a feeling or mood, leave the space blank.

The column for social situation is to be used to note family meals, business lunches, social gatherings of all kinds, and even times when you ate by yourself. The last column should be used to record your level of control over your food intake in each situation: 0 = no control, 1 = poor control, 2 = fair control and 3 = good control. Some people like to put the names of the people they eat with in the social situation column and rate their level of control with each person. That can be very useful information.

...become aware of what you normally do before you begin making changes!

Study the sample Food Data Record on page 24.

As you begin collecting these data you may discover the urge to not eat something rather than write it down. If those items are not recorded, you will have an inaccurate picture of your normal pattern. Therefore, **enter all food items whether or not you actually eat them,** and identify the ones you didn't eat by putting parentheses around them. When totaling the daily calorie intake, **do not add in the calories of the foods you didn't eat.**

It is important to record periodically throughout the day in order to achieve the most accurate information. Leave this book in a place where you are likely to see it and be reminded to write in it. If it is awkward to carry the book with you, simply remove the forms and carry them in your purse or pocket. If you have forgotten to record for the whole day, record as much information as you can from memory. That will be more helpful than not recording anything.

Remember, these records are for your own use, and the more accurate you are in gathering information about your eating behavior, the more successful you will be in implementing change. After all, a successful chemistry experiment cannot be performed from inaccurate or incomplete data. Neither can a successful experiment in human behavior be performed without complete, correct information from which to plan.

Data Analysis Form

On the evening or morning before coming to the next class complete the Data Analysis Form on pages 41-42. The purpose of this form is to aid you in condensing the information from the week's data sheets. First, average your daily calorie intake and record that plus the weight change from the previous week on the form. The blanks in Section 3 are provided for you to list the places where you most frequently ate your meals and snacks. Section 4 breaks the day up into two-hour time periods. Review each time period separately on your data sheets and note whether it was a time when you ate constantly, frequently, rarely, or never, and what your average hunger level was for that time period. Enter that information on the Data Analysis Form. If you ate only a regularly established meal within a two-hour time period, you can note it as "breakfast only," "lunch only," and so on. If you identify periods of time when eating frequency is high and hunger levels are low, the eating is most likely influenced by environmental factors, and those can be identified easily. Section 5 provides spaces for you to record the activities, objects or people, and moods or feelings which most often preceded unscheduled meals or snacks.

As you review your Food Data Records, you may notice movement patterns at

---

If eating frequency is high and hunger levels are low, the eating is most likely influenced by environmental factors...

---

home or at work which frequently result in extra food being eaten. Using a hallway at work which goes past a vending machine or using the telephone in the kitchen are two examples of such movement patterns. Record these patterns in the spaces provided in Section 6. For Section 7 list the social situations and people most frequently mentioned on your Food Data Records and write in your average control level for each of the situations and people. There is a sample Data Analysis Form on pages 39-40.

Completing this form may seem like a lot of work to you right now. The information condensed on it will be invaluable to you as you go through the lessons in this book. Besides, what good are all those data you collected for seven days if you can't use it?

Weight Record

The Weight Records, found on pages 45-47, are provided for you to keep an accurate, up-to-date account of all your weight changes. Each Record includes a chart for current weight, weekly weight change, average daily calorie intake and date. There is also a graph to make it easy to see the overall weight change pattern.

To use the Weight Record, first, weigh yourself on your home scale tomorrow morning, before breakfast and without clothes, and enter your weight and the date on the top line of the chart. Do not weigh again until the morning of the day you return for your second lesson. Enter that weight and the date on the second line of the chart. Figure out the change in your weight from the previous week and enter it in the second column. Use a "+" or a "-" to show whether your weight change represented a gain or a loss from the previous week. If you maintained your weight during the week, put a zero in the weight change column. Compute your average, daily calorie intake for the week and enter that figure in the third column. If you are not counting calories, leave that column blank or use it for recording other information. Review the sample Weight Record on page 43.

Two Weight Records have been provided: one for you and one for your instructor. Enter all weights and weight changes indicated by your home scale on your copy of the Record. If your instructor prefers that you use the scale he or she has provided, record those weights and weight changes on the instructor's copy. When the course is completed, your instructor will have a record of your weight according to his or her scale, and you will have a record of your weight according to your own scale. If you are using only a home scale or only the instructor's scale, use the same figures for both forms.

To plot your progress on the graph, write your beginning weight on the line to the left of the graph. The horizontal line beginning at 0 signifies no change in weight. Gains in weight above the beginning weight are recorded above the line and losses in weight are recorded below the line. If you lose some weight, regain a few pounds but still weigh less than your beginning weight, the lines of your graph will still be below the horizontal line. Study the graph on the sample Weight Record.

In closing this lesson I would like to add a few words about daily weighing. It is more helpful if you weigh yourself weekly. Daily weighing may cause you to focus more on the scale than on your habits, and the point of control is not in the scale—it is in the habits themselves. People comment about feeling depressed if their weight goes up, especially after a day of good control; if the weight is lower than expected, it occasionally leads to an extra doughnut or some other goodie.

Daily weighing may cause you to focus more on the scale...

Either way, daily weighing can be a problem. Weekly weighing will be sufficient to measure the effectiveness of the habit changes. Some people will lose weight after the first week of recording. Others will gain or maintain their weight. It is not expected that you will lose weight in the first week.

This lesson requires more work than any other lesson in the book, and yet in many ways it is the most interesting. It is a unique opportunity you have to be an original researcher in your own behavior patterns. The data you collect during this coming week will open up a fascinating series of experiences for you. The more you know about yourself, the easier it will be to set up successful experiments and establish long-term change. Some people look at this week as their last chance to enjoy their favorite foods; others become so conscious of everything they eat that they eat much less than usual. Whatever your response is, the importance of this lesson is not how much you eat, it is the identification of what causes you to eat both with and without control. So, watch what you do and don't be surprised by anything you see. Good luck!

(Continued from page 16.)

them and leave one copy with you at the end of the last class. If you are having the students weigh in class and at home, they can record the numbers on your scale for your copy of the weight record and the numbers on their scale for their copy.

Closing Comments for the Students:

1. Don't get discouraged by how much there is to do. This is the most time-consuming lesson but it lasts for only one week.
2. The fun of learning about yourself is worth the bother of writing everything down.
3. Don't let yourself get upset by how much or how often you're eating. If you weren't overeating to begin with, you wouldn't be taking this course. So expect yourself to eat. Don't be surprised by what you do.
4. This week's focus is not so much on what you're eating, as on the factors which influence what, how much, and how often you eat. If you have a binge this week, just write everything down so that you can learn from it.

Summary:

People eat differently according to the times of the day, their moods, the circumstances and the people they are with. Many of these responses are consistent and quite predictable. It is important for your students to be aware of how the various stimuli affect them, particularly the ones which produce consistent responses. In time they will learn to apply their knowledge of what results in controlled eating to augment and strengthen their over-all eating control. In this lesson they will learn what specifically affects them and in what ways. In subsequent lessons they will learn techniques for modifying or eliminating the stimuli which result in uncontrolled eating, and for building controlled eating responses through conscious planning.

FOOD DATA RECORD - INSTRUCTOR NOTES

For the First Lesson: Environmental Impact and Food Cues

Purposes:

1. Create an awareness of what is being consumed.
2. Provide a mechanism for collecting data on information related to food and beverage consumption.
3. Provide a mechanism for detecting food cues.
4. Provide a record of daily calorie consumption.
5. Provide the information necessary for assessing and analyzing food and hunger patterns.

Explanation of instructions: pages 20 and 21.

Sample form: page 24.

Appropriate lesson: the first lesson only.

Instructions: highlighted on pages 20 and 21.

(**INSTRUCTOR NOTES** for this form are on page 23.)

FOOD DATA RECORD (Sample)

List each food item and describe method of preparation (baked, fried, boiled, broiled, raw) Food Item/Beverage	Amount	Calories	Time of Day	Meal/Snack	Level of hunger before eating 0 = none to 3 = extreme hunger	Activity before eating	Feeling/mood before eating (bored, tired, depressed, happy)	Location of eating	Social situation (family meal, eating out, meal at work, alone, etc.)	Eating control level 0 = none to 3 = total
Raisin Bran	3/4 cup	101	7:30 AM	M	2	family breakfast prep.	hurried	kitchen table	family meal	3
Skim milk	1/2 cup	51	"	M	2	"	"	"	"	3
Sugar	1 tsp	16	"	M	2	"	"	"	"	3
orange juice	1/2 cup	55	"	M	2	"	"	"	"	3
Black Coffee	1 cup	—	"	M	2	"	"	"	"	3
McDonald's Hamburger	1/4 lb.	416	12:15 PM	M	2	Drive to Restaurant	happy	Restaurant	lunch w/ Judy	2
Coke	6 oz.	73	"	M	2	"	"	"	"	2
apple (raw)	1	80	3:30 PM	S	2	ran errand	bored	desk	work break, alone	2
Coke	6 oz.	73	4:00 PM	S	2	cleared off desk	tired	desk	"	2
6 Oreo cookies	6	228	5:43 PM	S	2 1/2	arrived home	tired rushed	kitchen counter	alone	1
chicken (roasted)	4 oz.	206	6:30 PM	M	2	family dinner prep.	wound up	kitchen table	family meal	2
green beans (boiled)	1/2 cup	20	"	M	2	"	"	"	"	2
Baked potato	1	92	"	M	2	"	"	"	"	2
1 tsp. butter	1 tsp.	33	"	M	2	"	"	"	"	2
Jello	1/2 cup	81	"	M	2	family dinner	relaxed	"	"	2
Binge	?	approx. 1200	12:30 AM	Binge	1	had phone call	depressed	kitchen	alone	0

Total Calories for day 2725

Date January 31

FOOD DATA RECORD

List each food item and describe method of preparation (baked, fried, boiled, broiled, raw) Food Item/Beverage	Amount	Calories	Time of Day	Meal/Snack	Level of hunger before eating 0 = none to 3 = extreme hunger	Activity before eating	Feeling/mood before eating (bored, tired, depressed, happy)	Location of eating	Social situation (family meal, eating out, meal at work, alone, etc.)	Eating control level 0 = none to 3 = total

Total Calories for day ____________________

Date ______________________________

FOOD DATA RECORD

List each food item and describe method of preparation (baked, fried, boiled, broiled, raw) Food Item/Beverage	Amount	Calories	Time of Day	Meal/Snack	Level of hunger before eating 0 = none to 3 = extreme hunger	Activity before eating	Feeling/mood before eating (bored, tired, depressed, happy)	Location of eating	Social situation (family meal, eating out, meal at work, alone, etc.)	Eating control level 0 = none to 3 = total

Total Calories for day ____________

Date ____________

FOOD DATA RECORD

List each food item and describe method of prep-aration (baked, fried, boiled, broiled, raw) Food Item/Beverage	Amount	Calories	Time of Day	Meal/Snack	Level of hunger before eating 0 = none to 3 = extreme hunger	Activity before eating	Feeling/mood before eating (bored, tired, depressed, happy)	Location of eating	Social situation (family meal, eating out, meal at work, alone, etc.)	Eating control level 0 = none to 3 = total

Total Calories for day ______________

Date ______________________

FOOD DATA RECORD

List each food item and describe method of preparation (baked, fried, boiled, broiled, raw) Food Item/Beverage	Amount	Calories	Time of Day	Meal/Snack	Level of hunger before eating 0 = none to 3 = extreme hunger	Activity before eating	Feeling/mood before eating (bored, tired, depressed, happy)	Location of eating	Social situation (family meal, eating out, meal at work, alone, etc.)	Eating control level 0 = none to 3 = total

Total Calories for day ____________________

Date ______________________________

FOOD DATA RECORD

List each food item and describe method of preparation (baked, fried, boiled, broiled, raw) Food Item/Beverage	Amount	Calories	Time of Day	Meal/Snack	Level of hunger before eating 0 = none to 3 = extreme hunger	Activity before eating	Feeling/mood before eating (bored, tired, depressed, happy)	Location of eating	Social situation (family meal, eating out, meal at work, alone, etc.)	Eating control level 0 = none to 3 = total

Total Calories for day ______________

Date ______________________

FOOD DATA RECORD

List each food item and describe method of preparation (baked, fried, boiled, broiled, raw)

Food Item/Beverage	Amount	Calories	Time of Day	Meal/Snack	Level of hunger before eating 0 = none to 3 = extreme hunger	Activity before eating	Feeling/mood before eating (bored, tired, depressed, happy)	Location of eating	Social situation (family meal, eating out, meal at work, alone, etc.)	Eating control level 0 = none to 3 = total

Total Calories for day ____________________

Date ______________________________

FOOD DATA RECORD

List each food item and describe method of preparation (baked, fried, boiled, broiled, raw) Food Item/Beverage	Amount	Calories	Time of Day	Meal/Snack	Level of hunger before eating 0 = none to 3 = extreme hunger	Activity before eating	Feeling/mood before eating (bored, tired, depressed, happy)	Location of eating	Social situation (family meal, eating out, meal at work, alone, etc.)	Eating control level 0 = none to 3 = total

Total Calories for day ____________________

Date ____________________

DATA ANALYSIS FORM - INSTRUCTOR NOTES

For the First Lesson: Environmental Impact and Food Cues

Purposes:

1. Provide a mechanism for condensing and analyzing the information recorded on the Food Data Records.
2. Provide a quick reference to the information collected for future use.

Explanation of instructions: page 21.

Sample form: page 39.

Appropriate lesson: the first lesson only.

Instructions: highlighted on page 21.

DATA ANALYSIS FORM (Sample)

1. Average daily calorie intake for the past week: 1650 calories/day.

2. Weight change for the past week: -½ lbs.

3. Eating places in the house and at work:

Meals	Snacks
kitchen table	bed
dining room table	family room
desk at work	kitchen counter
	hallway near vending machine
	drug store

4. Daily time and hunger patterns:

Time period	Frequency of eating (ate constantly, frequently, rarely or only a specific meal)	Average hunger level for that time period 0 = no hunger 1 = mild hunger 2 = moderate hunger 3 = extreme hunger
6:00 a.m.-8:00 a.m.	Breakfast only	2
8:00 a.m.-10:00 a.m.	Rarely	1
10:00 a.m.-12 Noon	Rarely	2
12:00 Noon-2:00 p.m.	Lunch only	2
2:00 p.m.-4:00 p.m.	Rarely	2
4:00 p.m.-6:00 p.m.	Frequently	2½
6:00 p.m.-8:00 p.m.	Frequently	2
8:00 p.m.-10:00 p.m.	Frequently	1½
10:00 p.m.-12 Midnight	Rarely	1

5. External food cues in the environment:

Activities	Objects	Moods/Feelings
Watching TV	food on counter	bored
Reading paper	cookie jar	tired
taking bath	chair in family room	up-tight
typing	vending machine	
	Winchell's Doughnuts	

6. Movement patterns:

coming into house through kitchen door

driving home on 196th St. (stop at Winchell's for a doughnut)

7. Eating control in social situations:

Social situations (Specify)	Control level 0 none 1 poor 2 fair 3 good
family breakfast	3
lunch out	2
family dinner	2
dinner out	1
eating alone (work)	1-2
Eating alone (home)	0-1

DATA ANALYSIS FORM

1. Average daily calorie intake for the past week:______calories/day.

2. Weight change for the past week:______lbs.

3. Eating places in the house and at work:

Meals	Snacks
____________________	____________________
____________________	____________________
____________________	____________________
____________________	____________________
____________________	____________________
____________________	____________________

4. Daily time and hunger patterns:

Time period	**Frequency of eating** (ate constantly, frequently, rarely or only a specific meal)	**Average hunger level for that time period** 0 = no hunger 1 = mild hunger 2 = moderate hunger 3 = extreme hunger
6:00 a.m.-8:00 a.m.	____________________	__________
8:00 a.m.-10:00 a.m.	____________________	__________
10:00 a.m.-12 Noon	____________________	__________
12:00 Noon-2:00 p.m.	____________________	__________
2:00 p.m.-4:00 p.m.	____________________	__________
4:00 p.m.-6:00 p.m.	____________________	__________
6:00 p.m.-8:00 p.m.	____________________	__________
8:00 p.m.-10:00 p.m.	____________________	__________
10:00 p.m.-12 Midnight	____________________	__________

5. External food cues in the environment:

Activities	Objects	Moods/Feelings

6. Movement patterns:

7. Eating control in social situations:

Social situations (Specify)	Control level 0 none 1 poor 2 fair 3 good
Eating alone	

(**INSTRUCTOR NOTES** for this form are on page 44.)

MASTER WEIGHT RECORD (Sample)

NOTE: Record information in morning of day of class.

Week	Current Weight	Weekly Weight Change (+/-)	Avg. Daily Calorie Intake	Date
1	165*			1/10*
2	163½	-1½	1200	1/17
3	164¼	+¾	2000	1/24
4	163¾	-1	1800	1/31
5	162	-1¼	1775	2/7
6	161	-1	1775	2/14
7	161	0	1900	2/21
8	159	-2	1500	2/28
9				
10				
11				
12				
13				
14				
15				
16				
17				
18				

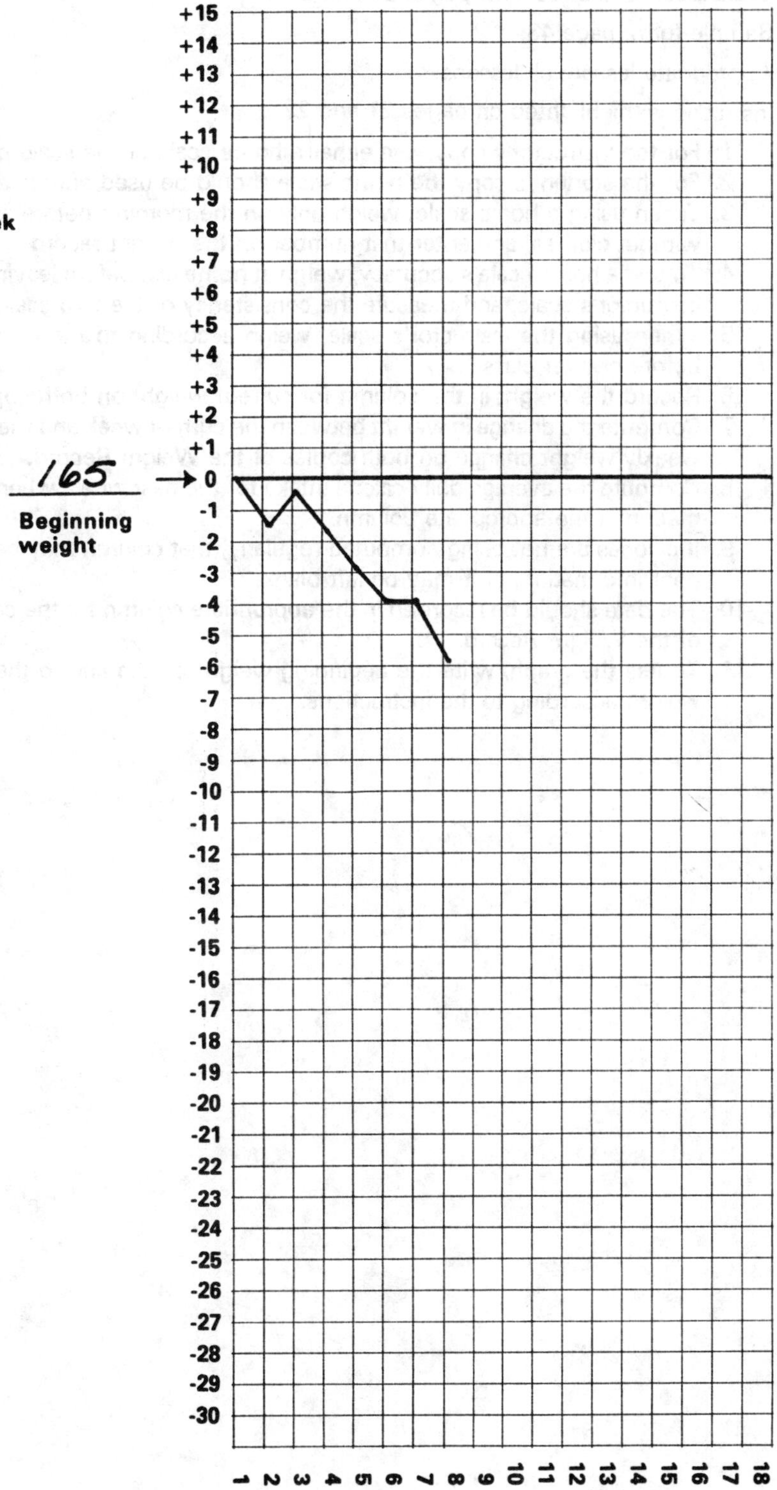

*Beginning date and weight.

MASTER WEIGHT RECORD - INSTRUCTOR NOTES

Purposes:

1. Provide an easy-to-use record of weight and weight changes.
2. Provide a record of average daily calorie levels.
3. Provide a means for seeing the relationship between the daily calorie averages and corresponding weight changes.

Explanation of instructions: pages 21 and 22.

Sample form: page 43.

Appropriate lesson: all lessons.

Instructions: highlighted on pages 21 and 22.

1. For the instructor's copy, use either a home scale or the scale provided by the instructor.
2. For the student's copy the home scale should be used and its accuracy tested against the instructor's scale.
3. When using a home scale, weigh only on the morning before attending a course session, before breakfast and without clothes, and enter that number on the weight record.
4. To test a home scale's accuracy, weigh at home just before leaving for the course session and weigh again on the instructor's scale, and measure the consistency of the two scales from week to week.
5. When using the instructor's scale, weigh according to the instructor's directions, e.g., with or without shoes, before or after class.
6. Record the weight in the column for current weight on both copies of the Weight Record.
7. Compute the change in weight between the current week and the previous week and record that in the column for weekly weight change on both copies of the Weight Record.
8. Compute the average daily calorie intake for the past week, when calories are being recorded, and enter the information in the appropriate column.
9. If calories are not being computed regularly, that column may be altered to record exchanges or any other pertinent information, or it may be left blank.
10. The date should be recorded in the appropriate column for the corresponding weight information on both copies of the Weight Record.
11. To use the graph, write the beginning weight on the line to the left of the graph, and plot gains and losses in weight according to the instructions.

MASTER WEIGHT RECORD (Student)

NOTE: Record information in morning of day of class.

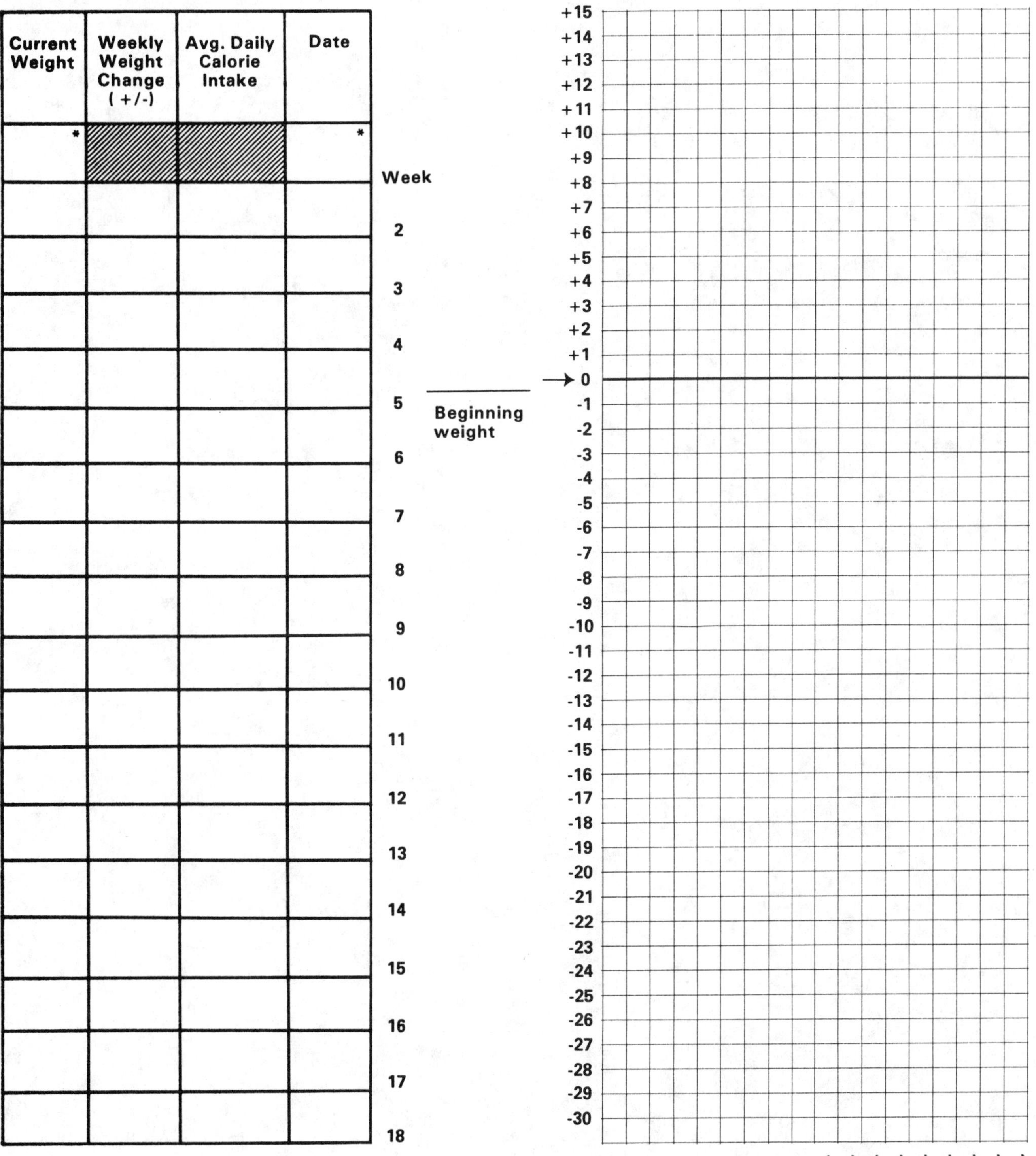

Current Weight	Weekly Weight Change (+/-)	Avg. Daily Calorie Intake	Date	Week
*			*	
				2
				3
				4
				5
				6
				7
				8
				9
				10
				11
				12
				13
				14
				15
				16
				17
				18

*Beginning date and weight.

MASTER WEIGHT RECORD (Instructor)

NOTE: Record information in morning of day of class.

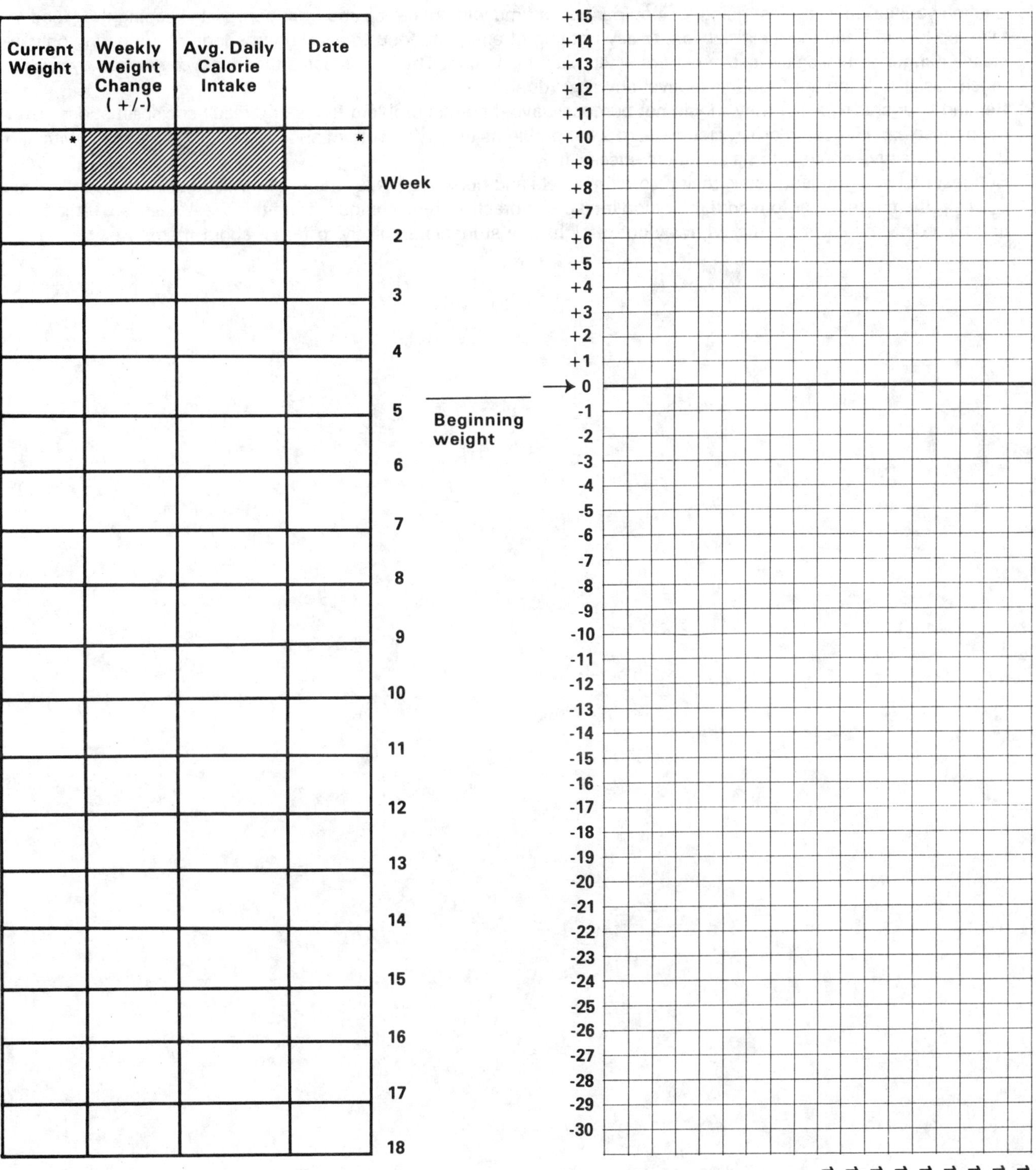

Current Weight	Weekly Weight Change (+/-)	Avg. Daily Calorie Intake	Date	Week
*			*	
				2
				3
				4
				5
				6
				7
				8
				9
				10
				11
				12
				13
				14
				15
				16
				17
				18

***Beginning date and weight.**

Chapter 2 - INSTRUCTOR NOTES

Suggested Techniques and Homework Assignments:
Read the instructions on pages 53 and 54.

Cautions and Reminders:

1. Caution your students against going for long periods of time without eating and from purposely keeping their food intake too low to bring them satisfaction, to say nothing of adequate food to eat. Long periods of not eating only increase hunger and instigate loss of control when eating is begun. That perpetuates the "feast or famine" cycle. It is much easier to bring the food intake level down **gradually.**
2. Remind your students that they should not purposely avoid normal problem foods or difficult social situations. They need those experiences in order, first, to learn what problems they will confront and, second, to experiment with and develop effective controls to handle them successfully.
3. Suggest that your students leave their recording sheets and book in a place where they will be seen frequently. This will help them remember to record their food intake and practice the techniques from this week's lesson. If the book and recording materials are tucked away out of sight, the students are likely to forget about them.

2

Target: Stimulus control.
Objectives:

1. Reduce (and eliminate where appropriate) food cues in the home environment which result in uncontrolled eating.
2. Restructure the home environment to make it easier to eat lower-calorie foods and correspondingly more difficult to eat higher-calorie foods.
3. Reduce or maintain calorie level; establish or maintain dietary plan.

Motto:

Out of sight, out of mind.

Controlling Your Home Environment

The analysis of your data from the first lesson should illustrate the process of stimulus response. People usually discover that they eat in a variety of places and for a variety of reasons. A logical method for reducing the eating response would be to eliminate or reduce the food cue stimuli in the environment. That is the primary objective of this lesson: to teach you to restructure your environment in order to reduce the number of external food cues, and, thereby, decrease your eating response.

In the first lesson an example was given illustrating an eating pattern related to doing the laundry. As the woman analyzed her data it became apparent to her that the existence of a pantry adjoining the laundry area was a powerful food cue. The chair and the book inside the pantry made eating there even more attractive. Her first environmental control project was to remove the book and the chair from the pantry. Then she took the food items out of the pantry and stored them in kitchen cupboards. She filled the pantry shelves with seldom used pots and small electrical appliances for which she needed storage space. The result of that project? She no longer ate when doing the laundry, and after a few days, she no longer felt the urge to do so.

Most people arrange things in their homes according to ease and convenience. Consequently, frequently eaten foods will be kept in the most convenient places. In addition people buy certain foods primarily because they require little or no preparation, in other words, they are easy to eat. Examples of these "convenience foods" are crackers, cookies, snack foods

---

Restructure your environment in order to reduce the number of external food cues.

---

in general, TV dinners, and canned spaghetti; most are high in calories. These easy-to-eat foods are then often stored in places of convenience; they may be put on kitchen counters, in cookie jars or on the easiest-to-reach shelves in the cupboard where they are also easily seen. Even tempting leftovers in plain sight in the refrigerator become targets for random snacking both because they are convenient and because their visibility creates a desire for them. Contrast the eating of a convenience food to that of a fresh carrot which has to be pulled out of a vegetable bin and cleaned before eating. When people are hungry, tired, or hurried they will often not go to the extra effort to look for or prepare something. The environmental structure is such that it is easier to eat high-calorie foods and harder to eat low-calorie foods.

One approach toward restructuring the environment would be to make it very easy to eat low-calorie foods, and correspondingly more difficult to eat those higher in calories. The desired foods should be prepared and stored in ways that make them easy to see, convenient to reach and ready to eat. High calorie foods

---

Leftovers in plain sight become targets for random snacking.

---

should be stored in ways that make them difficult to see or reach, a nuisance to prepare and difficult to open. Placing tempting foods at the back of the top shelves of the cupboards requires the bothersome aid of something to stand on. If the extra slice of bread has to be taken from the freezer and toasted before it is eaten, and if the butter has been placed in the refrigerator where it gets hard, instead of on top of the refrigerator where it stays soft, snacking on buttered bread may be too much work. A little fingernail polish painted on the inside of the lid of a peanut butter jar before it is put back on the shelf increases the time it takes to open the jar. The convenience of eating peanut butter is reduced and its usefulness as random snack food is decreased. All of these suggestions pertain to random, unstructured eating, "grazing" as it was referred to in the first lesson. When the inconveniently stored foods are needed for meals, planned snacks or even food binges, people will make the effort and take the necessary time needed to fix them.

One of the biggest problems in keeping tempting foods conveniently placed is that their high visibility is a powerful cue mechanism. If, when opening a cupboard door to get a bottle of vinegar, a person sees a bag of cookies and thinks how good those cookies would taste, that person has inadvertently been cued to want to eat a tempting but high-calorie food. If the cookies are eaten, extra calories have been consumed; if the cookies are reluctantly not eaten, feelings of deprivation often result. For some people this leads to eating out of control later in the day or evening. Thus the person has been "set up" by the placement of those foods to either want or eat them.

I can remember just such an experience of my own. Feeling hungry one evening, I went to the refrigerator for an apple. While getting the apple I saw some left-over macaroni on the top shelf. The macaroni looked better to me than the apple, but I dutifully ate the apple anyway and thought about the macaroni. I next decided to eat some carrot and celery sticks, but while in the refrigerator, I saw the macaroni again, and this time it looked even better to me. I held to my plan, ate the carrots and celery, and tried to forget about the macaroni. I still wanted it so this time I decided to eat a piece of cheese, thinking that cheese would satisfy the craving. While getting the cheese I had another look at the macaroni, but ate the cheese as planned. Twenty minutes later I went back and ate the macaroni!

The "out of sight, out of mind" motto would certainly have been helpful in my situation. If that macaroni had been placed in an opaque container or wrapped in a brown paper bag, I might not have even remembered that it was in the refrigerator.

Many of my students have similar experiences and have reported that when they place low-calorie foods on the top shelf of the refrigerator where they are easily visible, they are cued to eat them instead of high-calorie foods. One idea is to store the tempting foods in the vegetable and fruit bins in the refrigerator and keep the fruits and vegetables in containers on the refrigerator shelves. One lady removed the light bulb from her refrigerator. She said that her whole family snacked less that week because they couldn't see anything!

People frequently mention that they don't want to deprive others in the house of tempting snack foods. One way to handle that is to assign out-of-the-way storage areas to other family members for their snack foods. These could be areas of the kitchen other than those where ingredients for cooking or foods for daily use are kept. Thus they would not be seen in the usual process of food preparation.

One lady removed the light bulb from her refrigerator. . .her whole family snacked less that week because they couldn't see anything!

Some people have asked other family members to keep their snack foods in private, non-visible storage areas outside of the kitchen. One woman had changed her shopping routine to exclude purchase of high calorie snack foods. Her three sons had all graduated from high school and were living away from home. During the spring break from college all three sons returned home for a week. They asked their mother to buy their favorite snack foods for them. With those foods in sight, she began eating them at random. An old pattern had returned. Her solution: she purchased snack foods for each son and distributed all of them to the boys at the same time. Then she said, "All the time you were growing up I never let you keep food in your bedrooms. Now I've changed my mind. I want you to store your goodies in your rooms, throw away the wrappers when you are through and give me a list for shopping when you have eaten all of it. I don't want to see those foods anywhere!" She reported that the boys thought her plan was terrific, and she was no longer cued to eat those foods. "In fact," she said, "I didn't even miss them."

When activities unrelated to eating or food preparation take place in the kitchen, they provide another type of environmental trigger for unplanned eating. One woman had been having a frustrating conversation with someone on the telephone in the kitchen and began eating to reduce her tension while talking. High school and college students often report that they eat more often while typing or studying in the kitchen. Both men and women find that playing cards or other table games in the kitchen results in greater eating frequency than when playing in the family or living room. It is logical, then, that if people eat more when doing non-food related activities in the kitchen, they will have better control of their food intake by confining these activities to other rooms in the house. To insure that people are free of food cues in those other rooms, there should be no visible food items in sight anywhere except in the kitchen and pantry. The adage, "out of sight, out of mind," applies here as well. If tempting foods are not visible, people will not be constantly reminded to eat them.

Students often eat more while typing or studying in the kitchen.

In the first lesson the concept of "paired associations" was introduced. By the end of the first week, people have usually identified at least one paired association. One man discovered that he became hungry whenever he got into his car. Another man identified a pattern that included lots of beer, peanuts, popcorn and potato chips with every football game and other sporting event on television. He found that the more exciting the action was, the more he ate. One close game resulted in 2100 calories consumed in excess of his average daily calorie intake! To help people break their paired associations, they need to sever any relationship between the cue and eating. As in Pavlov's experiment, when the dogs stopped salivating at the sound of the bell it was because they were no longer fed when the bell sounded. The association between the bell and eating had been broken. The bell was not a food cue anymore.

You can achieve the same result by assiduously doing two things. The first is to confine all eating to the kitchen and dining room table at home or in other people's homes. The result is a step in environmental structure which reduces eating frequency, increases control, and causes you to be aware of when you are eating. You may drink a non-caloric beverage in places other than the kitchen/dining room table, but *never eat* in those places. In this way, if you are used to eating in a lot of different places in the house, you eventually become free to sit in the family room, work at your desk at home, or putter in the workshop without suffering through hunger pangs at the same time.

The next step in eliminating paired associations is, when eating, to do only that and not to do other activities at the same time. Activities like reading or watching TV are often associated with eating so that the act of turning on the TV or picking up a book can become a powerful food cue. Try reading or watching TV

Extended eating can become boring.

---

without eating for this week as an experiment. You may drink a non-caloric beverage if desired. When eating at the table with others, talking is, naturally, permissible. If your family likes to watch TV during dinner, sit with your back toward the TV set so that you can focus more attention on your food. If driving the car or talking on the telephone are associated with food, these activities should also be done without eating.

There are two additional benefits to eating without doing other activites. The first is that the book, magazine, or TV program captures people's attention and causes them to be much less aware of when they feel full or are simply tired of eating. How many times have you had the experience of reaching into a nearby bowl while reading or watching TV and discovering, to your surprise, that the bowl was empty and then thinking, "Did I eat all of that?" The more attention you can give to the eating process the more likely you are to be aware of when you've had enough and be able to stop eating. The second benefit is that when you are entertained while eating, it is possible to sit longer and consume more food than when doing nothing else. Once your initial hunger is reduced, and that usually happens in the first few minutes, extended eating can become boring. A number of people have claimed that they become too restless to eat all of what they had originally planned to eat.

One unforgettable experience for me was listening to a woman angrily reporting that she was eating her snack in the kitchen one evening, all alone, because of my assignment. Everyone else in the family was watching TV in the family room. She was so irritated at being stuck in the kitchen that she only ate half of her snack, leaving the rest uneaten on the table while she returned to the TV set. As she told her story others who were listening began to chuckle. The woman stopped, looked at the other people a moment, and then sheepishly said, "That was supposed to happen, wasn't it?" She had eaten fewer calories than usual that evening.

She was so irritated at being stuck in the kitchen that she only ate half of her snack.

Explanation of Homework

Assignment for this week: experiment with up to five of the environmental control exercises below, and record your progress and food intake daily.

1. Do all at-home eating at the kitchen or dining room table.

2. Eat without reading or watching TV.

3. Keep tempting foods out of sight, hard to reach and bothersome to prepare.

4. Have low-calorie foods accessible, visible, easy to reach and ready to eat.

5. Store tempting foods in containers which are opaque or difficult to open.

6. Give other family members their own snack food storage areas.

7. Do non-food related activities

outside of the kitchen, and stay out of the kitchen as much as possible.

Not all of these exercises will be useful to you and some may not even apply to your situation. Select only those you wish to experiment with and enter them on the Weekly Progress Record, explained on pages 257-260. Experiment with exercises one and two to see if they have particular importance for you. It is often difficult to predict their value until you have had a week of experience with them.

Weekly Progress Record

The instructions for how to use the Weekly Progress Record are on pages 257-260.

Daily Food Record

The instructions for how to use the Daily Food Record are on pages 261-263.

Weight Record

The instructions for how to use the Weight Record are on pages 21-22.

Remember that the objective of this week's assignment is to experiment. Don't expect perfection. Make note of what is and is not effective for you. Remember also to explain this week's lesson thoroughly to the support person you selected earlier. Good luck!

WEEKLY PROGRESS RECORD

BASIC SKILLS:	SUN	MON	TUES	WED	THURS	FRI	SAT	*
Read Progress Record in morning								
Record food intake								
Stay within calorie/ exchange total								
SPECIFIC TECHNIQUES/EXERCISES:								
Daily Totals								

*This column is for the weekly totals for each specific technique or exercise.

DAILY FOOD RECORD

Food Item/ Beverage	Amount	Calories/Exchanges	Time of Day

Total Calories for day ______

Date ______

Total Exchanges for day:

(1) Milk ______
(2) Vegetable ______
(3) Fruit ______
(4) Bread ______
(5) Meat ______
(6) Fat ______

DAILY FOOD RECORD

Food Item/ Beverage	Amount	Calories/Exchanges	Time of Day

Total Calories for day ________

Date ________________

Total Exchanges for day:
(1) Milk ______
(2) Vegetable ______
(3) Fruit ______
(4) Bread ______
(5) Meat ______
(6) Fat ______

DAILY FOOD RECORD

Food Item/ Beverage	Amount	Calories/Exchanges	Time of Day

Total Calories for day ________

Date ________________

Total Exchanges for day:
(1) Milk ______
(2) Vegetable ______
(3) Fruit ______
(4) Bread ______
(5) Meat ______
(6) Fat ______

DAILY FOOD RECORD

Food Item/ Beverage	Amount	Calories/Exchanges	Time of Day

Total Calories for day ________

Date ____________________

Total Exchanges for day:

(1) Milk ______
(2) Vegetable ______
(3) Fruit ______
(4) Bread ______
(5) Meat ______
(6) Fat ______

DAILY FOOD RECORD

Food Item/ Beverage	Amount	Calories/Exchanges	Time of Day

Total Calories for day ________

Date ____________________

Total Exchanges for day:

(1) Milk ______
(2) Vegetable ______
(3) Fruit ______
(4) Bread ______
(5) Meat ______
(6) Fat ______

DAILY FOOD RECORD

Food Item/ Beverage	Amount	Calories/Exchanges	Time of Day

Total Calories for day ________

Date ____________________

Total Exchanges for day:

(1) Milk ______
(2) Vegetable ______
(3) Fruit ______
(4) Bread ______
(5) Meat ______
(6) Fat ______

DAILY FOOD RECORD

Food Item/ Beverage	Amount	Calories/Exchanges	Time of Day

Copyright © Northwest Learning Associates, Inc., 1978. All rights reserved.

Total Calories for day ________

Date ____________________

Total Exchanges for day:

(1) Milk ______
(2) Vegetable ______
(3) Fruit ______
(4) Bread ______
(5) Meat ______
(6) Fat ______

Chapter 3 - INSTRUCTOR NOTES

Suggested Techniques:
Listed on pages 64 and 65.

Homework Assignments:
Read the instructions on page 65.

Cautions and Reminders:

1. Remind students that the focus of their homework is on what they are doing rather than on what they aren't doing. As they record how often they do each of the techniques listed on their Weekly Progress Records, they may find that they aren't doing some of them as often as they would like. Or they may be aware that the number of times they didn't do them exceeds the number of times they did them. That is to be expected in the beginning. Their performance with some techniques will be better than with others. The object of the homework is to experiment long enough with the selected techniques to determine their effectiveness in helping to control eating response. Later, when the course is completed, they will be taking the effective techniques and building them into strong habits.
2. It is particularly important for people not to arrive at work hungry nor to leave themselves without legitimate, satisfying food breaks. Controlling stimulus response is made much more difficult if the person is also having to deal with physical hunger cues.
3. Discourage your students from being overly rigid in their weekly plans. If they find that a technique isn't effective or relevant, they should trade it in for a different technique. The object is to discover which techniques are useful and which ones aren't. This information is necessary before they can start developing control strategies. On the other hand, it is far better to work consistently with a few techniques rather than risk becoming overwhelmed and frustrated when all are tried at once.

3

Targets: Stimulus control and preplanning.

Objectives:

1. Reduce and eliminate food cues in the work environment which result in uncontrolled eating.
2. Reduce exposure to food items and situations which result in uncontrolled eating.
3. Restructure the work environment to make it easier to eat lower-calorie foods and correspondingly more inconvenient to eat higher-calorie foods.
4. Reduce or maintain calorie level; establish or maintain dietary plan.

Motto:

Make it EASIER to do what you DO want to do and HARDER to do what you DON'T.

Controlling Your Work Environment

While a lot of people have more control over their food consumption at work than at home, for others the work environment possesses a variety of opportunities for unplanned and high-calorie eating. External food cues, the necessity for fast, ready-to-eat foods, and late afternoon hunger pangs are three frequently mentioned reasons for out-of-control eating at work.

Examples of external food cues in a work setting include open boxes of candy or nuts placed on counters or desks, plates of pastries sitting next to the main coffee pot, and food items stored in desk drawers. Quite a few of my students mention that vending machines and small snack bars or drug stores located in the building where they work are particularly potent food cues. Others talk about their vulnerability to the specialty food shops and fast-food establishments they pass on their route to and from work. As one man said, "I pass that drug store every day on my way to the parking lot, and every day I buy a few candy bars to eat on the way home. I don't know what I'd do without that place!"

For most people when the opportunity comes to eat a regular meal at work, there isn't much time available for lengthy preparation. The result is usually a dependence upon convenience foods, or upon restaurants or cafeterias where there is a temptation to eat both larger portions and high calorie foods. This is true for coffee breaks as well.

The work environment possesses a variety of opportunities for unplanned eating.

In these examples there is one common element: the environment or circumstance is the controlling force, leaving the person feeling victimized and not in control over what is eaten. Review your data from the first lesson and see where your work environment may be setting you up to eat more in either quantity or calories than you would like.

Most of my students experience a low energy point in mid to late afternoon that is sometimes accompanied by hunger, irritability, and the lack of patience that is associated with fatigue. Some of them try not to eat anything, to wait until they get home before eating. Then they go out of control, nibbling one item after another in random fashion. Others stop to purchase something to "tide them over" until dinner, often an item high in calories.

There are ten exercises to experiment with which could result in greater control over what, when and how much you eat during the work day.

1. Where possible, **do not eat at your desk,** especially if your desk has become associated with food and just sitting there makes you hungry. Confine your eating to staff lounges, cafeterias or other places where eating is appropriate. If you have no alternative and must eat at your desk, clear away your papers and set your food out as you would if you were sitting at a table. Try to eat without doing paperwork or talking on the telephone so that you have an opportunity to enjoy your meal.

2. **Do not keep tempting food in your desk drawers.** Each time the drawers are opened you will be reminded that the food is there and you will be likely to eat more often than you would if you had to go to the staff lounge, or wherever else you put your food, before eating.

3. **Pre-package meals and snacks and take them to work with you.** This will satisfy the need for readily available food but give you calorie control at the same time. If you anticipate that you will forget and leave the house without taking the pre-packaged food with you, leave your car keys or glasses in the bag with the food to help you remember! Keep one or two packages of instant soup or some diet soda at work in case you get unusually hungry or do forget to bring your lunch to work. It may help you to keep away from snack shops or short-order restaurants.

4. **Carry no change with you for vending machines or purchases from the candy or gift shop in the building.** Bring something from home to eat instead of using the vending machines. This will result in greater control. If vending machines are really a problem, try carrying no bills in denominations of $1.00 or $5.00. If getting change becomes a nuisance it may decrease the number of times you use the vending machines. If you ride a bus to and from work, buying pre-paid bus tokens or ticket books will reduce the need for carrying a supply of coins. If you do collect change during the day, save it and put it into a sealed coin bank at night. You will have the reward of extra money to spend on something for yourself later as well as the reinforcement not to take change to work the next day!

5. **Eat a planned snack before leaving work to increase control on the way home.** This will help you restore

your energy level in a controlled manner, and can be particularly helpful if you stop to have a drink with friends or co-workers before going home. Alcohol can be an appetite stimulant. If you are tired and hungry and then have a drink or two, your level of control over your later food intake may be severely reduced.

6. **Use exercise instead of food when you need to take a break from routine at work.** Try taking a short walk or climbing up and down a flight of stairs. The activity will give you the break you need, to help you feel "re-energized," and the short bit of exercise may act as an appetite depressant. Just be sure that your exercise break doesn't also take you past the vending machines, snack bar or candy shop!

7. **When eating in a cafeteria, plan your order in advance and bring only enough money to cover your order, plus tax.** If there is little or no extra money to spend you won't be tempted to buy more than you originally intended.

8. If pastries and other tempting items placed next to the coffee pot are a problem, **keep a small percolator or hot pot plugged in by your desk for coffee or tea.**

9. When you feel deprived by not having any of the food treats brought to work by someone else, **select one piece early in the day, wrap it up and store it in a locker or coat pocket to eat either before leaving work or for a snack later in the evening.** You may also need to have a low-calorie food to eat when others are eating the high-calorie treat, especially if it is at a social coffee-break time.

10. If you work in a bakery, food store or restaurant and find that you nibble all day long, the following ideas may be helpful. Select one item to be eaten later at home; follow an eating urge with a drink of a low-calorie beverage or a piece of a low-calorie food item, such as cut vegetables, bite-size shredded wheat biscuits, or any dry "chex" cereal; or suck on sugar-free candy or chew sugar-free gum during periods of poor control to make it inconvenient to nibble on high-calorie items.

During periods of poor control make it inconvenient to nibble on high-calorie items.

Explanation of Homework

Assignment for this week: experiment with up to five of the exercises presented above, and record your progress and food intake daily.

Weekly Progress Record

The instructions for how to use the Weekly Progress Record are on pages 257-260.

Daily Food Record

The instructions for how to use the Daily Food Record are on pages 261-263.

Weight Record

The instructions for how to use the Weight Record are on pages 21-22.

If you have not read the lesson entitled "Controlling your Home Environment," please look it over to add to your understanding of this lesson. If you are doing both lessons together, select up to five of the techniques suggested in either or both of the two lessons and practice them for the week. Do not try more than five or six techniques in one week. It is far more effective to do a few things consistently than it is to do a lot of things in a random, haphazard fashion. After the course is over you can go back and try the techniques you missed the first time. If a technique you originally selected turns out to be ineffective the first few times you use it, trade it for another technique. If you have some ideas of your own, use them instead of the suggestions in the book. It's fun to develop new techniques and try them out. Good luck!

WEEKLY PROGRESS RECORD

BASIC SKILLS:	SUN	MON	TUES	WED	THURS	FRI	SAT	*
Read Progress Record in morning								
Record food intake								
Stay within calorie/exchange total								
SPECIFIC TECHNIQUES/EXERCISES:								
Daily Totals								

*This column is for the weekly totals for each specific technique or exercise.

DAILY FOOD RECORD

Time of Day	Food Item/Beverage	Amount	Calories/Exchanges

Total Calories for day ____

Total Exchanges for day:
(1) Milk ____
(2) Vegetable ____
(3) Fruit ____
(4) Bread ____
(5) Meat ____
(6) Fat ____

Date ____

Copyright © Northwest Learning Associates, Inc., 1978. All rights reserved.

DAILY FOOD RECORD

Food Item/ Beverage	Amount	Calories/Exchanges	Time of Day

Total Calories for day ________

Date ________________

Total Exchanges for day:

(1) Milk ______
(2) Vegetable ______
(3) Fruit ______
(4) Bread ______
(5) Meat ______
(6) Fat ______

DAILY FOOD RECORD

Food Item/ Beverage	Amount	Calories/Exchanges	Time of Day

Total Calories for day ________

Date ________________

Total Exchanges for day:

(1) Milk ______
(2) Vegetable ______
(3) Fruit ______
(4) Bread ______
(5) Meat ______
(6) Fat ______

Copyright © Northwest Learning Associates, Inc., 1978. All rights reserved.

DAILY FOOD RECORD

Food Item/ Beverage	Amount	Calories/Exchanges	Time of Day

Total Calories for day ______

Date ______

Total Exchanges for day:
(1) Milk ______
(2) Vegetable ______
(3) Fruit ______
(4) Bread ______
(5) Meat ______
(6) Fat ______

DAILY FOOD RECORD

Food Item/ Beverage	Amount	Calories/Exchanges	Time of Day

Copyright © Northwest Learning Associates, Inc., 1978. All rights reserved.

Total Calories for day ______

Date ______

Total Exchanges for day:
(1) Milk ______
(2) Vegetable ______
(3) Fruit ______
(4) Bread ______
(5) Meat ______
(6) Fat ______

DAILY FOOD RECORD

Food Item/ Beverage	Amount	Calories/Exchanges	Time of Day

Total Calories for day ________

Date ________________

Total Exchanges for day:
(1) Milk ______
(2) Vegetable ______
(3) Fruit ______
(4) Bread ______
(5) Meat ______
(6) Fat ______

DAILY FOOD RECORD

Food Item/ Beverage	Amount	Calories/Exchanges	Time of Day

Total Calories for day ________

Date ________________

Total Exchanges for day:
(1) Milk ______
(2) Vegetable ______
(3) Fruit ______
(4) Bread ______
(5) Meat ______
(6) Fat ______

Copyright © Northwest Learning Associates, Inc., 1978. All rights reserved.

Chapter 4 - INSTRUCTOR NOTES

Suggested Techniques:

1. Shopping techniques listed on pages 76 and 77.
2. Preparation techniques listed on pages 77 through 80.
3. Clean-up and leftovers techniques listed on page 80.

Homework Assignments:

Read the instructions on page 81.

Cautions and Reminders:

1. If your students are feeling overloaded, suggest that they not concentrate on previous assignments. Have them select the area of greatest difficulty in this lesson and focus on the suggested techniques.
2. Remind the students to put the Reference Outline of Techniques and Exercises on a bulletin board or some other convenient place and use it for reinforcement and review.
3. Sometimes students become upset if they miss a day or two of recording. Some students find that they go out of control when this happens. Other students have a difficult time recording at all for the remainder of the week. Let your students know it is okay to miss occasional days of recording. The important point is that they resume recording again as soon as possible. One way to get themselves restarted is to leave their recording sheets in an easily visible, frequently seen place, and with a pen or pencil attached. Taping them to a cupboard door and leaving the pencil on an inside shelf is one example of what might be done. Placing the recording sheets and pencil (1) at the table where they eat, (2) on the counter of the bathroom, or (3) inside the cellophane wrapper of their cigarette packages will result in greater awareness and more consistent recording.
4. Many students do not record their food intake for days of poor control because they don't want to know how much food they've eaten. Suggest that they record what they eat, but not the calories (if the calorie information is too upsetting). Stress the importance of knowing what types of foods are usually eaten on poor-control days, as well as how often they want to eat. This very important information will be used later to study their poor-control-day patterns and to develop strategies for effective management of those days.

4

Targets: Stimulus control and preplanning.

Objectives:

1. Develop strategies for control of impulse response when shopping.
2. Reduce time spent in food-related activities.
3. Develop strategies to augment control during food preparation and clean-up.
4. Reduce inadvertent food cues through effective storage of leftovers.
5. Reduce or maintain calorie level; establish or maintain dietary plan.

Motto:

Buy less, prepare less, save less, see less, eat less, weigh less!

Daily Food Management

A necessary dimension to any overall plan for food-intake control involves the daily management of food: shopping, preparation and cleanup. Each of these activities offers multiple opportunities for automatic, unaware eating as well as for impulsive eating responses.

Two years ago I asked ten women with different daily routines to do a time-use assessment of their average day's activity and to estimate the amount of time spent on food-related tasks. Their answers surprised me. A young mother with three pre-school children reported that an average of 75% of her day was spent in action or thought which involved food. Another homemaker, without children, reported an average of 63% of her time was spent on food-related tasks. One part time secretary and homemaker estimated that 55% of her time involved food. The rest of the averages were: 40% for a college student, 48% for a full time nurse, 39% for a full time secretary, 58% for a pre-school teacher, 46% for a high school guidance counselor, 38% for a single sales clerk, and 41% for a full time dental hygienist. The only low average reported was 28% for a full time keypunch operator who was going to school at night, lived alone and didn't enjoy cooking for herself. Men who live alone or who enjoy cooking also report high percentages of their time spent on food related tasks. These figures illustrate the point that even when food is not a primary activity in a person's life it still consumes a lot of time each day.

. . . A young mother reported that 75% of her day was spent in action or thought which involved food . . .

It seems logical that the more time spent with food the more opportunity there is to eat, particularly when your control level is low. The two primary strategies used in planning for successful daily food management are: 1) minimize contact with food and 2) where involvement with food is necessary, limit it as often as possible to those times when your control level is likely to be high. Review the following ideas and strategies for shopping, preparation and cleanup.

Shopping

A few introductory words should be said about food stores. Millions of dollars a year are spent in advertising, packaging and marketing. You are up against experts, specialists with training in psychology, hired to place food items in stores in ways that promote impulse buying. If you are responsive to external cues, you need to be particularly careful of your buying habits.

1. **Do not shop when hungry.** The biggest detriment to shopping with control is hunger. It can be very hard to resist tempting food cues at any time; but when people are hungry, particularly in the late afternoon or evening, increased irritability and frustration levels contribute to the problem. The result is often impulsive purchasing of extra high-calorie foods, perhaps some ready-to-eat foods to eat right away, and maybe even greater quantities of food than usual. The impulse response problem is then brought home, when tempting food items purchased from the store are placed on counters or in other storage places where they continue to emit "eat" messages. Obviously one aid to shopping with control is to shop shortly after eating so that your responsiveness to food cues is decreased. It is also helpful to shop at those times of the day when your control is highest. Some people will shop only in the morning because of this factor.

If you are responsive to external cues, you need to be particularly careful of your buying habits.

2. **Shop from a specific list.** This will decrease the tendency to select food items impulsively. The list is also useful for those quick, "last minute" trips to the store to get the one or two items that are necessary for cooking the dinner meal. The use of a list will help you remember what you actually went into the store to buy.

3. **Shop quickly.** The longer you are exposed to strong food cues the harder it will be to maintain control. Some people play a game of "beat the clock" trying to finish their shopping and leave the store before the clock reaches a specified time. Some people plan a pleasant activity for a little later in the day or evening. This has the effect of refocusing their attention on the need to shop quickly so that the food can be taken home and put away before leaving the house again for the planned activity. An example is to plan to meet someone at a predetermined time.

4. **Don't buy your favorite varieties or flavors of high-calorie foods,** such as best-loved types of cookies or favorite flavors of ice cream. If your favorite flavor is chocolate chip mint, but others in the family like raspberry marble ice cream, and you don't, purchasing the raspberry marble flavor will be helpful for control after the ice cream is brought home.

5. **Avoid buying the economy size in hard-to-resist foods.** People who respond to open bags by eating up what's left have better control when others in the family are snacking from individual, single-serving bags. People typically eat all of what is in the smaller bags, so that there are few tempting morsels left to trigger an impulsive eating response. Ice cream bars, dixie cups, and the like are examples of single serving items, and the selection of these items in preference to half gallon containers will be helpful to many people who have difficulty controlling their intake of ice cream. If you decide to have an ice cream bar or dixie cup, the amount is not large enough to create many problems, and being able to eat the whole thing may be sufficiently satisfying to allow you to stop after eating only one.

I will never forget one particular woman and the lesson she taught me about shopping to maintain control. I was standing in the checkout line of the neighborhood grocery store when my eye was attracted to this woman, who was two rows ahead of me. A large cake box had been put into her shopping bag, and she had removed it and was trying to give the cake to the man standing behind her. The man obviously didn't understand what she was trying to do. She was telling him to take the cake to his family as a gift from her. He didn't know her and wasn't sure whether the real problem was that she was too embarrassed to return a cake she didn't want or that something was wrong with the cake. She finally convinced him to take it.

My curiosity wouldn't let me alone, so I left my order and went over to ask the woman why she gave the cake away. Her answer was, "I've recently lost a lot of weight and don't want to regain it. My biggest pleasure in shopping is to spend half an hour in the bakery buying the best looking cake there is. If I try to take it home, I'll eat it all before I get there, even if I put it in the trunk first. So I decided that I would still give myself the fun of buying the cake but would give it away before I leave the store. That way I have the fun of buying it and the pleasure of giving it to someone who can enjoy it. Most people don't understand why I'm giving away the cake, but it doesn't bother me. I do it every week." I walked away thinking how smart that lady was. Her need was to buy the cake, not to eat it. She knew that and had figured out a way to have her cake and not eat it too.

Preparation

1. **Prepare foods during periods when your control is highest.** Some people have their best control in the mornings and their worst control

around supper time. The most logical, but not necessarily the most convenient, approach, if this is your pattern, is to assemble the ingredients for the dinner meal in the morning, leaving only the placement of the food in the oven for that difficult period at the end of the day.

A woman in one of my classes devised an elaborate scheme using this strategy. Her worst eating control was when she came home from work. If she allowed herself to be in the kitchen at that time, she tended to eat out of control. Her plan began in the morning when she assembled the ingredients for the dinner meal and placed them in the refrigerator for later. Immediately upon arriving home after work, she went straight to the bathroom (still wearing her coat) and turned the bath water on full force. She then went to the kitchen where she opened the oven, quickly moved the casserole dishes from the refrigerator to the oven, set the oven temperature and timer, and then dashed back to the bathroom in time to turn the water off before it overflowed. She settled into a hot bath until the timer rang on the stove, signalling the end of the cooking period. By the time she sat down to eat, she was relaxed and in much better control than earlier.

If you stay home during the day, you may appreciate being out of the kitchen at the end of the day as much as do people who work outside of the home. If you are able to relax, instead of cooking at that time, there is even more benefit to this strategy than just better control of food intake.

2. **Lunches and snacks can be prepared at the same time another meal is being cooked.** If every request to make a snack or a lunch results in extra food consumption or in a personal wrestling match over whether or not to eat something, the best approach is to minimize contact with food by preparing it in advance. Even pre-schoolers can take their snacks from the counter or table themselves if the food is ready to be eaten.

She knew that and had figured out a way to have her cake and not eat it too.

3. **If tasting is your downfall when cooking, wear a surgical mask, chew gum, suck on a dietetic sour lemon drop or drink diet soda to prevent nibbling.** If you occasionally do need a taste to judge the accuracy of your seasoning, a quarter teaspoon will be sufficient to taste, but not gain weight.

"My problem," declared one man, "is I'm a taster. I come home from work and hang around the kitchen listening to my wife and tasting everything I can find." Many people fall into the category of tasters. I asked students in three separate classes to run an experiment for me. They were each to take a surgical mask home and wear it every day from the time they entered the kitchen in the late afternoon until they sat down at the table for dinner. They were asked to count how many times a hand or eating utensil bumped into the mask and write each day's total on the mask.

Most people thought it was a weird idea that sounded like fun. One elderly, five-foot-tall lady, however, wasn't amused by the idea. She stood up and said, "My dear, I know I don't eat anything standing up and I NEVER taste food when I cook." I asked her if she would mind checking the accuracy of her perceptions, just for fun. She agreed and the next week in class said, with embarrassment, "It's hard for me to tell you this after what I said last week, but one day I bumped the mask 32 times!"

The tasters in the three classes experimented with a lot of ideas for keeping food items out of their mouths and found these four to be particularly effective: wearing a surgical mask (some people really liked them), chewing gum, sucking on dietetic sour lemon drops and drinking diet soda. When tasting is absolutely necessary, using a quarter teaspoon instead of a large cooking spoon "means I can taste and not get fat," chuckled one lady.

4. There are two basic strategies to use when preparing two dinner meals at the same time to insure that the second meal will not be eaten sooner than originally planned. One is to **prepare both meals at the same time, but cook only one portion then, storing the second portion, uncooked, in the refrigerator.** The uncooked ingredients are not nearly as tempting to snack on. The second strategy is to **place the total amount of food in two containers, cook both at the same time, but place one container in the freezer for storage as quickly after cooking as possible.**

5. **When baking for others, don't make your own favorite things.** Many people love to bake and the tendency is for them to bake their own favorites. It is much harder to control the consumption of favorite foods. How often I've heard people comment, "I don't care about cake so I don't eat it, but when I bake cookies I make a double recipe so I can eat the dough and still have enough cookies for everybody." That situation guarantees loss of control. If a person wants to bake, control will be best established with less tempting items.

For some people large items like cakes or pies are preferred for maintaining control over items like cookies. Missing cookies are not necessarily noticed, but slices or bites out of pies or cakes are obviously visible. People are sometimes reluctant to spoil the appearance of a freshly baked pie or cake by cutting into it. The result is less temptation.

"...when I bake cookies
I make a double recipe
so I can eat the dough..."

When baking exclusively for the fun of it, plan where the finished products will go before you begin baking. Food banks, convalescent homes and residential schools for handicapped children represent a few possible outlets for donations of freshly baked foods. In this way, the fun of baking is enhanced by the good feelings of giving the food to others. When baking for the family, dividing the recipes in half or using only half the amount of a prepared mix reduces the amount left over and eliminates a potential food cue.

6. **Use smaller containers for mixing and cooking.** This technique is particularly useful to people whose family size is reduced, as in the situation where children have moved away from home. Many of them cook without recipes and in the same pots and pans they've always used. Thus it is easy to continue to prepare the same quantities of food even though it results in unwanted leftovers. People who purchase smaller pots and casserole dishes often find that they prepare smaller amounts of food without having to think much about it, because they make their measurement judgments in relation to the size of the container.

Cleanup and Leftovers

1. Leftovers on plates or scraps of food left in bowls or pans set up a powerful automatic eating response in a lot of people. **A little water, salt, sugar, or hot sauce, poured over the leftovers reduces their desirability.**
2. If there is enough remaining of a particular food to be usable, the best approach is to **package and label it immediately for a specific snack or meal.** You can use labels such as "Sunday dinner supplement," or "my lunch, Tuesday." Food items which have an assigned use are less tempting to many people. Some people seal leftovers in plastic cooking pouches, which further helps them to leave the food alone.
3. **Keep large plastic containers of leftover vegetables and meat in the freezer for eventual use in soups or stews.**
4. **Make your own TV dinners out of leftovers.** Save empty TV-dinner trays and whenever there are some leftovers, put them into individual sections of the trays and place them in the freezer. Keep adding food items until the trays are full. In time, a variety of homemade TV dinners is established and available whenever a quick meal is desired.
5. **If there is no good use for a leftover food, don't eat it just to keep it from being thrown out.** Feed it to a pet. Toss it onto the compost heap. Dump it into the disposal. If you eat it up only to save it from being thrown out, **IT IS STILL GARBAGE**, particularly if you then have to worry about losing the extra weight gained from eating the leftovers. That may be a hard concept to accept, but it is very important that you learn to do so.

If you eat it up only to

save it from being thrown out,

IT IS STILL GARBAGE.

Explanation of Homework

Assignment for this week: experiment with up to five of the suggestions listed in this chapter, and record your progress and food intake daily.

Weekly Progress Record

The instructions for how to use the Weekly Progress Record are on pages 257-260.

Daily Food Record

The instructions for how to use the Daily Food Record are on pages 261-263.

Weight Record

The instructions for how to use the Weight Record are on pages 21-22.

It might be helpful to select the area of greatest difficulty, either shopping, preparation or cleanup, and concentrate only on the suggestions for that area. Whatever you decide, the objective is to try out some new ideas. If you are feeling overloaded by the number of techniques to experiment with, practice only one or two from earlier lessons and try only a few from this lesson. It will not be possible to practice everything thoroughly the first time you go through the book. When the course is completed you will be able to go through all of the lessons again, taking time to explore thoroughly and practice the techniques you weren't able to try during the course. When your spirits get low, remember the lady in the grocery store and laugh a little. Good luck!

WEEKLY PROGRESS RECORD

BASIC SKILLS:	SUN	MON	TUES	WED	THURS	FRI	SAT	*
Read Progress Record in morning								
Record food intake								
Stay within calorie/ exchange total								
SPECIFIC TECHNIQUES/EXERCISES:								
Daily Totals								

*This column is for the weekly totals for each specific technique or exercise.

DAILY FOOD RECORD

Food Item/ Beverage	Amount	Calories/Exchanges	Time of Day

Total Calories for day ______

Total Exchanges for day:
(1) Milk ______
(2) Vegetable ______
(3) Fruit ______
(4) Bread ______
(5) Meat ______
(6) Fat ______

Date ______

DAILY FOOD RECORD

Food Item/ Beverage	Amount	Calories/Exchanges	Time of Day

Total Calories for day ________

Date ________________

Total Exchanges for day:

(1) Milk ______
(2) Vegetable ______
(3) Fruit ______
(4) Bread ______
(5) Meat ______
(6) Fat ______

DAILY FOOD RECORD

Food Item/ Beverage	Amount	Calories/Exchanges	Time of Day

Copyright © Northwest Learning Associates, Inc., 1978. All rights reserved.

Total Calories for day ________

Date ________________

Total Exchanges for day:

(1) Milk ______
(2) Vegetable ______
(3) Fruit ______
(4) Bread ______
(5) Meat ______
(6) Fat ______

DAILY FOOD RECORD

Food Item/ Beverage	Amount	Calories/Exchanges	Time of Day

Total Calories for day ________

Date ____________________

Total Exchanges for day:

(1) Milk ______
(2) Vegetable ______
(3) Fruit ______
(4) Bread ______
(5) Meat ______
(6) Fat ______

DAILY FOOD RECORD

Food Item/ Beverage	Amount	Calories/Exchanges	Time of Day

Total Calories for day ________

Date ____________________

Total Exchanges for day:

(1) Milk ______
(2) Vegetable ______
(3) Fruit ______
(4) Bread ______
(5) Meat ______
(6) Fat ______

DAILY FOOD RECORD

Food Item/ Beverage	Amount	Calories/Exchanges	Time of Day

Total Calories for day ______

Date ______

Total Exchanges for day:

(1) Milk ______
(2) Vegetable ______
(3) Fruit ______
(4) Bread ______
(5) Meat ______
(6) Fat ______

DAILY FOOD RECORD

Food Item/ Beverage	Amount	Calories/Exchanges	Time of Day

Total Calories for day ______

Date ______

Total Exchanges for day:

(1) Milk ______
(2) Vegetable ______
(3) Fruit ______
(4) Bread ______
(5) Meat ______
(6) Fat ______

Copyright © Northwest Learning Associates, Inc., 1978. All rights reserved.

Chapter 5 - INSTRUCTOR NOTES

Suggested Techniques:

Listed on pages 92 and 93.

Homework Assignments:

Read the instructions on page 94.

Cautions and Reminders:

1. Refusing food when it is ordered is a difficult task for many people. If some of your students express worry or concern at the thought of trying this technique, a little bit of role-playing in class is helpful. Try some "wishy-washy" refusals first to illustrate how difficult it can be to transmit a definite "no." Elicit examples from students. Combine theirs with yours and role-play some definite, polite refusals. Divide the class into pairs to practice saying "no" politely to one another. Do this for five or ten minutes. Then suggest that they continue to practice at home, either by themselves or with a partner. The objective is not to teach them that they must always say "no" when food is offered. Rather, the purpose is to develop specific responses for the times when they really do want to refuse. This increases the likelihood that they will be able to decline successfully the offer of extra food.
2. Some of your students may ask why it is important to leave some food on their plates, if they are measuring the amount carefully beforehand. Remind them that they will not always be able to measure the amount of food on their plates, and, if there are times when they don't want to eat all of it, it will be important for them to know how to leave it uneaten. The best place to practice is at home. Urge those students who measure their portions to add slightly extra portions—a piece of bread crust, a couple of extra beans or peas, or a little extra amount of potato or rice—and then follow the directions in their books.
3. Many students resist the idea of refusing food, to say nothing of leaving it. To overcome such resistance, urge them to try these exercises to see what happens. If they don't like the results after a few trials, they don't have to do them anymore. If they like the results, they can make their own decisions about where and when to use them. Remind your students that the objective of these lessons is **experimentation.**

5

Target: Stimulus control.
Objectives:
1. Eliminate or reduce external factors from the mealtime environment which result in overconsumption and/or prolonged eating.
2. Identify and experiment with external factors which result in reduced portion sizes and/or number of servings, and which enhance satisfaction with the amount consumed.
3. Reduce or maintain calorie level; establish or maintain dietary plan.

Motto:

You control the environment; don't let the environment control you.

Controlling Your Mealtime Environment

The first lesson introduced the concept of internal and external food cues and their impact on eating behavior. It focused on external cues as trigger mechanisms which create a desire to eat. External cues influence eating behavior in other ways too. Some external cues have the effect of prolonged eating, as in the following examples: food in serving bowls on the table, a hostess' invitation to have just a little more or finishing the meal early and having a second serving for something to do while others are still eating.

Some external cues signal the completion of a meal: an empty plate, empty serving bowls on the table, watching others get up from the table, or having the waitress clear the dishes away in a restaurant. One lady mentioned that a cue for her was her son's question, "What's for dessert, Mom?" That was her signal to stop eating and serve the dessert. Until she heard it she kept on eating. Another woman discovered that standing up, as if to leave the table, was an effective end-of-the-meal signal.

External cues may even affect how satisfied people feel with what they have eaten. Consider how a cup of pudding looks when placed in a cereal bowl and when placed in a small custard cup. A cup of vegetables, a serving of meat, and a half cup of rice look relatively larger when placed on a salad plate than when placed on a plain, borderless dinner plate. The amount of food relative to the size of the container is the point of focus. The same amount of food in a smaller container appears larger and more satisfying.

A similar reaction takes place for some people when they take a small serving out of a large container, as in the example of one cup of sherbet taken from a full half-gallon carton. Compared to the half-gallon, the cup of sherbet doesn't seem to be very much. For many people this results in feelings of deprivation; for others it results in unplanned, additional servings. People sometimes mention that they use food items more sparingly when the amount in the bottle or jar gets low in contrast to full containers of the same items.

One of the major tasks for people in changing their mealtime eating patterns is to establish external cues which help them control their eating, and to eliminate or reduce those external cues which cause them to eat more than was originally planned. Strategies for altering these external cues are listed below.

Environmental Control Exercises For Meals

1. **Do not keep serving bowls at the table.** Extra food may be kept on the stove, the counter or on a serving cart. The underlying rationale is both to remove an effective food cue from sight and to make it more bothersome to take second servings.

2. **Use smaller plates, bowls, glasses and serving spoons.** Research studies have demonstrated that the size of the plate, bowl or glass a person's food is presented in significantly influences his or her perception of the amount of the food or beverage served. This perception, in turn, affects how much satisfaction the person feels.

   Many of my students have experimented with the same amount of food in plates and bowls of different sizes. For the bowls, one cup of pudding was used. For the plates, one half cup of peas, one half cup of rice and four ounces of meat were used. When using a cereal bowl for the pudding, most of the people reported feeling deprived because the amount of pudding seemed so little when compared to the size of the bowl. The same amount of pudding placed in a custard cup appeared to be larger, and almost everyone felt more satisfied.

   In the plate experiment, the least amount of satisfaction was felt when plain white dinner plates were used. One woman's comment was: "It looked like the dishwasher detergent ad. I had so much of my plate to see my reflection in!" Plates that had interwoven designs over the entire surface were preferred over the white plates, but dessert or salad plates were most effective in allowing people the greatest satisfaction from the measured amount of food. Some people, particularly men, object to the obvious appearance of a smaller plate. An effective solution for them is the use of a dinner plate with a wide, raised border. The actual eating surface is reduced in size and has the same effect as the smaller plate; that is, to make the same amount of food appear to be proportionately larger. This is a relatively easy habit for people to establish.

The same amount of pudding placed in a custard cup appeared to be larger.

   Many people are amazed at the number of calories they save by using smaller glasses. Once a beverage is poured, people usually drink the entire amount. If a nine ounce glass is used rather than a large tumbler, or a four or six ounce glass is used instead of a nine ounce glass, the need for something to drink is satisfied with fewer calories consumed.

There is another aspect to this exercise. If tempting foods are packaged in smaller amounts it is easier to take a single serving without feeling deprived. A one cup serving of ice milk, when taken from a full half-gallon, doesn't seem like very much compared to the total amount but seems far more reasonable when taken from a pint or quart container.

3. **Leave a little bit of food on your plate.** This is the hardest exercise of all for some people. Its purpose is to break the external cue of an empty plate signifying the end of a meal. People ask why this is important if they measured their food beforehand. The answer is that in some situations they may be given a plate of food which was served by someone else, or they may put more on their own plates than was desired, especially in buffet or cafeteria lines.

If the result of having too much food on the plate is that too much food has to be eaten, the person is not in control of his or her food intake. It is not essential that you leave a lot of food on your plate for this exercise. A couple of peas, a corner piece of bread crust, or a spoonful of potatoes left on the plate at the end of the meal will be sufficient to break the empty-plate cue.

4. **Remove the plate as soon as you finish eating.** This will help you stick to your original resolve to leave that little bit of food on your plate!

5. **For situations in which the plate cannot conveniently be removed, destroy the desirability of the food with a discreet, but liberal, sprinkling of salt, pepper, or hot sauce.** If you forget and take a bite, the result may be sufficiently unpleasant to curb all desire for that food for the duration of the meal.

6. **Practice polite refusals when extra food is offered to you.** A major eating problem for some people is an impulsive response when food is offered to them. Many people simply cannot say "no" to an invitation to eat. Often they eat something before they have even questioned whether or not they want to at all. The purpose of this exercise is to decrease these impulsive eating responses.

A man I know used to "define" himself by saying, "I can never pass up desserts. Whenever someone asks me if I want a piece of cake or pie, I know I'll say 'yes' even if I'm too full to really want it." By defining his actions in this way, the man had given himself permission to eat the dessert. Refusing the cake or

---

Many people simply cannot say "no" to an invitation to eat.

---

pie was made more difficult by the fact that he did not plan how to say "no" because he had really prepared himself to say "yes". Once he had seen that his response was impulsive and was asked to experiment with this exercise, his first reaction was, "What will I say?" He thought about it awhile, tried out a few different ideas and came up with a response he particularly liked. It was, "Oh, no, thank you. Your dinner was so delicious that I overate and couldn't possibly stuff in one more bite."

In order to practice his refusal he decided to refuse all offers of unplanned food especially when at his mother-in-law's house. The strategy he selected was to tell her before sitting down at the table that he probably wouldn't want any dessert that night, but if he changed his mind, he would ask for it. After two weeks he reported that he had had a hard time in the beginning, but that he was doing well at last and really felt much more in control of his eating response. He chuckled when adding that he had even turned down a couple of beers after work because he hadn't asked for them himself.

With this exercise it is important for you to decide when to ask for something so that if you want a particular food, you are able to ask for it before the hostess offers it. For a lot of people the result of this exercise is an increased feeling of control in choosing what, when or how much food they want and fewer *automatic* responses to extra food passed their way. The most important aspect of this exercise is that it forces you to think about how to say "no." Having done that, it is much easier to actually say it.

Explanation of Homework

Assignment for this week: experiment with up to five of the Environmental Control Exercises for Meals explained in this lesson, and record your progress and food intake daily.

Weekly Progress Record

The instructions for how to use the Weekly Progress Record are on pages 257-260.

Daily Food Record

The instructions for how to use the Daily Food Record are on pages 261-263.

Weight Record

The instructions for how to use the Weight Record are on pages 21-22.

Politely refusing food when it is offered is one of the most difficult exercises to do. Ask someone to practice with you. Ask that person to try many different ways of talking you into eating something and, each time, you practice refusing politely, but firmly. The more you practice, the easier it will be to refuse food when it is offered to you at a time when you really would prefer not to eat it. Good luck!

WEEKLY PROGRESS RECORD

BASIC SKILLS:	SUN	MON	TUES	WED	THURS	FRI	SAT	*
Read Progress Record in morning								
Record food intake								
Stay within calorie/ exchange total								
SPECIFIC TECHNIQUES/EXERCISES:								
Daily Totals								

*This column is for the weekly totals for each specific technique or exercise.

DAILY FOOD RECORD

Food Item/ Beverage	Amount	Calories/Exchanges	Time of Day

Total Calories for day ______

Date ______

Total Exchanges for day:

(1) Milk ______
(2) Vegetable ______
(3) Fruit ______
(4) Bread ______
(5) Meat ______
(6) Fat ______

DAILY FOOD RECORD

Food Item/ Beverage	Amount	Calories/Exchanges	Time of Day

Total Calories for day ________

Date ____________________

Total Exchanges for day:

(1) Milk ______
(2) Vegetable ______
(3) Fruit ______
(4) Bread ______
(5) Meat ______
(6) Fat ______

DAILY FOOD RECORD

Food Item/ Beverage	Amount	Calories/Exchanges	Time of Day

Total Calories for day ________

Date ____________________

Total Exchanges for day:

(1) Milk ______
(2) Vegetable ______
(3) Fruit ______
(4) Bread ______
(5) Meat ______
(6) Fat ______

Copyright © Northwest Learning Associates, Inc., 1978. All rights reserved.

DAILY FOOD RECORD

Food Item/ Beverage	Amount	Calories/Exchanges	Time of Day

Total Calories for day ______

Date ______

Total Exchanges for day:
(1) Milk ______
(2) Vegetable ______
(3) Fruit ______
(4) Bread ______
(5) Meat ______
(6) Fat ______

DAILY FOOD RECORD

Food Item/ Beverage	Amount	Calories/Exchanges	Time of Day

Total Calories for day ______

Date ______

Total Exchanges for day:
(1) Milk ______
(2) Vegetable ______
(3) Fruit ______
(4) Bread ______
(5) Meat ______
(6) Fat ______

DAILY FOOD RECORD

Food Item/ Beverage	Amount	Calories/Exchanges	Time of Day

Total Calories for day ________

Date ____________________

Total Exchanges for day:
(1) Milk ______
(2) Vegetable ______
(3) Fruit ______
(4) Bread ______
(5) Meat ______
(6) Fat ______

DAILY FOOD RECORD

Food Item/ Beverage	Amount	Calories/Exchanges	Time of Day

Total Calories for day ________

Date ____________________

Total Exchanges for day:
(1) Milk ______
(2) Vegetable ______
(3) Fruit ______
(4) Bread ______
(5) Meat ______
(6) Fat ______

Chapter 6 - INSTRUCTOR NOTES

Suggested Techniques:
Listed on page 105.

Homework Assignments:
Read the instructions on page 106.

Cautions and Reminders:

1. Caution your students against decreasing their portion size too rapidly. One potential outcome of this week's exercises is that by eating more slowly the hunger level may decrease sufficiently before the end of the meal to cause some people to eat less voluntarily.
2. Remind the students that improved performance, not perfection, is the objective of the lesson. If at first they don't do well with some of the exercises, that is to be expected. Their performance will improve with practice.
3. If some of the suggested techniques in this lesson are not applicable to individual students, or if some students are not having difficulty with this aspect of food habit control, suggest that they continue to practice techniques from an earlier lesson or that they experiment with some control ideas of their own.

6

Target: Reduced eating speed.

Objectives:

1. Reduce efficiency of eating patterns and thereby reduce eating speed.
2. Enhance enjoyment of mealtime eating.
3. Reduce or maintain calorie level; establish or maintain dietary plan.

Motto:

Savor the flavor; the slower you eat it the longer it lasts.

Eating Slowly: Reducing Efficiency

Efficiency is a highly valued asset in our culture. It allows for a maximum amount of accomplishment in a minimum amount of time. Many people have adopted a very efficient eating pattern which results in rapid food consumption. This pattern was best exhibited by a man I watched while eating in a restaurant one day. He held the knife in one hand, the fork in the other hand, never letting go of either utensil. While chewing one mouthful he was busily cutting food and loading up the next forkful, so that the next bite was ready and waiting before he had even swallowed what was already in his mouth! He spoke very little to the people he was eating with, appearing to be very intently focused on his meal. The result was that he was finished with his food far ahead of his companions.

A great many people report that eating more slowly results in significantly greater enjoyment of the meal. Beyond the satisfaction of basic hunger, much of the pleasure obtained in eating is sensual. People seem to need a certain amount of tasting, sucking, chewing and swallowing activity in order to achieve satisfaction from eating. When food is eaten rapidly there is less time spent in these activities, and for many people this results in greater amounts of food consumed in order to feel satisfied.

Some people have contrasted the difference in satisfaction between eating a plain Hershey chocolate bar and a Tootsie Roll. The Hershey bar is soft and usually eaten quickly, while a Tootsie Roll is chewy and takes considerably longer to eat. These people derived more enjoyment

. . . much of the pleasure obtained in eating is sensual.

and satisfaction from eating the Tootsie Roll.

That same type of comparison was made by another group of people using ice cream served in a dish and an ice cream cone. The cone required more time, offered greater "play" value from licking the ice cream, and was generally preferred to ice cream in a dish.

In both experiments, the consensus was that eating more slowly made it possible to taste and savor the food. As one of the experimenters said, "It was the difference between dining and 'wolfing'." As I listened to that comment, I had the instant visual image of my puppy, who gobbles his meal in less than two minutes and spends the rest of the day looking around for something else to eat. The lesson to be learned: if you enjoy eating, prolong the enjoyment.

Eating more slowly has an additional benefit for many people: it results in their needing to eat less food in order to feel full. Once you begin eating your body immediately starts converting the food into glucose, thereby raising the blood sugar level. Once that level reaches optimum the brain's regulator, located in the hypothalamus, stops sending "eat" messages to the brain and a reduction, or absence of hunger feelings occurs. An elevation of blood sugar sufficient to reduce hunger feelings is not related to the volume of food eaten. A small amount of food will work just as effectively as a large amount. The critical matter is time. The whole process, from beginning to eat to achieving an elevated blood sugar level, takes approximately twenty minutes no matter how much food is consumed.

"It was the difference between dining and 'wolfing'."

While there is some controversy over whether it is the actual rise in blood sugar which produces the feeling of satiety, it is clear that allowing an extended period of time for eating does result in greater satisfaction with smaller amounts of food.

Some of my students participated in an experiment to test the effect of time on their hunger feelings and they made the following observations.

One group selected ice cream as the experimental food. They found that when standing in front of the freezer eating ice cream out of the carton, it took roughly fifteen to twenty minutes before they felt satisfied. They then took one cup of ice cream to a table and waited a full twenty minutes from the time of the first spoonful to measure their hunger feelings, they found they were no longer hungry. Another group used salad as the experiemental food. The results were similar. Hunger pangs were gone in twenty minutes whether they had eaten continually for that period of time or had eaten one serving slowly and then waited until the full twenty minutes had passed.

What evolved can be called the Twenty Minute Rule: If you wait a full twenty minutes after beginning each meal or snack, you will feel satisfied and will not want additional food. Thus, eating more slowly at mealtimes not only increases sensual satisfaction, it uses up the twenty minutes required to reduce or eliminate the hunger feelings.

The specific procedures for reducing eating speed at mealtimes can be referred to as Efficiency Reduction Exercises. Their function is to reduce eating speed by reducing the efficiency of the person's eating pattern. There are six exercises listed below.

1. **Put the eating utensil down between bites.** This applies also to food items like sandwiches, chicken legs, or crackers. If the fork, spoon or food item has to be picked up again before each mouthful is taken, it reduces overall eating efficiency.

2. **Cut food as it is needed** rather than cutting it all in advance. Women who have young children are most prone to cutting food in advance since they are well practiced in preparing plates with bite-size pieces of meat and the like.

3. **Swallow what is in your mouth before preparing the next bite.** This is a particularly important step. Having a forkful of food ready for intake as soon as the previous mouthful is swallowed reduces the probability of any other action taking precedence over eating. To do anything else like taking a drink of water, conversing with someone, or even just resting would require putting a food laden fork down first. For most people the natural inclination is to eat what's on the fork before putting it down.

4. **Stop eating for a minute once or twice during the meal.** This will help you break your eating rhythm and allow you to keep pace with the slowest eaters.

5. **If second servings are desired, make each serving only half of the total planned amount.** This exercise provides a good opportunity to stress the importance of measuring the size of each serving. Using measuring cups and spoons to serve your food portions when at home makes the process of reducing portion size more accurate.

6. **Experiment with eating your meal in courses of one food at a time and in the following order: salad, hot vegetable, meat, rice or potato, and bread.** A number of people complain of difficulty controlling how much they serve themselves of high calorie foods. The strategy of beginning the meal with the least caloric foods allows a person to reduce the urgent hunger feelings before confronting those foods which require the most control. Many people report that they don't eat the bread or potato because they are no longer hungry. An adaptation of this strategy is very useful in situations where coming home from work is followed by uncontrolled eating.

A planned, low-calorie appetizer can be very effective in reducing urgent hunger and establishing control. One young wife cited the following problem. Her husband arrived home from work each day feeling tense, wound-up and unable to relax at the dinner table. He ate his food rapidly, leaving his wife to finish her meal alone. She was attempting to reduce her eating speed at mealtimes and found she couldn't eat slowly at dinner because of her husband's pattern. She experimented with the idea of having the salad ready as soon as her husband arrived home. He ate his salad rapidly, and by the time his wife served the rest of the meal at a more leisurely pace, he had begun to slow down and was able to finish in a more relaxed fashion.

Some people like the special feeling they have when serving one course at a time. One woman commented that she almost felt as though she were eating in a restaurant and liked it. Other people say that the one-food-at-a-time plan allows them to savor each food individually and to keep hot foods on the stove where they stay hot, thus increasing their enjoyment of the meal.

Explanation of Homework

Assignment for this week: experiment with up to five of the Efficiency Reduction Exercises explained earlier, and record your progress and food intake daily.

Weekly Progress Record

The instructions for how to use the Weekly Progress Record are on pages 257-260.

Daily Food Record

The instructions for how to use the Daily Food Record are on pages 261-263.

Weight Record

The instructions for how to use the Weight Record are on pages 21-22.

Remember that this week's assignment is an experiment to see whether eating more slowly enhances your enjoyment and allows you to be satisfied with smaller amounts of food. Record what you do and see what happens.

If you are not sure whether you eat rapidly, draw an extra column on your Daily Food Record and label it "Time Spent Eating." Each time you eat, record the time in minutes or seconds. When several items are eaten together, as in a meal or large snack, record the time for the whole meal rather than for each single item. As you practice this week's lesson you may find that you are spending more time with each meal and snack, and recording the time spent is a good way to measure your progress. Don't try too many techniques at one time. If you feel overloaded with too many ideas this week, select one to three ideas from your previous lessons for continued practice and add only a few ideas from this week's lesson. Don't work on more than you can comfortably handle. Good luck!

Beginning with this chapter, the number of Daily Food Record forms has been reduced to accustom you to using the Food Record forms located at the back of the book, beginning on page 273. The edge of the pages are marked with a gray stripe for quick reference.

WEEKLY PROGRESS RECORD

BASIC SKILLS:	SUN	MON	TUES	WED	THURS	FRI	SAT	*
Read Progress Record in morning								
Record food intake								
Stay within calorie/ exchange total								
SPECIFIC TECHNIQUES/EXERCISES:								
Daily Totals								

*This column is for the weekly totals for each specific technique or exercise.

DAILY FOOD RECORD

Food Item/ Beverage	Amount	Calories/Exchanges	Time of Day

Total Calories for day ______

Date ______

Total Exchanges for day:
(1) Milk ______
(2) Vegetable ______
(3) Fruit ______
(4) Bread ______
(5) Meat ______
(6) Fat ______

DAILY FOOD RECORD

Food Item/ Beverage	Amount	Calories/Exchanges	Time of Day

Total Calories for day ______

Date ______

Total Exchanges for day:

(1) Milk ______
(2) Vegetable ______
(3) Fruit ______
(4) Bread ______
(5) Meat ______
(6) Fat ______

DAILY FOOD RECORD

Food Item/ Beverage	Amount	Calories/Exchanges	Time of Day

Total Calories for day ______

Date ______

Total Exchanges for day:

(1) Milk ______
(2) Vegetable ______
(3) Fruit ______
(4) Bread ______
(5) Meat ______
(6) Fat ______

Copyright © Northwest Learning Associates, Inc., 1978. All rights reserved.

DAILY FOOD RECORD

Food Item/ Beverage	Amount	Calories/Exchanges	Time of Day

Total Calories for day ________

Date ________

Total Exchanges for day:
(1) Milk ____
(2) Vegetable ____
(3) Fruit ____
(4) Bread ____
(5) Meat ____
(6) Fat ____

DAILY FOOD RECORD

Food Item/ Beverage	Amount	Calories/Exchanges	Time of Day

Copyright © Northwest Learning Associates, Inc., 1978. All rights reserved.

Total Calories for day ________

Date ________

Total Exchanges for day:
(1) Milk ____
(2) Vegetable ____
(3) Fruit ____
(4) Bread ____
(5) Meat ____
(6) Fat ____

Chapter 7 - INSTRUCTOR NOTES

Suggested Techniques:

1. Write down your own personal guidelines for control.
2. Make a separate column heading for each regularly eaten meal and snack.
3. Develop a minimum of three variations of control meals in each column. Make certain to include foods that you are likely to want from time to time, like desserts or casseroles.
4. Experiment with your control meal plans for the week.
5. Modify your food options or guidelines as necessary.
6. Using separate 3″ x 5″ card for each meal and snack heading, write down the specific guidelines you wish to use. Carry them with you.

Homework Assignments:

Read the instructions on page 116.

Cautions and Reminders:

1. Students frequently fail to realize the importance of having their control meal plans developed and written down **before** they need to use them. If necessary, warn your students that they will be reviewing their specific plans in class the following week. The following week you can ask them to share their plans with the entire group, or break the group into diads or triads to share their plans.
2. Review your students' plans to make certain that they haven't developed unrealistically stringent, perfectionistic guidelines. These guidelines and specific meal options are designed for maintenance and will not be used or useful if they do not include options for favorite foods and for typically available items within their current life style. If some of your students eat out a lot or use convenience type foods, they must be included in the control meal plans or those plans will not be used because they are not relevant.
3. Once developed, the control meal plans must be available. If students choose not to carry them in purse or pocket, ask them to tape them to the inside of their kitchen cupboard doors where they will be seen and kept from being misplaced or thrown away. Suggest that your students take their control meal plans with them on vacations or extended weekends away from home.

7

Target: Preplanning (stabilization and restart planning).

Objectives:

1. Provide a structural guideline for easy meal planning and food selection.
2. Provide an alternative to calorie counting.
3. Supply a mechanism for "getting back on track" following an overindulgent meal or a binge.
4. Provide a guideline to be used on holidays or vacations, or when stress levels are high to reduce opportunities for random food selection or inclusion of too many high calorie foods.

Motto:

Reestablish control with personalized meal plans.

Control Meals

Have you ever wished, on a day of shaky control, that someone would come along and tell you what to eat? Or better yet, that someone would prepare and serve the appropriate foods to you in the appropriate amounts? The freedom of choice each of us has for daily food selection is important to most of us and probably helps more than we realize to keep us from rebelling against "the diet". However, that freedom can be a burden on some days. The effort to choose can feel overwhelming if you are under a great deal of stress, or if you are overly tired or depressed. Yet the comfort of a definite structure, of knowing exactly what to do can be very necessary at times. That structure is particularly important if you have overeaten and are having difficulty reestablishing control.

I have been asked hundreds of times whether a daily breakfast of plain grapefruit will melt away body fat. I have not seen a conclusive research study which suggests that grapefruit has definite fat dissolving properties. A little home kitchen experiment of my own, in which I placed 3 ounces of chicken fat and a full measure of grapefruit juice in a covered jar showed me the same result. After three weeks I still had 3 ounces of chicken fat and the same amount of grapefruit juice!

While there may not be a physiological benefit to grapefruit for breakfast, there can be a definite psychological benefit. If

The effort to choose can feel overwhelming.

you have had grapefruit for breakfast or any breakfast food which you consider to be appropriate for weight loss, would you be better able or less able to pass up doughnuts at the morning coffee break? If you had a poached egg, dry toast and juice for breakfast and it felt controlled, would it be easier for you to select an appropriate, "controlled" lunch? On the other hand if you had hash browned potatoes, sausage and a waffle with syrup for breakfast, what would you do with the doughnuts at coffee break, or with lunch at noon? Many of my students claim that a fattening breakfast causes them to give up control for the day. Other students try to make up for the excess food consumed and pass up the mid-morning goodies, eat little or no lunch, avoid late afternoon snacks but fall apart around supper time and overeat then and also later in the evening.

What this shows me is that many dieters function in an all or nothing way when it comes to food. They are either in excellent control or little-to-no control, and they are easily influenced by one inappropriate meal or snack. Since most dieters have very definite opinions about what is an OK, or controlled, meal and what is not, it is very important for each of us to know our own guidelines for control for each meal and snack we eat. How do you judge when a particular meal has been appropriate? What guidelines do you use?

Most people say that if they eat particular foods, like fish, vegetables or fruit, they feel in control. I remember listening to a woman complain angrily that she had stuffed herself on salad and felt just terrrible. The fact that she overate salad rather than higher calorie items was of some comfort but the real issue for her was volume. She ate too much and felt out of control. Once out of control, she had lots of trouble preventing further overeating during other meals and snacks.

Students in all of my classes devise their own lists of control guidelines for meals and snacks. Below is a list of guidelines developed during a class session by six of my students.

Guidelines for Controlled Meals and Snacks.

Specific foods (i.e., egg, salad, cereal, pizza, taco, etc.).

Specific food types (i.e., vegetable, protein, starch, protein sandwich, composite, dessert, etc.).

Portion size (volume control).

Number of food items allowable (i.e., 3 for breakfast, 4 for lunch, 5 for dinner, 1 per snack).

Related eating behaviors (i.e., sitting down to eat, eating slowly, etc.).

Calories

The word composite refers to foods like pizza, spaghetti, lasagna, casseroles, paella, oriental food, and so on in which several types of foods are combined. If you have ever used a food exchange plan to regulate your food intake you will notice that the guideline called "specific food types" is much like an exchange plan, with the inclusion of categories for sandwiches, composites, desserts. What are your specific control guidelines? What do you use to judge whether or not you have eaten correctly? List your guidelines on a separate sheet of paper.

These guidelines will be used in this next exercise which is to develop specific meal and snack food selections, called control meals. The purposes for developing specific control meals are the following:

1. **To provide a structure with definite guidelines** to be used as an al-

ternative to calorie counting;

2. **To give you a break from decision making** when you want or need it;
3. **To help you stabilize when your control feels wobbly**; and
4. **To build one dimension of a re-start program when loss of control has occurred.**

What are control meals? They are specific selections or plans, established for each meal and snack you routinely eat. Each meal should have 3 to 4 variations or options to give you an adequate range to meet your basic needs and preferences. Some samples of control meals are listed below. Explanation will follow the samples.

Breakfast

juice, poached egg, muffin, coffee

fruit, cereal, milk, coffee

juice, pastry, coffee

2-3 items

In these breakfast samples, no calorie guidelines were used. Sometimes calorie counting becomes tedious and people welcome a break from the recording. For some people if they cannot compute the calories accurately, on the spot, it sets them up to overeat. In this case, guidelines like any of the ones given above would be useful for stabilization when calorie counting is not possible. The inclusion of the 2-3 item guideline is for buffet or cafeteria selections where choices must be made quickly, or where so many options exist that you feel overwhelmed and can't think, or where you see so many favorite foods that you would feel cheated if you didn't eat some of them. In this latter case eating three favorite foods and nothing else, even if they are all fattening, is preferable to either eating lower calorie foods and having a binge later or eating a bunch of other items and then going back to the food line for your favorites.

Suppose you have been invited to someone's home for breakfast and the hostess serves platters of fruit, pastry, sausage and pancakes. What could you eat? According to option number one you could do some substitution of similar food types and have one piece of fruit (juice), one sausage link (poached egg), one plain pancake (muffin) and coffee. Using option number three you could have one piece of fruit (juice), one piece of pastry and coffee. Using option number four you could have one piece of fruit, one sausage link and maybe one pastry.

Lunch

soup, salad, roll, beverage

protein sandwich, salad or fruit, beverage

composite, vegetable or fruit slices, beverage

salad, dessert, beverage

3-4 items

This sample includes a protein sandwich. Using that definition, a simple fast-food hamburger, plain fish sandwich, or taco would qualify under the guidelines for option number two. A pizza could also be classified as an open face protein sandwich. Thus, if you prefer a fast-food or restaurant meal, you have a guideline for what to select. This will help you avoid temptations for adding french fries, milk shakes, etc. to the menu. The composite meal might refer to an omelet, casserole, side dish of spaghetti. A dessert option was included for dessert lovers who, on a long-term basis, need to have some goodies from time to time. The 3-4 items again refers to cafeteria or buffet style meals.

Dinner

1 protein, 1 starch, 2 vegetables, 1 fruit

1 composite, 1 vegetable or fruit, 1 starch or dessert, beverage

1 large salad, or 1 small salad and soup, dessert, beverage

4-5 items

In this sample, composite meals and desserts have been included. Suppose you are going to a PTA pot luck dinner. The menu includes spaghetti, lasagna, cole slaw, jell-o fruit salad, garlic bread, bread sticks, brownies and coffee. What would you select using option numbers two or four? With the high calorie density of this meal I would suggest using 4 instead of 5 items.

These samples do not represent all of the options which are possible, nor is it necessary for you to use the ones presented in this chapter. These are merely examples to provide a better illustration of what is meant by the term control meals. It is important for you to develop your own guidelines for snacks as well as meals, and to base those selections on your known needs, preferences, and life style. If lunch is the main meal in your day, plan accordingly, using the dinner guidelines at noon and the lunch guidelines for the evening meal. If you eat at fast-food restaurants frequently, plan with the typically available foods in mind. If you are a dessert lover, be sure to include a dessert option.

I cannot emphasize too strongly how important it is to have these control meal plans made up in advance. Then, on a day of shaky control, or a day when you've overeaten, take out the control meal options for the next meal and follow them exactly. If you overeat at lunch, for example, do not skip dinner, but eat according to one of your dinner options. In doing that you have given yourself an amount of food which feels customary, so it allows you to satisfy your physical needs for food and, at the same time, contains your tendencies to overeat because you have overeaten earlier. The control meals are also helpful when traveling, visiting other people, or any time when your routine is disturbed. When people break their daily activity routine they frequently eat out of control. Think, for example, of three-day weekends. The Monday holidays tend to be a big problem for many of my students. If this is true for you, use your control meal plans on those days.

Explanation of Homework

The homework assignment for this week is to write out control meal options for each meal and snack you customarily eat. Try them out this week to make certain that they meet your needs for control and for variation. Be sure to define what a serving is. For example, how many slices of meat equal one serving? How many spoonfuls of vegetable constitute one serving? How many serving spoonfuls of composite foods make one serving?

Modify your control meal options as necessary. When you have worked them through, write them down on 3 x 5 index cards and tape them to the inside of a kitchen cupboard door where you can find them quickly. When you think you'll need them, carry them with you in your purse or pocket. Be sure to take them along on trips, festive occasions or other situations where you anticipate difficulty in controlling your food intake.

Weekly Progress Record

The instructions for how to use the Weekly Progress Record are on pages 257-260.

Daily Food Record

The instructions for how to use the Daily Food Record are on pages 261-263.

Weight Record

The instructions for how to use the Weight Record are on pages 21-22.

The most important aspect of this week's assignment is the developing of your control meal plans. If you have sufficient time and energy to practice some of the techniques suggested in earlier lessons select no more than three or four and enter them on this week's Weekly Progress Record. Be sure to include entries for developing control meal plans and for experimenting with control meal plans. If the developing and the experimenting are all you have time for, do not add anything extra to your Weekly Progress Record. It usually works out best to do a few things thoroughly and consistently than to try to do too many things and become sporadic and haphazard in your efforts. Good luck!

Extra recording forms for this chapter may be found starting on page 273.

WEEKLY PROGRESS RECORD

BASIC SKILLS:	SUN	MON	TUES	WED	THURS	FRI	SAT	*
Read Progress Record in morning								
Record food intake								
Stay within calorie/ exchange total								
SPECIFIC TECHNIQUES/EXERCISES:								
Daily Totals								

*This column is for the weekly totals for each specific technique or exercise.

DAILY FOOD RECORD

Food Item/ Beverage	Amount	Calories/Exchanges	Time of Day

Total Calories for day ________

Date ________

Total Exchanges for day:

(1) Milk ________
(2) Vegetable ________
(3) Fruit ________
(4) Bread ________
(5) Meat ________
(6) Fat ________

DAILY FOOD RECORD

Food Item/ Beverage	Amount	Calories/Exchanges	Time of Day

Total Calories for day ________

Date ________________

Total Exchanges for day:

(1) Milk ______
(2) Vegetable ______
(3) Fruit ______
(4) Bread ______
(5) Meat ______
(6) Fat ______

DAILY FOOD RECORD

Food Item/ Beverage	Amount	Calories/Exchanges	Time of Day

Copyright © Northwest Learning Associates, Inc., 1978. All rights reserved.

Total Calories for day ________

Date ________________

Total Exchanges for day:

(1) Milk ______
(2) Vegetable ______
(3) Fruit ______
(4) Bread ______
(5) Meat ______
(6) Fat ______

DAILY FOOD RECORD

Food Item/ Beverage	Amount	Calories/Exchanges	Time of Day

Total Calories for day ________

Date ____________________

Total Exchanges for day:
(1) Milk ______
(2) Vegetable ______
(3) Fruit ______
(4) Bread ______
(5) Meat ______
(6) Fat ______

DAILY FOOD RECORD

Food Item/ Beverage	Amount	Calories/Exchanges	Time of Day

Total Calories for day ________

Date ____________________

Total Exchanges for day:
(1) Milk ______
(2) Vegetable ______
(3) Fruit ______
(4) Bread ______
(5) Meat ______
(6) Fat ______

Copyright © Northwest Learning Associates, Inc., 1978. All rights reserved.

Chapter 8 - INSTRUCTOR NOTES

Suggested Techniques:

1. Wait 15 to 20 minutes before eating in response to an impulsive urge to eat (Time Delay).
2. Replace eating with a different activity listed on pages 126 and 127.
3. Additional techniques for delaying eating response listed on pages 127 and 128.

Homework Assignments:

Read the instructions on pages 128 and 129.

Cautions and Reminders:

1. Time delay techniques may be inappropriate and possibly harmful for students with hypoglycemia or diabetes. You should consult with these students' physicians prior to discussing this lesson in class, and follow the physicians' recommendations for safe snack control strategies.
2. These techniques are aimed at unscheduled, impulsive hunger pangs. They are not meant to be used to replace planned, scheduled snacks. Many people plan to eat frequently throughout the day in order to heighten control through prevention of physical hunger, or in accordance with a dietary regimen.
3. Caution your students against deliberately going without food for long periods of time. This aggravates the problem of eating control and contributes to perpetuation of the "feast or famine" cycle.
4. There are three aspects to replacing eating with other activities.
   a. One is the need for a short-term diversion; an activity to keep the hands or thoughts temporarily occupied. This type of activity replacement is most effectively used for restlessness, boredom, a work break, to put off doing something, and to unwind. Appropriate activities for these needs include: solitaire, auto-bridge, crossword puzzles, jigsaw puzzles, paper and pencil mazes, needlework, pasting photographs in albums, playing a musical instrument, letter writing, polishing fingernails and polishing shoes.
   b. Another is the need to fill up longer periods of time, such as afternoons, evenings or weekends. At these times there aren't other planned diversions, and the time ahead seems to stretch out endlessly. These are frequently times of loneliness, aimlessness, or boredom. Appropriate activities may include some of those mentioned earlier as well as some type of exercise, a movie, reading, running errands, working on a time-consuming project (e.g., sewing), tying flies for fishing, cleaning the tackle box, polishing the car, working on a coin or stamp collection, gardening, or working on any hobby. Sometimes major activities become possible only after some smaller tasks have been done first to "get the wheels moving." For example, shopping for a book or magazine may be the first step to reading; a couple of rounds of solitaire may be necessary before the sewing project can be started. These larger projects are much easier to accomplish if the initial work on them has been done beforehand. It is easier to cut out the material for a new clothing item if the pattern has already been pinned to the fabric. It is easier to work on any hobby or collection if the materials are readily accessible. This avoids the initial hurdle of searching through drawers and closets to locate the necessary items.
   c. Almost everyone needs to comfort, pamper, reward or console themselves at various times. Activities to replace eating during these times cannot be as accomplishment-oriented or energy-consuming as are many of the activities mentioned before. These are usually times of depression, anxiety, unhappiness, distraction, frustration or fatigue. What is really needed is time away from doing "useful" tasks and the permission to do something of a comforting nature. Taking a nap or a leisurely bath, browsing through magazines, recreational reading, looking at old home movies, listening to records or tapes, watching TV, or even doodling with coloring books, clay or jigsaw puzzles can be restorative to both the spirit and the energy level.
5. Ask your students to prepare their lists of replacement activities with each of these aspects in mind and to categorize them accordingly. Remind them to tape their lists in places where they can be seen easily and frequently. When a hunger pang arrives it can be very difficult to remember automatically any ideas for delaying that eating response!
6. Caution your students to take no more than five techniques from previous lessons for practice this week. Some students may wish to focus primarily on the snack control exercises; others may want to emphasize techniques from earlier lessons. The important factor is that they don't overload themselves with too many things to try to accomplish in one week. It is to their benefit to do a few techniques consistently and effectively.

8

Targets: Delayed eating response and activity replacement.

Objectives:

1. Delay eating response to impulsive desires for food.
2. Replace the activity of eating with other activities which are appropriate to the needs and circumstances.
3. Reduce or maintain calorie level; establish or maintain dietary plan.

Motto:

"Yes, I may eat it in twenty minutes, but first I'm going to. . ."

Snack Control: Delayed Eating Response

While we have looked at impulsive eating responses in other chapters of this book, nowhere is the dimension of impulsive eating greater than in the category of snacking. People frequently eat in response to an impulsive urge for food stemming from actual food cues as well as the need for an activity. "You know, if I didn't eat so much between meals, I wouldn't have gained all that weight." "Cleaning the house makes me so HUNGRY!" "I eat just to have something to do." "I get so uptight when I study I just have to eat." "Oh, if only I could stop eating at night.'" These are just a few of the frustrated comments heard daily from people who struggle with between-meal eating problems.

Many people mistakenly believe that all hunger pangs are caused by a low blood sugar level. While that undoubtedly causes many hunger pangs, there are several other sources to consider.

Environmental triggers, such as those discussed in the first lesson, often create hunger pangs. Thought associations provide a powerful stimulus for hunger sensations. An example of this was heard in a young girl's exclamation, "Aunt Martha, I love your cooking so much I get hungry every time I think about you!" When planning a family vacation, one woman reported feeling very hungry right after deciding upon flight departure and arrival times. She anticipated eating dinner on the plane and experienced a hunger pang.

Moods or feeling states are common instigators of between-meal urges to eat. Feelings of anger, frustration, anxiety, depression, boredom, loneliness, restlessness, joy, anticipation or excitement are paired with eating for many people. Therefore, the onset of a mood or feeling state may stimulate a desire for food. Illness and fatigue, if not too severe, can also make people hungry. The most frequently recognized and reported triggers for between-meal eating are fatigue, depression and boredom.

Many people believe that unless they eat, their hunger pangs will not subside. Others believe that they will become weak or may faint unless they eat when they feel hungry. Unless a person has diabetes or hypoglycemia or some other medical problems with special dietary considerations and regimens, that person is not likely to suffer harm from ignoring a hunger pang. People do it all the time when they are too busy, their hands are too dirty, or there is simply no food around to eat! Feelings of weakness are helped by sitting down and resting for fifteen to twenty minutes, or by drinking a small amount of fruit juice. If the hunger pangs are the result of low blood sugar levels, people with normal metabolism will increase their blood sugar levels from stored energy deposits within twenty minutes. The hunger pangs will then subside.

Hunger pangs which result from thought associations, moods, feeling states or fatigue will also disappear within twenty minutes without eating. If the hunger pang will disappear anyway, a logical approach would be to stay away from food long enough to not feel hungry anymore. The strategy is called **time delay**. The tricky part is to keep away from food for that long! Eating in these instances is actually an activity. It is something to do when feeling bored, something to do when feeling restless or anxious, or something to do for comfort or distraction. The need to do something is really the issue. If the activity of eating is taken away, it must be replaced with a different activity, or the overwhelming need to do something will cause the person to eat regardless of the original decision to avoid food.

When you feel the urge to eat, try doing something else for twenty minutes first.

If the activity of eating is taken away, it must be replaced with a different activity.

This is an adaptation of the Twenty Minute Rule, discussed on page 104.

1. **Do an activity which is incompatible with eating,** something that can't or won't be combined with food. The best example is playing a flute or other musical instrument which involves using your mouth and hands at the same time. Other examples are typing, talking on the telephone, taking a nap, gardening, working on the car, or polishing fingernails. I used to include showering as an example until one of my students exclaimed, "Not for me! If I didn't have my hard boiled egg and juice in the shower in the morning, I'd have no breakfast at all."

2. **Do something you particularly like to do, maybe even something you don't often give yourself time or permission to do.** Examples could be talking or reading, puttering in the workshop, playing solitaire, working on crossword or jigsaw puzzles, working on any hobby, taking a bubble bath or caring for plants.

3. **Do some small task,** such as sweeping the porch, running an errand, changing a light bulb, or

putting clothes into a washer or dryer. Or **do a small part of a bigger job,** such as washing a single window pane or straightening one cupboard shelf. The intent is not to lure yourself into completing a big project. The exercise is simply meant to engage you in a few minutes of activity while allowing time for the hunger pang to subside.

You need to identify the specific replacement activities with which you want to experiment and write them down. Then make sure you you have the necessary materials at home and stored in a very convenient spot so that they are at least as easy to get at as the food they are supposed to replace. If you have decided that putting together a jigsaw puzzle is a good replacement activity, but when it's needed there isn't one in the house, you are likely to eat instead. If sewing is going to be used as a replacement activity, but every time you want to sew you have to haul the sewing machine out of the closet and set it up on a table, the process may represent too much of a hassle and you may eat anyway. It is essential to the successful use of replacement activities that: 1) the necessary materials are in the house, 2) the materials are set up and ready to use, and 3) a list of activities is kept in a strategic spot where it can act as a reminder when you have the urge for a snack.

Do not expect yourself to remember automatically these activities; eating is far more automatic. Constant reminding will be necessary for a long time. After five years of practice, I still don't trust myself to remember to use them as often as I want, so I keep a few pieces of paper with suggested activities placed where I can see them easily.

When a hunger pang is felt you can say to yourself, "Yes, I may eat it in twenty minutes, but first I'm going to...." If you still want to eat at the end of the twenty minutes, you may. It is likely that if you decide to eat at that time, you will have greater control over the type and amount of food selected than would have occurred immediately after the hunger pang was felt. Many of my students have reported that they set the oven timer for twenty minutes, and when the bell sounded, they couldn't remember why the timer had been set and had no urge to eat at that time.

The replacement activity concept is liked by a majority of people. Some use it at times when they feel aimless; others report it helps them unwind and focus on another activity. For others it provides permission to take a break from chores or concentrated thinking like studying or writing. For some it represents having a choice between doing something or eating. And recognizing the element of choice is important.

There are other ways to accomplish time delay besides using replacement activities.

1. **Use a short burst of intense exercise immediately following a hunger pang.** The exercise will not only occupy you for the necessary twenty minute delay, but will also provide the additional benefit of actively depressing your appetite. Some of my students who doubted that idea set up an experiment of their own. They planned to exercise for ten minutes each time a hunger pang was felt. Using a scale of 0 for

no hunger to 3 for extreme hunger, they measured their hunger levels before and after the exercise. Five of the six students reported average ratings of 0 at the end of the exercise period. The sixth student had ratings of 1 and sometimes 2 following the exercise. The types of exercise used were jumping rope, walking, jogging, and situps.

Another group of students set up a different experiment using exercise. Their plan was to complete the dinner meal and exercise immediately after dinner to determine whether the exercise would decrease their desire for desert. They were to do this experiment for one week, and all dinner meals were to be eaten at home. The types of exercise used were bicycling, walking, and jogging slowly. Every student in the group found that their desire for dessert disappeared. But they discovered one additional result: the knowledge that they were going to exercise immediately after dinner caused them to eat less during the meal. What a bonus! As one woman commented, "I couldn't picture myself jogging down the street with a full stomach." What interested me the most was that all of them had reduced their portion size at dinner, and none of them missed the extra food or felt deprived of a full meal later on.

2. **Brush your teeth and use mouthwash.** The clean, fresh feeling that comes from the use of a toothbrush and mouthwash can be an effective deterrent to eating. One person commented, "Who wants to go through all that work again? I'd rather not eat." And another person responded, "Nothing tastes good, anyway, after the mouthwash and toothpaste.

3. **Make snacks difficult to get.** Keeping problematic snack foods out of sight, hard to reach, difficult to open or a nuisance to prepare increases the period of time between the recognition of a hunger pang and the response—eating. Increasing that time period allows you more opportunity to catch yourself in action and to make decisions about whether or not you really do want to eat, and if so, what foods and how much of them. Review some of the ideas discussed in the lesson, "Controlling Your Home Environment."

If the hunger pang is coming from something specific, such as the sight of chocolate candy in a store window, or the smell of freshly baked bread drifting out of the bakery door, **keep walking.** The longer you stay in contact with a strong hunger cue, the more opportunity you have to weaken and let temptation drag you inside. Once you are inside the store all control may be lost, with the result that the food is bought and consumed. For some people this may result in feelings of guilt or frustration, leading to depression or out-of-control eating.

Explanation of Homework

Assignment for this week: apply one or more of this week's suggestions to one snack urge each day, practice selected techniques from previous lessons, and record your progress and food intake daily.

Weekly Progress Record

The instructions for how to use the Weekly Progress Record are on pages 257-260.

Daily Food Record

The instructions for how to use the Daily Food Record are on pages 261-263.

Weight Record

The instructions for how to use the Weight Record are on pages 21-22.

Select the suggestions you want to use and write them down on two or three pieces of paper making two or three lists of time delay ideas. Tape one list in a place where you can see it easily and frequently: the medicine cabinet in the bathroom, the refrigerator door, or even inside a frequently used drawer at work. Other lists can be placed on the doors of your favorite snack cupboards, the door of the freezer, or anywhere else you are likely to go for high-calorie snacks. You are not likely to remember to try these things in the beginning, and one way to remind yourself about them is to see a list of ideas placed where you are sure to notice it. You won't always decide not to eat, but each time you successfully replace a snack with an activity it means that you ate fewer calories that day. Be sure to have any materials you need for replacement activities available and ready to be used. Good luck!

Extra recording forms for this chapter may be found starting on page 273.

Sample List:

yes, I may eat it in 20 minutes but first I'm going to...

jump rope until tired
brush my teeth and use mouthwash
play the piano
play a game of solitaire
play a game with the children
read a magazine

WEEKLY PROGRESS RECORD

BASIC SKILLS:	SUN	MON	TUES	WED	THURS	FRI	SAT	*
Read Progress Record in morning								
Record food intake								
Stay within calorie/ exchange total								
SPECIFIC TECHNIQUES/EXERCISES:								
Daily Totals								

*This column is for the weekly totals for each specific technique or exercise.

DAILY FOOD RECORD

Food Item/ Beverage	Amount	Calories/Exchanges	Time of Day

Total Calories for day ______

Date ______

Total Exchanges for day:
(1) Milk ______
(2) Vegetable ______
(3) Fruit ______
(4) Bread ______
(5) Meat ______
(6) Fat ______

DAILY FOOD RECORD

Food Item/ Beverage	Amount	Calories/Exchanges	Time of Day

Total Calories for day ________

Date ________

Total Exchanges for day:
(1) Milk ________
(2) Vegetable ________
(3) Fruit ________
(4) Bread ________
(5) Meat ________
(6) Fat ________

DAILY FOOD RECORD

Food Item/ Beverage	Amount	Calories/Exchanges	Time of Day

Total Calories for day ________

Date ________

Total Exchanges for day:
(1) Milk ________
(2) Vegetable ________
(3) Fruit ________
(4) Bread ________
(5) Meat ________
(6) Fat ________

Copyright © Northwest Learning Associates, Inc., 1978. All rights reserved.

DAILY FOOD RECORD

Food Item/ Beverage	Amount	Calories/Exchanges	Time of Day

Total Calories for day ________

Date ____________________

Total Exchanges for day:
(1) Milk ______
(2) Vegetable ______
(3) Fruit ______
(4) Bread ______
(5) Meat ______
(6) Fat ______

DAILY FOOD RECORD

Food Item/ Beverage	Amount	Calories/Exchanges	Time of Day

Total Calories for day ________

Date ____________________

Total Exchanges for day:
(1) Milk ______
(2) Vegetable ______
(3) Fruit ______
(4) Bread ______
(5) Meat ______
(6) Fat ______

Chapter 9 - INSTRUCTOR NOTES

Suggested Techniques:
Listed on pages 138 through 140.

Homework Assignments:
Read the instructions on page 140.

Cautions and Reminders:

1. Remind your students to read the section entitled "Food for Thought" on pages 150-151 of their book. This section contains information on food substitutions and calorie comparisons of related foods. This information was taken directly from Barbara Kraus's **Calories and Carbohydrates** (The New American Library, Inc.; Signet Books, 1975). The only factor considered in that section was the calorie level. Students having sodium, sugar, triglyceride, cholesterol, or other factors in addition to calories to consider, should consult a dietitian for guidance in appropriate food substitutions.
2. Also remind your students to read the chapter entitled "Nutritional Considerations in Weight Loss and Control" on pages 235-240 of the text. The information in that chapter was written by a registered dietitian. It is important for every student to read that chapter, and particularly so for those students who do not have contact with a dietitian.
3. Stress the importance of having one treat every day. It is much easier to accept restrictions placed on the types and amounts of food eaten if there is some allowance for an enjoyable, satisfying treat each day. Elimination of all daily treats usually results in feelings of deprivation which, for many people, is the forerunner of a binge. Some care has to be taken in the selection of and conditions surrounding that treat. The treat should be fixed in quantity, such as, for example, one specially purchased sweet roll (rather than one of the dozen sweet rolls brought home "for the family"), or two slices of a favorite bread. In the beginning it may be preferable for some students to have their daily treat outside of their home; for example, going to Baskin-Robbins for an ice cream cone. For students who decide to store their treats at home, caution them against keeping their very favorites in the house, for the cue mechanism may prove to be too strong. For example, if coffee fudge ice cream is a person's very favorite flavor, but peppermint stick ice milk is satisfying without being too tempting, the ice milk is more appropriate to store at home for daily treats. If some students decide that barbecue potato chips represent the desired treat food, buying a large bag of them to be gradually consumed over a period of two or three days would probably represent a significant control problem. A more effective alternative is the daily purchase of one single serving size bag of barbecue chips to be eaten at home. Discuss these ideas with your students and elicit their suggestions for daily treats.

FOOD SUBSTITUTION WORKSHEET FOR SNACK CONTROL - INSTRUCTOR NOTES

The Worksheet is on page 148 and the sample is on page 147.

The Worksheet is both a record and a reminder of food substitutions and the calories saved. It is most effective when removed from the book and taped to a cupboard door or other easily visible place, because it then becomes a quick reference.

9

Targets: Food substitutions and preplanning.

Objectives:

1. Reduce the amount of calories in snacks by the use of alternative foods and/or beverages.
2. Preplan and prepackage snacks for particularly difficult-to-control times (Emergency Kits).
3. Reduce or maintain calorie level; establish or maintain dietary plan.

Motto:

Get the most for the least.

Snack Control: Food Substitutions

Snacking is a very popular activity for the majority of people, and for many of them, it results in increased weight. One logical approach to weight reduction and control would be to eliminate snacks, but for most of us, that would be unappealing and maybe even impossible to do. A more realistic approach would be to reduce the number of calories consumed per snack. The strategy involved is called **food substitution.** The objective is to get the most food for the least number of calories by replacing high-calorie foods with lower calorie foods.

Have you ever had the experience of being hungry for something but not knowing what you really wanted, so you ate several different items before finding the one that hit the spot? My students often talk about the appeal of certain types of high-calorie foods and that giving them up completely usually results in an eating binge. For some of them salty, crunchy foods are important; for others cold, creamy foods are favorites. Some people crave chewy or sticky foods, while others look for sweet foods, or hot foods or smooth foods. The point I'm trying to make is that each of them has a fondness for particular food *characteristics.* When those characteristics are severely reduced or eliminated because the foods they are associated with are high in calories, the result is first deprivation, then a binge. The person is almost forced to go out of control to satisfy the need for certain food characteristics.

Did you notice that I have referred to specific food characteristics rather than specific foods? If there is a low-calorie way of obtaining the same characteristics found in a high-calorie food, the result is usually an acceptance of the low-calorie food without feeling the deprivation or indulging in a binge. For example, many people who love cold and creamy foods are often just as satisfied with one Creamsicle, at 78 calories. Other people who particularly like dry, crunchy foods find that spoon size, shredded wheat cereal eaten dry and seasoned with onion powder, a little grated cheese, or barbecue spices, can be an effective substitute for higher calorie Triscuits for a saving of 17 calories per biscuit! When one type of cookie is as good as any other, why not eat the lowest calorie cookie available? Arrowroot cookies are only 16 calories each, so you can afford to indulge in three or four of them, whereas three or four of any other cookie will raise the calorie level significantly. More ideas for lower calorie food substitutions can be found at the end of this lesson.

If you are not aware of the preferences you have for certain food characteristics, use the Alternate Food Record included with this lesson to help you gather that information. The instructions and forms are in the homework section of this lesson.

There are several additional techniques to consider when using a food substitution approach to the urge to snack.

1. **Use an unrewarding snack food.** There are times when an urge to eat is quickly satisfied by a small amount of food. Sometimes the act of chewing and swallowing is what is important rather than the food itself. In those instances the choice of food isn't important. If, however, a very pleasurable food is chosen, a person may eat more than is needed or planned, because it is so much harder to control the intake of a favorite food. If the selected food is not terribly desirable but is useful in answering the need to chew and swallow something, the person is not likely to eat more than is necessary to satisfy that need. I keep a small container of dry puffed wheat in my desk drawer at work. When I have a strong need to have some food in my mouth I eat the puffed wheat dry, without milk or sugar. After four or five handfuls, I've had enough. Any more and it begins to feel like sawdust in my mouth; it is no longer desirable to me. Thus I've answered the original need for food without instigating a mental wrestling match between the desire to eat more and the knowledge that I should stop.

2. **Precede snacks with a large glass of water or diet soda.** For many people this much liquid is sufficient to fill up the hollow spots and decrease the desire for food. This technique is also helpful for eating control while cooking, or at dinner parties with long cocktail hours. One couple planned their cocktail party strategy around the use of large glasses of diet soda without liquor. They brought the diet soda to the party and stored it in the kitchen. Each took turns fixing drinks for the other. The husband's comment was, "We sloshed our way to the table, but the diet pop helped curb our appetites so that we both ate reasonable dinners."

". . . the diet pop helped curb our appetites so that we both ate reasonable dinners"

3. **The problem of candy cravings** is brought up for discussion in almost

every one of my classes. The idea of substituting some other sweet food for candy is suggested first, but the response is usually that the person must have candy. Three suggestions which people have found effective for this type of craving are: **1) eat a dill pickle first to reduce the desire for candy, 2) use sugar-free candy, or 3) eat a candy that is so intensely sweet that it makes you nauseated if you eat too much of it.** When people experience candy cravings their usual procedure is to eat their favorite kinds, thus reducing the probability of controlling how much candy they eat. Some people have talked about particular types of candy that turn them off after a while because they become too sweet and otherwise cause feelings of nausea or extreme satiation. The examples most frequently mentioned are white chocolate, divinity, taffy and licorice. If a person has a candy craving and selects one which will, after a short time, become unpleasant to eat, he or she will have far less difficulty eating it in reasonable amounts. If all other ideas fail, a little artificial sweetner placed on your tongue should effectively reduce the desire for more candy!

4. People who talk about **cheese cravings** the same way others talk about candy cravings, often find that if they **eat a little of a very rich, strongly flavored cheese,** their desire is more quickly satisfied with fewer calories consumed.

5. **Have low-calorie snack foods which are enjoyable and readily available, or pre-package high-calorie foods in small amounts.** Even high-calorie foods can be eaten occasionally for snacks if there is an effective way of limiting how much is consumed. If those foods are pre-packaged in small, single-serving-size containers, a person can eat the whole amount, which is psychologically satisfying, without being cued to want more by the presence of the big bag or package from which the single serving was taken. People report significantly greater control from using small individual bags of potato chips than when trying to limit the amount eaten from a big bag or bowl. "Once the bag is open," commented one man, "I'll eat it all up no matter what size bag it is."

Even high-calorie foods can be eaten occasionally if there is an effective way of limiting how much is consumed.

Many of my students talk about periods when they feel almost driven to eat. Sometimes this is related to a special food characteristic and often it is triggered by a particular mood. I know that when I am depressed, I crave sweet things; and unless I've planned something ahead, I'll eat jam, marshmallows, honey or anything else I can find that is sweet. One man found that when he is nervous or angry, he needs to chew. He'll chew through all of the low-calorie foods first and then move right on to the high-calorie foods.

If you know that you crave certain foods when you are depressed, lonely, or angry, and that you are likely to eat out of control at those times, plan ahead by preparing an **Emergency Kit** for just those times. Emergency Kits contain limited amounts of long-lasting or low-calorie foods selected to satisfy the craving for certain food characteristics. For example, the man who needs to chew, stores items like beef jerky, licorice, and sugar-free gum in his Emergency Kit. He once tossed a bagel into his Emergency Kit, and it was two weeks before he needed to use his Kit. He claimed it took him 40 minutes to chew up that stale bagel! He said his jaws were so tired after eating the bagel that he didn't need to eat anything else!

While the Emergency Kit items described above are not all low in calories, they are highly concentrated in terms of the desired food characteristics. Thus a significantly smaller amount of food may be required to appease the craving, and a lot of excess eating is eliminated. The foods selected should NOT be your favorites. They should be acceptable, but not normally tempting foods. Otherwise, you'll never leave them for the times when you'll need them. You can also add non-food items which might be helpful to your Emergency Kit. For example, my Emergency Kit usually contains the following: 10 small buttermints, 1 can of chocolate diet soda, 2 packages of sugar-free bubble gum, and a movie magazine. When I am very depressed, I need lots of sweetness and lots of comforting. So I take my sweet foods, the movie magazine (which I don't otherwise allow myself to read) and crawl into a hot tub. By the time I'm through with my bath, I've had all the sweetness I can take, I've had a wonderful break from all my depressing thoughts, and I'm sleepy enough to brush my teeth and go to bed. And I've only consumed 151 extra calories! If you pack candy in your Emergency Kit, be sure to include a toothbrush and toothpaste to use afterwards, to help prevent the sugar from affecting your teeth.

Explanation of Homework

Assignment for this week: apply one or more of this week's suggestions to one snack urge per day, practice selected techniques from previous lessons, and record your progress and food intake daily.

Weekly Progress Record

The instructions for how to use the Weekly Progress Record are on pages 257-260.

Daily Food Record

The instructions for how to use the Daily Food Record are on pages 261-263.

Weight Record

The instructions for how to use the Weight Record are on pages 21-22.

There is a Food Substitution Worksheet on page 148, and a sample is on page 147. Use it to keep track of all of your good food substitution ideas. If you remove the page from your book and tape it up somewhere in the kitchen where you can see it easily, it can serve as both a reminder and a record of the food substitutions and the calories saved. For extra reading, look over the section entitled, "Food for Thought," on pages 150-151, for more suggestions for low-calorie food substitutes. Good luck!

Extra recording forms for this chapter may be found starting on page 273.

WEEKLY PROGRESS RECORD

BASIC SKILLS:	SUN	MON	TUES	WED	THURS	FRI	SAT	*
Read Progress Record in morning								
Record food intake								
Stay within calorie/ exchange total								
SPECIFIC TECHNIQUES/EXERCISES:								
Daily Totals								

*This column is for the weekly totals for each specific technique or exercise.

DAILY FOOD RECORD

Food Item/ Beverage	Amount	Calories/Exchanges	Time of Day

Total Calories for day ______

Date ______

Total Exchanges for day:

(1) Milk ______
(2) Vegetable ______
(3) Fruit ______
(4) Bread ______
(5) Meat ______
(6) Fat ______

Copyright © Northwest Learning Associates, Inc., 1978. All rights reserved.

DAILY FOOD RECORD

Food Item/ Beverage	Amount	Calories/Exchanges	Time of Day

Total Calories for day ________

Date ____________________

Total Exchanges for day:
(1) Milk ______
(2) Vegetable ______
(3) Fruit ______
(4) Bread ______
(5) Meat ______
(6) Fat ______

DAILY FOOD RECORD

Food Item/ Beverage	Amount	Calories/Exchanges	Time of Day

Total Calories for day ________

Date ____________________

Total Exchanges for day:
(1) Milk ______
(2) Vegetable ______
(3) Fruit ______
(4) Bread ______
(5) Meat ______
(6) Fat ______

Copyright © Northwest Learning Associates, Inc., 1978. All rights reserved.

DAILY FOOD RECORD

Food Item/ Beverage	Amount	Calories/Exchanges	Time of Day

Total Calories for day ______

Date ______

Total Exchanges for day:

(1) Milk ______
(2) Vegetable ______
(3) Fruit ______
(4) Bread ______
(5) Meat ______
(6) Fat ______

DAILY FOOD RECORD

Food Item/ Beverage	Amount	Calories/Exchanges	Time of Day

Total Calories for day ______

Date ______

Total Exchanges for day:

(1) Milk ______
(2) Vegetable ______
(3) Fruit ______
(4) Bread ______
(5) Meat ______
(6) Fat ______

Copyright © Northwest Learning Associates, Inc., 1978. All rights reserved.

FOOD SUBSTITUTION WORKSHEET FOR SNACK CONTROL
(Sample)

Reduced Calorie Food (to replace)	Higher Calorie Food	Calories Saved
1 Creamsicle	1 cup ice cream	186
3 arrowroot cookies	3 sugar cookies	230
2 oz. plain popcorn	2 oz. potato chips	98
chocolate milk drink	chocolate milkshake	140
2 oz. Velveeta cheese	2 oz. cheddar cheese	62
4 Cheez-Its	4 Ritz crackers	44

FOOD SUBSTITUTION WORKSHEET FOR SNACK CONTROL

Reduced Calorie Food (to replace)	Higher Calorie Food	Calories Saved

Take Alongs

This section of **Food Habit Management** contains some quick-reference materials which have been placed on perforated pages for easy removal. A variety of sources were used in gathering these materials and you may notice some discrepancies in calorie values of certain foods from one source to another. For the purposes of this course the relative calorie values (one food in relation to another) have more importance than the absolute calorie values. If you find more than one calorie value listed for the same food, select one value and use it consistently.

FOOD FOR THOUGHT

Food Comparisons and Substitution Ideas

One of the easiest and least stressful ways to reduce the number of calories in your daily diet is to substitute a lower calorie food for a higher calorie food. When making substitutions of this type it is important that the lower calorie foods have the same general characteristics or usages as the higher calorie foods they replace. A variety of foods and their calorie values are listed below and some suggestions are offered for food substitutions. The purpose is to stimulate your own thinking toward getting the most and the best foods possible within your daily calorie allotment. All calorie figures were taken from **Calories and Carbohydrates,** by Barbara Kraus, Signet Books, the New American Library, Inc. (New York: 1975.)

Food Comparison Ideas

MEAT

Lean = meat after all the fat that can be cut away is removed.
Lean and Fat = meat with one-half-inch layer of fat.

BROILED MEAT

4 oz., (lean/lean and fat)	Calories
Pork Roast	277/400
T-bone Steak	253/536
Hamburger Patty	248/324
Beef Rump Roast	236/393
Ham (uncured)	212/328
Leg of Lamb	211/316
Venison (raw)	143/—

SPECIALTY MEAT

4 oz., prepared as listed	Calories
Corned Beef	422
Calf's Liver (fried)	296
Beef Liver (fried)	260
Chicken Liver (simmered)	187
Beef Tongue (braised)	277
One Frankfurter (1.6 oz.)	136

POULTRY

4 oz., roasted or raw when specified	Calories
Goose	264
Chicken (light meat)	206
Turkey (light meat)	200
Pheasant (raw)	184
Wild Duck (raw)	156

SEAFOOD

4 oz., meat only	Calories
Scallops (steamed)	127
Crab (steamed)	105
Shrimp (raw)	103
Clams (raw)	91

FISH

4 oz. raw	Calories
Salmon	246
Perch	134
Bass	118
Trout	115
Halibut	113
Haddock	90
Sole	90
Cod	88

FRUIT

1 cup, fresh	Calories
Banana (sliced)	124
Orange (sections)	118
Grapes (whole)	104
Pear (sliced)	100
Sweet Cherries (whole)	82
Pineapple (diced)	82
Papaya (cubed)	71
Peach (sliced)	64
Apple (diced and pared)	59
Cranberries (whole)	52
Rhubarb (diced)	20
Blueberries (whole)	90
Blackberries (whole)	84
Red Raspberries (whole)	82
Strawberries (whole)	53
Honeydew Melon (diced)	55
Cantaloupe (cubed)	48
Watermelon (diced)	42
Raisins (seedless whole)	500

FRUIT JUICE

1 cup fresh or frozen	Calories
Grape Juice (sweetened)	230
Cranapple Juice	188
Cranapple, low calorie	38
Pear Nectar	140
Peach Nectar	140
Pineapple Juice	120
Apple Cider	116
Orange Juice	112
Orange-grapefruit Juice	110
Grapefruit Juice (unsweetened)	102
Tomato Juice (canned)	46

VEGETABLES

1 cup, raw or cooked without butter	Calories
Lima beans	188
Parsnips	140
Corn (kernels)	138
Green Peas (shelled)	116
Pea Pods	98
Brussels Sprouts	56
Beets (diced)	54
Carrots (sliced)	54
Green Onions	44
Broccoli	40
Tomato (sliced, peeled)	40
Eggplant (diced)	38
Green beans (sliced)	34
Crookneck squash	26
Cauliflower (sliced)	22
Cabbage (chopped)	22
Radishes (sliced)	20
Mushrooms (sliced)	20
Cucumber (diced, pared)	20
Celery (sliced)	18
Zucchini	18
Green Pepper (sliced)	18
Spinach (chopped)	14
Baked Beans in tomato sauce (canned)	286
Refried Beans (canned)	240

POTATOES

1 cup, prepared	Calories
Pan Fried	456
Hash Browned	446
Au Gratin (Betty Crocker)	320
Scalloped (Betty Crocker)	300

Food Comparison Ideas (cont.)

POTATOES *cont.*

	Calories
Mashed (milk & butter)	184
Mashed (milk only)	128
Boiled (plain)	102
McDonald's French Fries (one serving)	215

CHEESE

1 oz.	Calories
Parmesan (grated)	143
Cheddar	115
Edam	104
Kraft Philadelphia Cream Cheese	104
Brick	103
Monterey Jack	102
Muenster	100

CHEESE *cont.*

	Calories
Process Gruyere	93
Camembert	85
Kraft - Velveeta	84
Creamed Cottage Cheese	27

CRACKERS

1 cracker	Calories
1 Rye Krisp (whole cracker)	24
1 Hi Ho	18
1 Ritz	16
1 Buttery Flavored Sesame	16
1 Saltine	12
1 Bacon Thin	11
1 Chicken-in-a-Biscuit	10
1 Wheat Thin	9
1 Cheez-It	6

COOKIES

1 cookie	Calories
1 Stella D'Oro Chinese Almond	178
1 Hey Day	122
1 Chocolate Fudge Sandwich	99
1 Sugar	86
1 Pecan Sandie	85
1 Peanut Butter	79
1 Fig Newton	57
1 Raisin	55
1 Chocolate Chip	51
1 Oreo	51
1 Shortcake	46
1 Lorna Doone	37
1 Cinnamon Crisp	17
1 Arrowroot	16

Food Substitution Ideas

CRUNCHY FOODS

	Calories		Calories	Calories Saved
One oz. Lay's potato chips	158	One oz. plain popped corn	109	49
One oz. Fritos corn chips	159	One oz. Corn Chex cereal (dry)	111	48
One Triscuit	21	One spoon size shredded wheat biscuit	4	17
One Nabisco shortcake cookie	46	One Arrowroot cookie	16	30
One Sunshine applesauce cookie	86	One bag Weight Watchers Apple Snacks	50	36

CREAMY FOODS/BEVERAGES

	Calories		Calories	Calories Saved
One oz. Kraft Philadelphia cream cheese	104	One oz. Kraft Neufchatel cheese	70	34
One oz. Kraft American or cheddar cheese	113	One oz. Borden Gouda cheese	86	27
One cup regular cottage cheese	213	One cup low-fat cottage cheese	155	58
One 9.5 oz. chocolate milkshake	318	One 8.6 oz. chocolate milk drink	178	140
One cup vanilla ice cream	296	One cup vanilla ice milk	194	102
One vanilla Good Humor Bar	197	One Creamsicle	78	119
One cup whole milk	152	One cup skim milk	103	49
One cup sour cream	485	One cup plain low fat yogurt	122	363
One cup plain low fat yogurt	122	One cup low-fat buttermilk	88	34

SYRUP AND JAM

	Calories		Calories	Calories Saved
One Tbs. Log Cabin Maple Honey syrup	54	One Tbs. S&W Imitation Maple syrup	12	42
One Tbs. strawberry jam	54	One Tbs. S&W Imitation Strawberry jam	12	42

SPREADS, DRESSINGS AND OIL

	Calories		Calories	Calories Saved
One Tbs. cooking oil	126	One Tbs. whipped margarine	67	59
One Tbs. Fleischmann's regular margarine	101	One Tbs. Fleischmann's diet margarine	50	51
One Tbs. butter	100	One Tbs. apple butter	33	67
One Tbs. butter	100	One Tbs. Durkee butter flavoring	9	91
One Tbs. Good Seasons Italian salad dressing	84	One Tbs. Good Seasons low calorie salad dressing	9	75
One Tbs. mayonnaise	101	One Tbs. Frenchette Mayonette Gold	32	69

CALORIE COUNTER
Fast Food Restaurant Convenience Foods

These are approximate values and may vary depending on reference source.

ARBY'S

	Calories
Junior Roast Beef	220
Roast Beef	350
Super Roast Beef	620
Beef 'n Cheese	450
Ham 'n Cheese	380
Swiss King	660
Turkey	410
Turkey Deluxe	510
Club	560

ARTHUR TREACHER'S

	Calories
Fish (2 pieces)	355
Chicken (2 pieces)	369
Shrimp (7 pieces)	381
Chips	276
Krunch Pups	203
Coleslaw	123
Lemon Luvs	276
Chowder	112
Fish Sandwich	440
Chicken Sandwich	413

BASKIN-ROBBINS

	Calories
Ice Creams, all flavors (one scoop)	133-148
Sherbets and Ices	139

BURGER CHEF

	Calories
Regular Hamburger	260
Cheeseburger	300
Double Cheeseburger	430
Big Shef	540
Super Shef	600
Skipper's Treat	600
French Fries	190
Shake	330
Mariner Platter	680
Rancher Platter	640

BURGER KING

	Calories
Cheeseburger	305
French Fries	220
Hamburger	230
Hamburger, Double	325
Hot Dog	291
Whaler	486
Whopper	630
Whopper Junior	285
Shake, Chocolate	365

DAIRY QUEEN

	Calories
Hamburger	260
Cheeseburger	320
Big "Brazier"	460
Big "Brazier"/cheese	550
Super "Brazier"	780
Big "Brazier" Deluxe	540
"Brazier" Barbecue	280
"Bosn's Mate" Fish Sandwich	340
Super "Brazier" Chili Dog	570
Super "Brazier" Dog	500
Hot Dog	270
Hot Dog/chili	330
Hot Dog/cheese	330
Fish Sandwich	400
Fish Sandwich/cheese	440
French Fries	200
French Fries—Large	320
Onion Rings	300
Small Cone	110
Regular Cone	230
Large Cone	340
Small Dipped Cone	160
Medium Dipped Cone	310
Large Dipped Cone	450
Chocolate Sundae—	
Small	170
Regular	290
Large	400
Chocolate Malt—	
Small	340
Regular	600
Large	840
Float	330
Banana Split	540
Parfait	460
"Mr. Misty" Freeze	500
"Mr. Misty" Float	440
"Dilly" Bar	240
"DQ" Sandwich	140
"Mr. Misty" Kiss	70

DUNKIN DONUTS

	Calories
Donuts (including rings, sticks, crullers)	240
Donuts, Yeast-Raised (add 5-10 calories for glaze)	160
Fancies (includes coffee rolls, Danish, etc.)	215
Munchkins, Yeast-Raised	26
Cake, including Chocolate Cake	240

(Add 40-50 calories per Donut for filling and topping combined; add 10-15 calories per Munchkin for filling and topping combined. Figures are approximations.)

GINO'S

	Calories
Cheeseburger	300
Sirloiner	441
Cheese Sirloiner	532
Giant	569
Heroburger	647
Cheese Heroburger	738
Fish Sandwich	450
Fish Platter	650
French Fries	156
Apple Pie	238
Vanilla Shake	310
Chocolate Shake	324
Coke (regular)	117
Coke (giant)	181
Dinner Roll	51
Fry (regular)	195
Fry (giant)	274
Hamburger	289
Kentucky Fried Chicken (1 piece)	290
Orange (regular)	140
Orange (giant)	217
Root Beer (regular)	122
Root Beer (giant)	190

JACK IN THE BOX

	Calories
Hamburger	263
Cheeseburger	310
Jumbo Jack Hamburger	551
Jumbo Jack Hamburger /cheese	628
Regular Taco	189
Super Taco	285
Moby Jack Sandwich	455
Breakfast Jack Sandwich	301
French Fries	270
Onion Rings	351
Apple Turnover	411
Vanilla Shake	342
Chocolate Shake	365
Strawberry Shake	380
Ham and Cheese Omelette	425
Double Cheese Omelette	423
Ranchero Style Omelette	414
French Toast Breakfast	537
Pancakes Breakfast	626
Scrambled Eggs Breakfast	719

KENTUCKY FRIED CHICKEN

	Calories
Three Piece Dinner, Original Recipe	830
Three Piece Dinner, Extra Crispy	950

KENTUCKY FRIED CHICKEN *cont.*

	Calories
Wing	151
Drumstick	136
Breast	283
Rib	241
Thigh	275
Chicken, 9 pieces	1,892
Dinner (Fried Chicken, Mashed Potatoes, Coleslaw, Rolls):	
2-Piece Dinner, Original Recipe	595
2-Piece Dinner, Extra Crispy	665

LONG JOHN SILVER'S

	Calories
Fish/batter (2 pieces)	366
Peg Legs/batter (5 pieces)	350
Treasure Chest	506
Shrimp/batter (6 pieces)	268
Clams/batter	617
Oysters/batter	441
Fries	288
Coleslaw	138
Corn On The Cob	176
Hush Puppies (3 pieces)	153
Fish & Chips, Coleslaw	
2-Piece Dinner	955
3-Piece Dinner	1,190

McDONALD'S

	Calories
Hamburger	257
Cheeseburger	306
Quarter Pounder	418
Quarter Pounder w/cheese	518
Big Mac	541
Filet-O-Fish	402
French Fries, regular	210
Egg McMuffin	352
Pork Sausage	184
English Muffin, buttered	186
Scrambled Eggs	162
Hot Cakes/butter & syrup	472
Chocolate Shake	364
Vanilla Shake	323

continued

McDONALD'S *cont.*

	Calories
Strawberry Shake	345
Apple Pie	300
Cherry Pie	298
Hamburger, Double	350
Hot Cakes with Butter	272
Muffin	136

PIZZA HUT

	Calories
½ of 13-Inch Cheese Pizza—	
Thick Crust	900
Thin Crust	850
½ of 15-Inch Cheese Pizza—	
Thick Crust	1,200
Thin Crust	1,150
½ of 10-Inch Pizza (Thin Crust)	
Beef	488
Cheese	436
Pepperoni	459
Pork	466
Supreme	475
½ of 10-Inch Pizza (Thick & Chewy)	
Beef	620
Pork	640
Cheese	560
Pepperoni	560
Supreme	640

RUSTLER STEAK HOUSE

	Calories
Baked Potato	231
Dressing (Blue Cheese)	151
Dressing (French)	122
Dressing (Italian)	166
Dressing (Thousand Island)	150
Jell-O, Cherry	75
Pickle	2
Potato Chips	82
Pudding, Chocolate	144
Roll (Butter)	40
Roll (Rustler)	120
Roll (Twisted)	182
Rib Eye	369
Rustler's (Strip)	1,086
Salad	13

continued

RUSTLER STEAK HOUSE *cont.*

	Calories
Steak (Chopped) 4 oz.	327
Steak (Chopped) 8 oz.	653
T-Bone	1,532

TACO BELL

	Calories
Taco	159
Tostada	206
Enchirito	391
Bellbeefer	243
Pintos 'n Cheese	231
Bean Burrito	345
Beefy Tostada	232
Burrito Supreme	387

WENDY'S

	Calories
Single	470*
Double	670*
Triple	850*
Single/cheese	580*
Double/cheese	800*
Triple/cheese	1,040*
Chili—Single serving	230
French Fries	330
Frosty Dairy Dessert	390

*Lettuce, tomato, onion, pickle, mustard, ketchup included.

WHITE CASTLE

	Calories
Cheeseburger	198
Fish Sandwich	200
French Fries	219
Hamburger	165
Milk Shake	213
Onion Rings	341

REFERENCES:

Excerpted by permission of Rawson, Wade Publishers from *The Partnership Diet Program* by Kelly Brownell, Ph.D. with Irene Copeland. Copyright © 1980 by Kelly Brownell, Ph.D.

Excerpted by permission of Jordan, Henry A.; Levitz, Leonard S., and Kimbrell, Gordon M., *Eating is Okay!* New York: Signet Books, 1978.

CALORIE COUNTER

For Frozen Foods

The names of the products in our charts are registered trademarks. All calorie counts are approximate.

These are approximate values and may vary depending on reference source.

BANQUET

	Amount	Calories
MAN-PLEASER: DINNERS		
Chicken	17 oz.	1026
Turkey	19 oz.	620
Meat Loaf	19 oz.	916
Salisbury Steak	19 oz.	873
ENTREES		
Spaghetti/Meat Sauce	8 oz.	311
Macaroni and Cheese	8 oz.	279
MEAT PIES		
Beef	8 oz.	409
Turkey	8 oz.	415
Chicken	8 oz.	427
Tuna	8 oz.	434
DINNERS		
Beef Chop Suey	12 oz.	282
Beef	11 oz.	312
Spaghetti and Meatballs	11.5 oz.	450
Ocean Perch	8.8 oz.	434
Haddock	8.8 oz.	419
Macaroni and Beef	12 oz.	394
Chopped Beef	11 oz.	443
Chicken and Noodles	12 oz.	374
Mexican Style	16 oz.	608
Turkey	11 oz.	293
Meat Loaf	11 oz.	412
Macaroni and Cheese	12 oz.	326
Salisbury Steak	11 oz.	390
Corned Beef Hash	10 oz.	372
Veal Parmigiana	11 oz.	421
Fried Chicken	11 oz.	530
Chicken Chow Mein	12 oz.	282
Cheese Enchilada	12 oz.	459
Italian Style	11 oz.	446
Beef Enchilada	12 oz.	479
Beans and Franks	10.8 oz.	591
Ham	10 oz.	369
Mexican Style Combo	12 oz.	571
Fish	8 oz.	382
Chicken and Dumplings	12 oz.	282
Western	11 oz.	417
BUFFET SUPPERS		
Veal Parmigiana	32 oz.	1563
Gravy & Salisbury Steak	32 oz.	1454
Macaroni and Beef	32 oz.	1000
Chicken and Noodles	32 oz.	764
Spaghetti and Meatballs	32 oz.	1127
Chicken and Dumplings	32 oz.	1209
Giblet Gravy & Turkey	32 oz.	564
Beef Stew	32 oz.	700
Chicken Chow Mein	32 oz.	345
Gravy and Sliced Beef	32 oz.	782
Noodles and Beef	32 oz.	754

continued

BANQUET *cont.*

Buffet Suppers *cont.*	Amount	Calories
Beef Chop Suey	32 oz.	418
Beef Enchilada/Cheese and Chili Gravy	32 oz.	1118
Meat Loaf	32 oz.	1445
Macaroni and Cheese	32 oz.	1027
COOKIN' BAG		
Gravy and Sliced Beef	5 oz.	116
Giblet Gravy and Sliced Turkey	5 oz.	98
Sloppy Joe	5 oz.	199
Chicken A La King	5 oz.	138
Salisbury Steak and Gravy	5 oz.	246
Creamed Chipped Beef	5 oz.	124
Two Beef Enchiladas and Sauce	6 oz.	207
B.B.Q. Sauce/Sliced Beef	5 oz.	126
Macaroni and Cheese	8 oz.	261
Chicken Chow Mein	7 oz.	89
Beef Chop Suey	7 oz.	73
Meat Loaf	5 oz.	224
Veal Parmigiana	5 oz.	287

BIRDS EYE

	Amount	Calories
FROZEN VEGETABLES		
Artichoke Hearts	3 oz.	20
Asparagus, any style	3.3 oz.	25
Baby Butter Beans	3.3 oz.	140
Green or Wax Beans, any style	3 oz.	25-30
Baby Lima Beans	3.3 oz.	120
Fordhook Lima Beans	3.3 oz.	100
Broccoli, any style	3.3 oz.	25
Brussels Sprouts	3.3 oz.	30
Cauliflower	3.3 oz.	25
Corn on the Cob	1 ear	130
Little Ears Cob Corn	2 ears	140
Sweet Whole Kernel Corn	3.3 oz.	70
Mixed Vegetables	3.3 oz.	60
Chopped Onions	3 oz.	24
Small Whole Onions	4 oz.	40
Black-Eye Peas	3.3 oz.	130
Sweet Green Peas	3.3 oz.	70
Tender Tiny Peas	3.3 oz.	60
Peas and Carrots	3.3 oz.	50
Chopped Spinach	3.3 oz.	20
Leaf Spinach	3.3 oz.	20
Cooked Squash	4 oz.	50
Sliced Summer Squash	3.3 oz.	18
Zucchini Squash	3.3 oz.	16
Succotash	3.3 oz.	80

continued

BIRDS EYE *cont.*

	Amount	Calories
COMBINATION VEGETABLES		
French Green Beans/Mushrooms	3 oz.	30
French Green Beans/Almonds	3 oz.	50
Broccoli/Cheese Sauce	3.3 oz.	110
Broccoli Spears/Hollandaise Sauce	3.3 oz.	100
Carrots/Brown Sugar Glaze	3.3 oz.	80
Cauliflower/Cheese Sauce	3.3 oz.	110
Green Beans and Pearl Onions	3 oz.	35
Mixed Vegetables/Onion Sauce	2.6 oz.	110
Small Onions/Cream Sauce	3 oz.	100
Peas and Cauliflower/Cream Sauce	3.3 oz.	120
Peas and Pearl Onions	3.3 oz.	60
Peas and Potatoes/Cream Sauce	2.6 oz.	140
Peas/Cream Sauce	2.6 oz.	130
Peas/Mushrooms	3.3 oz.	70
Rice and Peas/Mushrooms	2.3 oz.	100
Creamed Spinach	3 oz.	60
Corn Jubilee	3.3 oz.	120
INTERNATIONAL VEGETABLES		
Bavarian Style Beans and Spaetzle	3.3 oz.	70
Chinese Style	3.3 oz.	20
Danish Style	3.3 oz.	30
Hawaiian Style	3.3 oz.	40
Italian Style	3.3 oz.	45
Japanese Style	3.3 oz.	45
Parisian Style	3.3 oz.	30
STIR-FRY VEGETABLES		
Chinese Style	3.3 oz.	30
Japanses Style	3.3 oz.	30
Cantonese Style	3.3 oz.	50
Mandarin Style	3.3 oz.	25
AMERICANA VEGETABLES		
New England Style	3.3 oz.	70
New Orleans Creole Style	3.3 oz.	70
Pennsylvania Dutch Style	3.3 oz.	45
San Francisco	3.3 oz.	50
Wisconsin Country Style	3.3 oz.	45
FROZEN POTATO PRODUCTS		
Cottage Fries	2.8 oz.	120
Crinkle Cuts	3 oz.	110
French Fries	3 oz.	110

continued

BIRD'S EYE *cont.*

Frozen Potato Products *cont.*	Amount	Calories
Hash Browns	4 oz.	70
Hash Browns O'Brien	4 oz.	60
Shredded Hash Browns	3 oz.	60
Shoestrings	3.3 oz.	140
Steak Fries	3 oz.	110
Tasti Fries, French Fries	2.5 oz.	140
Tasti Puffs, Potato Puffs	2.5 oz.	190
Tiny Taters, Potato Bites	3.2 oz.	200

CELESTE PIZZA

	Amount	Calories
PIZZA		
Sausage Pizza	5.5 oz.	380
Pepperoni Pizza	5 oz.	360
Deluxe Pizza	5.9 oz.	370
Cheese Pizza	4.8 oz.	320
Sausage and Mushroom Pizza	6 oz.	380
Cheese and Mushroom Pizza	5.4 oz.	300
Sausage Pizza	4 oz.	280
Pepperoni Pizza	3.6 oz.	270
Deluxe Pizza	4.5 oz.	300
Sausage and Mushroom Pizza	4.5 oz.	290
Cheese and Mushroom Pizza	4 oz.	230
Cheese Pizza Sicilian Style	5 oz.	350

GREEN GIANT

	Amount	Calories
BOIL-IN-BAG VEGETABLES		
Asparagus/Butter Sauce	1 cup	90
Green Beans/Butter Sauce	1 cup	70
Green Beans, Onions/ Bacon Bits	1 cup	80
Baby Lima Beans/Butter Sauce	1 cup	220
Broccoli/Butter Sauce	1 cup	90
Broccoli/Cheese Sauce	1 cup	130
Broccoli, Cauliflower, Carrots/Cheese Sauce	1 cup	140
Brussels Sprouts/Butter Sauce	1 cup	110
Brussels Sprouts/Cheese Sauce	1 cup	170
Carrot Nuggets/Butter Sauce	1 cup	100
Cauliflower/Cheese Sauce	1 cup	130
Niblets Golden Corn/Butter Sauce	1 cup	190
Mexican Golden Corn, Peppers/Butter Sauce	1 cup	190
Golden Corn, Cream Style	1 cup	180
White Corn Kernels/Butter Sauce	1 cup	190
Mixed Vegetables/Butter Sauce	1 cup	130

continued

GREEN GIANT *cont.*

Boil-In-Bag Vegetables *cont.*	Amount	Calories
Onions/Cheese Flavor Sauce	1 cup	140
Le Sueur Early Peas/Butter Sauce	1 cup	150
Sweet Peas/Butter Sauce	1 cup	150
Le Sueur Tiny Peas, Onions, Carrots/Butter Sauce	1 cup	160
Le Sueur Tiny Peas, Pea Pods, Water Chestnuts/ Sauce	1 cup	180
Spinach/Butter Sauce	1 cup	90
Spinach, Creamed	1 cup	190
Chinese Style Vegetables	1 cup	130
Hawaiian Style Vegetables	1 cup	200
Japanese Style Vegetables	1 cup	130
BOIL-IN-BAG TOAST TOPPERS		
Gravy and Sliced Beef	5 oz.	130
Gravy and Sliced Turkey	5 oz.	100
Chicken A La King	5 oz.	170
Sloppy Joe	5 oz.	160
Cream Tuna/Peas	5 oz.	140
Welsh Rarebit	5 oz.	220
BOIL-IN-BAG ENTREES		
Macaroni and Cheese	9 oz.	330
Macaroni and Beef	9 oz.	240
Salisbury Steaks/Tomato Sauce	9 oz.	390
Chicken and Noodles	9 oz.	250
Lasagna/Meat Sauce	9 oz.	310
Beef Stew	9 oz.	160
Spaghetti and Meatballs	9 oz.	280
Chicken Chow Mein	9 oz.	130
BOIL-IN-BAG RICE ORIGINALS		
Continental	1 cup	230
Medley	1 cup	200
Pilaf	1 cup	230
White and Wild Rice	1 cup	220
White and Wild Oriental Rice	1 cup	230
White and Wild Rice Medley	1 cup	320
Rice 'n Broccoli/Cheese Sauce	1 cup	250
Verdi	1 cup	270
BAKE AND SERVE VEGETABLES		
Cut Broccoli/Cheese Sauce	1 cup	260
Cauliflower/Cheese Sauce	1 cup	220
Creamed Peas/Bread Crumb Topping	1 cup	300
Spinach Souffle	1 cup	300
Potatoes Au Gratin	1 cup	390
Potatoes Vermicelli	1 cup	390
OVEN BAKE ENTREES		
Macaroni and Cheese	8 oz.	290
Salisbury Steak/Gravy	7 oz.	290

continued

GREEN GIANT *cont.*

Oven Bake Entrees *cont.*	Amount	Calories
Stuffed Green Peppers	7 oz.	200
Stuffed Cabbage Rolls	7 oz.	220
Lasagna	7 oz.	300
Breaded Veal Parmigiana	7 oz.	310
Chicken and Biscuits	7 oz.	200
Beef Stew and Biscuits	7 oz.	190
POLY BAG VEGETABLES		
Baby Lima Beans	1 cup	150
Cut Broccoli	1 cup	30
Brussels Sprouts	1 cup	50
Cauliflower	1 cup	25
Golden Corn	1 cup	130
White Corn	1 cup	130
Peas	1 cup	100
Mixed Vegetables	1 cup	90

JENO'S PIZZA

	Amount	Calories
PIZZA		
Cheese	6.5 oz.	420
Sausage	6.8 oz.	450
Pepperoni	6.5 oz.	450
Hamburger	6.8 oz.	440
PIZZA ROLLS		
Sausage and Cheese	3 oz.	260
Pepperoni and Cheese	3 oz.	260
Cheeseburger	3 oz.	270
Shrimp and Cheese	3 oz.	220

LA CHOY

	Amount	Calories
DINNERS		
Beef	11 oz.	342
Chicken	11 oz.	354
Pepper Oriental	11 oz.	349
Shrimp	11 oz.	325
ENTREES		
Beef Chow Mein	16 oz.	97
Chicken Chow Mein	16 oz.	108
Fried Rice and Pork	12 oz.	216
Pepper Oriental	15 oz.	110
EGG ROLLS		
Chicken (4)	6.5 oz.	120
Lobster (4)	6.5 oz.	108
Meat and Shrimp (4)	6.5 oz.	108
Meat and Shrimp (6)	7.5 oz.	102
Shrimp (4)	6.5 oz.	104

MORTON

	Amount	Calories
FROZEN DINNERS		
Beans and Franks	10.8 oz.	530
Beef	10 oz.	260
Boneless Chicken	10 oz.	230
Chicken Croquette	10.3 oz.	410
Chicken 'N Dumplings	11 oz.	300
Chicken 'N Noodles	10.3 oz.	220
Fish	8.8 oz.	260

continued

MORTON *cont.*

Frozen Dinners *cont.*	Amount	Calories
Fried Chicken	11 oz.	460
Haddock	9 oz.	350
Ham	10 oz.	440
Italian Style	11 oz.	300
Macaroni and Beef	10 oz.	260
Macaroni and Cheese	11 oz.	320
Meat Loaf Dinner	11 oz.	340
Meat Ravioli	10 oz.	330
Salisbury Steak	11 oz.	290
Shrimp	7.8 oz.	400
Spaghetti and Meatball	11 oz.	360
Spaghetti and Sauce	11 oz.	240
Turkey	11 oz.	340
Turkey Tetrazzini	11 oz.	470
Western Round-Up	11 oz.	400
Fried Chicken	6.4 oz.	440
PIES AND CASSEROLES		
Beef Pot Pie	8 oz.	320
Chicken Pot Pie	8 oz.	320
Tuna Pot Pie	8 oz.	370
Turkey Pot Pie	8 oz.	340
Macaroni and Cheese	8 oz.	270
Spaghetti and Meat	8 oz.	220

MRS. PAUL'S

FISH PRODUCTS	Amount	Calories
Deviled Crabs	3 oz.	174
Deviled Crab Miniatures	3.5 oz.	210
Fried Scallops	3.5 oz.	210
Fried Fish Fillets	4 oz.	220
Fried Haddock Fillets	4 oz.	230
Fried Flounder Fillets	4 oz.	220
Fried Perch Fillets	4 oz.	250
Buttered Fish Fillets	5 oz.	310
Fish Cakes	4 oz.	210
Beach Haven Fish Cakes	4 oz.	220
Clam Sticks	4 oz.	240
Fried Clams	2.5 oz.	270
Deviled Clams	3 oz.	180
Fried Shrimp	3 oz.	170
Shrimp Sticks	3.2 oz.	190
Shrimp Cakes	3 oz.	150
Fish Sticks	3 oz.	150
Fish Parmesan	5 oz.	220
Fish Au Gratin	5 oz.	250
Light Batter Fish Sticks	3.5 oz.	280
Light Batter Scallops	3.5 oz.	200
Sole/Lemon Butter	4.5 oz.	160
Flounder/Lemon Butter	4.5 oz.	150
Scallops/Butter and Cheese	7 oz.	260
Supreme Light Batter Fish Fillets	3.6 oz.	220
Crab Crepes	5.5 oz.	240
Shrimp Crepes	5.5 oz.	250
Clam Crepes	5.5 oz.	280
Scallop Crepes	5.5 oz.	220
FROZEN VEGETABLES		
Candied Sweet Potatoes	4 oz.	180
Candied Sweets 'N Apples	4 oz.	160
Fried Onion Rings	2.5 oz.	150

continued

MRS. PAUL'S *cont.*

Frozen Vegetables *cont.*	Amount	Calories
Fried Eggplant Sticks	3.5 oz.	260
Fried Eggplant Slices	3 oz.	230
Eggplant Parmesan	5.5 oz.	250
Light Batter Zucchini Sticks	3 oz.	180
Corn Fritters	4 oz.	260
Apple Fritters	4 oz.	240
Light Batter Broccoli and Cheese	2.5 oz.	150
Light Batter Cauliflower and Cheese	2.6 oz.	120

ORE-IDA

POTATO PRODUCTS	Amount	Calories
Golden Crinkles or Fries	3 oz.	130
Shoestrings	3 oz.	170
Pixie Crinkles	3 oz.	170
Country Style Dinner Fries	3 oz.	120
Cottage Fries	3 oz.	140
Crispers	3 oz.	230
Heinz Self-Sizzling Fries or Crinkles	3 oz.	160
Heinz Self-Sizzling Shoestrings	3 oz.	220
Southern Style Hash Browns	3 oz.	70
Shredded Hash Browns	6 oz.	120
Tater Tots Plain	3 oz.	160
Tater Tots/Onions	3 oz.	160
Tater Tots/Bacon Flavor	3 oz.	150
Small Whole Peeled Potatoes	3 oz.	70
O'Brien Potatoes	3 oz.	60
Potatoes/Butter Sauce	3 oz.	120
Potatoes/Butter Sauce and Onions	3 oz.	130

RONZONI

FROZEN ENTREES	Amount	Calories
Lasagna	4 oz.	140
Linguine/Clam Sauce	4 oz.	120
Fettuccine Alfredo	4 oz.	190
Baked Ziti	4 oz.	115

STOKELY-VAN CAMP

VARIETY VEGETABLES	Amount	Calories
Succotash	3.3 oz.	100
Vegetables, Mixed	3.3 oz.	60
Vegetables, Stew	4 oz.	60
Broccoli Florentine	3.3 oz.	30
Chuckwagon Corn	3.3 oz.	90
Vegetables Del Sol	3 oz.	25
Vegetables Milano	3 oz.	45
Vegetables Orient	3 oz.	25
Vegetables Rio	3 oz.	35
Vegetables Romano	3 oz.	40
FRUIT		
Red Raspberries	5 oz.	160

continued

STOKELY-VAN CAMP

Fruit *cont.*	Amount	Calories
Strawberry Halves	5 oz.	160
Whole Strawberries	4 oz.	110

STOUFFER'S

ENTREES & SIDE DISHES	Amount	Calories
Macaroni and Beef	5.8 oz.	190
Macaroni and Cheese	6 oz.	260
Creamed Chicken	6.5 oz.	300
Tuna Noodle Casserole	5.8 oz.	200
Stuffed Peppers	7.8 oz.	225
Creamed Chipped Beef	5.5 oz.	235
Lasagna	10.5 oz.	385
Beef Stroganoff	9.8 oz.	390
Salisbury Steak	6 oz.	250
Beef Stew	10 oz.	310
Spinach Souffle	4 oz.	135
Chicken A La King	9.5 oz.	330
Green Pepper Steak	10.5 oz.	350
Potatoes Au Gratin	3.8 oz.	135
Scalloped Potatoes	4 oz.	126
Turkey Tetrazzini	6 oz.	240
Corn Souffle	4 oz.	155
Broccoli Au Gratin	5 oz.	170
Escalloped Chicken	5.8 oz.	250
Chicken Divan	8.5 oz.	335
Noodles Romanoff	4 oz.	170
Spaghetti	14 oz.	445
Shrimp and Scallops	10.2 oz.	400
Ribs of Beef	5.8 oz.	350
Swedish Meatballs	11 oz.	475
Teriyaki	10 oz.	365
Chicken Cacciatore	11.2 oz.	310
Chicken Paprikash	10.5 oz.	385
Beef Hash	5.8 oz.	265
PIZZA		
Cheese	5.1 oz.	330
Deluxe	6.2 oz.	400
Pepperoni	5.6 oz.	410
Sausage	6 oz.	420
MEAT PIES		
Chicken	10 oz.	500
Beef	10 oz.	550
Turkey	10 oz.	460

Stouffer's *Lean Cuisine* entrees have not been included in this list because the calorie values appear on the package.

SWANSON

FROZEN TV DINNERS	Amount	Calories
Barbecue Flavored Fried Chicken	11.3 oz.	530
Beans and Beef Patties	11 oz.	500
Beans and Franks	11.3 oz.	550
Beef	11.5 oz.	370
Beef Enchiladas	15 oz.	570
Chopped Sirloin Beef	10 oz.	460
Crispy Fried Chicken	10.8 oz.	650

continued

SWANSON *cont.*

Frozen T.V. Dinners *cont.*	Amount	Calories
Fish 'N Chips	10.3 oz.	450
Fried Chicken	11.5 oz.	560
German Style	11.8 oz.	430
Ham	10.3 oz.	380
Italian Style	13 oz.	420
Loin of Pork	11.3 oz.	470
Macaroni and Beef	12 oz.	400
Macaroni and Cheese	12.5 oz.	390
Meat Loaf	10.8 oz.	530
Meatballs	11.8 oz.	400
Mexican Style	16 oz.	700
Noodles and Chicken	10.3 oz.	390
Polynesian Style	13 oz.	490
Salisbury Steak	11.5 oz.	500
Spaghetti and Meatballs	12.5 oz.	410
Swiss Steak	10 oz.	350
Turkey	11.5 oz.	360
Veal Parmigiana	12.3 oz.	510
Western Style	11.8 oz.	440
THREE COURSE DINNERS		
Beef	15 oz.	490
Fried Chicken	15 oz.	630
Salisbury Steak	16 oz.	490
Turkey	16 oz.	520
HUNGRY-MAN DINNERS		
Barbecue Fried Chicken	16.5 oz.	760
Boneless Chicken	19 oz.	730
Chopped Beef Steak	18 oz.	730
Fish 'N Chips	15.8 oz.	760
Fried Chicken	15.8 oz.	910
Lasagna/Meat	17.8 oz.	790
Salisbury Steak	17 oz.	870
Sliced Beef	17 oz.	540
Spaghetti and Meatballs	18.5 oz.	660
Turkey	19 oz.	750

continued

SWANSON *cont.*

Hungry Man Dinners *cont.*	Amount	Calories
Veal Parmigiana	20.5 oz.	990
Western Style	17.8 oz.	840
FROZEN TV ENTREES		
Chicken Nibbles/French Fries	6 oz.	370
Fish 'N Chips	5 oz.	290
French Toast/Sausages	4.5 oz.	300
Fried Chicken/Whipped Potatoes	7 oz.	360
Gravy and Sliced Beef/ Whipped Potatoes	8 oz.	190
Meatballs/Gravy and Whipped Potatoes	9.3 oz.	330
Meatloaf/Tomato Sauce and Whipped Potatoes	9 oz.	330
Pancakes and Sausage	6 oz.	500
Salisbury Steak/Crinkle Potatoes	5.5 oz.	350
Scrambled Eggs and Sausage/Coffee Cake	6.3 oz.	460
Spaghetti in Tomato Sauce/Breaded Veal	8.3 oz.	290
Turkey-Gravy-Dressing and Whipped Potatoes	8.8 oz.	260
FROZEN MEAT PIES		
Beef	8 oz.	430
Chicken	8 oz.	450
Turkey	8 oz.	460
Macaroni and Cheese	7 oz.	230
HUNGRY-MAN MEAT PIES		
Beef	16 oz.	770
Chicken	16 oz.	780
Sirloin Burger	16 oz.	830
Turkey	16 oz.	800

continued

SWANSON *cont.*

	Amount	Calories
HUNGRY-MAN ENTREES		
Barbecue Fried Chicken	12 oz.	550
Fried Chicken	12 oz.	620
Lasagna	12.8 oz.	540
Salisbury Steak	12.5 oz.	640
Sliced Beef	12.3 oz.	330
Turkey	13.3 oz.	380

TASTE O'SEA FROZEN FISH PRODUCTS

	Amount	Calories
COD FISH		
Raw Breaded Cod Portions	4 oz.	130
Breaded "Banquet Style" Cod Portions	4 oz.	140
Golden Fried Moby Dicks	5.2 oz.	310
Golden Fried Skinless Cod Sticks	4 oz.	260
Golden Fried Cod Portions Long	4 oz.	190
Batter Dipt Cod Wedgies (Oven Bake)	3 oz.	210
Batter Fried Cod Wedgies	3 oz.	170

WEIGHT WATCHERS

Weight Watcher's and Stouffer's *Lean Cuisine* entrees have not been included in this list because the calorie values appear on the package.

REFERENCES:

Excerpted by permission of Rawson, Wade Publishers from *The Partnership Diet Program* by Kelly Brownell, Ph.D., with Irene Copeland. Copyright © 1980 by Kelly Brownell, Ph.D.

Chapter 10 - INSTRUCTOR NOTES

Suggested Techniques:

Restart Plan

1. Make a list of readiness activities and enter one or two of them at the base of the Restart Plan in the spaces provided.
2. Make a list of basic control techniques. Use the Reference Outline of Techniques and Exercises for review if necessary.
3. List control techniques by priority from easiest to most difficult, and enter them on the Restart Plan. Place the easiest technique in the space labelled 1; the next easiest in space labelled 2; and so on, with the most difficult technique placed at the top in space labelled 8. Write in pencil.
4. On the first day following loss of control do **only** what is listed on the bottom one or two levels of the Restart Plan.
5. On successive days move upward or downward on the Restart Plan as necessary until you can move comfortably upward to the level of resuming your regular control plan.
6. If a level seems too difficult to achieve, remove the technique or exchange it for a different one. Modify the levels as necessary.

Stress Plan

1. Use the Restart Plan as a Stress Plan also.
2. When you are under stress, begin at whatever level of the Restart/Stress Plan which is appropriate for your achievement ability at that particular moment.
3. Move upward or downward on the Restart/Stress Plan until the stress is reduced and full control can be resumed.

Homework Assignments:

Read the instructions on page 164.

Cautions and Reminders:

1. Instruct your students to put aside their Weekly Progress Records or Performance Graphs when using the Restart/Stress Plan. The purpose of the Restart/Stress Plan is to reduce the load and enable people to gradually reintroduce the techniques they had been using to initially establish control. Weekly Progress Records may be used once control has been reestablished.
2. Insist that your students develop their Restart/Stress Plans and experiment with them before your next scheduled class session. Plan to review each person's Restart/Stress Plan during the discussion section of the next class session. This is an assignment which many students put off doing because they don't recognize the necessity of advance planning. In-class sharing of plans provides a little incentive to complete the assignment on schedule.
3. Once developed, the Restart/Stress Plan should be kept in a readily accessible, easily remembered place. The insides of kitchen cupboard doors work exceptionally well as a place to tape strategy cards, Restart/Stress Plans and other written tools like Performance Graphs. Many students misplace their Plans and become overly frustrated when trying to find them during periods of already shaky control. The objective, when control is wobbly, is to provide easy-to-follow directions, developed and tested in advance, and kept in easily visible places so that students can find them quickly.

10

Target: Preplanning (stabilization and restart planning).

Objectives:

1. Develop specific plan for restarting control following temporary loss of control.
2. Develop flexibility in control routine to allow for periods of stress, unusually high activity, depression, illness or fatigue.

Motto:

If at first you don't succeed, try again, and again, and again!

Restart/Stress Plan

To control means to regulate, to exercise authority over, to curb, restrain, or hold back. Those are the dictionary meanings, but to a dieter the word "control" takes on some emotional aspects. A survey of 150 overweight men and women in my Food Habit Management classes brought out the following definitions of control: doing without, being deprived, perfection, abstinence, punishment, and being good. A quick look at these definitions shows an underlying sense of judgement, of validation of a person's worth as in "being good", but they also show a strong degree of rigidity which allows only for an extreme degree of control.

The human animal, alas, is not a perfect creature and days of excellent control are typically followed by days of shaky control as well as days of no control whatsoever. Further, in any one day a person could experience the whole range of control ability from excellent at breakfast, for example, to shaky control in the late afternoon, to total loss of control in the evening, as in a binge. Control can be further influenced by the presence of a particular person, like an "eating buddy"; a mood; stress, tension or fatigue; the easy availability of particular food items.

The human animal is not a perfect creature.

What I am suggesting here is that control is a valuable commodity, influenced by circumstantial factors, and is given more importance than is useful on a day-to-day level. Dieters frequently regulate their self-esteem or sense of self-worth according to their level of eating control. When asking my students the question, "If you had a successful day at work or in your daily routine at home, but an unsuccessful day controlling your food intake, how do you rate the day when you go to bed at night? Successful or unsuccessful?" The overwhelming response: unsuccessful. When I ask, "If you had a partly successful day at work or in your home routine, but an excellent day of eating control, how do you rate that day?" The response most typically given: successful. "How do you feel about yourself on that successful control day? The typical answer: great. The sense of self-worth on poor eating control days is rated by nearly everyone as very low, and their feelings about themselves are very negative.

What this tells me is that dieters give their eating control level an inordinate amount of power to determine their feelings about themselves, and to tell them whether or not they are valuable and worthwhile. Not everyone does this, of course, but for people who do place such high value on eating control some help is needed for dealing more effectively with the whole aspect of maintaining that very personal sense of self-worth.

I frequently ask my students if they are able to sense when an out-of-control day or period of time is coming. Answers vary but what comes across is that people do have a vague, uneasy feeling which, as time goes by progresses to anxiety and generalized "jumpiness". When asked to be specific about obvious signposts which tell them that loss of control could happen, most of my students are able to identify very definite clues. One woman said that when the breakfast dishes are left on the kitchen counter, she always overeats when she returns home. The unsightly mess tells her, in effect, that she is not keeping up with her daily tasks. She feels pressured and depressed and turns to food for comfort. Another woman talked about the importance of washing her hair and putting on her make-up. When she sees herself looking disheveled and her hair is oily, she doesn't feel good about herself, feels fat and ugly in her mind's eye, and decides that regulating her food intake wouldn't help anyway. One person mentioned that whenever she feels like she has to do everything for everyone and that no one appreciates her, she finds herself feeling revengeful. Unable to let herself have any other type of pleasure to soothe her feelings, she tries to be even more of a martyr and pushes herself into a binge. One gentleman in my class referred to leisurely Sunday mornings as his signpost. If he has breakfast in his bathrobe with the morning paper, it's noon to 1:00 before he gets around to starting his day and the morning has slipped past along with a lot of unnecessary calories eaten while reading the paper. He becomes angry and frustrated, and tends to overeat for the rest of the day. Do you have some definite signposts of your own for showing you that an out-of-control day is on its way? What are they?

Maintaining long-term control is a continuing challenge.

Maintaining long-term control is definitely a continuing challenge to personal skill and determination. Once a flexible, easy-to-follow plan of action is devised, maintaining and reestablishing control becomes a source of deep satisfaction. The keys to this entire project are simplicity and flexibility, both of which must be built into the plan if it is to be usable.

At this point I would like to make an analogy between climbing a mountain and establishing eating control. Picture a big mountain in your mind. Most mountains follow the same pattern, beginning at the base with a slow, gradual upward slope. There is usually vegetation underfoot and overhead, making the journey a little more difficult than a pleasant, woodsy walk. Continuing onward, the slope of the mountain becomes steeper, the vegetation sparser, and eventually you find yourself climbing on switchback trails of rock beneath your feet and open sky above your head. After a while you get to loose rock and then to the bare rock face of the mountain where further climb is possible only with the proper equipment and physical condition. Wind and weather can further increase the difficulty of the climb. And if you lose your footing and begin to fall, is your first thought how to reclimb? Probably your very first thoughts concern ways of stopping the fall. Once stopped, you would logically take a few moments to collect your breath and your wits before planning how to reclimb that mountain.

What does mountain climbing have to do with eating control? Simply this. Good eating control represents a gradual, progressively more difficult procession of tasks which place a person higher and higher in skill level. From what was said earlier in this book about how people learn, you have related eating control skills to the acquisition of skills in any area of learning in your life: skiing, typing, playing piano, making bread. All learning is sequential, with each new task learned providing a basis of skill and knowledge to do the next task. Before you can climb the bare mountain face, in my analogy, you must have first climbed a goodly distance from the bottom and have acquired a level of physical condition which makes the climb possible.

When people develop eating control they pass through some basic learning tasks, as represented by the techniques listed in the chapters which precede this one. Many of those techniques become part of the total control plan. Putting tempting food out of sight, shopping from a list, sitting down to eat, using smaller plates and bowls, putting the fork down between bites, and so on from the first six chapters of this book represent the gradual, woodsy walk at the base of the mountain. They are the easiest techniques because they are concrete and easy to apply. They provide the basic training necessary to be able to handle variations, periodic challenges to your typical routine, and unexpected obstacles to your control. Chapters 7 through 14 teach methods for dealing with the variations and challenges, and are analogous to the switchbacks and loose rock on the mountain climb. If you begin to slide down the mountain you pass by some of what you have already climbed. To get back up to where you began your fall, you have to reclimb the original path. So it is with your personal climb to good eating control. When you slide down in performance from where you are now, you have to climb back up in the same way, using the same techniques. Most dieters, however, feel that because of their extensive study and experience in the area of weight reduction, they should not have to retrace their early steps. They feel that they should be able to reach their highest level of control, perhaps represented by counting calories or not eating specific foods, right away. If you were a mountain climber you could not get to the pinnacle without reclimbing the same or similar path unless you had a helicopter. It is equally true for eating control. You cannot resume full control in one giant step, which might be evident to you if you have ever tried to get back into control by counting calories and not getting around to doing it. Day after day goes by with the same thought: "I'll start counting calories again tomorrow."

Below is a triangular diagram drawn to simulate my mountain analogy. Notice the various steps, beginning at the base with non-eating related tasks resulting from awareness of the signposts discussed earlier.

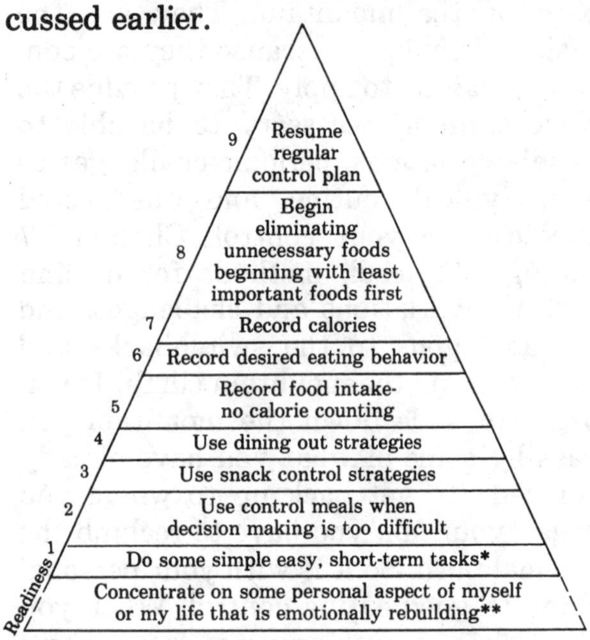

9 Resume regular control plan

8 Begin eliminating unnecessary foods beginning with least important foods first

7 Record calories

6 Record desired eating behavior

5 Record food intake-no calorie counting

4 Use dining out strategies

3 Use snack control strategies

2 Use control meals when decision making is too difficult

1 Do some simple easy, short-term tasks*

Readiness: Concentrate on some personal aspect of myself or my life that is emotionally rebuilding**

***Examples:** Sit down to eat, get problem foods out of house, carry no loose change for vending machines, etc.

****Examples:**

Pleasure based—do something fun like going out, working on a hobby, read a good book.

Appearance based—take bath, get dressed, have hair styled.

Accomplishment based—get some bothersome project or task completed and out of the way, like putting dishes in dishwasher, run necessary errands.

Socially based—talk on the telephone or get together with someone.

Do you see how the difficulty of the steps progresses from the base to the top of the triangle? Some of these steps may not be in the correct sequence for you. For example it may be necessary for you to reduce portion size before eliminating certain foods, so add in the extra step. It may be easier for you to control your eating away from home, so your sequence should have the dining out strategies below snack control strategies. The section at the very base of the triangle has broken lines to signify that it is a readiness step in the mental preparation and commitment to resume, or restart, control of your eating behavior. Giving a horse a carrot before placing the saddle on him puts him in a better frame of mind and will probably cause him to be more cooperative. Most people work in the same way. A little reward or positive input goes a long way to helping people feel better inside and causes them to be more charitable toward themselves and thus, be more willing to put in some effort on their own behalf.

In climbing your personal "food habit control" mountain what would be your first step? Would it be a readiness level task? If so, enter it at the base of the diagram at the end of this chapter in the area designated "readiness". What is the very easiest concrete technique you have used in this course to control some aspect of your food intake? Is it sitting down to eat, putting tempting food out of sight, or something else? If you are not sure, consult the Reference Outline of Techniques and Exercises, located on pages 267-270 of this book, and review the techniques you have studied. Select five to ten of them and put them in sequential order with number one being the very easiest, number two being the next easiest, and so on with your highest number alongside the most difficult task. Not all useful techniques need to be represented on the restart diagram. Just include the ones which are the most concrete and which have the most meaning and enjoyment for you. Once you get yourself moving in the direction of greater control, you will be able to branch out and include tasks you haven't written down.

Next, enter each technique, according to number, in the space provided for it on the diagram at the end of this chapter. Write in pencil so that necessary changes can be made at a later time. Look at the sample restart plan below.

Sample Restart Plan:

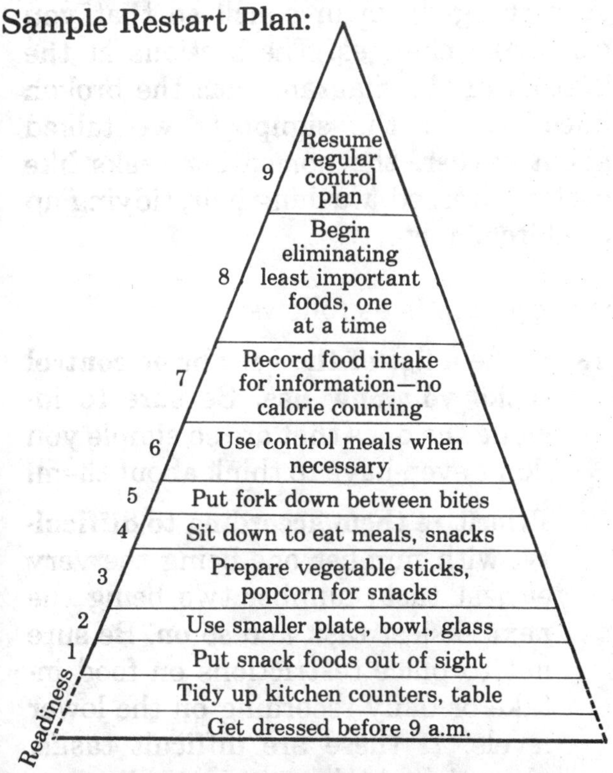

On the first day following loss of control work only at level 1. If you are not ready for level 1, work at the readiness level first. Stay at that level until you are ready to climb to the next level. On the following day move up to the next level. Continue upward at a rate that is comfortable. Don't rush. If you need to spend two or three days at one level that is OK. You may find that one level seems more difficult than the level above it. This means that the difficult level is either too complex or out of sequence. Remember that for each level you work on you must also be doing the tasks on the levels below. Do not add more than two levels at a time in the beginning. You may stay at any level for more than one day if necessary. In time you may be able to climb three or four levels in one day, but never attempt to climb all of them at one time. Do not restrict food intake until you are restarted. Don't be afraid to revise your plan periodically. Some of my own best plans needed several revisions.

Before leaving this chapter let's look for a few minutes at the effects of stress on our daily eating control. By definition the word stress implies strain, pressure, intensity, urgency, exertion. Increased stress results in decreased ability to maintain typical levels of performance in all aspects of daily life. When stress levels increase most people let up on things which don't absolutely have to be done. Dieters, however, frequently become perfectionists during stress periods and put extra pressure on themselves to do everything well, including their eating control. When stress becomes too great, the least essential or "elective" tasks are abandoned first, and those tasks which are most necessary to relieving the stress or tasks which must be done to fulfill job or family obligations are given the most effort. How you eat at any one time is not usually essential to the basic demands which must be answered. Look at this example. Suppose your uncle is in the critical care ward of your local hospital and you and your relatives have been told that his condition is momentarily stable. You all decide to go to the cafeteria for a quick bite to eat. All that remains for purchase is a few salads with "rusty" edges on the lettuce, some day old cottage cheese, macaroni and cheese, meat balls and gravy, corned beef hash and doughnuts. Would you decide to wait and eat later? Would you eat the lettuce or the cottage cheese? Would you just pick out something from the entree selection and tell yourself that you're hungry and just can't be choosy right now? Most of my students select the last option because, after all, how much does that one meal really matter anyway? It matters a lot if you give yourself a bad time over it, reduce your sense of self-worth and promote greater loss of control. It is preferable to maintain whatever level of control is possible rather than to shoot for perfection, miss the goal, and settle for no control at all. It is easier to slide down to the bottom levels of your control plan, doing those few tasks you feel capable of, and maintaining partial control than it is to fall away from all semblance of control and have to get psychologically and emotionally back into a control routine again.

The restart plan you work out for yourself can be used as a stress plan as well. When eating control feels wobbly, drop down to whatever level of control you can comfortably handle and remain at that level until the stress lets up and you can slowly climb back up to your usual control routine. Do you remember the popular poster of a kitten hanging by one claw from a tree with the caption, "Hang in there baby!"? That's exactly what I'm referring to here. If you can hang on to some portion of control at a very basic, easy-to-do level, what you are in effect saying to yourself is, "I can't do everything right now, but I am doing what I'm able to do. I haven't given up or lost control. I will increase my control when I can." In this way it is possible to feel good about yourself. If you can protect and preserve a positive mental attitude, better control will come sooner and more easily.

Explanation of Homework

Your assignment for this week is to work out a restart/stress plan using the diagram at the end of this chapter. Write everything down in pencil so that you can make changes. The sections at the bottom of the diagram with the broken lines are for the signposts we talked about earlier, the non-eating tasks like getting dressed, washing hair, tidying up the kitchen, etc.

The procedure is as follows:

1. **Make a list of the very basic control tasks you now use.** Be sure to include the ones that are so simple you don't even have to think about them.
2. **Prioritize them according to difficulty,** with number one being the very easiest task, number two being the next easiest task and so on. Be sure not to place restrictions on food intake or daily recording on the lower levels. If these are difficult tasks, place them higher up on the diagram as explained earlier in the chapter.
3. **Experiment with the plan this week to see if the steps seem to be in cor-**

rect sequence. Modify the plan as necessary.

4. **Post the plan where you can see it easily when you need to use it;** otherwise tape it to the inside of a kitchen cupboard door where you will be able to find it when you need it.

Weekly Progress Record

The instructions for how to use the Weekly Progress Record are on pages 257-260. Enter the four steps listed in the procedure explained in this week's homework assignment on your Weekly Progress Record.

Daily Food Record

The instructions for how to use the Daily Food Record are on pages 261-263.

Weight Record

The instructions for how to use the Weight Record are on pages 21-22.

When setting up your experimental restart/stress plan be sure to avoid the pitfall of putting difficult tasks like calorie counting, elimination of foods, **avoidance of particular events** at the lower levels. People often feel these tasks are so essential to good food control that they cannot restart without them. They explain that they have their best control when they are counting calories and avoiding certain foods. This is because they are also doing other, basic, necessary tasks like putting problem foods out of sight, having appropriate snacks readily available, and so on. If you are one who puts off counting calories or eliminating precious foods, then, for certain, these should not be listed at the bottom of your plan. To be useful, the Restart/Stress plan must be worked out **before** it is needed. Because it is so important to have this plan worked through, this is your only assignment for this week. Bring your plan to class next week and review the levels with your instructor. Good luck!

Extra recording forms for this chapter may be found starting on page 273.

Restart/Stress Plan

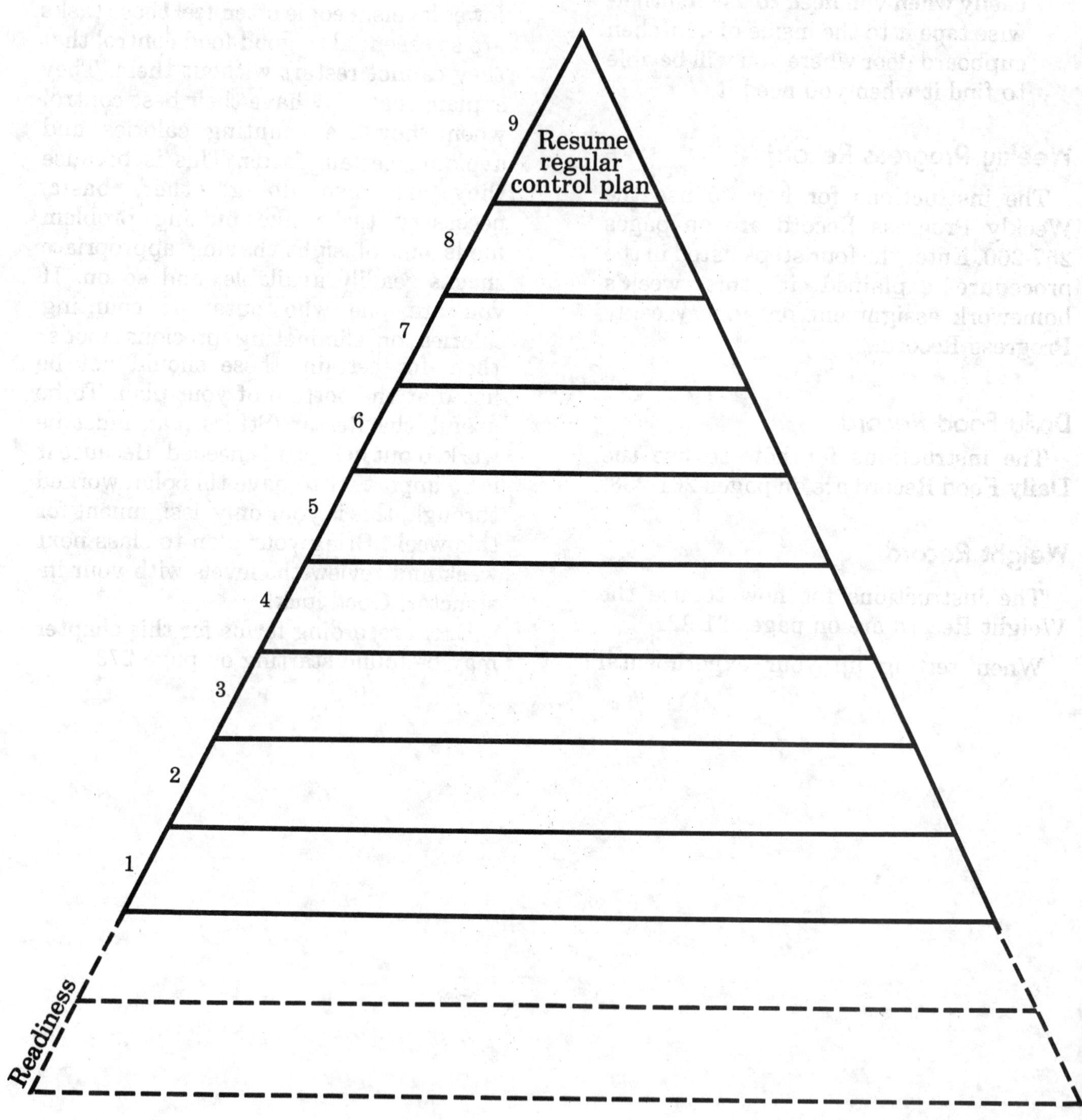

WEEKLY PROGRESS RECORD

BASIC SKILLS:	SUN	MON	TUES	WED	THURS	FRI	SAT	*
Read Progress Record in morning								
Record food intake								
Stay within calorie/ exchange total								
SPECIFIC TECHNIQUES/EXERCISES:								
Daily Totals								

*This column is for the weekly totals for each specific technique or exercise.

DAILY FOOD RECORD

Food Item/ Beverage	Amount	Calories/Exchanges	Time of Day

Total Calories for day ______

Date ______

Total Exchanges for day:

(1) Milk ______
(2) Vegetable ______
(3) Fruit ______
(4) Bread ______
(5) Meat ______
(6) Fat ______

DAILY FOOD RECORD

Food Item/ Beverage	Amount	Calories/Exchanges	Time of Day

Total Calories for day ______

Date ______

Total Exchanges for day:

(1) Milk ______
(2) Vegetable ______
(3) Fruit ______
(4) Bread ______
(5) Meat ______
(6) Fat ______

DAILY FOOD RECORD

Food Item/ Beverage	Amount	Calories/Exchanges	Time of Day

Copyright © Northwest Learning Associates, Inc., 1978. All rights reserved.

Total Calories for day ______

Date ______

Total Exchanges for day:

(1) Milk ______
(2) Vegetable ______
(3) Fruit ______
(4) Bread ______
(5) Meat ______
(6) Fat ______

Chapter 11 - INSTRUCTOR NOTES

Suggested Techniques:

Listed on pages 173 through 176.

Homework Assignments:

Read the instructions on page 176.

Cautions and Reminders:

1. Stress the importance of not deliberately starving all day for the purpose of saving all of those calories for the restaurant meal. Both heightened physical hunger (from lowered blood sugar level) and the rationalization that everything can be eaten "because I starved all day for it" lead to loss of control. In addition, those first bites of food provide a powerful stimulus to continue to eat. If a little food is eaten before traveling to the restaurant, the stimulus to continue eating is broken. When eating is resumed in the restaurant, the person is not as uncontrollably hungry or as overwhelmed by the stimulus to eat.
2. Remind your students that if a plan is tried and fails, it simply means that a new plan needs to be made. Each plan is an experiment. A plan which is effective under one set of conditions may not be as effective under different conditions. The procedure is to determine specifically what went awry and then plan a new strategy taking that information into account.
3. Caution your students to plan very carefully when they are going out to eat with their "eating buddies." Wearing an outfit with a not-too-roomy waistband may be a helpful reminder to limit food intake. Sharing the control strategy with a member of the group who is usually supportive might also be helpful. And when staying in control becomes too difficult, taking "time out" for a few minutes by going to the bathroom and getting away from the food cues may prove to be the most useful technique of all.

11

Target: Preplanning.

Objectives:

1. Develop strategies for control of food intake in restaurants.
2. Develop effective food selection strategies based upon anticipated needs, problems and preferences.
3. Reduce or maintain calorie level; establish or maintain dietary plan.

Motto:

Eat the BEST of what there is, not all of what there is.

Social Eating: Restaurants

Effective control of eating behavior depends upon a conscious awareness of what and how much is being eaten. The need for conscious awareness is particularly important in social situations where the person's attention is often directed away from food and the environment is filled with an attractive array of powerful food cues. All of this may be even further complicated by the insistence of other people to have a little more. No military general worth his medals would go into a battle without a plan. Neither can a person who wishes to control how much he or she eats go out to eat without a previously determined plan of attack.

The battle plan, or strategy, need not be elaborate. It can be very simple, involving only one or two techniques, but it must be specific enough to be written down. I ask my students to use 3x5 file cards for their plans. These strategy cards, as we call them, can be put into a purse or pocket and reviewed whenever needed. The value in making strategy cards is to help you avoid the helplessness you feel when your only plan is to wait and see what happens. It forces you into the position of problem solving. The feeling of control increases whenever action takes place; and making a plan, even a bad plan, denotes action. A plan can be revised if it isn't workable, and having a written plan gives you something to work from. Many of my students have adopted the policy of going into the bathroom if the going gets rough; they get away from the food cues, re-read and possibly revise their plans; and then return to the battleground with more concrete ideas of what they want to do next. "The best part of this whole idea," said one woman, "is that no one ever argues with me when I say I'm going to the bathroom, and no one can come with me. I can get away from people and food and have a chance to think for a minute."

Eating out is fun, and that aspect shouldn't have to change just because of the need to lose weight. The motto, "Get the best of what there is, not all of what there is," signifies the general approach to be used when going out to eat. One of the complaints frequently heard about eating out when on a diet is that the person selects food according to the diet plan and feels deprived of the more interesting, but fattening, foods. For some people this approach results in out-of-control eating later that night as the person attempts to compensate for the earlier deprivation. Others declare that they would prefer to eat at home rather than struggle through a restaurant meal of foods they would not choose to eat if they weren't dieting. If, however, the person selects *the best* of what is offered, and eliminates those food items that are unimportant, the feeling of deprivation is removed. "I can't eat all of it anyway," said one person, "so when I eat only what I like the most, I feel really good about it."

Eating out is fun,
and that aspect shouldn't
have to change
just because of the need
to lose weight.

Of all dining out situations, restaurants probably offer the greatest possibilities for control. Once an order is placed, there are few unexpected problems to handle. Deciding upon and placing the order can be major obstacles, however, and planning strategies for doing these tasks is very important. There are a number of questions to ask before deciding what to eat. First, is the meal going to be the whole evening's activity, or will it be followed by some other activity like a movie or sports event? Is it likely that the group will want to go somewhere to have drinks or pizza or pie later in the evening? Is today a good or poor control day in terms of food intake? The answers to these questions will supply some guidelines for decisions about what to order.

The next set of questions concerns what foods the specific resturant offers, methods of preparation, and the like. If you are familiar with the restaurant's menu, the decisions about what to order can be made in advance. If you are unfamiliar with the restaurant, you can call them at a slow time of day, perhaps midafternoon. Talk with someone who can explain what foods are available and answer questions about their preparation. Find out, for example, if the fish is fried or baked, and whether it comes with or without sauce. Ask whether à la carte entrées come with or without potatoes, and so on. Most restaurant personnel are very willing to provide this information if the call comes at a time when they are not rushed and if the person calling has stated that he or she has dietary restrictions and needs to have that information in advance. This information is particularly helpful if you have a special dietary regimen, such as low sodium or low fat, to follow.

Once all the preliminaries have been considered the final question is, "What am I in the mood to eat?" Using the "Eat the best of what there is, not all of what there is" motto, do the following exercise. After each food course listed below you will see a blank line. Imagine that you are going out for dinner tonight. Select a restaurant you know. Use your information of what foods are particularly good in that restaurant, together with what things you are in the mood for today, to numerically rate the desirability of each food course by number. Number 1 is the most desirable; number 11 is the least desirable. Each number may be used only once. Therefore, only one food is rated 1, and only one food is rated 2, and so on.

Cocktails ________

Hors d'oeuvres ________

Bread and rolls ________

Soup ________

Salad ________

Potato or rice ________

Specify ____________________

Hot vegetable ________

Meat, poultry, seafood, fish ________

Specify ____________________

Wine ________

Dessert ________

After dinner drinks ________

If you ate only the items marked 1 through 5 or 6 you would have selected "the best of what there is." This strategy allows you to be selective without feeling deprived, since the foods you rated below 6 are less important to you. This preplanning process may seem laborious and unnecessarily time consuming in the beginning, but once the procedure is learned it can be done quickly. The purposes of this procedure are to define the basic structure of the meal and to select specific techniques which will be useful in maintaining that structure effectively.

Here are some techniques for controlling your eating in restaurants:

1. Perhaps the most important technique to remember for all dining out situations is: **avoid starving yourself all day in anticipation of the dinner meal.** This often has disastrous results in terms of eating control. The first scent of food is a strong assault upon the resolve to eat carefully, particularly if your blood sugar level is low. This may be followed by the rationale, "It's OK for me to eat a lot. After all, I starved all day for it and I deserve it!" The strategy of saving up calories to be used at the restaurant can work well as long as you **eat some small amount of food before leaving the house, to increase your initial control.** A little cottage cheese, a salad, or some cold meat eaten in advance will raise your blood sugar level as well as reduce frantic hunger feelings before you arrive at the restaurant.

2. **Order a la carte** based upon the decision making process described

above. Avoid ordering the restaurant "special" if it includes food items that have low preference ratings. It is very important that

The first scent of food is a strong assault upon the resolve to eat carefully.

you not be tempted by the presence of low preference items on your plate. If the food is on the plate it is a powerful cue, particularly if you are inclined to eat what you paid for. Furthermore if every extra food item raises the bill, there is some inducement to limit how much is ordered.

3. If you have trouble placing the order that you originally planned, **ask someone else at the table to place the order for you.** One woman discussed her tendency to change her order once she heard what everyone else was going to eat. She liked the idea of asking someone else at the table to order for her. She found, however, that she still changed the order that the other person placed. A lively class discussion followed and a new strategy emerged: she would again ask someone to place the order for her, but this time she planned to get up from the table when the waitress arrived to take the orders, go to the bathroom and spend five minutes combing her hair, and return after the waitress had left. She thought that once the order was placed she would have no problem feeling satisfied with the meal. This strategy worked beautifully and she used it frequently.

4. **Plan what to order in accordance with the anticipated length of the meal and whether or not you will eat again later on.** If the dinner is to be the evening's activity, you may do well to order food items that require extra time to eat. Artichokes, seafood left in the shell, and poultry all require more time to eat than do foods like broiled fish fillets and sliced tomatoes. The longer it takes to eat, the longer you are occupied and the greater your satisfaction is likely to be. One man used the following plan. He ordered four hors d'oeuvres instead of an entrée and asked to have each one of them

Food on the plate is a powerful cue, particularly if you eat what you paid for.

brought to the table separately. By eating only one hors d'oeuvre at a time he managed to make his meal last a very long time. And because each dish was brought after the previous one had been eaten he had the added benefit of eating his food while it was still hot. On the other hand if the meal needs to be quickly eaten because another activity is planned, easy to eat foods are more appropriate.

5. There are times when the decision not to eat something is very difficult to uphold. For some people this is particularly true of the bread and crackers served during the pre-dinner cocktail hour. If necessary, **order some vegetables or a salad to be brought to the table** so that you will have something to eat other than bread and rolls. One lady stashed some cut vegetables in her purse and placed them on her bread plate in the restaurant. Her companions thought that was a great idea and promptly ate them all up! The next time she went out with the same friends, she managed to save some vegetables for herself.

6. **A chef's salad may be more satisfying if the meat, cheese and egg are eaten separately from the greens.** A common complaint about chef's salads is that the meat, cheese, and egg get all mixed up with the greens, leaving the person with the impression that the meal consisted only of lettuce and salad dressing. Some people derive more sensual satisfaction from separating those items from the salad greens and eating them separately. Ordering salad dressing to be brought in a separate dish will allow you to put on only as much as you want. You may prefer to bring low-calorie salad dressing with you or use lemon wedges instead.

7. **When "something sweet" is necessary to end the meal, several approaches may be helpful: ask for a three cent, chocolate covered mint to be brought to the table with the coffee; share a dessert order with another person; or save up the calories from other meal items and have a dessert or sweet after dinner drink** like a Brandy Alexander or Grasshopper. If eaten slowly a small amount of a sweet food will yield a lot of satisfaction.

8. **Share orders of high-calorie items with someone.** Many restaurants have built their reputations on the ample size of their portions. A number of people have discovered that sharing an order of a high-calorie food with someone allows each of them to have a sufficient amount without eating too much. One method for sharing is the following: one person orders the entrée, the other person orders a large salad or salad bar, and they share the orders with each other. Some people prefer to order one entrée and one dessert to share; other people like to order one large salad and one dessert.

The longer it takes to eat,
the longer you are occupied.

---

9. **If you don't want to eat all of what you ordered but don't want to waste it, ask for a "doggy bag"** to take the extras home in. One lady goes to one of Seattle's most exclusive restaurants and always asks to have a doggy bag brought to the table *with* her order. She places half the amount served in

the bag immediately and puts the bag next to her purse. "I get twice as much fun out of one meal that way," she explains, "because I can have the same thing for lunch the next day. Even if I might want to eat more in the restaurant, once that extra food is in the doggy bag I would be too embarrassed to pour it back on my plate."

10. **Pour salt, pepper or sugar over foods you want to leave uneaten on your plate if you find it next to impossible to leave food on your plate.** No matter how carefully an order is placed, there are times when there is too much food on the plate. If you don't want to eat all of it, but struggle to leave it uneaten, a generous sprinkling of salt, pepper, or sugar over the top of the food will spoil its taste and reduce its desirability.

11. **If you've eaten quickly in a short order restaurant and are still hungry, make a deal with yourself: you can order something else ONLY after waiting twenty minutes.** By that time you probably won't want anything more, but if you do, your control will be better. People frequently comment about residual hunger feelings after finishing a meal in a short order restaurant like McDonald's. Restaurants of this type offer abundant food cues. If the meal has been eaten quickly you may remain responsive to those cues for several more minutes. Many people approach this problem by promising themselves that if they are still hungry fifteen or twenty minutes after leaving the restaurant they can stop somewhere else for something to eat. This strategy makes it easier to leave the restaurant because of the assurance of more food later; and when the time period has passed, the desire for food may have completely disappeared.

Alcohol is both an appetite stimulant and a control depressant.

12. **Use alcoholic beverages sparingly before the meal.** Alcohol is both an appetite stimulant and a control depressant. A number of people have reported significantly better control when little or no alcohol was consumed in advance of the meal. When eating control is important, the drinking is best done at the end of the meal. There are several ways to handle the cocktail hour: 1) order a non-alcoholic beverage, 2) order a mixed drink but ask to have the liquor brought in a separate glass so it can be used in smaller amounts, or 3) order a drink that doesn't taste good, thereby reducing the urge to drink it.

Explanation of Homework

Assignment for this week: eat at least one meal in a restaurant using a planned strategy, continue practicing techniques from previous lessons, and record your progress and food intake daily.

Weekly Progress Record

The instructions for how to use the Weekly Progress Record are on pages 257-260.

Daily Food Record

The instructions for how to use the Daily Food Record are on pages 261-263.

Weight Record

The instructions for how to use the Weight Record are on pages 21-22.

The selection of which techniques to try when planning your resturant strategy should be based upon what you know about yourself in social eating situations, what sounds appealing and useful, and what seems most appropriate according to where and with whom the meal will be eaten. Write out a strategy card and take it with you. Have a good time!

Extra recording forms for this chapter may be found starting on page 273.

Sample Strategy Card:

Dinner at Main Street Cafe

1. Call restaurant in afternoon and find out what foods are available.
2. Eat a small amount of cottage cheese before leaving the house.
3. Order 1 glass of wine during cocktail hour.
4. Bring celery & carrot sticks to eat instead of bread.
5. Ask someone to place order for me.
6. Instead of dessert eat one mint with coffee.
7. Pour salt on leftovers I don't want to eat.

WEEKLY PROGRESS RECORD

BASIC SKILLS:	SUN	MON	TUES	WED	THURS	FRI	SAT	*
Read Progress Record in morning								
Record food intake								
Stay within calorie/ exchange total								
SPECIFIC TECHNIQUES/EXERCISES:								
Daily Totals								

*This column is for the weekly totals for each specific technique or exercise.

DAILY FOOD RECORD

Time of Day	Calories/Exchanges	Amount	Food Item/ Beverage

Total Calories for day ______

Date ______

Total Exchanges for day:

(1) Milk ______
(2) Vegetable ______
(3) Fruit ______
(4) Bread ______
(5) Meat ______
(6) Fat ______

Copyright © Northwest Learning Associates, Inc., 1978. All rights reserved.

DAILY FOOD RECORD

Food Item/ Beverage	Amount	Calories/Exchanges	Time of Day

Total Calories for day ________

Date ________________

Total Exchanges for day:

(1) Milk ______
(2) Vegetable ______
(3) Fruit ______
(4) Bread ______
(5) Meat ______
(6) Fat ______

DAILY FOOD RECORD

Food Item/ Beverage	Amount	Calories/Exchanges	Time of Day

Total Calories for day ________

Date ________________

Total Exchanges for day:

(1) Milk ______
(2) Vegetable ______
(3) Fruit ______
(4) Bread ______
(5) Meat ______
(6) Fat ______

Copyright © Northwest Learning Associates, Inc., 1978. All rights reserved.

Chapter 12 - INSTRUCTOR NOTES

Suggested Techniques:

1. Techniques for Buffets and Cafeterias listed on pages 183 through 185.
2. Techniques for Entertaining at Home listed on pages 185 and 186.
3. Techniques for Dinner Parties at Other People's Homes listed on page 186.

Homework Assignments:

Read the instructions on page 186.

Cautions and Reminders:

1. Urge your students to read (or review) the lessons on Social Eating: Restaurants; Daily Food Management, and Eating Slowly for suggestions which are applicable to this lesson.
2. A little advance thought and careful preplanning make a significant contribution to control in all social eating situations. Caution your students to remember that they cannot maintain good control in a difficult eating situation if they wait until they have trouble before making a plan. They must anticipate their problems and decide upon some specific control strategies, **before** they get into trouble. Then, if an unanticipated problem arises, they won't be overwhelmed. They will be much better prepared to handle it effectively.
3. Remind your students to think of these strategies as experiments. If an experiment (strategy) fails and the person eats too much, **no extra calories should be taken out of the next day's calorie level.** Just chalk the experience up to the need for a new strategy, write one out, and then forget about it. It's hard enough to have overeaten without also having to face the thought of eating almost nothing the next day! To try to make up for the extra calories consumed would only perpetuate the "all or nothing" approach many people are used to and may result in a food binge lasting one or more days. Many people are amazed to discover that they can have a night, or even a day, of higher calorie consumption and still maintain or lose a little weight. It's not the one day or night out of control that is so critical; it is the period of several days and/or nights out of control that do the real damage. So, if a person can face the day following a temporary loss of control with a full calorie allotment, the prospect of returning to control seems much brighter.

12

Target: Preplanning.

Objectives:

1. Develop strategies for control of food intake in social eating situations.
2. Develop effective food selection strategies based upon anticipated needs, problems and preferences.
3. Apply strategies for control during times of preparation and clean-up when entertaining at home.
4. Reduce or maintain calorie level; establish or maintain dietary plan.

Motto:

Eat the best and skip the rest.

Social Eating: Buffets, Cafeterias, Entertaining at Home

There are some common elements in all social eating situations, so if you haven't read the lesson "Social Eating: Restaurants," please study it carefully. Many of the suggestions in that lesson apply equally well to this lesson.

Buffets and Cafeterias

When considering the special challenges of buffets and cafeterias, make certain not to confuse quantity with quality. Many cafeterias attract people because of their "all-you-can-eat" policy. Home-style pot luck dinners and buffet tables often contain a tempting assortment of the cook's finest dishes, making it easy to say to yourself, "It all looks so good that I think I'll have a little of everything." If that results in a large amount of food on the plate, and if you are accustomed to eating everything on your plate, it becomes very easy to overeat.

The selection of what to eat can be very difficult when a whole array of attractive foods is spread out on a large table. Many foods are chosen because they look particularly good; others are taken because they "should" be eaten for one reason or another. The desire to sample different items may lead to extra food on the plate. If your desire is for quality rather than quantity, remember the motto from the previous lesson and try to eat only the *best* of what is offered. The following suggestions are intended to help you regulate the amount and selection of foods according to this philosophy.

> *"It all looks so good that I think that I'll have a little of everything."*

1. **Eat a plate of salad first to take the edge off of your hunger.** Then go back through the line for the three,

four or five food items that look the best to you. Eating a full plate of green salad first, before taking servings of other food items, increases control for three reasons: 1) the salad reduces the initial, strong hunger feelings, 2) going through the line allows you to see all of what is available, and 3) the time spent eating the salad can be used to make final decisions about the specific foods to take. Select the three, four or five food items that are the most desirable. "Since I can eat anything I want on that table anyway," declared one man, "I might as well have what I really want."

2. **Use a serving spoon for servings; use only half of a teaspoon for a taste.** A common problem with cafeterias and buffet tables is the desire to taste a number of different foods in addition to the planned food items. When the tastes are dished up with serving spoons, more food appears on the plate than had been anticipated. If you are then triggered to eat everything on the plate, the final result is overconsumption. If the tastes were measured in half-teaspoon amounts you would have the fun of tasting without the cost of overeating. Some people take a teaspoon along when they get the salad and put several taste-size servings of different foods on the salad plate to sample before deciding upon the best items to serve themselves for the entree.

3. **Use a salad plate instead of a dinner plate.** The use of a smaller plate, salad size rather than dinner size, can be helpful in limiting the amount of food taken as well as allowing you to feel as though you have a full plate of food. If only large plates are available, filling up half of it with green salad effectively reduces the amount of space available for higher calorie foods.

If the tastes were measured in half-teaspoon amounts you would have the fun of tasting without the cost of overeating.

4. **If limiting yourself is difficult, ask someone to get your food and you get theirs.** It will be easier for you to control what goes on someone else's plate rather than on your own! If you take time to see what foods are available and decide upon the specific choices first, another person will have no problem following the plan.

5. **After eating, clear away the dishes before having coffee** so you won't nibble on the leftovers on your plate. Once you have eaten the desired amount of food, it is important that the plate be removed as quickly as possible to prevent inadvertent nibbling on the leftovers while talking. One helpful idea is to get a cup of coffee or tea at the time the plate is cleared away rather than bringing it to the table earlier. If you like a hot drink at the end of the meal, you will

make the effort to get it, and leaving the table serves as a reminder to remove the plate.

6. **For added awareness, wear an outfit with a waistband that is not too roomy.** When you feel the need to loosen a belt or undo a button, it will remind you that you've eaten enough. A man once commented in class, "I can always tell I've had enough to eat when I have to move my belt out a notch." Contrast that with the comfort of an outfit that is sufficiently loose around the waist to cause no constriction when eating. If the intent is to eat freely, a roomy outfit is preferable; if the object is to control how much is eaten, a tighter fitting waistband acts as a reminder to stop eating.

"I can always tell I've had enough to eat when I have to move my belt out a notch."

Entertaining at Home

Entertaining at home has its own set of problems, particularly at preparation and cleanup times. As in all situations, a little pre-planning makes a big difference in eating control.

1. **There are many excellent cookbooks on the market with reduced calorie recipes.** Many of them list the calorie totals and include menus in addition to the recipes. The trick to teaching yourself to use new recipes is to wrap up all of the old, high-calorie cookbooks and recipe cards and store them in the attic or basement. When the old, familiar resources aren't readily available you will be more receptive to experimenting with the new ones.

2. **Single serving foods like chicken breasts allow you to prepare a specific amount per person** without having a lot of extra food. If your cooking philosophy is "It's better to have too much than too little," and leftovers are a problem, it can be helpful to prepare single serving food items like chicken breasts or meat and vegetables on a skewer instead of multiple serving food items like casseroles, spaghetti, and lasagna. In this way the amount prepared can be adjusted to the number of people available to eat it.

3. **Keep appetizers more than one arm's distance away.** If you can reach it easily, you are likely to eat more than you realize.

4. **Take a serving of only one or two items each time you pass the serving platters around.** It will help you pace yourself and allow you to savor each food separately. This is a useful tactic to employ when eating in someone else's home too.

5. **Immediately place all mixing bowls and utensils in a sink filled with soapy water before licking them clean.** The only thing to remember is to dunk the bowl into the sink before questioning whether or or not to do it! The longer the period of temptation, the more opportunity there is to give in. Many

people find that having something else in their mouths reduces the snacking while cooking habit. Sugar free hard candy, sour lemon drops, and gum are all helpful, as are having a low-calorie beverage to drink, some cut vegetables to eat and someone with whom to talk.

6. The greatest challenge to control for many people comes after the meal is finished, when anxiety or tension diminish, and the kitchen is empty except for the dirty dishes and the bits of food left over. You may find it very helpful to ask someone else in the house to put the food items away, leaving you free to vacuum or straighten up another room.

Dinner Parties at Other People's Homes

Many of the ideas presented in this lesson and in the preceding lesson apply also to dinners in other people's homes.

1. **Eat something before you leave home.** Don't arrive on an empty stomach!
2. **Keep alcohol consumption low until after dinner** if liquor weakens your food control!
3. **Keep all appetizers more than one arm's distance away.**
4. **Eat your green salad first.**
5. **Take a helping of only one or two items each time the serving bowls are passed.**
6. **Share your serving of a particularly high-calorie dessert with someone.**
7. **Wear an outfit with a waistband that is not too roomy.**
8. If a hostess is particularly insistent about having you take more of something you don't want, smile at her, tell her that her food was "soooo" delicious that you're really stuffed and that **perhaps you'll have a bit more later on.** Hopefully, you'll both forget about it!

If a hostess is particularly insistent, tell her that her food was "soooo" delicious that you're really stuffed, and that perhaps you'll have a bit more later on.

Strategies for eating slowly are very useful in all social eating situations. The slower you eat, the longer it lasts, and the longer it lasts, the less you'll need to eat! See the chapter entitled "Eating Slowly: Reducing Efficiency" for ideas to reduce eating speed.

Explanation of Homework

Assignment for this week: plan a specific strategy for an upcoming buffet or dinner party at home, or go to a cafeteria for dinner using a strategy; continue practicing techniques from previous lessons; and record your progress and food intake daily.

Weekly Progress Record

The instructions for how to use the Weekly Progress Record are on page 257-260.

Daily Food Record

The instructions for how to use the Daily Food Record are on pages 261-263.

Weight Record

The instructions for how to use the Weight Record are on pages 21-22.

Use ideas from previous lessons as well as this week's lesson in planning a strategy for control. Write your plan on an index card or piece of paper and take it with you. See the sample below. Enjoy yourself and good luck!

Extra recording forms for this chapter may be found starting on page 273.

Sample Strategy Card:

Dinner at Cafeteria

1. Eat a small amount of raw vegetables before leaving the house.
2. Look at all the food first and select the five best items.
3. Put the salad on the dinner plate instead of using a salad bowl.
4. Use half a teaspoon for tastes.
5. Don't take coffee to the table with the entrée; get it after I finish eating and remove my plate from the table on my way to coffee pot.

WEEKLY PROGRESS RECORD

BASIC SKILLS:	SUN	MON	TUES	WED	THURS	FRI	SAT	*
Read Progress Record in morning								
Record food intake								
Stay within calorie/ exchange total								
SPECIFIC TECHNIQUES/EXERCISES:								
Daily Totals								

*This column is for the weekly totals for each specific technique or exercise.

DAILY FOOD RECORD

Food Item/ Beverage	Amount	Calories/Exchanges	Time of Day

Total Calories for day ______

Date ______

Total Exchanges for day:
(1) Milk ______
(2) Vegetable ______
(3) Fruit ______
(4) Bread ______
(5) Meat ______
(6) Fat ______

DAILY FOOD RECORD

Food Item/ Beverage	Amount	Calories/Exchanges	Time of Day

Total Calories for day ________

Date ____________________

Total Exchanges for day:

(1) Milk ______
(2) Vegetable ______
(3) Fruit ______
(4) Bread ______
(5) Meat ______
(6) Fat ______

DAILY FOOD RECORD

Food Item/ Beverage	Amount	Calories/Exchanges	Time of Day

Copyright © Northwest Learning Associates, Inc., 1978. All rights reserved.

Total Calories for day ________

Date ____________________

Total Exchanges for day:

(1) Milk ______
(2) Vegetable ______
(3) Fruit ______
(4) Bread ______
(5) Meat ______
(6) Fat ______

Chapter 13 - INSTRUCTOR NOTES

Suggested Techniques:

1. Vacation techniques highlighted on page 194.
   a. Set time aside to plan your vacation eating strategies.
   b. Before writing the strategies (plans), think carefully about the points listed on page 194.
   c. Review all of the lessons in your book for pertinent ideas.
   d. Write the strategies out in detail.
   e. Purchase and/or pack any items necessary to your control plans.
   f. Record food intake daily.
2. Holiday techniques highlighted on page 195.
   a. Follow the procedure outlined above.
   b. When planning, take some additional factors into account:
      1. Look at the customary way the holiday is celebrated.
      2. Look at your old patterns.
      3. Identify your specific food-related desires for the holiday.
   c. Record your intake daily.
3. Suggestions for Holiday Weight Control (Christmas Season) listed on pages 196 and 197.
   a. Home Environment
   b. Holiday Baking
   c. Keeping Food Around for Guests
   d. Work Environment
   e. Keeping Track of Yourself
   f. Holiday Dinners and Parties
4. Food Holiday techniques listed on page 199.
   a. This procedure should NOT be used by people who have medical complications or who must follow a carefully regulated dietary plan!
   b. Select a date for the holiday.
   c. Prepare all snacks and meals for one to two days following the food holiday.
   d. Begin the holiday with, or after, dinner and end it at bedtime.
   e. Select items from your holiday food list and begin a new list when the holiday is over.
   f. Resume normal plan after completion of holiday plan.

Homework Assignments:

Read the instructions on page 199.

Cautions and Reminders:

1. Remind your students to record their food intake during the entire vacation or holiday. They may omit the calorie count, if that would prevent them from recording. But they must continue to list whatever they eat and drink in order to be aware of how much they are having and to pace their consumption rates. Recording is a control factor for most people. It is especially necessary when people are not following their usual routines.
2. The critical factor in controlling food intake during holidays and vacations is planning in advance. Tension, stress, social pressures, and changes in routine all contribute to changes in eating response. Without a predetermined plan for control all of the old automatic vacation and holiday eating patterns will take over.
3. Your students may find the Reference Outline of Techniques and Exercises, located on pages 267-270 of their book, helpful when reviewing the lessons and making their plans.

13

Target: Preplanning.

Objectives:

1. Anticipate needs and problems and plan appropriate control strategies in advance.
2. Use pertinent techniques from other lessons to develop control strategies.
3. Reduce or maintain calorie level; establish or maintain dietary plan.

Motto:

Plan ahead!

Vacations and Holidays

Have you noticed a difference in your eating control between weekdays and weekend days, or between special days and routine days? Students in my classes talk about this and cite many examples of controlling elements within the pattern and structure of their regular days which guide them toward greater control of their food intake. One example is the limited availability of food and of opportunities to eat during a work day as contrasted to a non-work-day. Another is the difference in the content of specific meals from weekdays to weekend days when larger breakfasts or more elaborate lunches or dinners may be planned. Many women who are home during the day talk of differences in eating patterns because of changes in the routines of other family members. This is especially noticeable when the children are out of school and at home wanting to eat frequently throughout the day. Many working people find that being at home with a more relaxed schedule of activities, perhaps less well defined eating times for meals, and a wider range of food choices makes maintaining control on weekends much more difficult. For some people the real lack of planned activity or planned contact with other people on weekends leads to greater food consumption.

Vacations and holidays provide a welcome break from our usual routines, and most of us look forward to the change of pace, activities, surroundings or people that are associated with them. Vacations and holidays are also a time of changed eating structure and each has its own set of obstacles to controlled food consumption. Each holiday has its own particular food cues. Look at Halloween, Thanksgiving, Christmas and July Fourth as examples. Vacations, too, frequently involve significant changes in eating structure. For both, the holiday atmosphere adds to the fun and frequently relaxes the determination to regulate food intake. Neither vacations nor holidays should represent an "either-or" choice between deprivation or inevitable weight gain. All that is necessary to comfortably handle special days is to plan control strategies in advance. Without a predetermined, written plan, you may fall into your old automatic holiday routine because there are no specific alternatives. If you do plan ahead, however, you will know how to handle specific situations, what foods to request, and so on.

Vacations

At least once every week I receive a panicky call or visit from someone saying, "I'm going on a trip. WHAT'LL I DO?!" The very first thing to do is to set a block of good thinking time aside to plan for the vacation. Then, before writing the plan, think carefully about each of the points listed below:

1) where you are going;
2) where and with whom you will stay;
3) how long and by what means you will travel;
4) what activities you think you'll be doing;
5) what the patterns are of the people you'll be traveling or staying with;
6) what your anticipated needs are; and
7) what problems you think you will have in controlling your food intake.

The next step is to review all of the lessons in your book for ideas to use, and the final step is to write the plan based upon the information you have gathered. Let's look at some specific ideas.

Staying in someone's home offers a special type of challenge. People express their concern about not wanting to impose upon the host family's hospitality by making special food requests. The need for some type of structure is necessary in order to achieve a sense of control without being inconsiderate of the host or hostess.

Guests can mentally assign designated eating places by watching where the family gathers to eat and making plans not to eat in other places, like the family room or living room. Most people are not offended if a guest brings along some specific items like diet soda, extra fruit, or sugar-free gum. Guests can still put the fork down between bites, cut food as it is needed, make each serving one-half of the total planned amount, and so on. Several students have taken needlework, crossword puzzles or other small projects to do while sitting around and talking for long periods of time. Some of the fly fishermen in my classes take along their fly-tying materials, so they can tie flies while they talk. One man who makes jewelry took his tools and supplies with him on a three day visit to his parents' home and completed several pieces while sitting around and talking. "I made something for my mother and sister, which made them happy; and I didn't snack all day, which made me happy." Another student commented, "By keeping my hands busy, I didn't get so restless, and besides I couldn't watch what everyone else was eating. I chewed gum, drank iced tea and crocheted two sweaters for my granddaughter." Alternate activities and food substitution ideas need to be planned so that the necessary items and foods can be purchased and packed along with the clothes.

Plans for car or airplane travel are also most successfully made in advance. For automobile or bus travel, it is helpful to store all food items in the trunk, keeping only low-calorie beverages, gum, or low-calorie hard candy available for immediate consumption. If all eating occurs at roadside picnic areas or restaurants, the association between driving and eating will diminish. Sometimes alternate activities such as driving, reading aloud or talking to the driver, and doing crossword puzzles or handwork can effectively replace eating as an activity. For airplane travel, low-calorie meals can be ordered on most major airlines when the flight reservations are made. The collective experience of many people in my classes is that the low-calorie meals on planes are enjoyable and of good quality.

For camping and hiking trips low-calorie foods can be used easily. It is necessary to decide upon the specific food items early enough to shop and pack them. When staying in hotels and motels, you may prefer not to bring food items into your room. If you enjoy frequent cups of tea or coffee, however, you might find that taking a small electric pot for boiling water, plus supplies of coffee, or tea will allow you to have hot drinks without going to coffee shops or snack bars where the temptation to have a doughnut, a piece of cake, or some ice cream is hard to resist.

If you are spending your vacation at home, first consider what you will be doing; who, if anyone, will be staying at your home; what the patterns are of the people you will be spending time with; and what your anticipated needs and problems are. Then plan accordingly.

Holidays

Holiday planning involves the same general procedure described earlier. However, it is also necessary to look at the ritualized way each holiday is celebrated. Thanksgiving is an excellent example with turkey, dressing, mashed potatoes and gravy, sweet potatoes, cranberry sauce, and pumpkin and mince pies. Whatever particular foods are part of your custom, the overall theme of Thanksgiving is food, and the main reason for people to get together is to eat.

Look at your old patterns and the specific desires you have for that holiday and then plan accordingly. If your usual Thanksgiving pattern is to have a big meal on Thursday and then have a free-for-all with the leftovers all day Friday, plan a strategy which either eliminates the leftovers, or allows you to eat them with control. One of my students plans a controlled Thanksgiving meal on Thursday, choosing the four best items and taking a serving of only one food at a time. She prefers to eat leftovers the next day, so she plans for it by packaging up small amounts of turkey and dressing on Thursday night. She sets the specific times of the day when she may eat each package of food. Her comment after the first experience with this plan was, "I had more fun than I ever had before. I had lots of leftovers, but I didn't overdo it because I ate only a small amount each time. The leftovers lasted longer too!"

The holiday which usually causes the most trouble for people wishing to control their food intake is Christmas. Actually, Christmas Day is only part of the problem. Beginning with Thanksgiving and ending after New Year's Day, the winter holiday season is the time of year when the normal environment of homes and stores changes to include a tempting variety of special holiday foods. People see them, buy and receive them as gifts, prepare them as part of their holiday routine, and stockpile them at home to have for guests to enjoy. That is also the time of year when people over-extend themselves, getting tired, hassled, and frazzled. A just-this-once atmosphere prevails. Even people who normally do not have trouble keeping their weight in control often overeat and gain a few pounds. Because the Christmas season provides such a challenge to food habit control, a variety of suggestions from my Holiday Weight Control class are presented below.

Suggestions for Holiday Weight Control: Christmas Season

1. Home environment
   a. Keep tempting foods out of sight in an out-of-the-way place.
   b. Decorate the house without using food. Use greens, wreaths, candles and flowers. You might even paint your windows with Christmas motifs.
2. **Holiday Baking**
   a. When baking with children, make special, decorated dough ornaments instead of cookies.
   b. Bake only in amounts you need or can use up quickly. Try tarts instead of pies, half cakes instead of whole cakes, or bake your fruit breads in smaller loaf pans.
   c. If you want to bake but haven't anyone but yourself to eat the product, donate your baked items to neighborhood or church sponsored food banks, convalescent homes, workshops for the handicapped, and other places where there are people who might not have opportunities to enjoy special holiday treats.
   d. If eating the dough or the batter is the best part of baking for you, set a measured amount aside and eat it after you finish baking. You will probably eat less but enjoy it more.
   e. Rather than sneak a cookie while baking or lick the spoon on the sly, allow for a specified amount, then sit down and enjoy it at leisure. If you allow for it, you may have it; and if you can have it openly, you'll feel much better about yourself.
   f. Wear a surgical mask, chew a double stick of gum, or suck on a low-calorie hard candy to help you control the urge to taste.
3. Keeping food around for guests
   a. Keep non-problem foods on hand for unexpected guests. Don't stock up on hard-to-control items like sweets, nuts or eggnog. You can always make an emergency trip to a 24-hour food store if necessary.
   b. Have low-calorie foods and drinks on hand for yourself and others.
   c. Keep items on hand that need to be assembled before they are appealing. For example, unsweetened baker's chocolate isn't

nearly as pleasing as the chocolate fondue you can make with it.

4. Work environment
   a. Take acceptable snacks to work with you.
   b. Stay away from the holiday treats set out for everyone to eat.
   c. Keep a small electric pot or percolator at your desk for your hot drinks if going to the main coffee pot puts you in contact with tempting foods.
5. Keeping track of yourself
   a. Write down *everything* you eat —with or without the calories!
   b. Plan established times throughout the day for meals and snacks. This is especially important if your schedule is irregular, or if you are so rushed that you are not likely to eat regularly.
   c. Keep low-calorie snacks prepared and visible.
   d. Pre-packaging meals and snacks in advance for the day's use is especially helpful if you are going to be very busy or rushed.
   e. Allow yourself to have one planned treat each day, preferably late in the day or the evening. Save that one piece of candy, or cookie, or whatever, and have it later. That may help you reduce the feelings of being cheated out of all of the treats and may keep you from having a binge.

For all of the holiday parties and dinners both at home and away from home, review the lessons on social eating. Plan to indulge in two or three specific meals or parties during the holiday season, so you won't feel deprived, but go to all the rest of them **with strategy cards in your hand.**

In these and all other anticipated situations **planning is the essential ingredient for assuring success.** Lots of plans fail or cannot be used for one reason or another, but a bad or inadequate plan is better than no plan at all. Any plan can be altered or rewritten, but if there isn't any plan at all, the old automatic, out-of-control behavior patterns take over.

Food Holidays

No discussion of holidays would be complete without mentioning my very favorite holidays of all: food holidays. To understand what they are, let's look at a common source of concern to many people: food binges. A food binge is defined as a period of uncontrolled eating. Some people have an established binge cycle. Once it begins the cycle follows a regular pattern. One individual may be able to predict the day the binge will begin while another may be able to predict the number of days the binge will last. Anyone who has ever taken a "mental health" day off from work, skipped a class, anxiously awaited the arrival of a holiday or vacation, or who has hired a last-minute babysitter to escape from the kids for a few hours understands the human need for breaks from routine. People need periodic vacations from food routines too. When these vacations are called food holidays, and are planned for and looked forward to, there is no reason to have either failure or guilt feelings. Allowing yourself these holidays and planning for them may prevent real out-of-control binges lasting much longer.

The procedure described in this lesson for food holidays is designed for people who have no medical complications such as heart disease, hypertension, diabetes or diagnosed hypoglycemia. If you do have medical complications, you must first consult with your physician or dietitian for specific guidelines for building your own food holiday plan.

Part of the fun of going on a holiday is the advance preparation: choosing a date, making plans for travel and accommodations, and packing the things you'll need to enjoy the trip. The fun of planning is part of a food holiday as well. In fact, the basis for the success of food holidays is the advance planning and preparation.

Part of the fun of going on a holiday is the advance preparation.

First, select a date for your food holiday. Food holidays usually begin with, or immediately after, dinner and last until you go to bed that night. Food holidays may be planned around specific events. Some of my students plan to have a food holiday on Thanksgiving, Christmas or other traditional holidays. Others plan their food holidays around specific dinner parties or social events, but you can select the ones which are most important to you. If your holiday meal is earlier in the day than your normal dinner, plan to end your holiday one to two hours after the meal. Pre-package all of your food for the rest of the day, as well as for the next one or two days as described below, and eat only what you have planned once the holiday is over.

Next, plan for the days AFTER the holiday. This means that all meals and snacks for one or two days after the holiday must be planned and prepared in advance. If you think you are likely to be very hungry on the day after a holiday, your plan should include something to eat that is high in bulk and low in calories as often as every 2½ hours or so. If you think you won't feel like eating until noon on the day after a holiday, the first meal should be planned for that time. When the foods are packaged and labeled for each snack or meal, a sequential list should be made which specifies when each item is to be eaten. On the day after the holiday consult your list. If the list begins with that day's breakfast packaged in a blue container labeled "Monday breakfast," that is what you will eat. If a mid-morning snack was planned, find the bag or container labeled "10:00 a.m. snack, Monday" and eat what is in it.

This procedure is designed to prevent the need for independent decisions about food. The object is to break any existing pattern of a night off followed by a thought process like, "I overate so much last night that there's no point in trying to control myself today," or a statement like, "One night out of control means two weeks out of control for me." There is no need to question whether or not control can or will be established. By eating the pre-packaged foods, control is re-established. It is usually much easier to eat what is already packaged than to hunt around for something else and then prepare it. The ease and convenience help people slide back into routine. By the third day most people have returned to their regular routine with positive feeling and a strong sense of "I can do it!"

Once the date for the holiday has been

set and the work completed for the days after the holiday, the next question to answer is, "What will I eat on my holiday?" Many of my students keep a list of all the high-calorie items they have chosen not to eat for one reason or another. This list then becomes the holiday menu. As one woman said, "Whenever I don't eat some goodie, I feel cheated unless I know that I can eat it some time in the future. If I write it down on a list and tell myself I can eat it on my food holiday, I don't have any trouble giving it up on a regular control day."

Not all of my students take a food holiday. A lot of them just keep their lists of holiday foods, adding new items as they go along, and tell themselves that when they really need to eat those foods, they'll plan a holiday. For these students the permission to have those foods is more important than it is to actually eat them.

In short, the food holiday plan works as follows:

1. Select a date.
2. Prepare all snacks and meals for one or two days following the food holiday.
3. Begin the holiday with, or following dinner, or time your holiday to coincide with a special event and end it at bedtime.
4. Select items from the holiday food list and begin a new list when the holiday is over.
5. Resume your regular plan after completion of the holiday plan.
6. Pat yourself on the back for reestablishing control!

It is not essential that you record calories or exchanges during the holiday itself. Many of my students do keep track of what they eat and look up the calories several days later. For a lot of them, the knowledge that they consumed fewer calories than they thought was a marvelous morale booster! For the days following the holiday, plan your foods with calorie information in mind. The first day can be 200 to 300 calories higher than your usual level. The second day's calorie total can be 100 calories higher than usual, if necessary. You should resume your usual calorie level by the third day. While it is true that your calorie intake goes up during this time, compare the totals with those of previous binges.

The purpose of the food holiday is to reduce the need for a binge and to ultimately replace out-of-control binges with controlled food holidays. The idea of a food holiday may scare you a bit right now, and you may prefer not to have one. In time, though, you may want to work with the food holiday concept. As you do, your anxiety will decrease as you gain confidence in your ability to successfully restart control the very next day.
To repeat my earlier warning, if you have diabetes, hypoglycemia or other medical problems which would be adversely affected by food holidays, do not use this strategy. Consult with your physician or dietitian for guidance on possibilities for safe alterations of your usual food routine.

Explanation of Homework

Assignment for this week: prepare a strategy card for your next holiday or vacation, continue practicing techniques from previous lessons, and record your progress and food intake daily.

Weekly Progress Record

The instructions for how to use the Weekly Progress Record are on pages 257-260.

Daily Food Record

The instructions for how to use the Daily Food Record are on pages 261-263.

Weight Record

The instructions for how to use the Weight Record are on pages 21-22.

Look at the sample strategy cards below. Review all of the previous lessons for ideas before preparing your own strategy cards. One fun idea is to purchase a recipe box and divide it into three sections: one for plans that worked, one for plans that failed and need revision, and one for new plans to try. Use recipe or index cards for recording your strategy plans. You may want to add sections labeled for each holiday, for vacations at home, and for vacations away from home. Add sections to include your eating-out strategy cards too. You probably take time to read recipes, so why not take time to read ideas? This is a handy way to keep track of what you've been doing and are planning to do. If all of your good ideas are in one place, you'll have a much easier time finding them when you need them. Good luck!

Extra recording forms for this chapter may be found starting on page 273.

Sample Strategy Cards:

Plan for the Week Before Christmas

1. Keep tempting foods OUT OF SIGHT!
2. Bake only ornaments for the tree (no cookies).
3. Keep low-calorie foods on hand for unexpected guests and make emergency trips to the store if necessary.
4. Do not buy gifts of food for others - avoid unnecessary temptation.
5. Set money aside to buy something nice for myself after Christmas as a reward for good food control.
6. Record food intake daily.
7. When eating out, take a strategy card with me and follow it!

Weekend Trip to Vancouver

1. Take something to read in the car; do not eat in the car.
2. Take a small electric pot, tea, coffee and instant soup for use in the motel room.
3. Eat only two meals a day in restaurants: mid-morning lunch and dinner.
4. Share orders of high calorie foods whenever possible.
5. Keep a large supply of sugar-free gum and sour lemon drops on hand for hunger pangs.

WEEKLY PROGRESS RECORD

BASIC SKILLS:	SUN	MON	TUES	WED	THURS	FRI	SAT	*
Read Progress Record in morning								
Record food intake								
Stay within calorie/ exchange total								
SPECIFIC TECHNIQUES/EXERCISES:								
Daily Totals								

*This column is for the weekly totals for each specific technique or exercise.

DAILY FOOD RECORD

Food Item/ Beverage	Amount	Calories/Exchanges	Time of Day

Total Calories for day ______

Date ______

Total Exchanges for day:

(1) Milk ______
(2) Vegetable ______
(3) Fruit ______
(4) Bread ______
(5) Meat ______
(6) Fat ______

DAILY FOOD RECORD

Food Item/ Beverage	Amount	Calories/Exchanges	Time of Day

Total Calories for day ________

Total Exchanges for day:
(1) Milk ______
(2) Vegetable ______
(3) Fruit ______
(4) Bread ______
(5) Meat ______
(6) Fat ______

Date ________________

DAILY FOOD RECORD

Food Item/ Beverage	Amount	Calories/Exchanges	Time of Day

Total Calories for day ________

Total Exchanges for day:
(1) Milk ______
(2) Vegetable ______
(3) Fruit ______
(4) Bread ______
(5) Meat ______
(6) Fat ______

Date ________________

Chapter 14 - INSTRUCTOR NOTES

Suggested Techniques:

1. Restart Skills
   - **a.** Make a specific Restart Plan by listing, from lowest to highest, the easiest techniques.
   - **b.** On the first day following loss of control do only what is listed on the bottom one or two levels of the Restart Plan.
   - **c.** On successive days move comfortably upward on the Restart Plan until the regular plan can be resumed.
2. Building Flexibility
   - **a.** Use Restart Plan as a Stress Plan also.
   - **b.** When you are under stress, begin at that level of the Restart/Stress Plan which is appropriate.
   - **c.** Move upward or downward on the Restart/Stress Plan until the stress is reduced and full control can be resumed.
3. Establishing and Maintaining New Habits
   - **a.** Review each lesson in your book, taking a week or two to experiment thoroughly with each one.
   - **b.** Select the specific techniques which you wish to build into habits. Star them on the Reference Outline. Also, pencil in your own Restart/Stress Plan.
   - **c.** Select a different section on the Outline every one to two weeks and work on the starred techniques. Record them on a Weekly Progress Record.
   - **d.** Go back through each relevant section of the Outline again and again, taking some sections on rotation and others according to need. You will need to practice those techniques for weeks and/or months in order to establish them as habits.
4. Techniques for recording food intake highlighted on page 206.
   - **a.** Continue to record food intake until your desired weight is reached and maintained for at least one month. Then try letting up for a day or two at a time.
   - **b.** Whenever you begin regaining weight, record your food intake faithfully until you figure out what the problems are and reestablish control.
5. Techniques for keeping track of weight highlighted on page 207.
   - **a.** Weigh only once a week.
   - **b.** Use weight-loss increments of five to ten pounds at a time until you approach your desired weight.
   - **c.** Allow for a two- to three-pound fluctuation in stabilized weight.
6. Maintaining control techniques listed on pages 207 and 208.

Cautions and Reminders:

1. Instruct your students to follow the same homework procedures they have used throughout the course, rotating through the lessons as explained previously. Additional record forms and Outlines can be ordered from the publisher. Their use is recommended to help people maintain the routines they have developed in the course.
2. Let your students know how they can contact you for help at future times.
3. Remind your students to keep their books, inventories, recording forms and reminder notes visible. The tendency, when a course is over, is to put the books and other materials away and then begin the process of forgetting what has been learned. Old habits are strong and not easily replaced. **Continued practice is essential to the establishment and maintenance of new habits.** For your students the real job is just beginning. They have experimented throughout the course; now they have to begin building effective new habits.
4. Remind your students to continue to talk about their projects and progress with the people with whom they have been sharing information about the course. If they are kept aware of their friend's continued efforts and progress, it will be easier for them to be supportive and reinforcing.
5. Stress the importance of improved, rather than perfect, performance. Perfection is an unrealistic goal. Remind them that mistakes, bad plans, or basic loss of control will happen from time to time. These should be expected and not mistaken as signs of personal failure.
6. Instruct them to review what happened, figure out specifically what went awry, and then write a new plan or follow a Restart Plan.
7. If the Restart/Stress Plan isn't effective, revise it or make a new one. There is nothing magical about the techniques. The real value is in the process of awareness, definition of problems, development of specific control strategies, experimentation with the strategies (and techniques), evaluation of the experiments, modification or revision of the strategies, and the continued application and practice of those strategies and techniques to build new habits. When subsequent revisions are necessary due to changes in circumstances, needs, etc., the same process is used. The result of all of that is ongoing effective Food Habit Management.

14 Last Lesson

Target: Preplanning.

Objectives:

1. Develop specific plan for restarting control following temporary losses of control.
2. Develop flexibility in control routine to allow for periods of stress, unusually high activity, depression, illness or fatigue.
3. Develop specific plan(s) for food holidays.
4. Build over-all plan for establishing and maintaining new habits.
5. Reduce or maintain calorie level; maintain dietary plan.

Motto:

The more you practice, the more skilled you will become.

Maintaining Control

Congratulations! You have reached the final lesson of this book, which marks the end of the formal instruction phase of your behavior change program. What lies ahead of you now is perhaps your most challenging task: to keep your progress and support system going until the goals you have set are realized.

Most of my students, at this point in time, are feeling overwhelmed by the task of trying to blend all that they have learned into a single, comprehensive plan of action. Many of them worry that the changes they have made are temporary. Others feel that the course has gone by too quickly and that they have too little experience with the techniques to be able to do anything with them.

Developing a Basic Routine

The first task in bridging the distance between formal instruction and independent programming is to review the material you have previously studied. Review each lesson in your book, taking a week or two to experiment more throughly with each one. This is especially important if you feel that the course progressed rapidly and that you were not able to try as many ideas as you would have liked.

When you have decided which techniques you want to concentrate on, continued practice will be required to establish them as habits. People often make the assumption that when new habits have been established, they will just maintain themselves automatically.

You do best
what you practice most.

Remember that those old habits you've been working so hard to get rid of have been established too and have been practiced much longer than your new habits. They are stronger and tougher than your fragile new habits, and in the beginning, the old habits will be more automatic than the new ones. You do best what you practice most, so the task will be to give all, or at least most, of your practice time to your new habits.

To ensure that you practice your new habits more than the old ones, periodic recording of each habit is essential. It will force you to concentrate on the habit and will keep your overall awareness of what you're doing much sharper. It is not necessary to concentrate on every habit each week. That is too formidable a task! In addition, the tendencies to overload yourself and become bored by the same routine must be accounted for in your maintenance program.

Lots and lots of practice will be required to build techniques into habits.

Consult the Reference Outline of Techniques and Exercises. Review each section of the Outline and make any changes you wish in the techniques listed for each section. Add some ideas of your own, and perhaps, put a star alongside those techniques and exercises you intend to develop into habits. Also, write your Control Meals and Restart/Stress Plan in the spaces provided on the Outline.

Vary your routine by selecting a different section of the Outline every one to two weeks. You may wish to select some sections according to your needs, for example using the Vacations and Holidays section for the time you are on vacation. The Social Eating sections can be referred to when planning ahead for a special meal with friends or relatives. Other sections, like the ones concerning control of home, work, and mealtime environments, or the ones on snack control can be taken in rotation with a week or two spent on each one. This procedure will keep you from becoming bored by doing the same things all the time and will allow you to maintain your skill with many habits. You may wish to remove or change some suggestions in the Outline to meet your own particular needs.

When you have selected the section of the Outline you want to focus on for the week, enter the techniques listed in that section on a Weekly Progress Record and use it in the same way you've been using it throughout the course. Continue recording your progress in this manner for as long as you feel it is necessary or helpful to do so. Additional ideas for using the Outline are in the Instructional Supplement Section of your book.

Recording Food Intake

I always advise people to record their food intake daily. It is essential that you stay aware of what, how much and when you are eating. People tend to increase their food intake when they do not record. You should record what is eaten and the calorie or exchange values until you have reached goal weight and for at least a month after goal weight has been maintained. Then you can try letting up for a day or two at a time. If you can only write down the foods and not the calories or exchanges, that will still be important in maintaining awareness. Whenever you experience weight regain, record your food intake faithfully until you figure out what the problems are and reestablish control.

Keeping Track of Weight

Continue to weigh yourself once a week. Weighing more often is not necessary. You may continue to use the Weight Record. Some people become discouraged when thinking about the total amount of weight they want to lose. Setting weight loss goals in increments of five to ten pounds can be very helpful for this problem. A reduction of nine out of ten pounds is a more rewarding and exciting comparison than is nine pounds out of thirty. Consult with your instructor about ideas for deciding upon a final weight to maintain. Factors which should be considered include: how healthy you feel, how you look, whether or not a standard clothing size will fit without major alteration, and how difficult it is to maintain that weight. Sometimes a two or three pound difference in weight significantly affects the ease and comfort with which weight stabilization is achieved. Allow for a two to three pound fluctuation in stabilized weight, particularly if you have water retention problems or are menstruating. Allowance for these fluctuations will help you avoid unnecessary discouragement. If the control plan is maintained, temporary weight gains will disappear quickly. Periodic adjustments in your calorie intake level may be necessary as you come down in weight. Review the instructions for calorie counting on pages 251-255.

Maintaining Control

Continue the control patterns you have set with yourself. Weigh weekly and record daily. Go through the Outline again and again, taking each relevant section slowly and carefully. Lots and lots of practice will be required to build techniques into habits. The more you practice the more skilled you will become. Some specific suggestions for maintaining control are listed below.

1. **Vary your routine by rotating through the different sections of your Outline**, as explained earlier in this lesson. This reduces boredom and allows you to maintain a broader range of skills.
2. **If you exceed your calorie limit, do not take the extra calories out of any other day's total.** Review your mistakes to see what you could do differently next time, write your ideas down, and forget about the extra calories. If you take those calories out of another day you perpetuate the pattern of mistake→guilt→binge. Conversely, when your calorie level is lower than your usual limit, you may not add those calories onto the limit for any other day. To do so would perpetuate the "feast or famine" cycle.
3. **Keep recording forms and the Outline visible.** If you see them you will be likely to use them. If they are put away in a drawer or some other out-of-the-way place, you will probably forget all about them. Remember the adage: "Out of sight, out of mind."
4. **Make separate plans for special events, holidays, or other changes of routine.** People visiting in your home, holiday weekends, and other times requiring extra effort like inventory week at work, or final exam week, all require plans which meet your specific needs at those times.

5. **Talk about your plans and your progress with other people.** Their interest can be very helpful; besides, your performance may be more reliable if others know what you are doing and ask you about it.

Changes in Daily Routine

Once the basic routine is established the next task is to develop flexibility. Vacations, holidays, special occasions of all types, visitors at your home, and stress periods like inventory or final exam week all create changes from your usual day-to-day routine. Even weekends provide a change from the normal weekday structure. Most of my students readily identify a weekday routine of fairly regular time use and activity patterns, generally established meal times and for some people, routine selections of foods for one or more meals (for example, a standard daily breakfast of cereal, juice and coffee). This structure, around which eating times and food choices are made, often changes on weekends or special days. Sometimes there appears to be no recognizable structure for those special days, to which many people respond by eating in random, unplanned ways. A recognizable structure supplies a sense of continuity and provides a focal point for decision making around eating times and food choices. Thus, it is logical that the loss of such a structure would result in impulsive or unplanned eating responses.

Looking at weekends first, it might be helpful to review your Food Data Records from several previous weekends. As you study them look for any patterns. Some people notice that their Sunday routines and activities are fairly similar from one weekend to the next as, for example, going to religious services in the morning, then either to a restaurant or home for a large meal, and then a dinner or supper later in the afternoon. Saturdays seem to be less consistent for many people, involving a great variety of activities like shopping, running errands, taking children to lessons or watching them perform in sporting events, exercise, maintenance tasks in house and yard, recreational and social events, and so on. The Sunday routine, if reasonably regular, can be planned around a guideline for meal times, and food selections can be developed in accordance with that routine. The Saturday routine may require a very different guideline for when and what types of things to eat. If the routine is irregular, a little advanced thought the day before will allow you to anticipate when it will be logical and likely for you to eat and what kinds of food you are likely to choose. A very basic plan can then be made which will provide a sense of structure and help you gauge your food intake appropriately.

Similarly, holidays, vacations, special occasions and visitors in your home can all be thought about in advance of their occurrence, and appropriate guidelines can be developed which will meet your specific needs at those times. All you need to do to develop a guideline is to write down a few notes about your anticipated needs, schedule demands, social activities, changes in your home environment such as having different foods available for your guests, and anything else which is pertinent. Following that, make a list of five or six suggestions to help you control your eating responses and to determine when and what types of food you will eat.

This may seem like a very laborious and time-consuming process to you right now but it all becomes easier and faster to do the more often you do it. In time, you will evolve some very general guidelines which can be modified a little to fit each specific situation. For example, I have a general vacation plan which I use for every vacation, with appropriate changes for different circumstances.

Continue the control patterns you have set with yourself.

Most of my holiday plans are very similar also, with only slight modifications for where and with whom I will be eating. You will be able to do the same as you learn to know yourself better and are able to indentify your typical needs and problems. Use your walking or jogging time, driving time, bus riding time, waiting for appointments time, or even your bath time at home to do some leisurely thinking and planning in advance of these occasions. Keep a piece of paper with you and jot down the basic ideas as you think of them so that you will have them for reference when necessary. Then tape it to the inside of a kitchen cupboard door where you can find it easily whenever needed.

Changes in Circumstances

As you progress from one year to another, various circumstances in your life will change from time to time. You may get into or out of school, change jobs or working hours, move from one residence to another or spend your time on a variety of different things. You may acquire new friends and lose others, or relationships with various people may change. You may become married or divorced or widowed, children may move into or out of your life, or other family members may become more closely or more distantly involved in your life. Your physical health or dietary requirements may change.

Each change brings about a change in the circumstances which influence your eating habits and patterns. A number of my former students have called to ask me for help following many months of good control. When we analyzed what was happening, most of them discovered that various circumstances had changed in their lives and their old control plans didn't quite fit their current needs and problems. What was needed was a week of basic data collection, isolation of relevant needs and problems, and the development of new control strategies, experimentation and revision where necessary. Does that sound like a familiar process? It is the very same process you used initially to begin changing your eating habits.

The message here is that whenever you realize that you are not controlling your food intake to your satisfaction, keep track of your food and calorie intake for a week, taking care to also record the time of day, hunger level, activity before eating, mood or feeling before eating, location of eating, social situation and eating control level for each time you eat. Isolate your needs and problems, and then place them on a list arranged in sequential order so that you are working on the easiest ones first. Review your resources and develop control strategies for the first one or two items on your list and proceed to try the strategies out a few times. If they don't work, change them completely; if they only require a little modification to be effective, change them as desired. When you find some effective strategies and techniques, tape some reminder notes to strategic places to help you remember to do them and keep track of your progress on Weekly Progress Records or graphs. Continue practicing them until they become a consistent part of your daily routine. And when you again realize that your control plan is out of date, use this same process all over again.

Periodic Plateaus in Progress

As you progress toward your goal you will discover that you have periods of intense energy output followed by seeming plateaus in your progress. These plateaus, or maintenance periods, are important for many reasons. They allow for periods of rest, change of pace and opportunities to delve deeply into other areas of life. Periodic life events like moving, changing jobs, vacations, visitors, holidays and the like take precedence over weight reduction and control efforts. The maintenance periods enable people to focus on other needs while retaining the progress they had made.

Weight plateaus are also normal and should be expected. Sometimes you may find that you don't lose any weight for one to three weeks and then, all of a sudden, you lose a few pounds all at once. Plateaus of this type occur, and frequently they signal an upcoming need to reduce calorie intake slightly or increase the exercise accordingly. Wait until you have been at the same weight for three full weeks before making any changes in your calorie level. When you reduce your daily calorie intake level, do it slowly. Begin with a 100 to 200 calorie reduction in the daily amount for a week or two and see what happens. If you need to bring it down further, shave away another 100 to 200 calories. Be sure not to allow the daily calorie consumption to drop below 1000 per day for women, or 1500 per day for men without guidance from a dietitian or physician.

Resistance to Change

Perhaps one of the most common problems in establishing new habits and patterns is resistance to change. Periodic resistance to change is normal and natural. Most students experience it at least once during their weight reduction period and many times following attainment of their desired weight.

People resist change for a variety of reasons. Let's look at some of them.

1. **The periodic need for a day or night away from the usual control routine.** We all need breaks from routine and a planned break like a food holiday may be all that is necessary to reestablish positive feelings toward your control plan.
2. **Discomfort with the new, less familiar patterns** which customarily feel awkward and strange for a while. As familiarity with the new patterns increases, there will be less need to fall back into the old routines for temporary comfort and security.
3. **The occasional need to break the tension** created by long and unaccustomed periods of good behavior. Expect this to happen periodically and plan how you will reestablish your control.

4. **Worry that we or our new behavior will not be accepted by other people.** The fear of loss of other people's approval is a powerful weapon each of us uses in maintaining our old patterns. It is the fear of what will happen, and not the reality of what people actually do think, that most often causes us to return to our old behavior.

5. **Difficulty in accepting how we, as individuals, operate and work within those guidelines.** Many of us spend a great deal of time uselessly wishing we were different, more like specific people and less like ourselves. Consequently a lot of time and effort is spent trying to get ourselves to act or react in ways which are foreign to our basic ways of doing things. I am fond of saying, "You can't play Monopoly by Scrabble's rules". What I mean by that is that if you typically resist all efforts to be regimented and highly organized, forcing yourself to make weekly menu plans and shopping accordingly, you are not likely to produce lasting change. Perhaps stocking key items and letting yourself invent your meals as you need them is more appropriate. Stocking low calorie frozen dinners can be helpful too in the event that your creativity produces a high calorie meal for your family which you would prefer not to eat.

6. **Interference from the old reputation earned by the old behavior patterns.** "Second serving" eaters, for example, have to deal with people's adherence to those old expectations. New behavior is not recognized easily or accepted as fact by other people until it has been verbally acknowledged and performed consistently for an extensive period of time.

7. **Fatigue.** When people are tired they have difficulty making that extra effort to plan, set the stage for, observe and record their desired behavior. A nap or a period of time to do something relaxing may help restore the energy and increase the control capability. If not, adherence to the control meal or restart/stress plan may prevent significant loss of control.

8. **Being overwhelmed by the enormity of the task** or by the extent, complexity, or sheer number of life events in general. If this happens to you, work at the bottom levels of your restart/stress plan until you feel capable of increasing your effort.

9. **Real or imagined feeling of lack of support.** People who attempt to make change in an area of previous failure or difficulty often say little or nothing when trying some new plan for change. Thus, they lose the support of others because the other people aren't aware of what they're trying to do.

10. **Fear of all the new expectations attached to the attainment of a goal.** People frequently set "rider clauses" to their weight loss as when, for example, a person says, "after I lose the weight I'll have to get a job." If that person has reluctant feelings about getting a job, there would be little motivation to lose the weight. Look at your own "rider clauses". If there are some undesirable tasks or goals attached to your successful

weight loss, separate them from the weight issue, and deal with them in advance of reaching your desired weight.

11. **Other people's resistance to the new behavior.** For example, if you have typically gone out to lunch Friday with two overweight friends and now you are trying to lose weight, your friends have a dilemma: should they order diet food so you won't be tempted by their meal or should they overeat as usual and run the risk of making you feel badly? Either way, the choice is difficult. They may seek an easy solution and refuse to eat with you until you are finished dieting. The resistance is less toward your weight loss than to their discomfort about meal selection. If situations like this one happen to you, discuss it with the person if possible. Otherwise, maintain consistent behavior on your part and, in time, the other people will adjust to your changes.

Developing a Positive Mental Attitude

Have you ever listened to a teacher "coach" a student through a particular task? There is a sound of encouragement in the words used and a smile is heard in the voice. "That's right. Now try this one. Good. Push it a little harder. No, not that way. Try this way instead. Excellent. You're doing a great job!" Contrast the coaching format with the inner voice which directs many of us in an area of uncertain success. "Why did you do that?! You know better. Haven't you learned anything yet? You're really hopeless. You know that, don't you? Worthless. I don't know why anybody even bothers with you. You'll never be any better either." If you had a boss who sounded like the inner voice described here, how long would you work for him? Yet if your critical inner voice sounds anything like the example, you can't quit and get away from it. That voice is a constant, static noise in your life, telling you what you can't, won't, couldn't, shouldn't, wouldn't and don't want to do. It interprets positive events in a negative way, causing you to feel that your successes are minor exceptions to the basic routine of mistakes.

Critical self-talk can be particularly damaging when you are attempting to change long-standing, difficult patterns.

Learn to talk to yourself in positive terms.

One of the first steps in developing a positive mental attitude is to neutralize the negative self-talk and learn to talk to yourself in positive terms. Statements like "I'm getting much better at leaving food on my plate," instead of "I should be leaving food on my plate everytime—I just can't seem to do it right," will help you feel good about your progress. It's what you **are** doing, not what you aren't doing, that is most important. It feels better to increase positive actions than to decrease negative actions, so focus your attention on the positives. Give yourself a pat on the back whenever possible. Changing your eating patterns is hard work and you deserve lots of credit for every success!

Few people who have agreed to long-term weight reduction programs escape the eventual realization that every reduction of food intake represents a loss of a very real, tangible pleasure. Self-critical overweight or perfectionistic people put off giving themselves tangible rewards

---

Give yourself a pat on the back whenever possible.

---

for their progress, preferring to wait until the goal is reached and maintained for a while. (See Chapter 15 for more information and ideas.) What are the rewards, then, which replace the rewards of eating? Typically they are described as intangible benefits like feeling better, having more energy, looking better in clothes, better health, less pain, better self-image, and so on. Not only are these rewards intangible and distant, they are hard to recognize. Because weight reduction tends to be gradual it is difficult to pinpoint its contribution to improvements in health, self-image or energy levels.

Intangible rewards are useful in changing behavior but they tend to be poor motivators when discouragement sets in, or when achievement of the goal seems a long way away. What tends to excite people the most is deciding what concrete benefits they will achieve as a result of losing the weight. Some of my students provided the following examples of tangible rewards: being able to buy clothes in a specific department of a particular store, wearing a bathing suit, participating in particular sports activities, being able to slide easily behind an automobile steering wheel, being able to roll over in bed without waking the other person, and being able to sit in any adult size chair. One of my tangible goals was to be able to cross one leg over the other far enough to be able to hook the foot of my crossed leg around my other leg. You can't do that if your thighs are too big!

Once you have the rewards in mind look for pictures of them, for example, ads for sports equipment; sporting activity pictures; brochures depicting beaches, bathing suits, slim line chairs; newspaper ads for that clothing department where you want to shop; and so on. Next, tape those pictures to the freezer, refrigerator and kitchen cupboard doors where they will be seen daily. Every time you go to a food source, reminder pictures on the doors will help you keep focused on your goals and keep you excited about the benefits to come. Turning down excess food will become easier once you see the trade-off in benefits.

Chapter 15, in the Supplementary Lesson section of this book, deals with methods for developing a support network. Be sure to study and apply the techniques to reinforce and reward your progress.

Above all, be patient and understanding with yourself. All learning takes time, patience, commitment and lots and lots of practice. If you fall down when trying to skate backwards, well, that's part of the learning process. If you have a bad day and exceed the planned calorie limit, well, that's part of the learning process too. Expect things like that to happen and when they do happen, chalk it up to the learning experience or the need for a food holiday, and use your Restart/Stress Plan. Remember, do not try to make up for the extra calories by starving for the next day or two. That process only perpetuates the "all or nothing" approach and reinforces the old pattern of guilt, pressure and crash diets. So, have your full calorie allotment as usual.

Remember not to overload yourself with work. Do only as much as you realistically can. There is a lot of information for you to remember and you should not expect yourself to be able to keep track of it all. When people write little notes or messages to themselves and leave them taped to places where they can be easily seen, their progress tends to be better than when no reminders are used.

Freezers, refrigerators, doorknobs, bathroom medicine cabinets and the insides of cupboard doors all provide handy places to tape reminder notes. One woman found that the best place for her to tape notes and strategy cards was on the tile around the bathtub. She took a long bath every night and used that time for planning and writing strategy cards. She then taped them to the tile where she could review them frequently. She also kept her Daily Food Record next to her on the kitchen counter, and her Weekly Progress Record was taped to the refrigerator door. "There was no way I could forget about it," she said. She discovered, too, that other family members would read the notes or record sheets from time to time and would ask her specific questions about her projects and comment upon her progress. This was very reinforcing for her.

By being very open about what she was doing, this woman allowed those around her to learn and share her projects, thereby teaching the others how to be supportive, and at the same time making it more difficult for her to just abandon it all. She kept going, called me once in a while, and came in for two follow-up sessions. She lost a total of 38 pounds in six months and has not regained the weight. She still records everything daily and has reminder notes taped all over the house.

Remove the Reference Outline of Techniques and Exercises from the book and tape it to a door, mirror, or any place where you are likely to see it often and use it as a reminder.

At the end of the course there is a tendency for many people to stop talking about the ideas and projects and to put the books and notes away. Friends and relatives may stop asking about it, assuming that, once the course is over, there is nothing more to discuss or ask about. It becomes easy to forget the information and to get out of the habit of doing the projects.

One of the most helpful things you can do for yourself is to continue to talk about your food habit experiments and the progress you are making in controlling your food intake. Continue to discuss your projects with the person to whom you have explained the lessons. Share anecdotes, achievements and ideas with relatives and friends, and they will be reminded and encouraged to ask you how and what you are doing. Their awareness of your continued effort may be strategically helpful in keeping you from abandoning your projects when you are feeling frustrated or when progress is slower than usual.

Explanation of Homework

Assignment for this week: select one section for this lesson to work on or begin your review of earlier chapters in the book, read Chapter 15, record your progress and food intake daily.

Weekly Progress Record

The instructions for how to use the Weekly Progress Record are on pages 257-260.

Daily Food Record

The instructions for how to use the Daily Food Record are on pages 261-263.

Weight Record

The instructions for how to use the Weight Record are on pages 21-22.

You have embarked upon a lifetime project, but taken one week at a time, even one day at a time, it seems possible. If the concept of a lifetime change scares you, continue to look at each day as part of an ongoing experiment in Food Habit Management. All you need now is more time, continued commitment, a strong belief in your self, and that good sense of humor!

Since this is the last lesson, only two pages of recording forms have been included here to remind you of the importance of monitoring your food intake behavior during the transition from formal classroom reinforcement to independent performance. Additional Daily Food Record forms and Weekly Progress Records may be found at the back of the book on pages 273 through 309. The edges of the pages are marked with a gray stripe for easy identification.

WEEKLY PROGRESS RECORD

BASIC SKILLS:	SUN	MON	TUES	WED	THURS	FRI	SAT	*
Read Progress Record in morning								
Record food intake								
Stay within calorie/ exchange total								
SPECIFIC TECHNIQUES/EXERCISES:								
Daily Totals								

*This column is for the weekly totals for each specific technique or exercise.

DAILY FOOD RECORD

Food Item/ Beverage	Amount	Calories/Exchanges	Time of Day

Total Calories for day ____

Date ____

Total Exchanges for day:

(1) Milk ____
(2) Vegetable ____
(3) Fruit ____
(4) Bread ____
(5) Meat ____
(6) Fat ____

DAILY FOOD RECORD

Food Item/ Beverage	Amount	Calories/Exchanges	Time of Day

Total Calories for day ________

Date ____________________

Total Exchanges for day:

(1) Milk ______
(2) Vegetable ______
(3) Fruit ______
(4) Bread ______
(5) Meat ______
(6) Fat ______

DAILY FOOD RECORD

Food Item/ Beverage	Amount	Calories/Exchanges	Time of Day

Total Calories for day ________

Date ____________________

Total Exchanges for day:

(1) Milk ______
(2) Vegetable ______
(3) Fruit ______
(4) Bread ______
(5) Meat ______
(6) Fat ______

Supplementary Lessons

INSTRUCTOR NOTES FOR "DEVELOPING A SUPPORT NETWORK" (Text begins on page 223.)

by Julie Waltz

People who are unsure of themselves or who have previously been unsuccessful or unstable in the acquisition and maintenance of new eating habits are likely to be the ones to "diet in quiet". They are also most prone to be hard on themselves when their expected goals are not met. The very process of change creates a degree of insecurity as people lose their ability to predict their own behavior accurately, and become apprehensive of the reactions of other people to their changes. The normal resistance which most of us feel toward new things may create a negative emotional undertone which interferes with the enthusiasm and commitment to long term behavior change. For many people this results in sporadic, "behind the scene" efforts to change behavior which contributes to the high drop out rate of dieters in general. No change comes without effort and some discomfort. This supplementary lesson is designed to help your students with their "growing pains" and may be used as a separate lesson at any place in your course sequence, or it may be incorporated into the discussion or homework assignments for other lessons. It could be assigned to the students for extra reading upon completion of the course, or it could be used as lesson discussion material in a follow-up or reinforcement session after the basic course is concluded.

A useful first step to take in presenting this lesson is to first review the progressive levels of commitment to actively establishing change in one's life.

1. The first and weakest level of commitment to change is establishing your goals in your mind only and mentally reviewing your plan of action to achieve those goals.
2. The second level of commitment involves writing the goals and the related plan of action down so that it can be seen and reviewed frequently throughout each day.
3. The third level of commitment requires that you make your goals and plan of action known to other people. By simply saying to another person, while waiting in a cafeteria line, for example, what you intend to buy for lunch, you are far likelier to resist temptation to purchase additional or unwanted items.
4. The fourth, and most effective level of commitment is based upon visible action. It involves the setting up of the situation in advance to cause the desired behavioral response. Examples include: removing tempting, high-calorie food items from your home environment; having low-

(Continued on page 222.)

(Continued from page 221.)

calorie, acceptable foods available at home or work for easy access; having no loose change or single dollar bills with you for vending machines; taking a specific shopping list to the grocery store; leaving your place setting of smaller glass, bowl, plate in an easily visible, readily accessible place; taping reminder notes, specific plans, progress records in places where they can be seen daily, and so on.

This lesson focuses on all four levels of commitment. Positive self-talk addresses commitment level one; the Performance Graph relates to levels two, three and four, the sections on clothing and developing a new reputation apply to commitment levels three and four, while the section on gaining support from others refers to level three. When people learn how these tasks relate to gradually increasing levels of attachment to their goals, they are able to understand why some of the tasks are more difficult for them. This helps people develop more patience with themselves and results in a more positive and charitable attitude toward themselves.

This lesson can be taught effectively as a single unit. The material contained in it is equally useful when divided up and incorporated into other lessons. Suggestions for doing this are listed below.

1. The concept of positive self-talk may be taught whenever you think your students are in need of positive mental attitude development.
   a. Practice re-phrasing negative recitations of students' reports to include something positive that the students did.
   b. Assign the chapter entitled, "Cognitive Ecology: Cleaning Up What You Say to Yourself" from the book, **Permanent Weight Control,** for extra reading. See the citation in the Bibliography of this book.
   c. Teach an attitude of "coaching" oneself through a difficult situation. Example: "You don't need to eat any more right now. Let's get the plate to the sink. Good. Now run a little water over it. Good job. Just leave the dishes alone right now. Come on, out of the kitchen. Let's get some toothpaste and a brush. Come on, brush a little harder. Now for some cinnamon flavored mouthwash." It's a step-by-step set of directions, done in a coaching style which can be very effective with people once they get past how silly they feel when they talk to themselves.
2. The Performance Graph may be incorporated into any lesson, replacing the Weekly Progress Record. This reward structure is particularly helpful when your students have hit a slump in their performance and are looking for something more exciting than weight loss to get them going again. Even weight loss can become uninteresting at times!
3. Clothing and other aspects of appearance may be discussed wherever it seems relevant. Encourage your students to experiment with changes in clothing, hair and make-up styles while they are losing weight for several reasons: it provides some amusement to sustain their interest while waiting for the weight to come down; it forces them to invest in themselves while they are creating change rather than allowing them to feel they are not worthy of personal investment until after they have reached their goals; it forces them to become familiar with how and where to shop for appearance based items; and it helps them learn their own preferences for styles and colors.
4. The material on changing your reputation may be taught as a separate lesson in the course, or as subject material in a follow-up session for your students after completion of their study program with you. Periodic get-togethers with your old students provide an opportunity for you to get feed-back about their progress, and supplies them with a reason to get themselves moving if they have slacked off in effort.
5. The suggestions for gaining support from others can be applied in many ways.
   a. Ask your students to invite an "eating buddy" to attend the lesson on social eating and request that they then go out for a restaurant meal together using a strategy card.
   b. Tie the material into vacation and holiday planning sessions, and have students role play how they would like to handle other peoples' comments, needs, etc.
   c. Reinforce the suggestion that your students explain each week's lesson to at least one other person. This is explained in the Before You Begin section of the book. Refer to this periodically throughout the course to make sure your students haven't lapsed into silence once again.

Many ideas will occur to you for ways to use this lesson material. Your own ideas can be augmented by reading a variety of books on positive mental attitude development, available in most book stores and libraries. Keep in mind the adage: "You can if you think you can," and help your students develop that attitude for themselves.

15

(**INSTRUCTOR NOTES** for this chapter begin on page 221.)

Developing a Support Network

By Julie Waltz

No matter how hard and diligently you work on your control strategies and routines, much of the fun of achieving success is being rewarded in some way for your efforts. Most of us strive for reinforcement of some kind, whether it is attention, recognition, praise, specific rewards or assistance. Overweight people most typically avoid rewarding themseleves while they are losing weight, feeling that the reward isn't justified until the goal weight has been achieved. Many overweight people are reluctant to share news of their progress with others, often out of embarrassment, reluctance to outwardly commit themselves to continuation of their control plans, or fear of what others will think, especially if they don't reach their ultimate goals.

Most people are quick to notice and spend time on their errors, and slow to recognize and give themselves credit for their successes. Thus, the little successes and the moderate-to-significant victories may go unrewarded; as the quest for perfection continues, the small, moderate and significant mistakes remain in the spotlight. Unless at least equal time is given to the positive outcomes, the whole process of retraining becomes very discouraging. The "motivation" that people always seem to look for tends to decrease with increased attention upon error and rises with increased attention upon success.

↑attention + mistakes = ↓motivation
↑attention + successes = ↑ motivation

This chapter will focus on the process of developing a mechanism which reinforces the positives and discourages undue attention upon the negatives. Specific suggestions will be aimed at self-training for the development of a support network which includes input from yourself as well as from other people. Subtopics in this lesson include: being supportive of yourself, developing a new reputation, and obtaining support from others.

Being Supportive of Yourself

Much or most of the support in any weight reduction or control plan has to come from the person who is most involved: you. If you respond as most people who have lost or are losing weight do, you may demand that you accomplish too many changes too fast and without error. This "all or nothing approach" sets most people up to feel dissatisfied with themselves whenever they aren't doing everything perfectly. Because perfect performance rarely occurs, these people tend to be unhappy with themselves much of the time. Moreover, when they do achieve desired progress in one or two areas, they frequently discount, or devalue, their success by stating that they usually don't do that well, or by pointing out all the other areas of poor progress. Familiar phrases are: "Yes, I did well then, but you don't know how many times I didn't do it at all!", and "That doesn't count because it was easy for me to do." As one of my students once said, "Why give myself credit for what I was supposed to do? If I do something extra or better, then I can give myself a pat on the back."

Don't let negative statements interfere with your feelings of success.

If you find that negative or self-discounting statements interfere with your feelings of success, you may find it helpful to teach yourself to rephrase those statements. Let's take an example. Suppose you just had a food binge and began telling yourself, "I ruined everything because of my food binge." Were you able to get back into control within a day or two? If the answer is "yes", you could then rephrase the original negative self-statement to something like, "I did have a binge, but I was able to get back into control afterward, and that's the important part." If the answer, however, is "no" because control wasn't quickly reestablished, the original self-statement could still be rephrased to something like, "I had a food binge during the week, but I know a little more about my binge pattern. Now I can make a plan for getting back into control more quickly."

This is the difference between being self-supportive and being self-destructive. The negative self-statements undermine your progress and dim your enthusiasm for changing your behavior. Neutral or positive self-statements support your efforts to make and continue your behavior changes. One of my student's remarks will live in my memory forever: "I'm definitely not perfect but I certainly am better!"

An integral part of your support system for long-term maintenance of newly developed eating and control habits is your ability to regard those habits in a context which encompasses more than just weight loss or gain. A comment such as, "I only put food items away because I'll get fatter if I don't," puts that habit solely in the context of weight reduction. Thus, the habit is relegated to temporary status, the implication being that when the weight is lost, the food can be brought out again. If the statement is rephrased to, "I put all food items away because I don't want a messy kitchen," or simply, "I just don't like to have food sitting around," it allows the habit changes to be interpreted in a broader and more integrated context. Thus, if weight isn't lost for a week or two, the food is still kept out of sight, because putting food away is simply part of the daily routine. And further, the broader context frees you from having to view all activities in your life from the perspective of weight gain and loss.

Performance Graph

It seems that people continually strive to meet their ultimate performance goals. Often these goals remain unchanged, despite how much progress is made. If people only look ahead toward their goals and not backward to measure their progress, it may appear to them that very little success has been achieved. It is analogous, perhaps, to climbing a mountain, in that if the climber continually looks upward toward the peak, no matter how far he or she climbs it still looks as though there is a long way to go. If he or she looks downward periodically (from a safe vantage point!), a greater feeling of progress will emerge as the scenery at the base of the mountain diminishes in size.

An even greater feeling of progress emerges when rewards are coupled with performance of the desired techniques. Look at the sample of the performance graph on page 226. The graph itself provides a visualization of the progress being made with each technique. The diagonal line alongside each technique separates the full control technique from the partial control technique which is used when full control is not probable. The darkened squares indicate pay-off times for tangible rewards. Let's look at the sample graph on page 226.

Doing something
is preferable to doing nothing.

Notice that only six spaces are provided for techniques. To try to do more than that sets up a situation of becoming haphazard, overwhelmed and generally ineffective at everything. Not all six spaces need to be used at one time. You are the best judge of how many techniques you can handle.

Perfectionists, or "all-or-nothing" style people tend to set high performance standards. If you follow this tendency it will be important to identify a goal of partial strength to go alongside each high level goal you set. Look at the sample graph. Notice how the goal to the right of the diagonal line is less severe than the one to the left. The strategy here is to strive, as usual, for performance of the higher level technique. But on a day of stress, tension, fatigue, etc., when full performance would be too difficult, work with the lower level tasks. Doing something is preferable to doing nothing, for it maintains the sense of discipline and preserves your positive feelings about yourself. Review your Reference Outline for additional ideas for techniques if needed.

Notice that there are two horizontal rows of 25 squares each for each one of the techniques. This supplies a total of 50 squares available for each technique. Progress is recorded by darkening each square, beginning with square 1 and pro-

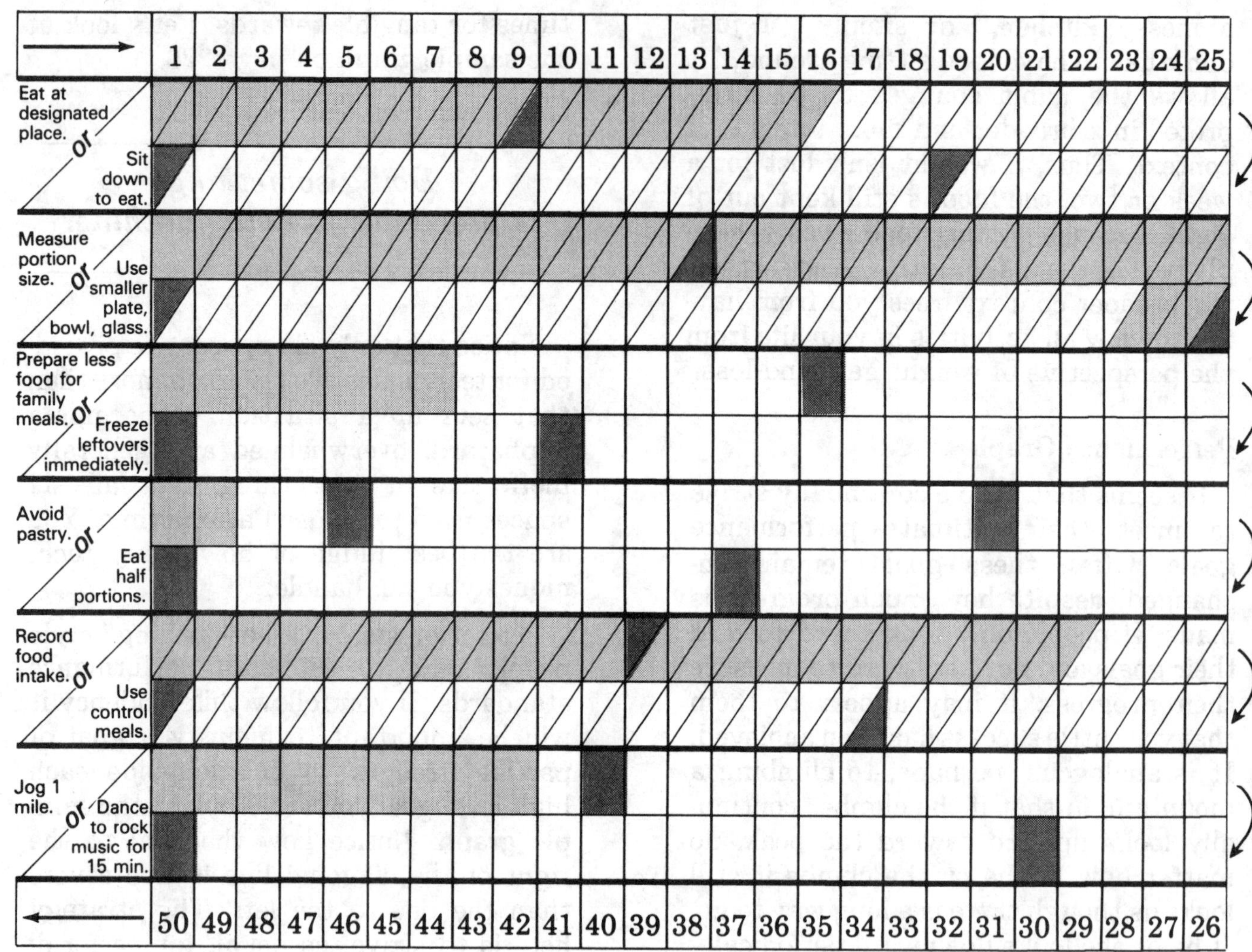

ceeding toward the right to square 25; then moving downward one row to square 26 and proceeding to the left, ending with square 50. Diagonal lines were added to the squares for those items which normally occur with greater frequency. This allows for twice as much recording space. The squares are **not** set up according to days of the month. Therefore do not skip any squares because you didn't work on that technique for a day or two. The next time you record, darken the square immediately next to the previous one darkened for that technique.

The squares which are already darkened in the sample are there as reward, or bonus, squares for progress made in the performance of **either** technique in the related box to the left. The darkened squares were spaced at random with the exception of the very last square for each pair of techniques. Thus, when you darken your own squares, do so for all squares numbered 50 and at random for the others.

Next, make a list of tangible rewards or little pleasures you would like to receive as a bonus for your good performance. Here are some ideas for tangible rewards.

Monetary Based

3-5 minute long distance phone call to someone special.

Purchase of some small item like a roll of camera film or a plant.

Have a facial, manicure, etc.

Purchase of sewing or hobby materials.

Purchase of new clothing item.

Purchase of book or record.

Purchase of tickets to some event.

Permission Based

An evening off to do whatever you want (no housework, bills, etc.)

Call a specific person to set a time to get together for fun.

Time period to work on hobby.

Trip to the library to borrow some books or magazines.

Museum or gallery looking.

Take a hike or bike ride.

Play a game with your kids.

There are many more possibilities than the ones listed here. What rewards create excitement for you? Write them down.

Once you've entered the techniques in the boxes and darkened your reward squares you are ready for action. If one or more of the techniques occurs frequently, you may wish to add some diagonal lines to the progress squares as illustrated. Post your performance graph and your reward list in an easy-to-see place and record your performance daily. Each time you reach a darkened square, select any bonus you wish from your reward list. You may use the same bonuses over and over again. You may wish to save a special bonus for the last square of the most difficult technique for extra incentive.

If you have an interested partner (spouse, parent, child, friend, relative), both of you could prepare your own performance graphs and attach the reward systems to favors or tasks each of you could do for the other. Each of you would need to make a list of what specific things you would like from your partner as rewards for your performance. Specific things could include having the partner scratch or rub your back, take out the garbage, wash your car, take you to a movie, bring you a flower, do an errand for you, write a letter for you, accompany you to some particular place, and so on. Your partner makes a similar list. You decide together what the point value should be for each reward. All rewards must be mutually agreed to. Then when you or your partner have totalled enough points for a particular reward, let the other person know and decide upon a time and date to "cash in" on the reward. This can be done very successfully with children who relate particularly well to the game aspect of it, but even adults find that the added incentive of tangible rewards for their efforts adds extra motivation to keep their performance improving.

The notion of tangible rewards is an important one for the basic reason that it makes the whole arduous process of change and retraining more fun. It allows you a means for specifically reinforcing the desired behavior and teaches you how to begin giving positive attention to yourself. People who invest in themselves and in the maintenance of their habit changes find that the investment reinforces and supports their commitment to reach for and maintain their goals. Each time you purchase something or do something specific and visible in support of the desired changes, you make a powerful statement that you are determined to reach your goals and that you want others to notice your progress.

Clothing

One tangible investment which many people who have gained and lost weight repeatedly have the greatest difficulty making is the purchase of new clothing or other appearance related items. Many of my students are reluctant to try on new clothing styles or even experiment with a new hair style. They talk about waiting until their goal weight is reached and when the investment of time and money seems more appropriate. Many of these same students also talk about how discouraged they feel when they look in a mirror and can't find visible changes in their appearance. This is counterproductive to establishing good feelings about themselves and the changes they have made.

Some people have clothes in their closets ranging from the smallest they've ever worn to the largest. Others wear the same ones no matter how loose they become. As they lose weight and their current clothes become too baggy, some people begin altering them to make them smaller. This is not only helpful but also it is preferred to the sloppy appearance of the larger clothes.

Many of my students discover that after they've altered their clothes they think they look just as overweight as before, even though the actual clothing size is smaller. It is often very difficult for the eye to distinguish the quantitative change in appearance, that the actual body size is smaller, when the same clothing items are worn at each size. A qualitative change, or actual difference in the appearance of the clothing items, is far more readily recognizable. If this notion of qualitative change in appearance appeals to you, my suggestion is that either you restyle the clothes as you cut them down in size so that they look different, or else exchange the larger clothing for completely different clothes of a smaller size. In both instances, the actual change in appearance will be far more uplifting than the change in size alone.

If you are one of the many people whose closets are filled with clothes of many sizes, the following suggestions may be helpful. First, group your clothes according to size, from largest to smallest. Then put all of the clothing items which are too small in a different closet. This is particularly important if you are disheartened by being continually reminded of all those clothes you used to wear when you were thinner. Besides, you may become so tired of seeing those clothes just hanging there in your closet that when you are at last able to wear them, a lot of the fun of having something new or different to wear is diminished.

Once the smaller clothes have been removed, those items which are too big have to be moved out of your closet also. I strongly suggest that you actually get rid of all the clothes which are too large. You can give or throw them away, sell them or exchange them for clothes of a smaller size. The point is that if those clothes are kept in the house "just in case they will be needed again," the expectation of weight regain has been reinforced. If, on a particular day or night, you have to put something on which is a little larger in order to be comfortable, it means that some weight has been regained. If you have bigger clothing items to wear and use them, the tendency is to rely on the bigger, more comfortable clothes more often until those clothes eventually fit. The result is that you have made it easier to regain the weight by keeping those clothes around. If, on the other hand, there were no larger clothing items available, a couple of days of discomfort may follow but there likely would be strong motivation to resume the weight reduction efforts.

If, like many of my students, you feel upset by the thought of parting with your old clothes, just put them in a package and wrap them for mailing, and then send them to a friend or relative who lives in another city for storage. In this way, the clothes are available, but not readily accessible. By the time the clothes are returned through the mail, the weight reduction efforts will most likely be established. The "make it easier to do what you want to do and harder to do what you don't want to do" adage applies well here.

Experiment with your appearance during the time you are losing weight. Try on different clothing styles and colors. When you reach a new size, or as your body proportions change, different styles may be more appropriate or attractive. If you wear bulky clothing, such as heavy sweaters, boxy jackets, and loosely fitting shirts or blouses, you may appear to be heavier than you actually are because the clothing adds bulk to your body size. Tucking blouses or shirts into skirts or pants, removing jackets and coats whenever possible, and using lightweight sweaters, sweater vests or jersey shirts will reduce the bulk, and consequently the physical space you take up. The overall result is a smaller appearance.

Buy a few little things for yourself when you reach a new size, or when you have achieved a desired performance level. This will help you feel good about yourself while you are still working hard to make changes. A small item of clothing, a bottle of cologne or after-shave lotion, a book or game, tickets to a play or sporting event, a record or tape, a piece of sheet music, or some item related to a hobby or recreational activity provides a psychological lift. And the incentive to continue to make changes is reinforced. The purchase of even a few items represent an investment in yourself. The greater your investment is in yourself, the more likely you will be to maintain control of your weight and your eating habits.

Tangible rewards make the process of change and retraining more fun.

Developing a New Reputation

Many of my students complain that their old, overeating reputations get in the way of establishing their new habit changes. Other people continue to respond to them as overeaters, and they find it easier to fall back into the old patterns. In addition, some students continue to regard themselves as overeaters who are temporarily controlling their food intake. The overeating responses have been predictable and people have learned how to elicit them either from themselves or from others.

Let's look at what happens with an old reputation. When a person has consistently behaved in particular ways he or she earns a reputation which is in accordance with the behaviors. For example, a person who eats large portions, takes two or more servings of each food item, accepts most offers of food or rarely leaves a scrap of food behind on the plate may earn the reputation of being a hearty eater. Once that reputation has been identified in specific terms, like "hearty eater", other people may refer to the person in those terms. The person may even use the same terms in referring to himself or herself. The terms themselves imply the performance of the related behaviors. Thus, comments like, "George is such a hearty earter; I know he'll have another helping," serve to reinforce continuation of those behaviors. Diagramatically, the process looks something like this:

Identifiable habits and patterns →
Reputation →
Expectations for specific behaviors →
Performance of those behaviors →
Reinforcement of same reputation →
Reinforcement of the same expectations →
Reinforcement of same behaviors →
Reinforcement of same reputation

When habits change the support mechanisms have to change too, in order to fit the new habits. If this doesn't happen, the old habits return. A person's own reputation can be a very powerful support mechanism. Thus, it becomes necessary to modify or change the reputation to fit the new habits.

The first task in changing a reputation is to define the terms associated with your old reputation, and then isolate the specific habits and behaviors which are associated with those terms.

Example:

Terms	Related Habits, Behaviors
Fabulous cook	Use new recipes often.
	Prepare complex dishes.
	Entertain often; serve a variety of special foods.
	Have well-stocked pantry and refrigerator.
	Often discuss food and recipes with friends.
	Spend free time browsing through cook books.
Eating buddy	Get together with friends over food.
	Am likely to say things like, "Let's get together and talk about it over dinner."
	Bring food whenever visiting other people.
	Suggest trying new restaurants or specialty food shops to friends.
	Keep others company by eating whenever they're eating.

The next task is to identify the terms you wish to have associated with your new and developing reputation. Once you have done that, isolate some specific behaviors which correlate strongly with those terms and list them as shown below.

Terms	Related Behaviors
Moderate eater	Take single servings of food.
	Choose fewer food items per meal.
	Decline offers of extra food.
	Order á la carte in restaurants.
	Leave a bite of food behind on the plate.
Planner	Plan snacks or specific meals in advance.
	Make shopping list for groceries.
	Plan strategies for specific hard-to-control situations.

Brainstorm as many examples of behaviors related to each term as possible. Then circle the ones which you want to consistently associate with yourself. If, for example, you think that leaving a scrap of food behind on the plate relates strongly to the term "moderate eater" but you just don't like doing that particular behavior, don't circle it. Circle only those you feel positive about.

The last, and hardest, task in changing a reputation is to perform the habit changes regularly and consistently. When other people notice the changes, their frequent response may be to try hard to push you back into the old, overeating habits. The real task, then, is to patiently retrain others to expect the new habits. Comments like, "I know I always used to eat in front of the TV, but now I prefer to sit at a table and pay attention to my food," teach others what to expect. It takes time to get used to new habits and to begin to feel comfortable with them. If the new habits are performed consistently, everyone eventually learns to expect them and then they don't feel strange anymore. I still remember one man's comment in class one day. "We went to my mother's for dinner last week and I was extremely hungry. I had decided to have a second helping of meat and, as I was taking it, my mother said, "I haven't seen you take a second helping for such a long time. Are you sure you really want it?" That made me realize that I had changed."

Improvement, rather than perfection, is the goal.

As in all habit changes, improvement, rather then perfection, is the goal. It is difficult to be regular and consistent with newly developing habits, particularly when there are other people involved. There are too many opportunities to slide back into the old habits or even to forget to do the new ones. Expect that changing reputations takes time and be patient with yourself and others during the retraining process.

Obtaining Support From Others

In the very beginning of the course you were asked to explain each lesson and related homework projects to at least one friend, relative or co-worker. One of the reasons given for that assignment was to reinforce your own knowledge by presenting the information logically to someone else. A second reason was to reinforce your commitment to doing your homework assignments by talking about them and sharing the results of your experiments.

Another reason for asking you to explain your lessons to someone else was to share exactly what you are and are not doing, **and why!** If you are able to share information about the particular techniques you are using, the progress being made with each of them, and even some of the problems encountered in developing effective strategies and in maintaining some of the newly changed habits, other people will be able to respond in more supportive and appropriate ways.

There may be times when you could use a little outside assistance to help you maintain or establish control. Make sure that your requests for help are **specific.** Generalized requests for help only leave other people confused and uncertain about what kind of help they should give you. A good example of this was provided by one of my students. Cocktail parties were particularly difficult for her, and she frequently felt the need for some help in maintaining control of her food intake. When she had asked her husband for help in the past, he ususally responded by taking the plate of food away from her or whispering to her that she shouldn't be eating. This angered her and she deliberately ate more, which only made her husband angry because he had, in his own way, answered her request for help. After talking about it in class, she realized that she needed to tell him specifically what to do. She made a plan for the next cocktail party, which was scheduled for the following weekend. She explained her control plan to him and said that whenever her control became shaky she would like to be able to restate her plan to him, right then, and would like him to praise her for maintaining control up to that time. He agreed and they worked out the signals together. Whenever she needed support, she tapped her husband on the arm; he excused himself from the conversation; they sat together while she restated her plan; and he praised her control efforts. By request, he said nothing about what she ate and did not take her plate away from her. Their subsequent evaluation was that they both felt much more comfortable than usual. The husband did not feel that he had to watch over his wife and he was free to enjoy himself. The wife was able to take responsibility for her own food intake and for getting some encouragement when it was needed. Consequently, she felt much better about herself and about her ability to be responsible for her own actions.

Many of my students complain that other people are always bringing them gifts of food, despite the fact that they have told these people how difficult it is for them to receive food gifts. Sometimes this represents a deliberate sabotage maneuver on the part of the other people, but often it is simply because the people want to give a gift of some kind and can't think of what else to give. Here again, specific information is important. For example, one husband was fond of bringing his wife candy and baked goods which she had always appreciated. She had made several requests that he stop bringing them to her. However, it wasn't until she presented him with a list of alternative small gift items that he was able to change his pattern. He had not known what to give her and, because he liked to bring her gifts, the idea list was very helpful.

When you feel the need to have someone give you praise or attention, take the responsibility yourself for asking the person for it. Other people can't readily tune into your needs for support, no matter how well they know you. When you feel that no one seems to care about what you're doing, make a request or statement which will elicit support from others. A comment like, "You never pay any attention to what I'm doing," is much less helpful than, "I would like to tell you about what I'm doing. Will you listen to me for a few minutes?" By saying something like, "Look, I've kept my food records complete for two weeks. Isn't that neat?", others will eventually learn to ask questions or to make comments about progress. More importantly, perhaps, taking responsibility for initiating the attention or support saves you from having to wait around for someone to anticipate your needs, and keeps you from becoming more unhappy or depressed. This may be all you need to short-circuit an impending food binge.

One more important thing to remember: be sure to show appreciation to others for any interest, questions, help and support they have given you. Everyone likes to be appreciated. When thoughtful gestures, attention, praise or encouragement are offered and then rewarded by a word or two of thanks, they will occur more often. And if the form of attention, help, etc., was not what you would have wished, make some kind of instructive comment like, "I appreciate your interest in what I'm eating, but you could help me more by putting that basket of rolls closer to your plate." In this way, you can recognize the person's efforts to be helpful and, at the same time, respond in a way which doesn't show resentment and teaches them how to be more appropriately helpful.

It may seem, as you read this chapter, that you are always placed in the position of taking an active role in your own support network, even when obtaining help from others. This is appropriate and necessary for a variety of reasons. Only you know what you want and need, and when you need it. You are the person in charge of your own control plans and eating habits. Giving other people the duty of determining what you need and when you need it only undermines your sense of capability. If others are given the job of controlling your food intake, they take over the management of your behavior. For most people this feels terrible and leads to disintegration of weight control and maintenance routines. The single most important aspect to remember is that you are the person who is totally in charge of all aspects of your eating and control habits. If you decide upon obtaining help for something, you do so in the same way a supervisor obtains help from an employee. A specific request is made, help is received and appreciation is shown. The supervisor remains in charge.

Homework Assignments

Select one or two areas for concentrated study. Make a specific plan for implementation and begin experimenting.

Explain this lesson to at least one other person.

Record food intake and progress with specific techniques daily.

Optional. A performance graph has been included with this lesson for your use.

The only form included with this lesson is a performance graph. Most of this lesson's work is involved in thinking, planning and sharing. The creation of your own personal support network may be one of the most challenging and rewarding assignments you have ever had. Good luck!

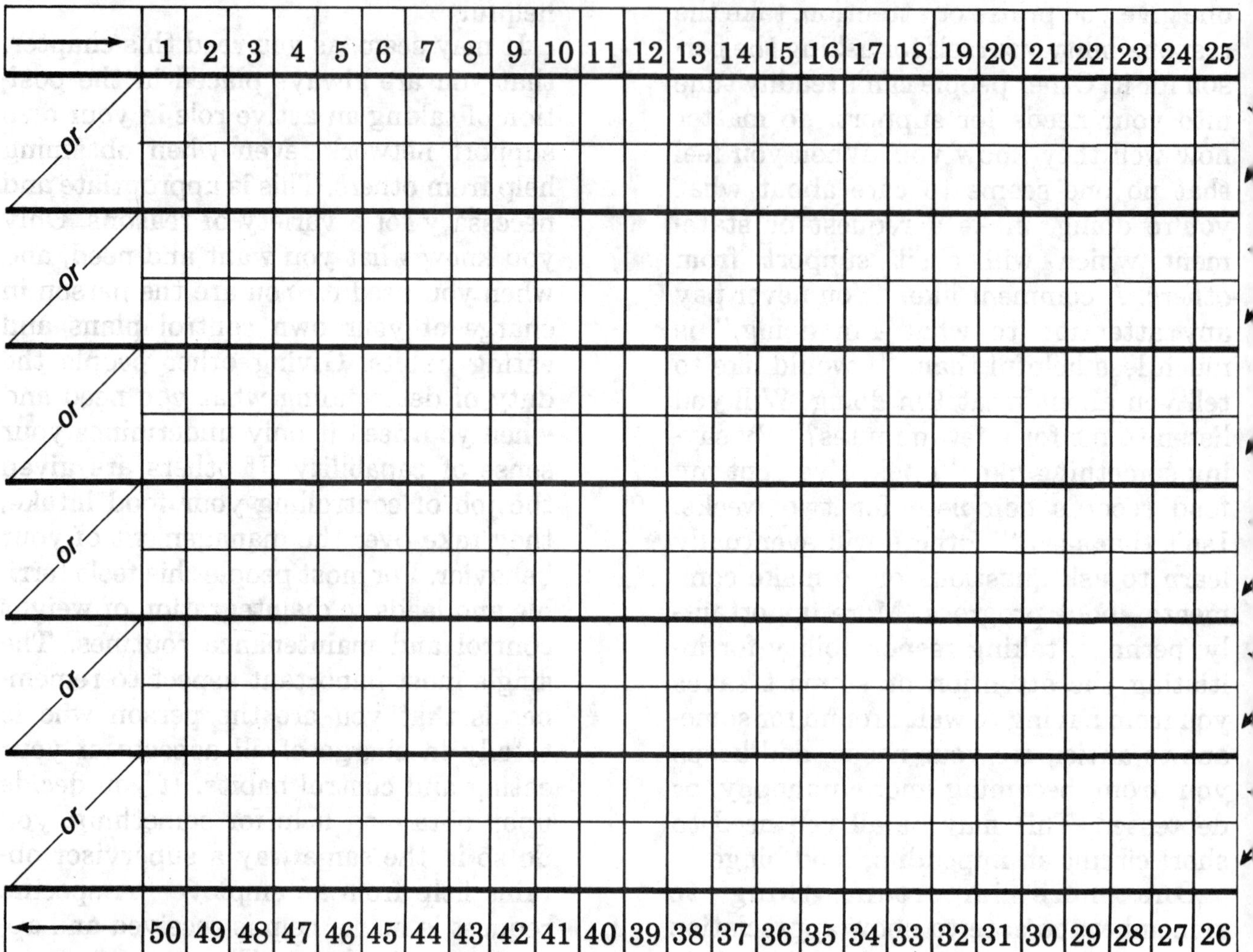
→ 1 2 3 4 5 6 7 8 9 10 11 12 13 14 15 16 17 18 19 20 21 22 23 24 25

or

or

or

or

or

or

← 50 49 48 47 46 45 44 43 42 41 40 39 38 37 36 35 34 33 32 31 30 29 28 27 26

INSTRUCTOR NOTES FOR "NUTRITIONAL CONSIDERATIONS IN WEIGHT LOSS AND CONTROL" (Text begins on page 235.)

by Luanne Anderson, R.D.

This information can be taught as a separate lesson, incorporated into several lessons, assigned for reading outside of class, discussed in a class (or individual session) or be assigned for students' use after the course is completed. If you are a dietitian, nutritionist or physician, you may want to expand this lesson by adding information of your own.

Either a calorie count or exchange system can be used with this lesson. If you are not thoroughly comfortable teaching the exchange system, instruct your students to count calories. If they are interested in learning more about the nutritional composition of their daily food plans, consult the Nutrient Tables on page 271, and the bibliography for other resources.

Some projects for homework assignments or class discussions are listed on page 235. An excellent resource for your own use is **The Obese Patient,** by George Bray, M.D., listed in the bibliography. Consult your local Department of Agriculture office or County Extension Agent for additional information.

16

Homework Assignments or Class Discussion:

1. Have students identify sources of fat in their diets.
2. Ask each student to revise a recipe, shopping list, guest dinner, sack lunch or restaurant meal (using an actual menu), to lower the fat and simple sugar content (thus calories) without destroying enjoyment.
3. Have students experiment with different meal patterns, keeping in mind the satiety value of carbohydrate, protein and fat, and identify which works best for them.
4. Have students evaluate their daily food plans according to each of the basic four food groups.
5. Expand discussion of vitamins, minerals, food fads, fad diets and various reducing plans by consulting the books by Jean Mayer, M.D., and Ronald Deutsch, M.D., listed in the bibliography.

Nutritional Considerations in Weight Loss and Control

By Luanne Anderson, R.D.

While it is true that environmental factors like cue mechanisms, paired associations and convenience influence your ability to manage your food intake, the way your body digests and uses, that is, metabolizes the foods you do eat also influences your control over your food habits. This is your internal environment. A basic understanding of some simple nutritional concepts will help you plan your meals and snacks to reduce your calorie intake, avoid actual physical hunger, and perhaps even increase your enjoyment of the food consumed.

Only three nutrients furnish calories: carbohydrate, protein and fat. Carbohydrate and protein furnish approximately 4 calories per gram or 20 calories per level teaspoon. Fat, on the other hand, furnishes 9 calories per gram or 45 calories per level teaspoon. A teaspoon of butter, margarine, mayonnaise, oil or fat in food supplies more than twice as many calories as a teaspoon of sugar, honey, jelly or jam. One slice of bread will range from 40 to 60 calories; a restaurant cube or one **level teaspoon** of margarine or butter will add 45 calories, one level teaspoon of jelly, jam or honey will add 20 calories.

Let's look more closely at these three nutrients. Carbohydrates can be broken down into two types. First, there are the concentrated, or simple, carbohydrate foods such as sugar, honey, syrup, soft drinks and sugar candies. These are sometimes referred to as "empty-calorie" foods because they have little nutritional value except calories or energy. Next are the complete carbohydrates, or starches. They include foods such as bread, potatoes, corn, and cereal grains. Many foods like bakery products, fruits, vegetables and many prepared cereals contain a combination of complex and simple carbohydrates.

Protein foods include meat, milk, eggs, cheese, poultry, fish and legumes. Like carbohydrates, most of these are not 100% protein but rather a mixture of carbohydrate, protein and fat. Fats include butter, margarine, oils and the fat in other foods. Especially high in fat are mayonnaise and most salad dressings, nuts, avocados, bacon and sausages. It is important to note that almost all protein foods common in the American diet are also very high in fat. Skim milk is the one outstanding exception.

The basic function of carbohydrate is energy; the basic function of protein is body building and repair; and the basic function of fat is concentrated energy. Excess protein will be used for energy, but it is more expensive to buy and a less efficient source of energy than carbohydrate. If you use more energy than usual, as in athletics, you need more carbohydrate. If you are growing or repairing your body, as in the childhood and teenage years, or following an illness or injury, you need more protein. If you are going to engage in a long period of activity with little or no food intake, you will need some extra fat for longer-lasting, more concentrated energy.

The concentrated or simple carbohydrates are the fastest source of energy because they are quickly absorbed. Complex carbohydrates take a little more "breaking down" in the digestive process and thus take a little longer to supply energy. Proteins are even slower to supply energy and fats take the longest time to digest and are therefore the slowest to release energy.

If you eat a breakfast at 7:00 a.m. consisting of fruit juice, toast, jelly or honey, coffee with sugar, or perhaps a sugar-coated cereal with very little milk, you may find that you're hungry again by 10:00 or 10:30. All you ate, except for the little bit of milk, was simple carbohydrate. If you want your breakfast to last you three to four hours, you can use carbohydrate plus protein with very little or no fat. Your menu might be unsweetened juice, whole-grain cereal or toast, one cup skim milk, or one egg cooked without fat, one teaspoon sugar, jelly, jam or honey, and coffee or tea if desired. If your breakfast needs to last you four to six hours, you will need to include some fat, like margarine, peanut butter, cheese, meat, or 2% or whole milk. Remember, fats are very concentrated sources of energy or calories. A very little will go a long way. Two strips of crisp bacon, thinly sliced, will add 90 to 100 calories, one ounce of sausage will add approximately 100 calories, and one level tablespoon of peanut butter will add approximately 90 calories to the total for that meal.

"I thought as long as it was protein, I didn't have to worry about calories."

Overweight people are often referred to as being "insulin sensitive." This simply means that they overreact to an intake of simple sugars or concentrated carbohydrate. Concentrated carbohydrate will cause a quick rise in blood sugar. An overweight person's body often overreacts to this quick rise, causing his or her blood sugar to drop below normal which again causes hunger symptoms: headache, weakness, tiredness, trembling, and a desire to eat. Because of this it is best to avoid eating just concentrated carbohydrate or "empty calories." If you are going to have some simple carbohydrate, use very little and combine it with a protein food. This also applies to alcoholic beverages.

Many Americans tend to worship protein. I often hear: "I thought as long as it was protein, I didn't have to worry about calories," or "The best diet is a protein diet," or even "But I need more protein" for one reason or another. The 1974 revision of the **Recommended Dietary Allowances**[1] states that the protein requirement for a 154-pound man is 56 grams, and for a 128-pound woman the requirement is 46 grams. Typical American diets generally greatly exceed this requirement.

Students ask, "If protein furnishes 4 calories per gram and carbohydrate also furnishes 4 calories per gram, does it make any difference if I get my calories from protein rather than carbohydrate?" One important difference is that almost all protein foods are combined with fat, which runs 9 calories per gram. Remember, the only common American high-quality protein food without fat is skim milk. So a high-protein diet is usually also a high-fat diet and thus a high-calorie diet as well.

I am not suggesting that you cut out all protein. Protein is extremely important and we all need it, but we need a good balance between protein, carbohydrate and fat. A simple formula to use in trying to achieve that balance is to apportion your daily intake of food to include at least **two to four times as much carbohydrate, and one-half to equal amounts of fat, as protein.** For example, if you eat 50 grams of protein a day you should have **at least** two times that amount, or 100 grams, or carbohydrate, and one-half that amount, or 25 grams or fat. Since most of our common protein foods are high in fat, this is a hard ratio to achieve, and you may go as high as 50 grams of fat in this example. Fifty grams of protein, 100 grams of carbohydrate and 26 grams of fat will furnish only 825 calories. This is too low a food intake to supply adequate energy for most people. Amounts can be increased but the ratio should remain approximately the same. This applies to a physically healthy person with normal metabolism. If you have metabolic or physical health problems, consult with a dietitian or physician for proper guidance.

"does it make any difference if I get my calories from protein rather than carbohydrate?"

One of the most common mistakes "dieters" make is trying to reduce their calorie intake so drastically that they experience real hunger. This weakens their self-control and results in the typical pattern of crash diets, with quick weight loss followed by binges and just as quick weight gain. While you are learning new food habits, it is very important to protect that self-control, so re-read the chapter on counting calories and don't try to reduce your calorie consumption by too much.

---

[1]**Recommended Dietary Allowances**, Eighth Edition, (Washington, D.C.: National Academy of Sciences, 1974).

If the calorie intake required to maintain your present weight is in the range of 2,000 to 3,000 calories, you can probably cut out 500 to 600 calories a day without experiencing severe hunger, provided that you set up your nutritional situation correctly. If the daily intake necessary to maintain your weight is in the range of 3,000 to 4,000 calories, you

Weight loss of one to two pounds a week will be safer and more permanent than more rapid weight loss.

can probably cut out 1,000 to 1,150 calories. Remember, weight loss of one to two pounds a week will be safer and more permanent than more rapid weight loss.

Another common mistake "dieters" make is in the uneven distribution of food intake throughout the day. This results in increased hunger and reduces the chances of successful food habit management. A common pattern is no breakfast, no lunch, and no other eating until about 4:00 p.m. when eating begins and continues throughout the evening.

Whenever your calorie intake exceeds your energy need the excess is stored as fat. When you eat an excess in the evening and then have little or no exercise, fat storage takes place. The next morning when you still feel full from the night before and your will power is strong, you are likely to feel that you don't need or want breakfast. Maybe by mid-morning you are feeling hungry but decide to use an alternate activity instead and get by longer without eating. Perhaps you even skip lunch. However, as the day wears on your body is going to need fuel. Your body could break down the fat you stored the night before, but that is the hard way. It is easier for your body to get you to eat something, so a very strong signal is sent out from the appetite center in the brain saying, "Feed me!" Usually your hunger level is so high at this point and your control level is so low that you go into the same overeating pattern as the night before and store more fat.

Finally, a word about vitamins, minerals and food supplements. As a woman, if you are eating 1,000 calories (1,500 for a man) or more and are using a wide variety of foods, chances are pretty good you are getting the vitamins and minerals you need. If your calorie intake is below 1,000 for a woman or 1,500 for a man, you would be well advised to take a vitamin and mineral supplement that contains 50% to 100% of the Recommended Dietary Allowance for vitamins and minerals. Women who are constantly "dieting" are often low on iron. If you are concerned about the adequacy of your diet, consult with a dietitian or physician. Do not take more than the Recommended Dietary Allowance of any vitamin or mineral without guidance from your physician. Do **not** go by the motto, "If a little is good, a lot is better." Overdoses of vitamins and minerals can be harmful and are not uncommon today. Food supplements are expensive and unnecessary and many do contain calories. Personally, I would rather get my calories from well-prepared, attractive, tasty food.

How do you apply all of this information? Simple. Plan, shop, prepare order and eat with the idea in mind to eliminate as much fat and concentrated carbohydrate as possible. Make a game o t and have fun with it. For an example, et's take the following company meal and change it to cut calories, but not the quality or enjoyment.

Original

	Calories
Chips and dip (calories vary greatly on type and amount)	100-500+
Alcoholic cocktail	120-300 each
or 12 oz. regular beer	140-165
6 oz. broiled sirloin steak	660
Mushrooms sautéed in butter (depends on amount)	50-300+
Baked potato with butter, sour cream, chives, bacon bits	300+
Asparagus with ¼ cup hollandaise sauce	100
Molded jello salad with mayonnaise dressing	100-300+
Apple pie	400
Total calories:	1,730-2,680

Substitute

	Calories
Raw Vegetables with a low-calorie dip	Calculate according to recipe and vegetables
Pre-dinner cocktail, try one of the following.	
3 oz. grapefruit or orange juice on the rocks	30
3½ oz. dry red or white wine on the rocks	70-80
3½ oz. apple cider on the rocks	35
3½ oz. cranberry juice cocktail	50-60
3 oz. tonic water on the rocks	35-40
Club soda on the rocks	0
3-4 oz. tomato or V8 juice on the rocks	20-30
12 oz. Lite Beer or low-calorie beer	70-100
2-3 oz. cranberry or other fruit juice, soda, ice (This makes your own diet soft drink. If desired use 1 level tsp. sugar and add 20 cal.)	20-40
6 oz. broiled top round steak (marinated in wine vinegar marinade or low-calorie dressing)	450
Mushrooms sautéed in bouillon with a hint of garlic, or raw with a low-calorie dip, or added to green salad or hot vegetables	Negligible
½ cup rice pilaf with onion, celery, green pepper—use your imagination!	100
Broccoli or asparagus with seasoned salt or with 1 T sour half & half	10 20
Tossed green salad with oil & vinegar or low-calorie dressing	20-100
½ cup orange sherbet	150
2 small sugar cookies	100
Total calories:	810-1,110+

Here are some ideas for how to plan, shop and prepare food in order to eliminate extra fat and concentrated carbohydrate from your diet.

1. Buy lean meat. Trim away all visible fat before cooking. Roast or broil meat to remove more fat. If you stew meat, do it the day before and then refrigerate it so that the fat becomes solid and easily removable. Remember, every teaspoon of fat you remove cuts out 45 to 50 calories!
2. Use more poultry and fish in your meal plans. They are lower in fat than beef, pork or lamb.
3. Plan a smaller serving of meat with plenty of fresh or cooked vegetables for satiety and eye appeal, and to add bulk or volume to your meal.
4. If you fry, do it slowly. Add no fat. If necessary, use a pan with a non-stick finish.
5. Rather than sauté vegetables in butter, cook them just until crisp in a small amount of water. If desired, add herbs, bouillon or soy sauce.
6. Buy a good chunk-style tuna and remove it from the can directly into a strainer. Rinse well under cold water and drain well. You can also use waterpack tuna. Add chopped celery or apple to the tuna for flavor and add as little mayonnaise as possible.
7. Add low-calorie vegetables like lettuce, celery, tomatoes, water chestnuts or sprouts to sandwiches.
8. Use wine, bouillon or lemon juice instead of butter when broiling or baking fish or poultry. Cover the food during most of the cooking period to keep the moisture in and remove the cover toward the end of cooking time to brown it.
9. Do not cook stuffing inside of poultry, because it absorbs extra fat in the cooking process. Cook the stuffing in a casserole dish and moisten it with bouillon.
10. Add more vegetables like celery, onions, green peppers, bean sprouts, mushrooms, water chestnuts, broccoli, carrots, beans and zucchini to casseroles, stuffings and omelets. Add smaller amounts of high-fat products like cheese, nuts, mayonnaise, eggs, meat, butter or margarine.
11. Substitute skim milk for whole or evaporated milk. To save money and calories, use non-fat dry milk.
12. Avoid the dark meat and the skin of poultry.
13. When making gravy use a commercial dry mix and bouillon. Do not use pan drippings unless you cool them first and remove all fat.
14. Use fresh or unsweetened canned fruit. When canning your own fruit, use a light syrup made of one part sugar to four parts water. You may want to reduce the processing time a little since the lighter syrup tends to make the fruit softer.
15. Unsweetened juices, low-calorie jellies and low-calorie canned fruit make delicious meat glazes.
16. Serve sauces and salad dressings in separate bowls.

Remember, the less fat you put in or on your food, the fewer calories you consume!

17

(INSTRUCTOR NOTES for this chapter begin on page 247.)

Developing Your Personal Exercise Program

By Denis Skog

As people increase in weight they find that moving around becomes more cumbersome, more tiring, and perhaps even more awkward. The result is that they move around less, becoming much more inefficient in their movements. Bending down and climbing becomes uncomfortable as weight increases, so the tendency is to do these actions less and less. The less they move, the more weight they gain from the same amount of food, and the less they feel like moving.

You don't have to become a superstar to become physically fit. Increasing activity doesn't have to mean daily calisthenics, jogging, cycling or handball. But it does mean becoming more active in a lot of little ways like taking a walk each day, using the stairs as much as possible, bending down, and becoming less efficient in your movement patterns.

If you are not active now, the first objective is to increase your current movement patterns. Here are some ideas to help you do this.

1. Stand, rather than sit, while dressing or undressing.
2. Instead of lying down on a couch while watching TV, sit up or perhaps even try standing up through the first half of the program.
3. Rather than sitting down immediately after a meal, do something more active like playing with your children, or working on a hobby or craft project.
4. Increase your opportunities to bend down by perhaps dropping things or storing frequently used kitchen or workshop items in the cupboards below the counter.
5. Make two trips out of every one trip by carrying fewer items.
6. Use the telephone and the

bathroom farthest away to increase your movement patterns inside your home or work setting.

7. Get rid of the remote control channel selector on your television set so that every time you wish to change the channel, you'll have to get up and do it yourself.

8. When going to the store, find a parking spot as far from the door as possible to increase your opportunity to walk.

9. Get off the bus three or four blocks before your usual stop so that you can add the extra blocks to your walking schedule.

10. Use the stairs instead of elevators and escalators. If you are not using stairs at all, begin by climbing only the first flight of stairs and then use the elevator or escalator for the remaining flights. After a few days, gradually increase the number of flights until you no longer need the elevator or escalator.

11. Take a walk break instead of a coffee break at work. Add a ten-minute walk at noon and another fifteen-minute walk in the evening.

12. Wash and wax your car yourself instead of using a commercial car wash.

13. Housework and yard work offer excellent opportunities for exercise. Do your work more briskly and vigorously. Bend, reach and stretch as much as possible. Remember, the more active you are, the more calories you will burn.

When you have established a more active daily routine and are ready to increase your energy expenditure a little more, give some careful thought to what you like to do and what you are likely to do on a long-term basis. If your previous pattern for exercise is to do situps and leg raises for two weeks and then quit, those exercises are probably not appealing to you. If you can get enthused about joining a volleyball, bowling or softball league, or a square-dance group, do that instead. If you wouldn't mind swimming but hate to do it alone, find a friend to go with you, or enroll in a swimming program where you'll have other people to keep you company. If you need to pay for an exercise program to keep you going, register for it and pay your fees in advance. If you prefer to do daily muscle stretching and toning exercises at home, establish a definite routine. Some people find that the exercise programs on television satisfy their need for company while exercising, and also provide a regular time for doing the exercises.

The more you move, the more you'll find that you can move. In other words, by being more active you become more limber and more flexible, your muscle tone improves and the tiredness you may feel in the beginning lessens as your condition improves. Many people tell me that *it wasn't their weight that kept them inactive as much as it was their poor physical condition.*

If you have been following a previously established, regular activity plan and are now ready to add more strenuous types of exercise to your routine, here are some guidelines for you to follow.

First, get examined thoroughly by your physician which includes a review of your personal and family history for the presence of heart disease, a chest x-ray, and tests of blood glucose, serum cholesterol and tri-glycerides. It is recommended that a multi-grade exercise stress test accompany the physical exam for all adults regardless of age, and is essential for those over 35. The physical exam combined with the stress test identifies a number of coronary risk factors, which may indicate that you should undertake a more moderate or more closely supervised exercise program. Primary coronary risk factors include: elevation of blood pressure, elevation of cholesterol and triglyceride levels and diminution of vital lung capacity usually due to cigarette smoking. The results of this graded exercise test can also be extremely important in determining the extent to which you should increase your daily activity level. Ask your physician where you can take a multi-grade exercise stress test.

The second step in starting an exercise program is to investigate your community resources. Local YMCAs, park and recreation departments, fitness clubs, community colleges and universities usually offer good programs with trained personnel. Some factors to consider in selecting a program include the education and qualifications of the personnel, the type and frequency of physical evaluations included in the program, and whether participants are given individualized exercise routines. Many people discover that they exercise more consistently and successfully when they are enrolled in an organized program.

If you prefer tc develop your own exercise program, there are some specific factors to consider. The first is the type of exercise you want to do. The most active type of exercise is called aerobic exercise and it increases heart and respiratory action for a sustained period of time. Examples of aerobic activities are running, jogging, jumping rope, cycling, stationary cycling, paddleball, handball, tennis, swimming, or anything that involves continued movement for a period of time. Aerobic exercise burns calories at a faster rate than the second type of exercise called isotonic exercise which allows for the movement of the muscle over its full range of motion and includes calisthenics, or muscle relaxation and stretching. It is essential for you to conclude each aerobic exercise period with ten to fifteen minutes of isotonics.

If you have decided upon an aerobic exercise program, the next step is to *determine your training rate.* This is done by taking your pulse, using the radial or temporal artery. If you do not know how to take your pulse, ask your physician or your physician's nurse to teach you how to do it at the time of your physical examination. You need to determine your resting heart rate first and you can do that by taking your pulse after you have been sitting quietly, undisturbed, for thirty minutes, or just before you get up in the morning. Take your pulse for fifteen seconds and multiply the number of beats by four. This is your resting heart rate.

After you find your resting heart rate, you must calculate your training heart rate. Your training heart rate is the range your heart will beat while you are exercising. This range will be between sixty and eighty per cent of your maximum heart rate. This is computed by the Karvonnen method. First, take the number 220 which is a standard maximum pulse rate and subtract your age, then subtract your resting heart rate, multiply that number by 60 per cent, and then add your resting heart rate. This formula will give you your 60 per cent level heart rate.

To determine your 80 per cent level heart rate, take the number 220, subtract your age, then subtract your resting heart rate, multiply the number by 80 per cent and add your resting heart rate.

Example:

Sample Training Heart Rate Range

220	standard maximums
– 40	subtract your age
180	
– 72	subtact your resting heart rate
108	
x .60	times 60 percent
65	(rounded to nearest whole number)
+ 72	add back in your resting heart rate
137	60% of your maximum heart rate

220	standard maximums
– 40	subtract your age
180	
– 72	subtract your resting heart rate
108	
x .80	times 80 percent
86	(rounded to nearest whole number)
+ 72	add back in your resting heart rate
158	80% of your maximum heart rate

Calculate Your Training Heart Rate Range Here

220	standard maximums
–	subtract your age
–	subtact your resting heart rate
x .60	times 60 percent
	(rounded to nearest whole number)
+	add back in your resting heart rate
	60% of your maximum heart rate

220	standard maximums
–	subtract your age
–	subtract your resting heart rate
x .80	times 80 percent
	(rounded to nearest whole number)
+	add back in your resting heart rate
	80% of your maximum heart rate

Before you can safely realize cardiovascular benefits from exercise, you must work at 60 per cent of your maximum heart rate and no more than 80 per cent of your maximum. Let's look at an example. A 40 year old person with a resting heart rate of 72 would have a training heart rate of 137 to 158. During a sustained exercise period that person's heart rate should be up to a minimum of 137 and no more than the maximum of 158. To keep track of your own heart rate during a period of sustained exercise, *take your pulse periodically while you are exercising.* Take your pulse for 10 seconds each time and multiply the number of beats by 6. After a little practice you will have no difficulty taking your pulse while you are exercising.

The next factor to consider is the length, or duration, of each exercise period. This is primarily determined by your physical condition when you start the exercise program. If you have not been exercising previously on a regular basis, begin with three or four-minute walks and gradually increase the duration as you progress weekly.

Keep records of your activity. Record the type of exercise, the distance, the duration of your exercise period, your pulse immediately after finishing and again five minutes after finishing your aerobic exercise. You should measure your pulse before beginning the stretching exercises which conclude the exercise session.

If you want to begin an aerobic exercise program on your own, look in the bibliography for suggested resources and read them over carefully.

Whatever type of activity you select, whether it is mild or strenuous, adherence to a few basic practices will increase your enjoyment and help you establish a regular pattern.

1. **Pick an exercise routine which suits you.** If you enjoy being out of doors, make sure that you have a program with that in mind. If you prefer being inside, choose an exercise which can be done indoors. If you enjoy being with other people, design your program to include others. If you like to be by yourself, plan your exercise program accordingly.

2. **Develop an exercise habit.** My suggestion is that you try to exercise on a daily basis. You may not be able to excerise every day, but generally three to five exercise periods per week are sufficient to maintain cardiovascular benefits and to make a significant increase in your caloric consumption.

3. **Arrange your schedule so that your exercise periods will come at logical and regular times.** Some people exercise before work, some at noon, and others on their way home from work. If exercising in the evening presents a problem because it interferes with other activities or because you prefer to relax in the evening, do your exercise before dinner. People who have stationary bicycles often establish their exercise periods around specific TV programs and cycle while watching them. "I cycle through the six o'clock news every day," said one woman. "Then I don't get bored, the weather doesn't keep me from

doing it and I'm not in the kitchen, eating." The specific times you choose may be different for week days, week-ends, and holidays. What is important is that you identify specific exercise times. If you choose them logically, so that they fit into your routine, it will be easy to make them a regular, daily part of your life.

4. **Dress the part**. It is very difficult to be active in a pair of high heels and a skirt, or a suit and tie. Find something comfortable to wear, like a pair of shorts or jeans, or buy yourself a sweatsuit, leotard or tights. If you start a walking or jogging program, find yourself a good pair of shoes. It's how you feel, not how you look, that is most important. By selecting clothes designed for exercise, you are saying to yourself, "I mean business, and I really intend to collect all of the rewards of my activity."

5. **Think the part**. Enjoyment and understanding of yourself in physical activity will help you to begin a regular program without having to force yourself. What happens in your head is as important to the success of your program as what happens to your body. If you do not enjoy what you are doing, you will find all kinds of excuses for not doing it at all. You must think positively and adopt an "active" frame of mind. As you become more active, focus on what is happening to your body. Feel your muscles work. Notice how sluggishness and tension disappear as you exercise, and how refreshed you feel afterward. Exercise can be a very pleasurable, even sensual, experience.

6. **Make it fun**. If you worry about becoming bored while you are exercising, play games with yourself. If you are walking, look for specific things along the way. For example, look for things which begin with a particular letter or which have a particular color or use. Vary the length of your stride and the particular route you take. If you are swimming, vary the strokes you use; make up rhymes or slogans which fit the rhythm of your strokes and repeat them in your mind as you swim. Compete with yourself and try to go a little farther or a little longer each time. If you are indoors jumping rope, riding a stationary bike or running in place, turn on the radio or phongraph and exercise to music.

Some people think that if they make themselves perspire more they will lose more weight, so they buy rubberized suits or belts to wear while exercising. For one thing, the rate of perspiration has no lasting relationship to weight loss since it represents loss of water and and not loss of fat. You have to burn calories to lose fat weight and that comes from movement, or exercise. The other thing to remember is that sweating is a functional part of the body's cooling mechanism. Wearing rubberized suits or belts while exercising prevents evaporation of the perspiration and thereby prevents your body from cooling itself properly. If sweating and evaporation do not occur, heat exhaustion may result.

Whatever means you choose for increasing your activity, the rewards will be worthwhile. As your muscle tone improves, you'll look slimmer and healthier, and more than likely you'll feel better too. Exercise cannot make up for overeating, but it can accelerate your rate of weight loss if done consistently and for sufficiently long periods of time. The more you move, the more you'll be able to move. And the more fun you have doing it, the more you'll want to do it. Being more active will not guarantee that you will add more years to your life, but it will probably add more life to your years.

INSTRUCTOR NOTES FOR "DEVELOPING YOUR PERSONAL EXERCISE PROGRAM" (Text begins on page 241.)

by Denis Skog

If you are planning to include an exercise component to your Food Habit Management course, there are several options to consider. If you have expertise in conducting exercise programs, you may prefer to write your own material. Or you may make arrangements with an exercise facility, such as the YMCA. Many instructors enjoy teaching the exercise lessons themselves. If this is true for you, the suggestions which follow are intended to help develop those lessons.

As you question your students about their movement and exercise patterns, you may discover that some have very sedentary patterns. Others have already established regular exercise routines. In that case, your lessons must be individualized to meet each student's particular needs.

STUDENTS WITH SEDENTARY PATTERNS

Students who have sedentary patterns usually respond more favorably to the concept of increasing movement than to the idea of "exercising." Some students will have developed negative attitudes about exercise. Consequently, they may resist your efforts toward helping them become more active in a scheduled way. Most students can understand intellectually that increasing caloric expenditure plays an important role in the total weight reduction plan. They also understand why, if they are uncomfortably overweight, movement of any kind is cumbersome or unpleasant. For these reasons a good place to begin is to ask your students to observe themselves for a week and to keep track of their responses to the following questions.

1. Do you keep all frequently used items within arm's reach?
2. Do you avoid bending or stretching?
3. Do you answer the telephone or use the bathroom closest to where you are?
4. Do you use the stairs when there is an available elevator or escalator?
5. Do you usually sit down when talking to others?
6. Do you sit down as much as possible when changing clothes?
7. Do you park as close as possible to your destination?
8. Do you usually lie down when you read or watch TV?
9. Do you ask someone else to fetch things for you?
10. Do you accept invitations to go for a walk or to do any other form of activity?

When students have completed their week of observation, discuss what they learned and establish a few simple, practical goals. The suggestions contained on pages 241 and 242 make excellent goals. Students may select a small number of suggestions, develop ideas of their own, and enter them on their Weekly Progress Records. They should record their exercise performance in the very same way they record their progress with food habit management techniques. As your students progress, the exercise goals may be changed or the frequency increased. The important objective is to help your students avoid the "all or nothing" approach to exercise by setting too many goals, or by making those goals unrealistically demanding. Some of the same pitfalls of sabotage and of trying to do too much too fast have as much application to exercise efforts as they have to reduction of food intake. Follow a step-by-step exercise plan which begins at a low level and progresses at a gradual pace. If your students are able to incorporate increased activity into their daily routines, they are much likelier to maintain their commitment and develop more positive attitudes about exercise.

STUDENTS WHO WANT TO BEGIN A REGULAR EXERCISE PROGRAM

No matter what type of sustained exercise program a person establishes, there are four basic, sequential components: warm-up, stretching, muscle tone exercises or aerobic exercise, and cool-down. Each of

(Continued on page 248.)

(Continued from page 247.)
these components, or phases, will be discussed separately.

Warm-up

The general purpose for warming up is to prepare the body, primarily the joints, muscles and heart, for vigorous activity. The warm-up is particularly important in prevention of muscle injury. The warm-up will normally be accompanied by heavier breathing, which will indicate that the heart is working a bit harder in order to supply the working muscles with more oxygen. There will also be an increase in body temperature, an increase in muscle pliability and a gradual increase in heart rate.

The warm-up phase should consist of exercises for each of the six major joints involved in movement: the neck, shoulders, lower back, hips, knees and ankles. Here are some suggested exercises for each of the six joints.

1. Neck: slow rotation of the head from side to side, then from front to back. If muscle tightness is noticed, hold the position for 15 seconds to accomplish increased stretching of the tight muscles.
2. Shoulders: arm circles over the head, followed by arm circles at shoulder level.
3. Lower back and hips: rotation of the upper half of the body from side to side first, and then in rotation from front to side to back to side to front, with hands on the hips.
4. Knees: place hands on the knees and rotate the knees in circular fashion.
5. Ankles: circular rotation of the foot in clockwise and counterclockwise directions.

With all of these exercises, the movement should be slow and controlled, with full range of motion in each joint area. Bouncing or bobbing motions should be avoided. The entire warm-up session should take approximately 3 to 4 minutes. Thus, each exercise should be done for no more than 30 seconds.

Stretching

The purposes of stretching exercises are to maintain a full range of motion in all muscle groups and to prevent muscle soreness. Muscles tighten during activity and when this happens, range of motion is decreased. Muscle soreness resulting from activities such as gardening, house painting, cleaning and snow shoveling may be prevented by doing 10 minutes of muscle stretching before and after the activity. In general, stretching exercises should be done for 10-15 minutes.

Before planning specific stretching exercises for your students, thoroughly review the first twenty pages of **Stretching,** by Robert and Jean Anderson, cited in the bibliography. This book outlines specific stretching programs for all types of activity. The guidelines in that book may be followed as written.

Improving Muscle Tone (Isotonic Exercise)

If some students wish to develop a program to improve muscle tone and do not wish to engage in sustained aerobic exercise, an excellent resource is the **Royal Canadian Air Force Exercise Plans for Physical Fitness,** cited in the bibliography. This book contains a specific, progressive program for improvement of muscle tone for men and women, and it may be followed as written.

Improving Cardiovascular and Respiratory Capacity (Aerobic Exercise)

For people who wish to increase their cardiovascular and respiratory capacity, it is necessary to do a form of exercise which produces a sustained increase in metabolic, cardiovascular and respiratory function. Activities of this type include vigorous walking, stationary and regular cycling, swimming, jogging, skating, dancing, bench-stepping, rope-jumping, hiking, some types of continuous, rhythmic calisthenics, and selected active sports.

Highly competitive game situations, or activities which demand bursts of energy, sudden, rapid movement or body contact should be avoided when beginning an exercise routine. Activities requiring effort against heavy resistance, such as weight lifting at near maximum exertion, and isometric exercises (tensing one set of muscles against another or against an immovable object), do little to improve cardiovascular function.

The intensity and duration of an exercise session will depend upon an individual's capacity for the type of exercise he or she plans to do. To achieve minimal cardiovascular endurance, the aerobic exercise must be done for a minimum of 20 minutes, at least twice a week and on nonconsecutive days. Ideally, the aerobic program should be performed for 30-40 minutes, three or more times a week, and on nonconsecutive days where possible. Two excellent references which may be used to determine the intensity and duration of aerobic exercise are: **The New Aerobics** and **Aerobics for Women,** written by Dr. Kenneth Cooper, cited in the bibliography.

Cool-down

One of the most important components of the overall exercise program is the cool-down phase and it is, perhaps, the one which is most frequently overlooked. The purposes of cool-down are to reduce muscle tension, to return the heart rate to approximately 110 to 120 beats per minute, to promote return of blood to the heart from the upper and lower extremities and to reduce body temperature.

The cool-down phase should last for a minimum of

(Continued on page 249.)

(Continued from page 248.)

5 minutes. Two of the 5 minutes should be spent on the major exercise activity performed at a slower pace. For example, if the major exercise is running, 2 minutes should be spent walking; if the major exercise is muscle toning, side stretches and overhead arm extensions may be used. The remaining 3 minutes of cool-down should be spent doing stretching exercises. The same stretching exercises which were used in the second phase of the over-all exercise program may be used for cool-down.

A phenomenon called "blood pooling" can occur in the lower extremities for anyone involved in strenuous exercise. During exercise, muscle contraction helps to move blood throughout the body to meet the body's demands for oxygen. When exercise is suddenly stopped, the muscle contraction also stops. This causes pooling, or accumulation, of blood in the lower extremities. There is, consequently, a reduced blood supply available to the heart to maintain effective pumping pressure. This may result in oxygen deprivation to the heart and brain which, in turn, may lead to dizziness or fainting. For individuals with certain kinds of coronary disease, it could lead to a heart attack. The cool-down exercises provide a continuation of muscle contraction, thereby eliminating the blood pools.

Supplementary Instructions and References

STUDENTS WHO HAVE PREVIOUSLY ESTABLISHED REGULAR EXERCISE PLANS

For those students who established their exercise programs prior to their contact with you, review the four exercise components with them to make sure they understand the role of each one, and review some specific exercises related to each component. Make sure that they know how to take their pulse accurately; that they establish their training heart rate; and that they monitor their heart rate as described below.

ESTABLISHING TRAINING HEART RATE

No matter what type of exercise your students select, they must be taught to work within their training heart rate. To determine this training heart rate, have each student take his or her pulse after sitting for a period of 30 minutes. Have them take their pulse for 15 seconds and multiply that number by four. Following the procedure explained on pages 243 and 244, have your students establish their training heart rate. Students should be taught to take their pulse immediately after the sustained, strenuous exercise and again after cool-down. The pulse should be taken at the radial or temporal arteries. If you need instruction in how to take an accurate pulse, consult a physician, nurse or exercise physiologist. Have your students practice taking their pulse in class to ensure that they know how to do it correctly.

CAUTIONS AND PRECAUTIONS

There are some cautions and precautions to consider in any exercise program. Anyone over the age of 35 should have a thorough physical examination which includes a stress test prior to beginning a strenuous exercise program. To make sure that your students do not exercise too strenuously, emphasize that they stay within their training heart rate during exercise and that the heart rate recovers to at least 120 beats per minute within five minutes, and to 100 beats per minute within ten minutes. Some variations of these numbers may occur, particularly if the person does not reach 60 percent of his or her maximum training heart rate during sustained exercise.

Caution your students not to exercise strenuously during periods of illness. Symptons of dizziness, chest pains or arm pains during exercise should be brought to the immediate attention of the person's physician.

RECORDING PROGRESS

As with the recording of food habit techniques, recording exercise progress can be very reinforcing. For those students who are unaccustomed to doing the warm-up, stretching or cool-down exercises, it might be particularly helpful for them to enter all four exercise components on a Weekly Progress Record and keep track of how often they do each separate component. By seeing the components listed individually, they will be reminded to do each one.

Some of your students may prefer to graph the actual progress they are making in terms of speed, distance, number of repetitions or whatever else is relevant. Any means of recording a student prefers would be appropriate to help them measure progress and reinforce their desired behavior.

INSTRUCTOR NOTES FOR HOMEWORK ASSIGNMENTS

The fundamental learning in this course is accomplished through the homework assignments. As with piano lessons, the sessions with the instructor set the student up to be able to practice the lessons at home. It is during piano practice that the real skills are developed and polished. The more time spent on practicing the faster annd more accomplished the skills become. The homework assignments in this course work in the same way: the class or individual sessions serve as a guide to set the students up to be able to experiment and practice at home. The practice has to come where the food is, and that is wherever the students' eating action takes place.

Once the initial data have been collected, there are three aspects to the homework assignments: pacing and recording food intake, experimenting with new techniques and strategies, and practicing those techniques and strategies previously determined to be helpful until they become habit.

Students should understand the importance of the homework and set aside sufficient, consistent time to do the assignments. Keeping the students motivated to do the work may be difficult, and instructors have devised various strategies for this. Some use a payment system whereby the students deposit a certain sum of money at the beginning of the course and then earn a specific amount of money back for each week of completed data sheets. Other instructors discount the cost of tuition for the course for completion of homework assignments. And some instructors set a rule that the students cannot attend a class or individual session unless the previous week's homework is completed.

I have experimented with a variety of approaches to the homework problem. Here are my thoughts. First of all, the initial motivation to do the work has to come from the students. You can't inject enough conviction and enthusiasm into nonmotivated or uncommitted students to cause them to do the work consistently, or for very long. For this reason, it is important to tell your interested, prospective students, before they enroll, that the course involves a heavy commitment of time and effort.

Although you, as the instructor, cannot take responsibility for your students' performance on their assignments, there are many ways to make it easier for them to follow through on their own. The first is to make sure that they understand clearly what to do and how to do it. They also need to understand thoroughly how to use the recording forms. So demonstrations of how to use them are very helpful. It is also useful to explore ways they can remember to record; for example, leaving the forms where they are clearly visible and taping reminder notes on car visors, medicine cabinet mirrors, the kitchen window over the sink and refrigerator and cupboard doors.

A second way to help your students is to encourage them to discuss their lessons and assignments with at least one supportive relative, friend or co-worker. As students share their experiences and get attention and feedback on their progress from other people, their interest in their assignments increases. Students are eager to prove that their experiments will work, and verbalizing them serves to reinforce their commitment to doing them.

Another way to help students is to stress that they implement only those ideas they can realistically accomplish. If they are anticipating a busy week, they should try fewer techniques; if they are anticipating an easier week, they can try more. In general, five or six techniques in the same week is ample. It is far more effective to practice a few things consistently than it is to attempt many things in random, haphazard fashion. As students add more and more lessons which require daily practice, they may experience feelings of panic and frustration associated with being overwhelmed. By having the students fill out their Weekly Progress Records in class you will be able to offer guidance in limiting the number of techniques each one selects.

When students find effective techniques, they should be encouraged to practice them until they become habit. However, some of the lessons in the book require more consistent daily work than others. When students are working on the lessons for controlling the environment, daily food management, changing mealtime patterns and snack control, they may find they have so many techniques they want to experiment with that they haven't time to practice selected techniques from earlier lessons. When this happens, it may be necessary either to reduce the number of techniques for continued practice, or to eliminate the practice of earlier techniques for one or two weeks. This will allow them time for experimentation with the new material. If you suggest elimination of earlier techniques, be sure to guide the students back to practicing those techniques in the lessons which don't require daily practice of the material. Some lessons may be less difficult or relevant for students. When this is the case, suggest that they practice techniques from earlier lessons and perhaps even experiment with some different techniques from those earlier lessons.

In summary, the primary purpose of homework assignments is to experiment with new techniques

(Continued on page 264.)

INSTRUCTOR NOTES FOR INSTRUCTIONS FOR CALORIE COUNTING

If you are planning to have your students count calories throughout the course, it is essential that they have an accurate, easy-to-use calorie book. It is important that the book includes a sufficiently wide variety of foods and preparations to allow for differences in food selections. Unless you have a reason to have your students do an ongoing analysis of the nutritional components of everything they eat, it is preferable to use a simplified calorie book which won't overwhelm them with lengthy entries on the vitamin and mineral content of every food and beverage listed. If your students are also to record the grams of sodium, carbohydrate, protein, or fat in addition to the calories, select your reference materials accordingly. Some useful books for this purpose are listed in the bibliography.

Some of your students may have been given specific calorie levels to follow by their physicians. Don't change them unless they are too low for the students to maintain with reasonable consistency or too high to result in weight loss. If either is the case, consult the student's physician and work out the modifications together.

For those students who will determine their calorie levels with your guidance, their collection of accurate calorie and weight data during the first week of the course will provide the information necessary to recommend an appropriate calorie level to experiment with during the following week. Follow the guidelines explained in the chapter on Instructions for Calorie Counting. That first week's calorie recommendation will be somewhat arbitrary for everyone, and many ad-

(Continued on page 256.)

Instructions for Calorie Counting

Calorie counting is suggested in this course for two reasons: as a pacing device to regulate calorie intake throughout the day and as a mechanism for learning the relative caloric value of foods. It is easy to make assumptions about the calorie content of foods based on likes, dislikes, whether it is a "healthy" or a "junk" food, and so on. No matter how familiar people are with the caloric values of foods it is still important for them to count calories in order to regulate their daily food consumption. A lot of people want to drastically lower their calorie intake to between 500 and 900 calories per day. This is too low for most people to maintain consistently, and their attempts to do so often result in a "feast or famine" cycle of low intake followed by uncontrolled high intake, followed again by low intake, then high intake, etc. This is not only unhealthy, it is counterproductive to achieving long-term food habit control. A woman should not drop her calorie intake below 1000 calories per day, or a man below 1500 calories per day without guidance from a dietitian or physician. People must take in enough food to maintain nutritional balance and have enough food choices to allow for experimentation and for feelings of satisfaction from what they do eat.

Most people are understandably in a hurry to lose weight. Research studies demonstrate, however, that the most long-lasting results are achieved through a slow, steady weight loss rate of approximately one pound per week. To help people curb their impatience, I often tell a story out of my experience and relate it to

Most long-lasting results are achieved through a slow, steady weight loss rate of one pound per week.

their weight reduction goal. Several years ago I enrolled in a beginning pottery class where my instructor made me sign an agreement that I would destroy the first ten pots I made, and if I couldn't destroy them, he would do it for me. Amazed, I asked him why. His response was to ask me if, when my first blob of clay looked like it might become a pot, I would experiment and stretch the clay up so far that the sides would collapse, or if I would use tools I had not used before, or if I would experiment by attached handles or pouring spouts or lids. I said that I probably wouldn't. He asked me why. I answered that I wouldn't want to spoil my chance of making it into a pot. That was the answer he was looking for. "In that case," he said, "you'll never learn to make a pot. You might accidentally create a pot or two, but unless you *learn* to use all of the tools, stretch the clay until it collapses, and attach handles and spouts, you won't be able to make pots consistently. If you can't keep your first ten pots anyway, you have nothing to lose by doing all these things. After that, and with practice, you will be able to make pots all the time because you'll know what you're doing."

This lesson, as it relates to weight reduction, is that, if a person is in a hurry to lose weight, he or she may not want to experiment with new ideas or techniques because some of them might not work, and weight loss might not occur that day. In that situation a person is encouraged to continue to use what is already known to be effective, thereby perpetuating old learning and hindering opportunities for new learning. People don't need more practice with what they already know. They need to expand their repertoires to include a lot of new ideas and techniques to increase their effectiveness in managing their food habits.

In adjusting calorie levels in accordance with a one pound per week weight loss, a rule of thumb to apply is 3500 calories equal one pound of weight. Therefore, if a person's weekly intake is 3500 calories more than what is needed to maintain his or her weight, the result is a one pound weight gain. Conversely, a reduction of 3500 calories below what is needed to maintain a person's body weight should result, for the average person, in a one pound weight loss. While individuals vary and the calorie level will have to be adjusted for each person, beginning with a 3500 calorie per week reduction is a good place to start. Calorie levels may have to be readjusted next week based upon what happens this week. It is preferable for people to drop their calorie levels gradually and readjust as necessary. As people lose weight it will take progressively fewer calories to maintain their body weight, so they will have to readjust their weekly totals when they are no longer losing at their current intake levels. For some people an increase in calorie expenditure through exercise will be required to achieve consistent weight loss without dropping daily calorie intake below recommended levels.

A weekly calorie total is used in this course, and daily totals are planned as pacing devices. Some people want the same calorie intake level every day of the week; others prefer two days of higher intake each, with five days of correspondingly lower intake for the rest of the week. The two-day/five-day approach is planned for people who want a small increase in calories to allow for dining out, social or family activities, being at home with more opportunities to eat, or just for a little variety in their weekly routine. Whatever the reason, the difference between the five-day average and the two-day average should not exceed 350 calories per day. If there is too great a difference in calorie totals from one day to the next it may trigger the old "feast and famine" cycle and would thereby defeat the purpose of building flexibility without loss of control. In a two-day/five-day plan, any two days may be used for the higher intake level. Thus if Saturday and Sunday were the days planned for higher intake, but the person was unexpectedly invited out on a Wednesday and would like some extra calories to work with, he or she could trade a Wednesday total for a Saturday total, using the higher intake on Wednesday and the lower intake on Saturday.

Establishing Your New Calorie Level

Your new calorie level will be based upon the results of your first week of data collection. Look at the calorie level and weight change recorded on your Data Analysis Form. Then, depending upon whether you lost, gained or maintained your weight, follow the instructions which apply to you.

Instructions Based Upon Weight Loss

If you lost one or two pounds during the week of data collection, you may continue to use the same calorie level providing that it isn't too low or too difficult to maintain. Do not subtract any additional calories. If you lost more than two pounds, ask your instructor for help in selecting a calorie level for each day of the week. If you prefer, you may change it to fit the two-day/five-day plan by using this formula. Subtract 100 calories from the daily calorie level you decided upon

Examples:

1,500 cal/day for 7 days (weekly total: 10,500 calories)

OR

1,500 cal/day
- 100 cal.
1,400 cal/day for 5 days

and

1,500 cal/day
+ 250 cal.
1,750 cal/day for 2 days

(five-day total: 7,000 calories
+ two-day total: 3,500 calories
weekly total: 10,500 calories

Compute your new calorie level:

__________cal/day for 7 days

OR

__________cal/day
- __________cal.
__________cal/day for 5 days

and

__________cal/day
+ __________cal.
__________cal/day for 2 days

and that total will be your calorie level for each of five days. For each of the remaining two days, add 250 calories to the original calorie level.

Instructions Based Upon Weight Gain

If you gained weight during the week of data collection your first task would be to compute the approximate number of calories you need to maintain your current body weight. If you are a woman involved in mild to moderate daily activity, take your current weight and multiply it by the number 12. The answer may be used as an approximation of the calories needed daily to maintain your current weight. If you are more active, you may find that multiplying your weight by the number 13 or 14 is more accurate; if you are extremely active, the number 15 may be more appropriate. If you are a man, multiply your current body weight by 15 for light to moderate activity: or by 16, 17 or 18, based upon the amount of daily energy expenditure. The calorie level you end up with is not necessarily accurate, but it does provide a number with which to begin experimenting. If the calorie level seems too low or too high in comparison with the data you collected during the first week, ask your instructor for assistance. Once you have decided upon a calorie level which you think will maintain your current weight, use the procedure explained in the following section.

Instructions Based Upon Weight Maintenance

If you maintained your weight during the first week of data collection, use that daily calorie average as the level necessary to maintain your current body weight. If you would like to to have the same calorie level each day of the week, subtract 500 calories from the daily average. The total is the new calorie level to be used for each of the seven days. If you prefer a two-day/five-day plan, use the following procedure. Subtract 600 calories from the daily calorie average, and that total will be your calorie level for each of five days. For each of the two remaining days, subtract 250 calories from the original daily calorie average.

Treat each day as a separate entity. If you make a mistake and go over your calorie limit, do not take the extra calories out of any other day. Review your mistake to see what you could do differently next time, write your ideas down and forget about it. If you take those calories out of another day, you perpetuate the pattern of mistake→guilt→binge. Conversely, when your calorie level is lower than your usual limit, you cannot add those calories onto the limit for any other day. It would perpetuate the "feast or famine" cycle. If you have the two-day/five-day plan, you can trade a higher calorie day for a lower calorie day, but you can only do that twice in one week.

Review your daily/weekly calorie totals and weight changes with your instructor and make adjustments if necessary. If you are losing a pound a week, don't change anything. If you are losing more than that, make sure your average daily total isn't too low or too difficult or uncomfortable to maintain. If you have maintained or gained weight, bring the daily amount down slowly: specifically, 100 or 200 calories per day for a total weekly reduction of 700-1400. Remember, do not allow the daily calorie consumption to drop below 1000 per day for women, or 1500 per day for men, without guidance from a dietitian or physician.

Examples:

2,000 cal/day (daily average needed to maintain current weight)
\- 500 cal.

1,500 cal/day for 7 days (weekly total: 10,500 calories)

OR

2,000 cal/day (to maintain weight)
\- 600 cal.

1,400 cal/day for 5 days

2,000 cal/day (to maintain weight)
\- 250 cal.

1,750 cal/day for 2 days

five-day total: 7,000 calories
\+ two-day total: 3,500 calories

weekly total: 10,500 calories

Compute your new calorie level:

__________cal/day (daily average needed to maintain current weight)
\- 500 _____cal.

__________cal/day for 7 days

OR

__________cal/day (to maintain weight)
\- 600 _____cal.

__________cal/day for 5 days

__________cal/day (to maintain weight)
\- 250 _____cal.

__________cal/day for 2 days

(Continued from page 251.)

justments may have to be made at the end of the second week.

Sometimes it is difficult to know just where to have the students begin if that first week of data collection resulted in weight gains of two or more pounds. You might use the formula described in the section entitled, Instructions Based Upon Weight Maintenance, on page 254. This is a very arbitrary formula and you will have to rely on your judgment in setting the calorie levels. Remind yourself and the students that these first calorie levels will require experimentation and that the necessary adjustments will be made at the next class session. If some of your students lost two or three pounds in the first week and their calorie levels aren't too low for health or comfort, you can let them experiment with those same levels for another week. If some of the students maintained their weight during the first week, follow the instructions exactly as they are written on page 254.

Some students may insist that they can only lose weight by adhering to a very low calorie limit, often between 500 and 900 calories per day. When this happens in my classes, I usually ask those students to run an experiment with me and adopt my suggested calorie level for a week just to see what happens. Many of the students lose weight at the higher calorie level, which often surprises them. For those who don't lose weight at or above the recommended minimum level of 1000 calories per day for women and 1500 calories per day for men, I work out an individualized alternative plan, usually involving an increase in activity or acceptance of a slower rate of weight loss.

The discussion on calorie counting provides an excellent opportunity to emphasize the difference between the approach used in your course and a traditional dieting approach. This is particularly important for students who have become so accustomed to stringent diets that they fail to understand that the objective of the course is not to avoid food; rather it is to learn how to control food intake. Stringent dieters quite logically avoid favorite high-calorie foods and problematic eating situations because they represent too much temptation and possible loss of eating control. If those dieters return to those foods and situations later on, they return to the same old problems. The key to long-term control of food intake is the development and practice of effective control strategies with the very foods and situations which present the problems. And because a good deal of experimentation has to occur before the effective strategies are worked out, there has to be some room for error which, in this case, may mean slightly higher calorie consumption. A gradual reduction of calorie intake below the levels required to maintain their current weight will allow your students sufficient room for experimentation, and will also allow them to cut out the unimportant calories first. It is terribly important that your students continue to eat the foods they want to be eating on a long-term basis.

Another traditional dieter's pattern which comes up during the discussion of calorie counting is the "feast and famine" cycle. Many students have established patterns of hoarding calories and then going on an eating spree which, for many of them, results in a food binge lasting several days. The guidelines recommended in the book are directed toward teaching students to regularize their food intake patterns. The two-day/five-day plan calls for a slight increase of no more than 350 calories for each of the two days of higher calorie intake. Stress the concept of treating each day as a separate entity in terms of calorie levels. If a mistake is made and the calorie level is exceeded on one day, the extra calories should not be taken out of any other day. Conversely, if fewer calories were consumed than is allowed for, the extra calories cannot be added onto the calorie intake for another day.

As the course progresses, advise your students to make their calorie adjustments gradually. If they have maintained their weight for a couple of weeks, sometimes a reduction of only 100 or 200 calories will be sufficient to reestablish a weight loss pattern.

You may find it helpful to review the three components of scale weight: water weight, muscle weight and fat weight. Rapid changes in scale weight often reflect an increase in the proportion of water weight, which is influenced by salt intake, menstrual cycles, medication, and perspiration. The higher weight reflected the morning after a night of overindulgence is more of an indicator of increased water weight than of increased fat weight. If people have increased their activity levels significantly over a period of several weeks, the maintenance of scale weight may reflect an increased proportion of muscle weight. Inasmuch as muscle weighs more than fat, it also represents a decrease in the proportion of fat weight. And because it is difficult to know for certain which factors are operating to produce the number on the scale, the less time spent on the scale, the better! The real measure of success is whether the person ate according to an effective control plan, and, if not, how quickly he or she was able to reestablish control.

(**INSTRUCTOR NOTES** for this section are on page 259.)

Instructions for the Weekly Progress Record

The Weekly Progress Record has two purposes. First, it provides a reminder of the specific techniques or exercises you want to experiment with for the week. It also serves as a scoring mechanism for keeping track of how often each one is done on a daily and weekly basis. The techniques and exercises you choose for each week's homework should be written on the form under the appropriate heading. It is not intended that you try everything at the same time. In fact, people who select too many things to do at one time frequently abandon the whole week's project out of frustration at not being able to do everything. *It is far better for you to do a few things consistently, on a daily basis, than it is to do a lot of them on a random, whenever-there-is-time basis.*

Use one Weekly Progress Record for each week. Select two to five of the new exercises for that particular week's assignment. Write each one down in the column labeled "Specific Techniques /Exercises." Read over the Progress Record every morning and when you have done so place a ✓ in the box on the top line under the appropriate day of the week. The daily scoring for each exercise and basic skill is best done later in the day or evening. If you stayed within your planned daily calorie intake, a ✓ should be placed in the appropriate box for that skill and day of the week. Similarly, ✓'s should be placed in the boxes indicating reading your Progress Record in the morning and daily recording of food intake. For each specific exercise, a ✓ is placed in the appropriate box for each time it was done on the day the record was scored. Thus, if you eat at the kitchen table or dining room table five times on Monday, five ✓'s should appear in the Monday box for that exercise. Some things may be done only once; for example, for giving family members a snack storage area a single ✓ is sufficient. Others, like making things difficult to open, or storing things in opaque containers, will occur periodically. They should be scored accordingly. Some exercises, like putting the fork down after each bite, will occur too frequently to be able to use a ✓ each time you do it. Use the ✓ to record every meal or snack where you consciously worked on putting the utensil down, rather than the number of times you actually put the utensil down. Thus, if you tried putting the fork down for two meals and three snacks on Monday, five ✓'s would appear on the square for Monday. There is no optimum

---

It is far better for you to do a few things consistently, on a daily basis, than it is to do a lot of them on a random, whenever-there-is-time basis.

---

score. The more often something is done the sooner it will strengthen into a habit. You may tally your scores on a daily basis in the bottom column marked Daily Totals, and on a weekly basis for each exercise in the right-hand column marked "*". See the example on page 260.

As you progress from the first assignment and add others, you will probably want to continue practicing some of your earlier assignments. Continue to record your progress on a smaller number of them and add only a few of the exercises for the new week. Do not try to record more than five or six exercises in one week! You will have plenty of time, when the course is completed, to go back through each chapter and experiment with the ideas you didn't have a chance to try out the first time.

If you think you have listed more exercises than you can effectively work on at one time, reduce the number. One effective way to sabotage your progress is to try to do too much, thus forcing yourself to abandon the whole project because of frustration. If two exercises are selected, they can both come from a previous week's lesson or one from an earlier week and one from the current week. One woman consistently lost 1-½ pounds a week for three months from working hard on only two exercises: keeping all tempting foods out of sight and storing everything else in opaque containers. A man achieved steady progress from just one project: not eating while watching TV. You may, however, do well with several exercises. Do not work on more than five or six exercises at one time.

You may wonder why it is necessary to continue practicing exercises for so long. Equate the learning process involved in developing new eating habits with learning to ski, ice skate, play a musical instrument or speak a foreign language. Skill development takes time, patience and constant practice no matter what type of learning is involved. There is one complicating factor in establishing new eating habits: eating is not a new activity. You already know how to eat and must replace old learning with new learning. For skiing, language training, and the like, you are likely to concentrate completely on those activities while doing them, but a lot of eating occurs when you are concentrating on something else such as conversation, or thought. This makes the establishment of new eating habits a little harder. Perfect performance is not expected—improved performance is the goal. If you ate at the designated eating place twice in the first week and six times in the second week, the improvement is the important aspect and should be focused upon, rather than the fact that you didn't eat at the designated place fifteen times. This concept is difficult for a lot of people to grasp initially, but by the end of the course most of them feel very good about their progress and have learned how to handle their unsuccessful experiments.

WEEKLY PROGRESS RECORD - INSTRUCTOR NOTES

Purposes:

1. Provide a daily reminder of the specific techniques and exercises for practice or experimentation.
2. Provide a scoring mechanism for keeping track of how often each technique and exercise is done on a daily and weekly basis.

Sample form: page 260.

Appropriate lessons:

All, except the first lesson, "Environmental Impact and Food Cues."

Instructions: highlighted on pages 257 and 258.

1. Use one Weekly Progress Record for each week.
2. Remove the form and keep it where it can be seen and used easily.
3. Select the specific techniques or exercises for experimentation from the current week's lesson and record them in the column labeled "Specific Techniques/Exercises."
4. Record the specific techniques or exercises from previous lessons for continued practice under those listed for experimentation.
5. There should not be more than five or six items listed, in total, for experimentation and practice.
6. Read the Weekly Progress Record over each morning and then place a ✓ in the box on the top line under the appropriate day of the week.
7. Each time a technique or exercise is done a ✓ should be placed in the box appropriate to that particular item and the day of the week.
8. To record progress for frequency of putting the fork down between bites, use ✓s to indicate the number of meals and snacks where conscious effort was made to put the fork down, rather than the actual number of times the fork was put down.
9. Do the daily scoring for each basic skill and technique later in the day or evening.
10. A ✓ should be placed in the appropriate box whenever the planned daily intake of calories or exchanges was maintained.
11. If food intake was recorded for a particular day, a ✓ should be placed in the appropriate box.
12. Tally the scores on a daily basis for each day in the bottom horizontal column labeled "Daily Totals."
13. Tally the scores on a weekly basis for each technique and basic skill on the right-hand vertical column marked with a *.

WEEKLY PROGRESS RECORD (Sample)

BASIC SKILLS:	SUN	MON	TUES	WED	THURS	FRI	SAT	*
Read Progress Record in morning	✓	✓	✓	✓		✓		5
Record food intake	✓	✓	✓		✓	✓	✓	6
Stay within calorie/ exchange total	✓	✓			✓	✓		4
SPECIFIC TECHNIQUES/EXERCISES:								
Eat at kitchen/dining room table	✓✓✓✓✓	✓✓✓✓✓✓	✓✓✓✓	✓✓✓✓✓	✓✓	✓✓✓✓	✓✓✓✓✓✓✓	33
Eat without TV or book	✓✓	✓	✓✓✓✓	✓✓✓✓	✓✓✓✓✓	✓✓✓	✓✓✓✓✓✓	25
Put tempting food in opaque container	✓	✓✓	✓✓✓	✓	✓✓✓✓	✓✓	✓✓✓	16
give other family members their own snack food storage area		✓						1
Put fork down between bites	✓✓	✓✓✓✓✓	✓✓✓✓	✓✓✓✓✓	✓✓✓✓	✓✓	✓	23
make lunches when preparing breakfast	✓	✓	✓	✓	✓	✓		6
Daily Totals	14	19	18	17	18	15	18	

*This column is for the weekly totals for each specific technique or exercise.

DAILY FOOD RECORD - INSTRUCTOR NOTES

Purposes: highlighted on page 261.

1. Create and maintain awareness of what is being consumed.
2. Provide a record of daily food consumption.
3. Provide a mechanism for pacing rate of food consumption.
4. Provide a mechanism for assessing and analyzing food patterns.

Sample form: page 263.

Appropriate lessons: All, except the first lesson, "Environmental Impact and Food Cues."

Instructions: highlighted on page 261.

1. Use one Daily Food Record for each day.
2. Remove the form and keep it where it can be seen and used easily.
3. Record all food items and beverages consumed each day.
4. Record the amount consumed of each food item and beverage.
5. Record the calories or exchanges of each item consumed.
6. Record the time of day each item was consumed.
7. Total the number of calories or exchanges consumed each day and enter that information plus the date on the lines provided at the bottom of the form.

Modifications: To record carbohydrate, protein, fat, or sodium grams in addition to, or instead of, the calories or exchanges, add the necessary number of columns to the form for recording that information. Or change the column headings as needed, and add blank lines to the bottom of the form for the daily totals.

Related supplementary instructions: For recording calories and adjusting calorie levels, read the "Instructions for Calorie Counting" on pages 251 throuth 255, and "Supplementary Instructions for Calorie Counting" on page 251.

NSTRUCTOR NOTES for this section are on page 60.)

Instructions for the Daily Food Record

Daily recording of all food intake is mandatory during the entire weight reduction period and for a minimum of one month after the goal weight has been achieved. Recording daily food intake can be bothersome and there is a tendency to "forget" to record. What usually happens when people stop recording is that their food intake increases. Awareness is a skill, often a poorly developed one. We have talked about the fact that a lot of eating happens when attention is focused elsewhere. Eating is not only automatic, it may also be unaware and thus not remembered later. Not only is it essential that you be fully aware that you are eating; it is terribly important to know how much food has been consumed since breakfast in order to know how to regulate food intake for the rest of that day. The Daily Food Record is designed to help you keep track of your daily food intake in the easiest way possible. Simply record the food item or beverage, the amount consumed, the calories or exchanges, and the time of day. If you are counting calories, use your calorie book to determine the correct number for each entry. If you are using an exchange system, consult your instructor for information on recording your exchanges correctly. An example of the Daily Food Record using each recording system is included at the end of this chapter.

The Daily Food Records are perforated for easy removal if you want to carry them with you. One page will usually be sufficient to record a single day of food intake. If you need more space to write, turn the page over and record on the back of it.

Eating is not only automatic, it may also be unaware.

Think of ideas for ways to make daily

recording easy to do and to remember. Some people leave their recording sheets at their designated eating places or on the kitchen counters. People who smoke sometimes tuck a food record inside the cellophane wrapper and record what has been eaten since the previous cigarette. Others leave notes for themselves as a way of remembering to record. One woman kept her food record sheets on her bathroom counter because, as she said, "that's the one place where I know I'll sit down several times a day and I can remember what I've eaten from one bathroom trip to another!"

As you use the Daily Food Recc forms you may notice that beginni with Chapter 6, the number of pages recording forms following each chap has been reduced to accustom studer to refer to page 273 at the back of t book for extra forms. There are also sufficient number of extra forms for cc tinued daily recording after completi of the course. A gray stripe runs alo the edge of the pages for easy identific tion.

DAILY FOOD RECORD (Samples)

DAILY FOOD RECORD (Exchanges)

Food Item/ Beverage	Amount	Exchanges*	Time of Day
Orange juice	½ cup	1 fruit	7:30 AM
Black coffee	1 cup	free	"
Boiled egg	1 large	½ fat 1 meat	"
Black coffee	1 cup	free	10:20 AM
Plain doughnut	1	1 fat 1 bread	"
Pea Soup	1 cup	1½ bread ½ fat	12:30 PM
Rye toast	2 pieces	2 bread	"
Butter	1 tsp.	1 fat	"
Diet Pepsi	6 oz.	free	2:30 PM
Cheese Kisses	4 pieces	½ fat 1 meat	4:00 PM
Celery stalks	3	½ veg.	5:30 PM
canned Beef stew	2 cups	4 meat 1 fat 1½ bread	6:30 PM
Corn on cob	1 ear	2 bread	"
Butter	4 tsp.	2 fat	"
Chocolate Pudding	½ cup	1½ bread ½ milk ½ fat	"

Total Calories for day 1488

Date January 31

Total Exchanges for day:

(1) Milk ½
(2) Vegetable ½
(3) Fruit 1
(4) Bread 9½
(5) Meat 6
(6) Fat 7½

*These exchanges are according to the 1976 revision of the Exchange List of the American Diabetes Association.

DAILY FOOD RECORD (Calories)

Food Item/ Beverage	Amount	Calories*	Time of Day
Orange juice	½ cup	55	7:30 AM
Black coffee	1 cup	—	"
Boiled egg	1 large	81	"
Black coffee	1 cup	—	10:20 AM
Plain doughnut	1	125	"
Pea Soup	1 cup	145	12:30 PM
Rye toast	2 pieces	34	"
Butter	1 tsp.	45	"
Diet Pepsi	6 oz.	—	2:30 PM
Cheese Kisses	4 pieces	72	4:00 PM
Celery stalks	3	21	5:30 PM
canned Beef stew	2 cups	436	6:30 PM
Corn on cob	1 ear	98	"
Butter	4 tsp.	180	"
Chocolate Pudding	½ cup	196	"

Total Calories for day 1488

Date January 31

Total Exchanges for day:

(1) Milk ½
(2) Vegetable ½
(3) Fruit 1
(4) Bread 9½
(5) Meat 6
(6) Fat 7½

*These exchanges are according to the 1976 revision of the Exchange List of the American Diabetes Association.

(Continued from page 250.)

and simultaneously maintain practice on relevant techniques from earlier lessons. When the ability to experiment is compromised by the increased number of techniques for continued practice, the objective is to condense the number of techniques to practice, thereby allowing room to try new techniques. If, however, practice and experimentation represent an overwhelming task in a particular week, eliminate the practice for that week only, and increase the experimentation. Guide the students back to practicing those earlier techniques in the following week, and especially during the lessons which don't require a lot of daily experimentation.

While it is ideal for all students to do their work every day, practically, many students will be inconsistent in their performance. Some of that inconsistency will be due to schedule problems, holidays, visitors or illness, or it may reflect periodic resistance to change, discouragement or frustration at having too much to do. Nonetheless, encourage students to attend all course sessions, whether or not they have done all of their homework. Keeping students out of sessions because of incomplete homework can cause them to drop out of the course. Allowing them to attend the sessions, share their experiences, perhaps get some helpful suggestions for how to do the assignments more regularly, and receive some support and encouragement for whatever efforts they have made usually results in greater application of time and effort to subsequent assignments.

Many students have an "all or nothing" approach to doing their assignments. Whenever they miss a whole day or a partial day of recording they may say, "Oh well, I haven't done it so I might as well wait until tomorrow." When tomorrow comes, some of those students will be unable to get started, thinking that they might as well put it off until the next session. I encourage my students to do as much as they can, saying that five days' effort is better than three days' effort, and that even two days of recording is better than none at all. I also praise their efforts to record for even half of a day, especially if it is the second half, because it represented their ability to restart their recording. I also encourage them to write down what they did when they didn't record. My experience has been that haranguing the students to record has only distanced them from me. By being supportive and firmly encouraging, students are more apt to tell me, for example, that they don't understand how to do the work. Or they may reveal what problems they encountered. With that information I can make appropriate suggestions.

Some students will sit through an entire course without doing much work, no matter how much reinforcement and help is offered. Many of these students may be very responsive in class and even quite enthusiastic about the course. When this happens, it may be helpful to consider that sometimes people have to sample somthing before they're ready to really commit themselves. There is also a point of readiness which has to be reached before people are psychologically prepared to actively apply themselves to a task. What I mean is that sometimes people have to hear the information and think about it before they are prepared to do something with it.

When these students are in a group situation, I consider that they are auditing the course, as opposed to taking the course, and allow them to continue coming to the class sessions. When the students are taking the course in individual sessions, I discuss the matter with them and suggest that they transfer to a group session where they can listen and experience the course more fully. Where there is a matter of interference of some type which prevents their active participation, I suggest that they postpone the remainder of the sessions until they have the time, settle the other problems, or feel that changing their eating behavior is a priority in their lives. The majority of my inactive students who preferred to continue in the course either returned for a refresher course later on, or proceeded to make active use of the course information on their own within a year after completion of the course.

As you prepare your weekly assignments, read the references to the homework assignments for each lesson, and read the cautions and reminders for the same lesson in the lesson outlines included in each chapter. There is also an outline of instructions for each of the recording forms used in the book. Each outline lists the specific pages where you will find detailed instructions and sample forms. All of the outlines have been prepared for ease of reference and are a condensation of the lengthier explanations in the student's chapters.

(**INSTRUCTOR NOTES** for this section are on page 266.)

Instructions for the Reference Outline of Techniques and Exercises

As you look at the Reference Outline you will see that each section of the Outline corresponds to a lesson in your book, with one exception: the first lesson in the book is not shown on the Outline. The Restart/Stress Plan section has been left blank so that you can write in your own plan. Thus, the Outline can serve as both a quick reference to some of the ideas in the book, and as a reminder of specific techniques to try or exercises to practice.

The Outline is designed to be removed from the book and tacked to a bulletin board, cupboard door, or any place where you are likely to see it daily. As you go through each lesson in the book, look at the corresponding section of the Outline periodically throughout the day. In this way you will be reminded of the specific techniques to practice for that lesson. If you need a refresher on some of the ideas from previous lessons, or you want to plan ahead for social occasions or vacations, look at the appropriate section of the Outline for ideas.

When you have finished your course and are on your own, the biggest task will be to remind yourself daily of the specific things you want to do. First, go over the Outline and make any necessary changes or additions. Place a star alongside the techniques you want to build into habits. Then put the Outline in an obvious place where you can see it easily and frequently. Make a habit of looking at it at least twice a day. If you put the Outline on the kitchen window over the sink, on the refrigerator door, on your closet door in the bedroom or even the medicine cabinet in the bathroom, it would probably be easy for you to see and read it at least twice a day. One woman covers hers with heavy plastic and uses it as a placemat. "I always look at my plate," she said, "so

I'm certain to see the Outline at the same time."

Select a different section of the Outline every one to two weeks and follow the instructions accordingly. Go through the Outline again and again, taking each section in order. You may prefer to select some sections according to your needs such as the social eating sections, the vacations and holiday section, or the Restart/Stress Plan section. It is very important to review and practice every section periodically in order to keep all of your skills intact.

At the beginning of each week select the section of the Outline you will concentrate on and write the specific suggestions listed in that section on a Weekly Progress Record. Additional recording forms may be ordered from the publisher. Record your progress in the same way you've been doing throughout the course.

Whether or not you are recording your progress, daily review of the Outline will help you remember what to do, and by taking only one section at a time, it will keep you from doing too many things at once.

REFERENCE OUTLINE OF TECHNIQUES AND EXERCISES - INSTRUCTOR NOTES

Purposes: highlighted on page 265.

1. Provide a daily reminder of specific techniques and exercises for practice and experimentation.
2. Provide a complete outline of the food habit management techniques and exercises listed in the book.
3. Provide a quick reference for planning strategies for specific occasions.

Reference Outline: pages 267 through 270.

Appropriate lessons:

All lessons, and particularly after completion of the course.

Instructions: highlighted on pages 265 and 266.

1. For use during the course,
   a. Remove the Reference Outline from the book and place it where it can be seen easily and frequently.
   b. Read the section of the Reference Outline relevant to each week's lesson for daily reinforcement.
2. For use after completion of the course,
   a. Remove the Reference Outline from the book and place it where it can be seen easily and frequently.
   b. Make any necessary additions, deletions or changes in the Reference Outline and complete the Restart/Stress Plan on the Outline.
   c. Focus on one section of the Reference Outline each week and practice the relevant techniques listed in that section.
   d. Record the techniques listed in the section selected for the week on a Weekly Progress Record and record the progress accordingly.
   e. Refer to specific sections of the Reference Outline as needed, e.g., read the sections on social eating when planning a strategy for a particular meal, or the section on vacations and holidays when preparing for a vacation.
   f. Take the Reference Outline on trips for quick review and daily reinforcement.
   g. Review the Reference Outline as often as possible to keep the information fresh in mind.

Reference Outline of Techniques and Exercises

CONTROLLING YOUR HOME ENVIRONMENT

Eat at the kitchen or dining room table.
Eat sitting down.
Eat without reading or watching TV.
Keep tempting foods out of sight.
Use opaque containers for tempting foods.
Make tempting foods hard to reach.
Make tempting foods bothersome to prepare.
Have low calorie foods ready to eat, in sight, and easy to reach.
Give other family members their own snack food cupboard.
When possible, stay out of the kitchen.

CONTROLLING YOUR WORK ENVIRONMENT

Do not eat at your desk.
Do not keep tempting food in your desk drawers.
Take pre-packaged meals, snacks and treats to work.
Carry no change for vending machines.
Eat a planned snack before leaving work.
Use exercise instead of food for a work break.
Plan your cafeteria order in advance.
Bring just enough money to pay for your planned order.
Keep a small percolator by your desk for hot drinks.
If you work around food: select one item to be eaten later at home; follow an eating urge with a low-calorie beverage or food; make it inconvenient to nibble on high calorie items by using sugar-free candy or gum.

DAILY FOOD MANAGEMENT

Shopping

Do not shop when hungry.
Do not shop when tired.
Shop from a specific list.
Shop quickly.
Don't buy your favorite varieties of high-calorie foods.
Buy small packages of hard-to-resist foods.

Preparation

Prepare food when your control is highest.
Prepare lunches and snacks when another meal is being cooked.
Use a quarter teaspoon for tasting.
To discourage tasting: wear a surgical mask; chew gum; suck on a sugar-free hard candy; or drink a low-calorie beverage.
If you prepare more than one meal at a time, cook each portion in a separate pot and freeze the extra portions immediately.
When baking for others, don't bake your favorites.
Use smaller containers for mixing, baking, and cooking.

Cleanup and Leftovers

Pour water, salt, sugar, or hot sauce over unwanted leftovers.

Package and label usable leftovers for a specific meal or snack.

Freeze containers of leftovers for soups or stews.

Make your own TV dinners out of leftovers.

If there is no good use for a leftover food, throw it out!

CONTROLLING YOUR MEALTIME ENVIRONMENT

Don't keep serving bowls at the table.

Use smaller plates, bowls and glasses.

Leave a little bit of food on your plate.

Remove the plate as soon as you have finished eating.

Politely refuse offers of extra food.

EATING SLOWLY: REDUCING EFFICIENCY

Put the utensil or food down between bites.

Cut food as it is needed.

Swallow your food before preparing the next bite.

Stop eating for a minute once or twice during the meal.

Allow for second servings by making each serving one-half of the original amount.

Serve yourself one food item at a time.

CONTROL MEALS

Write your control meal options for each meal and snack in the spaces below.

Breakfast	Lunch	Dinner	Snacks

SNACK CONTROL: DELAYED EATING RESPONSE

Wait 20 minutes before eating in response to an impulsive urge to eat.

Replace eating with a different activity.

Do something that can't or won't be combined with food.

Do something you particularly like to do.

Do a little task or a small part of a bigger job.

Use a short burst of intense exercise.

Brush your teeth and use mouthwash.

Move away from the sight, smell or sound of tempting food.

SNACK CONTROL: FOOD SUBSTITUTIONS

Use an unrewarding snack food.

Precede snacks with a large glass of water or diet soda.

For candy cravings: eat a dill pickle first, eat a sugar-free candy or eat a little of an intensely sweet candy.

For cheese cravings: eat a little of a very rich, strongly flavored cheese.

Keep enjoyable low calorie snack foods available.

Pre-package high-calorie foods in small amounts.

Pre-package food "Emergency Kits" for times when you are upset or likely to eat out of control.

RESTART/STRESS PLAN

Fill in the Restart/Stress Plan below. Put the easiest techniques on the bottom levels.

To restart control:

begin with the bottom one or two levels on the Restart/Stress Plan; and on successive days, move upward on the Plan, as is comfortable, until your regular plan can be resumed.

When under stress:

begin at whatever level of the Restart/Stress Plan is comfortable; and move upward or downward on the Plan, for as many days as is necessary, until the stress is reduced and full control can be resumed.

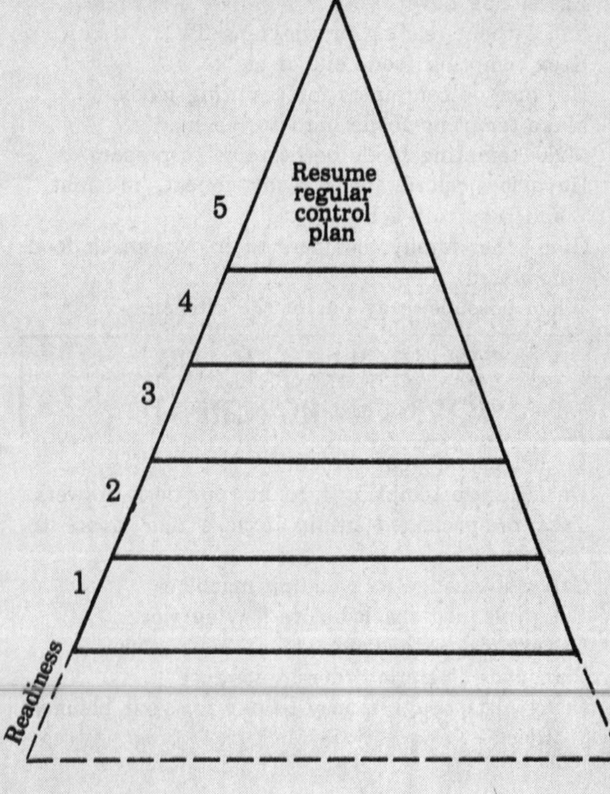

SOCIAL EATING: RESTAURANTS, BUFFETS, CAFETERIAS, HOME ENTERTAINING

Basics

Don't arrive hungry; eat something before you leave home.
Plan a control strategy.
Eat the best and skip the rest!
Pour salt, pepper or sugar over foods you want to leave uneaten.
Share orders of high-calorie items with someone.
If you are still hungry after the meal, wait at least 20 minutes before asking for more.
Use alcoholic beverages sparingly before the meal.
Wear an outfit with a not-too-roomy waistband.

Restaurants

Order à la carte.
Order according to the length of time you will spend in the restaurant and according to whether or not you will be eating again soon.
Ask someone to place your order for you.
Order some vegetables or a salad to be brought to the table right away.
Ask to have the salad dressing brought in a separate dish.
Instead of dessert, eat a chocolate-covered mint or have a sweet after-dinner drink.
Ask for a "doggy bag" to take the extra food home.

Buffets and Cafeterias

Eat a plate of salad first.
Use a serving spoon for servings; use a half-teaspoon for tastes.
Use a salad plate instead of a dinner plate.
Cover half of your dinner plate with green salad.
Ask someone to get your food, and you get theirs.
After eating, clear away your dishes before having coffee or tea.

Entertaining at Home

Use cookbooks with reduced calorie recipes.
Use single-serving foods, like chicken breasts.
Prepare a specific amount per person.
Keep appetizers more than one arm's distance away.
Take a serving of only one or two items at a time.
Immediately place all mixing bowls and utensils in soapy water before licking them clean.
Ask someone else to put the food items away while you clean up another room.

Dinner Parties at Other People's Homes

Use techniques listed earlier in the Social Eating section.
When coaxed to have more food, say that you'll have more later.

VACATIONS AND HOLIDAYS

Vacations

Set time aside to plan your vacation strategies, considering:
- where you are going;
- where, and with whom, you will stay;
- how long, and by what means, you will travel;
- what activities you think you will be doing;
- what the patterns are of the people you'll be travelling or staying with;
- what your anticipated needs are; and
- what problems you think you will have in controlling your food intake.

Review all of the sections in the Outline for more ideas.
Write the strategies out in detail.
Purchase and pack any items necessary to your control plans.
Record your food intake daily.

Holidays

Follow the procedure for vacations.
When planning, also consider:
- the customary way the holiday is celebrated;
- your old eating patterns; and
- your specific eating desires for the holiday.

Record your food intake daily.

Suggestions for Holiday Weight Control: Christmas Season

Home Environment

Keep tempting foods out of sight.
Put tempting foods in out-of-the-way places.
Decorate the house without using food.

Holiday Baking

Make dough ornaments instead of cookies.
Bake only in amounts you can use up quickly.
Donate your baked items to food banks for the needy.

Set aside a measured portion of dough or batter for yourself.

Set a small number of cookies aside to eat at your leisure.

To control the urge to taste, chew a double stick of gum or suck on a low-calorie hard candy.

Food for Guests

Keep non-problem foods on hand for unexpected guests.

Have lower-calorie foods and drinks on hand.

Keep items on hand that need to be assembled before they are appealing.

Work Environment

Take acceptable snacks to work.

Stay away from the treats other people bring.

Keeping Track of Yourself

Write down everything you eat.

Establish times throughout the day for planned meals and snacks.

Keep low-calorie snacks prepared and in sight.

Pre-package meals and snacks.

Allow yourself one planned treat each day.

Holiday Dinners and Parties

Review the Social Eating section for specific ideas.

Select two or three specific meals or parties where you plan to indulge.

Have written strategy cards with you.

MAINTAINING CONTROL

Establishing and Maintaining New Habits

Review each lesson in your book:

Take a week or two to thoroughly experiment with each lesson;

Select the techniques you want to build into habits;

Star those techniques on your Outline.

When you have completed your review:

Select a different section on the Outline every one to two weeks;

Work on the starred techniques;

List the starred techniques to be practiced for the current week on a Weekly Progress Record;

Record your progress;

Practice those techniques for weeks or months, if necessary, to establish them as habits.

Recording Food Intake

Record your food intake until your desired weight is reached and maintained for at least one month.

When you want to stop recording your food intake, do it gradually until you feel comfortable.

Whenever you begin regaining weight, record your food intake faithfully, until you have figured out what the problems are and have re-established control.

Keeping Track of Weight

Weigh only once a week.

Use weight loss increments of 5 to 10 pounds, until you approach your desired weight.

Allow for a 2- to 3-pound fluctuation in stabilized weight.

Maintaining Control

Vary your routine by rotating through the different sections of your Outline.

If you exceed your calorie limit, do not take the extra calories out of any other day's total.

When your calorie level is lower than your limit, do not add those calories onto the total for any other day.

Keep the Outline and the recording forms in sight.

Make separate plans for special events, holidays or other changes of routine.

Talk about your plans and progress with other people.

(INSTRUCTOR NOTES for this section begin on page 272.)

Nutrient Tables of Commonly Used Foods for Modified Dietary Plans

These tables are provided for persons who are interested or find it necessary for health reasons to change their intake of one or more nutrients in their normal eating patterns. Use these tables to help you to identify foods that contain significant amounts of the nutrient(s) in mind. Use the following evidence to guide you to increase or decrease your consumption according to your individual needs and food preferences.

Fat

Evidence by the Senate Select Committee on Nutrition and Human Needs states that Americans consume more fat than needed for optimal health. Reducing the total fat content of the diet is often desirable because of the high caloric value for weight control and/or because of an elevated serum cholesterol or triglyceride level. It is recommended that fat be limited to 30 percent of total calories with the remainder from protein (15 percent) and carbohydrates (45 percent).

Saturated and Polyunsaturated Fat

For optimal heart health, it is desirable to consume a greater proportion of polyunsaturated fat than saturated fat. Patients with hyperlipidemia are often instructed to consume twice as much polyunsaturated fat than saturated fat while reducing total fat.

Sodium

The average American diet contains about 6,000 to 9,000 milligrams of sodium. There is an increasing body of evidence that supports the thesis that the average American diet contains too much sodium. The Department of Agriculture recommends 5,000 milligrams or less. The American Heart Association recommends 3,000 milligrams or less. Patients with high blood pressure are usually advised to limit their sodium intake to 2,000 milligrams or less.

Potassium

Increasing potassium intake has become more important with the use of many diurectics to control blood pressure. There is also increasing evidence to support the thesis that increasing the ratio of potassium and sodium may be beneficial for hypertensives. A good level of potassium would seem to be 3,000 to 5,000 milligrams.

Luanne Anderson, R.D.
Naomi Urata, M.S., R.D.

References

Parfrey, P.S., et al. "Blood Pressure and Hormonal Changes Following Alteration in Dietary Sodium and Potassium in Mild Essential Hypertension." *Lancet,* 1:59-63, 1981.

Skrabal, F., et al. "Effect of Moderate Salt Restriction and High Potassium Intake in Pressor Hormones." *Clinical Science,* 59:157-160, 1980.

Nutrient Tables of Commonly Used Foods for Modified Dietary Plans. Data from:

Adams, Katherine, and Richardson, M. *Nutritive Value of Foods,* Home and Garden Bulletin No. 72. Washington, D.C.: USDA, 1981.

Sodium contents compiled by Naomi Urata, M.S., R.D. Information obtained from:

Adams, Katherine F. *Nutritive Value of American Foods in Common Units.* Agriculture Handbook No. 456. Washington, D.C.: Government Printing Office, 1975.

Kraus, Barbara. *The Dictionary of Sodium, Fats and Cholesterol.* New York: Gosset and Dunlap, 1974.

Marsh, A.C., Klippstein R.N., and Kaplan, S.D. *The Sodium Content of Your Food.* Home and Garden Bulletin No. 223. Washington, D.C.: USDA, 1980.

Pennington, J.A.T. and Church, H.N. *Bowes and Church's Food Values of Portions Commonly Used.* Philadelphia: J.B. Lippincott Company, 1980.

INSTRUCTOR NOTES FOR NUTRIENT TABLES OF COMMONLY USED FOODS FOR MODIFIED DIETARY PLANS

The Nutrient Tables are included for use with students concerned about particular nutrients in their diets. They are useful as a supplemental reference to an exchange system because they provide more exact information on nutrient content of foods. These tables can be used (1) to calculate total intake of a nutrient(s) for the day; (2) as a calorie counter; and (3) as a learning tool to familiarize students with the nutrient content of foods.

Persons who have been prescribed a modified diet by a health care provider, but have difficulty making food choices that suit their individual likes and needs may consider consulting with a registered dietitian. Dietitians can be contacted at local hospitals or found in the yellow pages of the phone book under dietitians or (State or Local) Dietetic Association. Ask for referrals to dietitians in your area who will provide individual service.

NUTRIENT TABLES OF COMMONLY USED FOODS FOR MODIFIED DIETARY PLANS

(Dashes (—) denote lack of reliable data for a constituent believed to be present in measurable amount)

Item No.	Foods, approximate measures, units, and weight (edible part unless footnotes indicate otherwise)			NUTRIENTS IN INDICATED QUANTITY				Fatty Acids					
				Water	Food energy	Protein	Fat	Saturated (total)	Unsaturated Oleic	Unsaturated Linoleic	Carbohydrate	Potassium	Sodium
			Grams	Percent	Calories	Grams	Grams	Grams	Grams	Grams	Grams	Milligrams	Milligrams
	DAIRY PRODUCTS (CHEESE, CREAM, IMITATION CREAM, MILK; RELATED PRODUCTS)												
	Butter. See Fats, oils; related products, items 103-108.												
	Cheese:												
	Natural:												
1	●Blue	1 oz	28	42	100	6	8	5.3	1.9	0.2	1	73	396
2	●Camembert (3 wedges per 4-oz container).	1 wedge	38	52	115	8	9	5.8	2.2	.2	Trace	71	319
	Cheddar:												
3	Cut pieces	1 oz	28	37	115	7	9	6.1	2.1	.2	Trace	28	198
4		1 cu in	17.2	37	70	4	6	3.7	1.3	.1	Trace	17	120
5	Shredded	1 cup	113	37	455	28	37	24.2	8.5	.7	1	111	791
	Cottage (curd not pressed down):												
	Creamed (cottage cheese, 4% fat):												
6	● Large curd	1 cup	225	79	235	28	10	6.4	2.4	.2	6	190	515
7	● Small curd	1 cup	210	79	220	26	9	6.0	2.2	.2	6	177	481
8	● Low fat (2%)	1 cup	226	79	205	31	4	2.8	1.0	.1	8	217	918
9	● Low fat (1%)	1 cup	226	82	165	28	2	1.5	.5	.1	6	193	918
10	● Uncreamed (cottage cheese dry curd, less than 1/2% fat).	1 cup	145	80	125	25	1	.4	.1	Trace	3	47	471
11	Cream	1 oz	28	54	100	2	10	6.2	2.4	.2	1	34	71
	Mozzarella, made with—												
12	Whole milk	1 oz	28	48	90	6	7	4.4	1.7	.2	1	21	104
13	Part skim milk	1 oz	28	49	80	8	5	3.1	1.2	.1	1	27	132
	Parmesan, grated:												
14	Cup, not pressed down	1 cup	100	18	455	42	30	19.1	7.7	.3	4	107	870
15	Tablespoon	1 tbsp	5	18	25	2	2	1.0	.4	Trace	Trace	5	44
16	Ounce	1 oz	28	18	130	12	9	5.4	2.2	.1	1	30	247
17	Provolone	1 oz	28	41	100	7	8	4.8	1.7	.1	1	39	245
	Ricotta, made with—												
18	Whole milk	1 cup	246	72	430	28	32	20.4	7.1	.7	7	257	208
19	● Part skim milk	1 cup	246	74	340	28	19	12.1	4.7	.5	13	308	310
20	●Romano	1 oz	28	31	110	9	8	—	—	—	1	—	340
21	Swiss	1 oz	28	37	105	8	8	5.0	1.7	.2	1	31	201
	Pasteurized process cheese:												
22	American	1 oz	28	39	105	6	9	5.6	2.1	.2	Trace	46	322
23	●Swiss	1 oz	28	42	95	7	7	4.5	1.7	.1	1	61	331
24	●Pasteurized process cheese food, American.	1 oz	28	43	95	6	7	4.4	1.7	.1	2	79	337
25	●Pasteurized process cheese spread, American.	1 oz	28	48	80	5	6	3.8	1.5	.1	2	69	461
	Cream, sweet:												
26	Half-and-half (cream and milk)	1 cup	242	81	315	7	28	17.3	7.0	.6	10	314	111
27		1 tbsp	15	81	20	Trace	2	1.1	.4	Trace	1	19	7
28	Light, coffee, or table	1 cup	240	74	470	6	46	28.8	11.7	1.0	9	292	103
29		1 tbsp	15	74	30	Trace	3	1.8	.7	.1	1	18	6
	Whipping, unwhipped (volume about double when whipped):												
30	Light	1 cup	239	64	700	5	74	46.2	18.3	1.5	7	231	86
31		1 tbsp	15	64	45	Trace	5	2.9	1.1	.1	Trace	15	5
32	Heavy	1 cup	238	58	820	5	88	54.8	22.2	2.0	7	179	76
33		1 tbsp	15	58	80	Trace	6	3.5	1.4	.1	Trace	11	5
34	Whipped topping, (pressurized)	1 cup	60	61	155	2	13	8.3	3.4	.3	7	88	14
35		1 tbsp	3	61	10	Trace	1	.4	.2	Trace	Trace	4	<1
36	Cream, sour	1 cup	230	71	495	7	48	30.0	12.1	1.1	10	331	96
37		1 tbsp	12	71	25	Trace	3	1.6	.6	.1	1	17	6

✱ Indicates foods with greater than 400 mg potassium per commonly used portions.

● Indicates foods with greater than 300 mg sodium per commonly used portions.

Food Energy = calories
Oleic = monounsaturated
Linoleic = polyunsaturated
Footnote explanations may be found at the end of the tables.

NUTRIENT TABLES OF COMMONLY USED FOODS FOR MODIFIED DIETARY PLANS

Item No.	Foods, approximate measures, units, and weight (edible part unless footnotes indicate otherwise)			Water	Food energy	Protein	Fat	Fatty Acids: Saturated (total)	Fatty Acids: Unsaturated: Oleic	Fatty Acids: Unsaturated: Linoleic	Carbohydrate	Potassium	Sodium
			Grams	Percent	Calories	Grams	Grams	Grams	Grams	Grams	Grams	Milligrams	Milligrams
	Cream products, imitation (made with vegetable fat):												
	Sweet Creamers:												
38	Liquid (frozen)	1 cup	245	77	335	2	24	22.8	.3	Trace	28	467	192
39		1 tbsp	15	77	20	Trace	1	1.4	Trace	0	2	29	12
40	Powdered	1 cup	94	2	515	5	33	30.6	.9	Trace	52	763	192
41		1 tsp	2	2	10	Trace	1	.7	Trace	0	1	16	4
	Whipped topping:												
42	Frozen	1 cup	75	50	240	1	19	16.3	1.0	.2	17	14	32
43		1 tbsp	4	50	15	Trace	1	.9	.1	Trace	1	1	2
44	Powdered, made with whole milk.	1 cup	80	67	150	3	10	8.5	.6	.1	13	121	192
45		1 tbsp	4	67	10	Trace	Trace	.4	Trace	Trace	1	6	12
46	Pressurized	1 cup	70	60	185	1	16	13.2	1.4	.2	11	13	14
47		1 tbsp	4	60	10	Trace	1	.8	.1	Trace	1	1	<1
48	Sour dressing (imitation sour cream) made with nonfat dry milk.	1 cup	235	75	415	8	39	31.2	4.4	1.1	11	380	240
49		1 tbsp	12	75	20	Trace	2	1.6	.2	.1	1	19	15
	Ice cream. See Milk desserts, frozen (items 75-80).												
	Ice milk. See Milk desserts, frozen (items 81-83).												
	Milk:												
	Fluid:												
50	Whole (3.3% fat)	1 cup	244	88	150	8	8	5.1	2.1	.2	11	370	122
	Lowfat (2%):												
51	No milk solids added	1 cup	244	89	120	8	5	2.9	1.2	.1	12	377	122
	Milk solids added:												
52	Label claim less than 10 g of protein per cup.	1 cup	245	89	125	9	5	2.9	1.2	.1	12	397	127
53 *	Label claim 10 or more grams of protein per cup (protein fortified).	1 cup	246	88	135	10	5	3.0	1.2	.1	14	447	145
	Lowfat (1%):												
54	No milk solids added	1 cup	244	90	100	8	3	1.6	.7	.1	12	381	122
	Milk solids added:												
55	Label claim less than 10 g of protein per cup.	1 cup	245	90	105	9	2	1.5	.6	.1	12	397	127
56 *	Label claim 10 or more grams of protein per cup (protein fortified).	1 cup	246	89	120	10	3	1.8	.7	.1	14	444	145
	Nonfat (skim):												
57 *	No milk solids added	1 cup	245	91	85	8	Trace	.3	.1	Trace	12	406	128
	Milk solids added:												
58 *	Label claim less than 10 g of protein per cup.	1 cup	245	90	90	9	1	0.4	0.1	Trace	12	418	130
59 *	Label claim 10 or more grams of protein per cup (protein fortified).	1 cup	246	89	100	10	1	.4	.1	Trace	14	446	144
60	Buttermilk	1 cup	245	90	100	8	2	1.3	.5	Trace	12	371	212
	Canned:												
	Evaporated, unsweetened:												
61 *	Whole milk	1 cup	252	74	340	17	19	11.6	5.3	0.4	25	764	297
62 *	Skim milk	1 cup	255	79	200	19	1	.3	.1	Trace	29	845	280
63 *●	Sweetened, condensed	1 cup	306	27	980	24	27	16.8	6.7	.7	166	1,136	343
	Dried:												
64 *	Buttermilk	1 cup	120	3	465	41	7	4.3	1.7	.2	59	1,910	620
	Nonfat instant:												
65	Envelope, net wt., 3.2 oz[5]	1 envelope	91	4	325	32	1	.4	.1	Trace	47	1,552	479
66	Cup[7]	1 cup	68	4	245	24	Trace	.3	.1	Trace	35	1,160	358
	Milk beverages:												
	Chocolate milk (commercial):												
67 *	Regular	1 cup	250	82	210	8	8	5.3	2.2	.2	26	417	149
68 *	Lowfat (2%)	1 cup	250	84	180	8	5	3.1	1.3	.1	26	422	150
69 *	Lowfat (1%)	1 cup	250	85	160	8	3	1.5	.7	.1	26	426	152
70 *	Eggnog (commercial)	1 cup	254	74	340	10	19	11.3	5.0	.6	34	420	138

(Dashes (—) denote lack of reliable data for a constituent believed to be present in measurable amount)

NUTRIENT TABLES OF COMMONLY USED FOODS FOR MODIFIED DIETARY PLANS

Item No.	Foods, approximate measures, units, and weight (edible part unless footnotes indicate otherwise)		NUTRIENTS IN INDICATED QUANTITY					Fatty Acids					
				Water	Food energy	Protein	Fat	Saturated (total)	Unsaturated Oleic	Unsaturated Linoleic	Carbohydrate	Potassium	Sodium
	(Dashes (—) denote lack of reliable data for a constituent believed to be present in measurable amount)												
	DAIRY PRODUCTS (CHEESE, CREAM, IMITATION CREAM, MILK; RELATED PRODUCTS)—Con.		Grams	Percent	Calories	Grams	Grams	Grams	Grams	Grams	Grams	Milligrams	Milligrams
	Malted milk, home-prepared with 1 cup of whole milk and 2 to 3 heaping tsp of malted milk powder (about 3/4 oz):												
71 *	Chocolate	1 cup of milk plus 3/4 oz of powder.	265	81	235	9	9	5.5	—	—	29	500	168
72 *	Natural	1 cup of milk plus 3/4 oz of powder.	265	81	235	11	10	6.0	—	—	27	529	214
	Shakes, thick:[8]												
73 *●	Chocolate, container, net wt., 10.6 oz.	1 container	300	72	355	9	8	5.0	2.0	.2	63	672	317
74 *●	Vanilla, container, net wt., 11 oz.	1 container	313	74	350	12	9	5.9	2.4	.2	56	572	317
	Milk desserts, frozen:												
	Ice cream:												
	Regular (about 11% fat):												
75	Hardened	1/2 gal	1,064	61	2,155	38	115	71.3	28.8	2.6	254	2,052	634
76		1 cup	133	61	270	5	14	8.9	3.6	.3	32	257	79
77		3-fl oz container	50	61	100	2	5	3.4	1.4	.1	12	96	29
78	Soft serve (frozen custard)	1 cup	173	60	375	7	23	13.5	5.9	.6	38	338	84
79	Rich (about 16% fat), hardened.	1/2 gal	1,188	59	2,805	33	190	118.3	47.8	4.3	256	1,771	865
80		1 cup	148	59	350	4	24	14.7	6.0	.5	32	221	108
	Ice milk:												
81	Hardened (about 4.3% fat)	1/2 gal	1,048	69	1,470	41	45	28.1	11.3	1.0	232	2,117	840
82		1 cup	131	69	185	5	6	3.5	1.4	.1	29	265	105
83 *	Soft serve (about 2.6% fat)	1 cup	175	70	225	8	5	2.9	1.2	0.1	38	412	163
84	Sherbet (about 2% fat)	1/2 gal	1,542	66	2,160	17	31	19.0	7.7	.7	469	1,585	712
85		1 cup	193	66	270	2	4	2.4	1.0	.1	59	198	89
	Milk desserts, other:												
86	Custard, baked	1 cup	265	77	305	14	15	6.8	5.4	.7	29	387	209
	Puddings:												
	From home recipe:												
	Starch base:												
87 *	Chocolate	1 cup	260	66	385	8	12	7.6	3.3	.3	67	445	162
88	Vanilla (blancmange)	1 cup	255	76	285	9	10	6.2	2.5	.2	41	352	162
89 ●	Tapioca cream	1 cup	165	72	220	8	8	4.1	2.5	.5	28	223	406
	From mix (chocolate) and milk:												
90 ●	Regular (cooked)	1 cup	260	70	320	9	8	4.3	2.6	.2	59	354	322
91 ●	Instant	1 cup	260	69	325	8	7	3.6	2.2	.3	63	335	940
	Yogurt:												
	With added milk solids:												
	Made with lowfat milk:												
92 *	Fruit-flavored[9]	1 container, net wt., 8 oz	227	75	230	10	3	1.8	.6	.1	42	439	133
93 *	Plain	1 container, net wt., 8 oz	227	85	145	12	4	2.3	.8	.1	16	531	159
94 *	Made with nonfat milk	1 container, net wt., 8 oz	227	85	125	13	Trace	.3	.1	Trace	17	579	174
	Without added milk solids:												
95	Made with whole milk	1 container, net wt., 8 oz	227	88	140	8	7	4.8	1.7	.1	11	351	105
	EGGS												
	Eggs, large (24 oz per dozen):												
	Raw:												
96	Whole, without shell	1 egg	50	75	80	6	6	1.7	2.0	.6	1	65	59
97	White	1 white	33	88	15	3	Trace	0	0	0	Trace	45	50
98	Yolk	1 yolk	17	49	65	3	6	1.7	2.1	.6	Trace	15	9
	Cooked:												
99	Fried in butter	1 egg	46	72	85	5	6	2.4	2.2	.6	1	58	170
100	Hard-cooked, shell removed	1 egg	50	75	80	6	6	1.7	2.0	.6	1	65	59
101	Poached	1 egg	50	74	80	6	6	1.7	2.0	.6	1	65	130
102	Scrambled (milk added) in butter. Also omelet.	1 egg	64	76	95	6	7	2.8	2.3	.6	1	85	167
	FATS, OILS; RELATED PRODUCTS												
	Butter:												
	Regular (1 brick or 4 sticks per lb):												
103	Stick (1/2 cup)	1 stick	113	16	815	1	92	57.3	23.1	2.1	Trace	29	119

NUTRIENT TABLES OF COMMONLY USED FOODS FOR MODIFIED DIETARY PLANS

(Dashes (—) denote lack of reliable data for a constituent believed to be present in measurable amount)

Item No.	Foods, approximate measures, units, and weight (edible part unless footnotes indicate otherwise)			Water	Food energy	Protein	Fat	Fatty Acids: Saturated (total)	Fatty Acids: Unsaturated: Oleic	Fatty Acids: Unsaturated: Linoleic	Carbohydrate	Potassium	Sodium
			Grams	Percent	Calories	Grams	Grams	Grams	Grams	Grams	Grams	Milligrams	Milligrams
	FATS, OILS; RELATED PRODUCTS—Con.												
104	Tablespoon (about 1/8 stick).	1 tbsp	14	16	100	Trace	12	7.2	2.9	.3	Trace	4	116
105	Pat (1 in square, 1/3 in high; 90 per lb).	1 pat	5	16	35	Trace	4	2.5	1.0	.1	Trace	1	49
	Whipped (6 sticks or two 8-oz containers per lb).												
106	Stick (1/2 cup)	1 stick	76	16	540	1	61	38.2	15.4	1.4	Trace	20	746
107	Tablespoon (about 1/8 stick).	1 tbsp	9	16	65	Trace	8	4.7	1.9	.2	Trace	2	93
108	Pat (1 1/4 in square, 1/3 in high; 120 per lb).	1 pat	4	16	25	Trace	3	1.9	.8	.1	Trace	1	32
109	Fats, cooking (vegetable shortenings).	1 cup	200	0	1,770	0	200	48.8	88.2	48.4	0	0	0
110		1 tbsp	13	0	110	0	13	3.2	5.7	3.1	0	0	0
111	Lard	1 cup	205	0	1,850	0	205	81.0	83.8	20.5	0	0	0
112		1 tbsp	13	0	115	0	13	5.1	5.3	1.3	0	0	0
	Margarine:												
	Regular (1 brick or 4 sticks per lb):												
113	Stick (1/2 cup)	1 stick	113	16	815	1	92	16.7	42.9	24.9	Trace	29	1,120
114	Tablespoon (about 1/8 stick)	1 tbsp	14	16	100	Trace	12	2.1	5.3	3.1	Trace	4	140
115	Pat (1 in square, 1/3 in high; 90 per lb).	1 pat	5	16	35	Trace	4	.7	1.9	1.1	Trace	1	50
116	Soft, two 8-oz containers per lb.	1 container	227	16	1,635	1	184	32.5	71.5	65.4	Trace	59	2,239
117		1 tbsp	14	16	100	Trace	12	2.0	4.5	4.1	Trace	4	138
	Whipped (6 sticks per lb):												
118	Stick (1/2 cup)	1 stick	76	16	545	Trace	61	11.2	28.7	16.7	Trace	20	750
119	Tablespoon (about 1/8 stick)	1 tbsp	9	16	70	Trace	8	1.4	3.6	2.1	Trace	2	70
	Oils, salad or cooking:												
120	Corn	1 cup	218	0	1,925	0	218	27.7	53.6	125.1	0	0	0
121		1 tbsp	14	0	120	0	14	1.7	3.3	7.8	0	0	0
122	Olive	1 cup	216	0	1,910	0	216	30.7	154.4	17.7	0	0	0
123		1 tbsp	14	0	120	0	14	1.9	9.7	1.1	0	0	0
124	Peanut	1 cup	216	0	1,910	0	216	37.4	98.5	67.0	0	0	0
125		1 tbsp	14	0	120	0	14	2.3	6.2	4.2	0	0	0
126	Safflower	1 cup	218	0	1,925	0	218	20.5	25.9	159.8	0	0	0
127		1 tbsp	14	0	120	0	14	1.3	1.6	10.0	0	0	0
128	Soybean oil, hydrogenated (partially hardened).	1 cup	218	0	1,925	0	218	31.8	93.1	75.6	0	0	0
129		1 tbsp	14	0	120	0	14	2.0	5.8	4.7	0	0	0
130	Soybean-cottonseed oil blend, hydrogenated.	1 cup	218	0	1,925	0	218	38.2	63.0	99.6	0	0	0
131		1 tbsp	14	0	120	0	14	2.4	3.9	6.2	0	0	0
	Salad dressings:												
	Commercial:												
	Blue cheese:												
132	Regular	1 tbsp	15	32	75	1	8	1.6	1.7	3.8	1	6	153
133	Low calorie (5 Cal per tsp)	1 tbsp	16	84	10	Trace	1	.5	.3	Trace	1	5	155
	French:												
134	Regular	1 tbsp	16	39	65	Trace	6	1.1	1.3	3.2	3	13	214
135	Low calorie (5 Cal per tsp)	1 tbsp	16	77	15	Trace	1	.1	.1	.4	2	13	110
	Italian:												
136	Regular	1 tbsp	15	28	85	Trace	9	1.6	1.9	4.7	1	2	116
137	Low calorie (2 Cal per tsp)	1 tbsp	15	90	10	Trace	1	.1	.1	.4	Trace	2	110
138	Mayonnaise	1 tbsp	14	15	100	Trace	11	2.0	2.4	5.6	Trace	5	78
	Mayonnaise type:												
139	Regular	1 tbsp	15	41	65	Trace	6	1.1	1.4	3.2	2	1	82
140	Low calorie (8 Cal per tsp)	1 tbsp	16	81	20	Trace	2	.4	.4	1.0	2	1	17
141	Tartar sauce, regular	1 tbsp	14	34	75	Trace	8	1.5	1.8	4.1	1	11	141
	Thousand Island:												
142	Regular	1 tbsp	16	32	80	Trace	8	1.4	1.7	4.0	2	18	109
143	Low calorie (10 Cal per tsp)	1 tbsp	15	68	25	Trace	2	.4	.4	1.0	2	17	153
	From home recipe:												
144	Cooked type[13]	1 tbsp	16	68	25	1	2	.5	.6	.3	2	19	?
	FISH, SHELLFISH, MEAT, POULTRY; RELATED PRODUCTS												
	Fish and shellfish:												
145	Bluefish, baked with butter or margarine.	3 oz	85	68	135	22	4	—	—	—	0	—	87

NUTRIENT TABLES OF COMMONLY USED FOODS FOR MODIFIED DIETARY PLANS

(Dashes (—) denote lack of reliable data for a constituent believed to be present in measurable amount)

Item No.	Foods, approximate measures, units, and weight (edible part unless footnotes indicate otherwise)			Water	Food energy	Protein	Fat	Fatty Acids: Saturated (total)	Fatty Acids: Unsaturated: Oleic	Fatty Acids: Unsaturated: Linoleic	Carbohydrate	Potassium	Sodium
	FISH, SHELLFISH, MEAT, POULTRY; RELATED PRODUCTS—Con.		Grams	Percent	Calories	Grams	Grams	Grams	Grams	Grams	Grams	Milligrams	Milligrams
	Clams:												
146	Raw, meat only	3 oz	85	82	65	11	1	—	—	—	2	154	102
147	Canned, solids and liquid	3 oz	85	86	45	7	1	0.2	Trace	Trace	2	119	—
148	●Crabmeat (white or king), canned, not pressed down.	1 cup	135	77	135	24	3	.6	0.4	0.1	1	149	1,700
149	Fish sticks, breaded, cooked, frozen (stick, 4 by 1 by 1/2 in).	1 fish stick or 1 oz	28	66	50	5	3	—	—	—	2	—	10
150	Haddock, breaded, fried[14]	3 oz	85	66	140	17	5	1.4	2.2	1.2	5	296	150
151	Ocean perch, breaded, fried[14]	1 fillet	85	59	195	16	11	2.7	4.4	2.3	6	242	128
152	Oysters, raw, meat only (13-19 medium Selects).	1 cup	240	85	160	20	4	1.3	.2	.1	8	290	319
153	●Salmon, pink, canned, solids and liquid.	3 oz	85	71	120	17	5	.9	.8	.1	0	307	443
154✱	●Sardines, Atlantic, canned in oil, drained solids.	3 oz	85	62	175	20	9	3.0	2.5	.5	0	502	552
155	Scallops, frozen, breaded, fried, reheated.	6 scallops	90	60	175	16	8	—	—	—	9	—	175
156	Shad, baked with butter or margarine, bacon.	3 oz	85	64	170	20	10	—	—	—	0	320	90
	Shrimp:												
157	● Canned meat	3 oz	85	70	100	21	1	.1	.1	Trace	1	104	1,955
158	French fried[16]	3 oz	85	57	190	17	9	2.3	3.7	2.0	9	195	159
159	●Tuna, canned in oil, drained solids.	3 oz	85	61	170	24	7	1.7	1.7	.7	0	—	303
160	Tuna salad[17]	1 cup	205	70	350	30	22	4.3	6.3	6.7	7	—	—
	Meat and meat products:												
161	Bacon, (20 slices per lb, raw), broiled or fried, crisp.	2 slices	15	8	85	4	8	2.5	3.7	.7	Trace	35	274
	Beef,[18] cooked:												
	Cuts braised, simmered or pot roasted:												
162	Lean and fat (piece, 2 1/2 by 2 1/2 by 3/4 in).	3 oz	85	53	245	23	16	6.8	6.5	.4	0	184	33
163	Lean only from item 162	2.5 oz	72	62	140	22	5	2.1	1.8	.2	0	176	33
	Ground beef, broiled:												
164	Lean with 10% fat	3 oz or patty 3 by 5/8 in	85	60	185	23	10	4.0	3.9	.3	0	261	57
165	Lean with 21% fat	2.9 oz or patty 3 by 5/8 in	82	54	235	20	17	7.0	6.7	.4	0	221	49
	Roast, oven cooked, no liquid added:												
	Relatively fat, such as rib:												
166	Lean and fat (2 pieces, 4 1/8 by 2 1/4 by 1/4 in).	3 oz	85	40	375	17	33	14.0	13.6	.8	0	189	41
167	Lean only from item 166	1.8 oz	51	57	125	14	7	3.0	2.5	.3	0	161	38
	Relatively lean, such as heel of round:												
168	Lean and fat (2 pieces, 4 1/8 by 2 1/4 by 1/4 in).	3 oz	85	62	165	25	7	2.8	2.7	.2	0	279	60
169	Lean only from item 168	2.8 oz	78	65	125	24	3	1.2	1.0	0.1	0	268	52
	Steak:												
	Relatively fat-sirloin, broiled:												
170	Lean and fat (piece, 2 1/2 by 2 1/2 by 3/4 in).	3 oz	85	44	330	20	27	11.3	11.1	.6	0	220	48
171	Lean only from item 170	2.0 oz	56	59	115	18	4	1.8	1.6	.2	0	202	32
	Relatively lean—round, braised:												
172	Lean and fat (piece, 4 1/8 by 2 1/4 by 1/2 in).	3 oz	85	55	220	24	13	5.5	5.2	.4	0	272	60
173	Lean only from item 172	2.4 oz	68	61	130	21	4	1.7	1.5	.2	0	238	48
	Beef, canned:												
174	Corned beef	3 oz	85	59	185	22	10	4.9	4.5	.2	0	—	893
175✱	● Corned beef hash	1 cup	220	67	400	19	25	11.9	10.9	.5	24	440	1,188
176	●Beef, dried, chipped	2 1/2-oz jar	71	48	145	24	4	2.1	2.0	.1	0	142	3,048
177✱	Beef and vegetable stew	1 cup	245	82	220	16	11	4.9	4.5	.2	15	613	91
178	●Beef potpie (home recipe), baked[19] (piece, 1/3 of 9-in diam. pie).	1 piece	210	55	515	21	30	7.9	12.8	6.7	39	334	596
179✱	●Chili con carne with beans, canned.	1 cup	255	72	340	19	16	7.5	6.8	.3	31	594	1,194

NUTRIENT TABLES OF COMMONLY USED FOODS FOR MODIFIED DIETARY PLANS

(Dashes (—) denote lack of reliable data for a constituent believed to be present in measurable amount)

Item No.	Foods, approximate measures, units, and weight (edible part unless footnotes indicate otherwise)			Water	Food energy	Protein	Fat	Fatty Acids: Saturated (total)	Fatty Acids: Unsaturated: Oleic	Fatty Acids: Unsaturated: Linoleic	Carbohydrate	Potassium	Sodium
			Grams	Percent	Calories	Grams	Grams	Grams	Grams	Grams	Grams	Milligrams	Milligrams
	FISH, SHELLFISH, MEAT, POULTRY; RELATED PRODUCTS—Con.												
180	✱ ● Chop suey with beef and pork (home recipe).	1 cup	250	75	300	26	17	8.5	6.2	.7	13	425	1,053
181	Heart, beef, lean, braised	3 oz	85	61	160	27	5	1.5	1.1	.6	1	197	87
	Lamb, cooked:												
	Chop, rib (cut 3 per lb with bone), broiled:												
182	Lean and fat	3.1 oz	89	43	360	18	32	14.8	12.1	1.2	0	200	57
183	Lean only from item 182	2 oz	57	60	120	16	6	2.5	2.1	.2	0	174	39
	Leg, roasted:												
184	Lean and fat (2 pieces, 4 1/8 by 2 1/4 by 1/4 in).	3 oz	85	54	235	22	16	7.3	6.0	.6	0	241	59
185	Lean only from item 184	2.5 oz	71	62	130	20	5	2.1	1.8	.2	0	227	46
	Shoulder, roasted:												
186	Lean and fat (3 pieces, 2 1/2 by 2 1/2 by 1/4 in).	3 oz	85	50	285	18	23	10.8	8.8	.9	0	206	59
187	Lean only from item 186	2.3 oz	64	61	130	17	6	3.6	2.3	.2	0	193	45
188	Liver, beef, fried[20] (slice, 6 1/2 by 2 3/8 by 3/8 in).	3 oz	85	56	195	22	9	2.5	3.5	.9	5	323	150
	Pork, cured, cooked:												
189	● Ham, light cure, lean and fat, roasted (2 pieces, 4 1/8 by 2 1/4 by 1/4 in).[22]	3 oz	85	54	245	18	19	6.8	7.9	1.7	0	199	637
	Luncheon meat:												
190	Boiled ham, slice (8 per 8-oz pkg.).	1 oz	28	59	65	5	5	1.7	2.0	.4	0	—	288
	Canned, spiced or unspiced:												
191	● Slice, approx. 3 by 2 by 1/2 in.	1 slice	60	55	175	9	15	5.4	6.7	1.0	1	133	422
	Pork, fresh,[18] cooked:												
	Chop, loin (cut 3 per lb with bone), broiled:												
192	Lean and fat	2.7 oz	78	42	305	19	25	8.9	10.4	2.2	0	216	46
193	Lean only from item 192	2 oz	56	53	150	17	9	3.1	3.6	.8	0	192	42
	Roast, oven cooked, no liquid added:												
194	Lean and fat (piece, 2 1/2 by 2 1/2 by 3/4 in).	3 oz	85	46	310	21	24	8.7	10.2	2.2	0	233	47
195	Lean only from item 194	2.4 oz	68	55	175	20	10	3.5	4.1	.8	0	224	45
	Shoulder cut, simmered:												
196	Lean and fat (3 pieces, 2 1/2 by 2 1/2 by 1/4 in).	3 oz	85	46	320	20	26	9.3	10.9	2.3	0	158	47
197	Lean only from item 196	2.2 oz	63	60	135	18	6	2.2	2.6	.6	0	146	43
	Sausages (see also Luncheon meat (items 190-191)):												
198	● Bologna, slice (8 per 8-oz pkg.).	1 slice	28	56	85	3	8	3.0	3.4	.5	Trace	65	369
199	● Braunschweiger, slice (6 per 6-oz pkg.).	1 slice	28	53	90	4	8	2.6	3.4	.8	1	—	310
200	● Brown and serve (10-11 per 8-oz pkg.), browned.	1 link	17	40	70	3	6	2.3	2.8	.7	Trace	—	193
201	● Deviled ham, canned	1 tbsp	13	51	45	2	4	1.5	1.8	.4	0	—	122
202	● Frankfurter (8 per 1-lb pkg.), cooked (reheated).	1 frankfurter	56	57	170	7	15	5.6	6.5	1.2	1	—	499
203	● Meat, potted (beef, chicken, turkey), canned.	1 tbsp	13	61	30	2	2	—	—	—	0	—	—
204	● Pork link (16 per 1-lb pkg.), cooked.	1 link	13	35	60	2	6	2.1	2.4	.5	Trace	35	168
	Salami:												
205	● Dry type, slice (12 per 4-oz pkg.).	1 slice	10	30	45	2	4	1.6	1.6	.1	Trace	—	226
206	● Cooked type, slice (8 per 8-oz pkg.).	1 slice	28	51	90	5	7	3.1	3.0	.2	Trace	—	184
207	● Vienna sausage (7 per 4-oz can).	1 sausage	16	63	40	2	3	1.2	1.4	.2	Trace	—	152
	Veal, medium fat, cooked, bone removed:												
208	Cutlet (4 1/8 by 2 1/4 by 1/2 in), braised or broiled.	3 oz	85	60	185	23	9	4.0	3.4	.4	0	258	55

NUTRIENT TABLES OF COMMONLY USED FOODS FOR MODIFIED DIETARY PLANS

Item No.	Foods, approximate measures, units, and weight (edible part unless footnotes indicate otherwise)			Water	Food energy	Protein	Fat	Fatty Acids: Saturated (total)	Fatty Acids: Unsaturated: Oleic	Fatty Acids: Unsaturated: Linoleic	Carbohydrate	Potassium	Sodium
					NUTRIENTS IN INDICATED QUANTITY (Dashes (—) denote lack of reliable data for a constituent believed to be present in measurable amount)								
			Grams	Percent	Calories	Grams	Grams	Grams	Grams	Grams	Grams	Milligrams	Milligrams
	FISH, SHELLFISH, MEAT, POULTRY; RELATED PRODUCTS—Con.												
209	Rib (2 pieces, 4 1/8 by 2 1/4 by 1/4 in), roasted.	3 oz	85	55	230	23	14	6.1	5.1	.6	0	259	57
	Poultry and poultry products:												
	Chicken, cooked:												
210	Breast, fried,[23] bones removed, 1/2 breast (3.3 oz with bones).	2.8 oz	79	58	160	26	5	1.4	1.8	1.1	1	—	50
211	Drumstick, fried,[23] bones removed (2 oz with bones).	1.3 oz	38	55	90	12	4	1.1	1.3	.9	Trace	—	33
212✱	Half broiler, broiled, bones removed (10.4 oz with bones).	6.2 oz	176	71	240	42	7	2.2	2.5	1.3	0	483	116
213	Chicken, canned, boneless	3 oz	85	65	170	18	10	3.2	3.8	2.0	0	117	268
214✱●	Chicken a la king, cooked (home recipe).	1 cup	245	68	470	27	34	12.7	14.3	3.3	12	404	760
215 ●	Chicken and noodles, cooked (home recipe).	1 cup	240	71	365	22	18	5.9	7.1	3.5	26	149	600
	Chicken chow mein:												
216✱●	Canned	1 cup	250	89	95	7	Trace	—	—	—	18	418	658
217✱●	From home recipe	1 cup	250	78	255	31	10	2.4	3.4	3.1	10	473	680
218 ●	Chicken potpie (home recipe), baked,[19] piece (1/3 or 9-in diam. pie).	1 piece	232	57	545	23	31	11.3	10.9	5.6	42	343	594
	Turkey, roasted, flesh without skin:												
219	Dark meat, piece, 2 1/2 by 1 5/8 by 1/4 in.	4 pieces	85	61	175	26	7	2.1	1.5	1.5	0	338	84
220	Light meat, piece, 4 by 2 by 1/4 in.	2 pieces	85	62	150	28	3	.9	.6	.7	0	349	70
	Light and dark meat:												
221✱	Chopped or diced	1 cup	140	61	265	44	9	2.5	1.7	1.8	0	514	127
222	Pieces (1 slice white meat, 4 by 2 by 1/4 in with 2 slices dark meat, 2 1/2 by 1 5/8 by 1/4 in).	3 pieces	85	61	160	27	5	1.5	1.0	1.1	0	312	77
	FRUITS AND FRUIT PRODUCTS												
	Apples, raw, unpeeled, without cores:												
223	2 3/4-in diam. (about 3 per lb with cores).	1 apple	138	84	80	Trace	1	—	—	—	20	152	2
224	3 1/4 in diam. (about 2 per lb with cores).	1 apple	212	84	125	Trace	1	—	—	—	31	233	2
225	Applejuice, bottled or canned[24]	1 cup	248	88	120	Trace	Trace	—	—	—	30	250	5
	Applesauce, canned:												
226	Sweetened	1 cup	255	76	230	1	Trace	—	—	—	61	166	6
227	Unsweetened	1 cup	244	89	100	Trace	Trace	—	—	—	26	190	5
	Apricots:												
228	Raw, without pits (about 12 per lb with pits).	3 apricots	107	85	55	1	Trace	—	—	—	14	301	1
229✱	Canned in heavy sirup (halves and sirup).	1 cup	258	77	220	2	Trace	—	—	—	57	604	3
✱	Dried:												
230	Uncooked (28 large or 37 medium halves per cup).	1 cup	130	25	340	7	1	—	—	—	86	1,273	34
231✱	Cooked, unsweetened, fruit and liquid.	1 cup	250	76	215	4	1	—	—	—	54	795	20
232	Apricot nectar, canned	1 cup	251	85	145	1	Trace	—	—	—	37	379	9
	Avocados, raw, whole, without skins and seeds:												
233✱	California, mid- and late-winter (with skin and seed, 3 1/8-in diam.; wt., 10 oz).	1 avocado	216	74	370	5	37	5.5	22.0	3.7	13	1,303	22
234✱	Florida, late summer and fall (with skin and seed, 3 5/8-in diam.; wt., 1 lb).	1 avocado	304	78	390	4	33	6.7	15.7	5.3	27	1,836	12
235✱	Banana without peel (about 2.6 per lb with peel).	1 banana	119	76	100	1	Trace	—	—	—	26	440	2
236	Banana flakes	1 tbsp	6	3	20	Trace	Trace	—	—	—	5	92	Trace

NUTRIENT TABLES OF COMMONLY USED FOODS FOR MODIFIED DIETARY PLANS

Item No.	Foods, approximate measures, units, and weight (edible part unless footnotes indicate otherwise)			Water	Food energy	Protein	Fat	Fatty Acids: Saturated (total)	Fatty Acids: Unsaturated: Oleic	Fatty Acids: Unsaturated: Linoleic	Carbohydrate	Potassium	Sodium
			Grams	Percent	Calories	Grams	Grams	Grams	Grams	Grams	Grams	Milligrams	Milligrams
	FRUITS AND FRUIT PRODUCTS--Con.												
237	Blackberries, raw	1 cup	144	85	85	2	1	—	—	—	19	245	1
238	Blueberries, raw	1 cup	145	83	90	1	1	—	—	—	22	117	1
	Cantaloup. See Muskmelons (item 271).												
	Cherries:												
239	Sour (tart), red, pitted, canned, water pack.	1 cup	244	88	105	2	Trace	—	—	—	26	317	5
240	Sweet, raw, without pits and stems.	10 cherries	68	80	45	1	Trace	—	—	—	12	129	1
241*	Cranberry juice cocktail, bottled, sweetened.	1 cup	253	83	165	Trace	Trace	—	—	—	42	25	1
242	Cranberry sauce, sweetened, canned, strained.	1 cup	277	62	405	Trace	1	—	—	—	104	83	1
	Dates:												
243*	Whole, without pits	10 dates	80	23	220	2	Trace	—	—	—	58	518	1
244*	Chopped	1 cup	178	23	490	4	1	—	—	—	130	1,153	2
245*	Fruit cocktail, canned, in heavy sirup.	1 cup	255	80	195	1	Trace	—	—	—	50	411	5
	Grapefruit:												
	Raw, medium, 3 3/4-in diam. (about 1 lb 1 oz):												
246	Pink or red	1/2 grapefruit with peel[28]	241	89	50	1	Trace	—	—	—	13	166	1
247	White	1/2 grapefruit with peel[28]	241	89	45	1	Trace	—	—	—	12	159	1
248	Canned, sections with sirup	1 cup	254	81	180	2	Trace	—	—	—	45	343	8
	Grapefruit juice:												
249	Raw, pink, red, or white	1 cup	246	90	95	1	Trace	—	—	—	23	399	2
	Canned, white:												
250*	Unsweetened	1 cup	247	89	100	1	Trace	—	—	—	24	400	4
251*	Sweetened	1 cup	250	86	135	1	Trace	—	—	—	32	405	1
	Frozen, concentrate, unsweetened:												
252	Undiluted, 6-fl oz can	1 can	207	62	300	4	1	—	—	—	72	1,250	4
253*	Diluted with 3 parts water by volume.	1 cup	247	89	100	1	Trace	—	—	—	24	420	1
254*	Dehydrated crystals, prepared with water (1 lb yields about 1 gal).	1 cup	247	90	100	1	Trace	—	—	—	24	412	2
*	Grapes, European type (adherent skin), raw:												
255	Thompson Seedless	10 grapes	50	81	35	Trace	Trace	—	—	—	9	87	1
256	Tokay and Emperor, seeded types	10 grapes[30]	60	81	40	Trace	Trace	—	—	—	10	99	1
	Grapejuice:												
257	Canned or bottled	1 cup	253	83	165	1	Trace	—	—	—	42	293	8
	Frozen concentrate, sweetened:												
258	Undiluted, 6-fl oz can	1 can	216	53	395	1	Trace	—	—	—	100	255	6
259	Diluted with 3 parts water by volume.	1 cup	250	86	135	1	Trace	—	—	—	33	85	3
260	Grape drink, canned	1 cup	250	86	135	Trace	Trace	—	—	—	35	88	3
261	Lemon, raw, size 165, without peel and seeds (about 4 per lb with peels and seeds).	1 lemon	74	90	20	1	Trace	—	—	—	6	102	2
	Lemon juice:												
262	Raw	1 cup	244	91	60	1	Trace	—	—	—	20	344	2
263	Canned, or bottled, unsweetened	1 cup	244	92	55	1	Trace	—	—	—	19	344	1
264	Frozen, single strength, unsweetened, 6-fl oz can.	1 can	183	92	40	1	Trace	—	—	—	13	258	1
	Lemonade concentrate, frozen:												
265	Undiluted, 6-fl oz can	1 can	219	49	425	Trace	Trace	—	—	—	112	153	2
266	Diluted with 4 1/3 parts water by volume.	1 cup	248	89	105	Trace	Trace	—	—	—	28	40	Trace
	Limeade concentrate, frozen:												
267	Undiluted, 6-fl oz can	1 can	218	50	410	Trace	Trace	—	—	—	108	129	Trace
268	Diluted with 4 1/3 parts water by volume.	1 cup	247	89	100	Trace	Trace	—	—	—	27	32	Trace
	Limejuice:												
269	Raw	1 cup	246	90	65	1	Trace	—	—	—	22	256	Trace
270	Canned, unsweetened	1 cup	246	90	65	1	Trace	—	—	—	22	256	Trace
	Muskmelons, raw, with rind, without seed cavity:												
271*	Cantaloup, orange-fleshed (with rind and seed cavity, 5-in diam., 2 1/3 lb).	1/2 melon with rind[33]	477	91	80	2	Trace	—	—	—	20	682	24

(Dashes (—) denote lack of reliable data for a constituent believed to be present in measurable amount)

NUTRIENT TABLES OF COMMONLY USED FOODS FOR MODIFIED DIETARY PLANS

Item No.	Foods, approximate measures, units, and weight (edible part unless footnotes indicate otherwise)			NUTRIENTS IN INDICATED QUANTITY									
				Water	Food energy	Protein	Fat	Fatty Acids: Saturated (total)	Fatty Acids: Unsaturated: Oleic	Fatty Acids: Unsaturated: Linoleic	Carbohydrate	Potassium	Sodium
			Grams	Percent	Calories	Grams	Grams	Grams	Grams	Grams	Grams	Milligrams	Milligrams
	FRUITS AND FRUIT PRODUCTS—Con.												
272	Honeydew (with rind and seed cavity, 6 1/2-in diam., 5 1/4 lb).	1/10 melon with rind[33]--	226	91	50	1	Trace	—	—	—	11	374	14
	Oranges, all commercial varieties, raw:												
273	Whole, 2 5/8-in diam., without peel and seeds (about 2 1/2 per lb with peel and seeds).	1 orange----------------	131	86	65	1	Trace	—	—	—	16	263	1
274	Sections without membranes------	1 cup-------------------	180	86	90	2	Trace	—	—	—	22	360	1
	*Orange juice:												
275*	Raw, all varieties--------------	1 cup-------------------	248	88	110	2	Trace	—	—	—	26	496	2
276*	Canned, unsweetened-------------	1 cup-------------------	249	87	120	2	Trace	—	—	—	28	496	5
*	Frozen concentrate:												
277	Undiluted, 6-fl oz can--------	1 can-------------------	213	55	360	5	Trace	—	—	—	87	1,500	4
278	Diluted with 3 parts water by volume.	1 cup-------------------	249	87	120	2	Trace	—	—	—	29	503	2
279*	Dehydrated crystals, prepared with water (1 lb yields about 1 gal).	1 cup-------------------	248	88	115	1	Trace	—	—	—	27	518	2
	Orange and grapefruit juice:												
	Frozen concentrate:												
280	Undiluted, 6-fl oz can--------	1 can-------------------	210	59	330	4	1	—	—	—	78	1,308	4
281*	Diluted with 3 parts water by volume.	1 cup-------------------	248	88	110	1	Trace	—	—	—	26	439	Trace
282	Papayas, raw, 1/2-in cubes--------	1 cup-------------------	140	89	55	1	Trace	—	—	—	14	328	4
	Peaches:												
	Raw:												
283	Whole, 2 1/2-in diam., peeled, pitted (about 4 per lb with peels and pits).	1 peach-----------------	100	89	40	1	Trace	—	—	—	10	202	1
284*	Sliced------------------------	1 cup-------------------	170	89	65	1	Trace	—	—	—	16	343	2
*	Canned, yellow-fleshed, solids and liquid (halves or slices):												
285	Sirup pack--------------------	1 cup-------------------	256	79	200	1	Trace	—	—	—	51	333	5
286	Water pack--------------------	1 cup-------------------	244	91	75	1	Trace	—	—	—	20	334	5
	Dried:												
287*	Uncooked----------------------	1 cup-------------------	160	25	420	5	1	—	—	—	109	1,520	26
288*	Cooked, unsweetened, halves and juice.	1 cup-------------------	250	77	205	3	1	—	—	—	54	743	13
	Frozen, sliced, sweetened:												
289	10-oz container---------------	1 container-------------	284	77	250	1	Trace	—	—	—	64	352	6
290	Cup---------------------------	1 cup-------------------	250	77	220	1	Trace	—	—	—	57	310	5
	*Pears:												
*	Raw, with skin, cored:												
291	Bartlett, 2 1/2-in diam. (about 2 1/2 per lb with cores and stems).	1 pear------------------	164	83	100	1	1	—	—	—	25	213	3
292	Bosc, 2 1/2-in diam. (about 3 per lb with cores and stems).	1 pear------------------	141	83	85	1	1	—	—	—	22	83	3
293	D'Anjou, 3-in diam. (about 2 per lb with cores and stems).	1 pear------------------	200	83	120	1	1	—	—	—	31	260	4
294*	Canned, solids and liquid, sirup pack, heavy (halves or slices).	1 cup-------------------	255	80	195	1	1	—	—	—	50	214	3
	*Pineapple:												
295*	Raw, diced----------------------	1 cup-------------------	155	85	80	1	Trace	—	—	—	21	226	2
*	Canned, heavy sirup pack, solids and liquid:												
296	Crushed, chunks, tidbits-------	1 cup-------------------	255	80	190	1	Trace	—	—	—	49	245	3
	Slices and liquid:												
297	Large-----------------------	1 slice; 2 1/4 tbsp liquid.	105	80	80	Trace	Trace	—	—	—	20	101	1
298	Medium----------------------	1 slice; 1 1/4 tbsp liquid.	58	80	45	Trace	Trace	—	—	—	11	56	1
299	Pineapple juice, unsweetened, canned.	1 cup-------------------	250	86	140	1	Trace	—	—	—	34	373	3
	Plums:												
	Raw, without pits:												

(Dashes (—) denote lack of reliable data for a constituent believed to be present in measurable amount)

NUTRIENT TABLES OF COMMONLY USED FOODS FOR MODIFIED DIETARY PLANS

(Dashes (—) denote lack of reliable data for a constituent believed to be present in measurable amount)

Item No.	Foods, approximate measures, units, and weight (edible part unless footnotes indicate otherwise)			Water	Food energy	Protein	Fat	Fatty Acids: Saturated (total)	Fatty Acids: Unsaturated: Oleic	Fatty Acids: Unsaturated: Linoleic	Carbohydrate	Potassium	Sodium
			Grams	Percent	Calories	Grams	Grams	Grams	Grams	Grams	Grams	Milligrams	Milligrams
	FRUITS AND FRUIT PRODUCTS—Con.												
300	Japanese and hybrid (2 1/8-in diam., about 6 1/2 per lb with pits).	1 plum	66	87	30	Trace	Trace	—	—	—	8	112	1
301	Prune-type (1 1/2-in diam., about 15 per lb with pits).	1 plum	28	79	20	Trace	Trace	—	—	—	6	48	Trace
	Canned, heavy sirup pack (Italian prunes), with pits and liquid:												
302	Cup	1 cup[36]	272	77	215	1	Trace	—	—	—	56	367	3
303	Portion	3 plums; 2 3/4 tbsp liquid.[36]	140	77	110	1	Trace	—	—	—	29	189	1
	Prunes, dried, "softenized," with pits:												
304	Uncooked	4 extra large or 5 large prunes.[36]	49	28	110	1	Trace	—	—	—	29	298	4
305*	Cooked, unsweetened, all sizes, fruit and liquid.	1 cup[36]	250	66	255	2	1	—	—	—	67	695	9
306*	Prune juice, canned or bottled	1 cup	256	80	195	1	Trace	—	—	—	49	602	5
	*Raisins, seedless:												
307	Cup, not pressed down	1 cup	145	18	420	4	Trace	—	—	—	112	1,106	39
308	Packet, 1/2 oz (1 1/2 tbsp)	1 packet	14	18	40	Trace	Trace	—	—	—	11	107	4
	Raspberries, red:												
309	Raw, capped, whole	1 cup	123	84	70	1	1	—	—	—	17	207	1
310	Frozen, sweetened, 10-oz container	1 container	284	74	280	2	1	—	—	—	70	284	3
	Rhubarb, cooked, added sugar:												
311*	From raw	1 cup	270	63	380	1	Trace	—	—	—	97	548	5
312*	From frozen, sweetened	1 cup	270	63	385	1	1	—	—	—	98	475	8
	Strawberries:												
313	Raw, whole berries, capped	1 cup	149	90	55	1	1	—	—	—	13	244	1
	Frozen, sweetened:												
314	Sliced, 10-oz container	1 container	284	71	310	1	1	—	—	—	79	318	3
315	Whole, 1-lb container (about 1 3/4 cups).	1 container	454	76	415	2	1	—	—	—	107	472	5
316	Tangerine, raw, 2 3/8-in diam., size 176, without peel (about 4 per lb with peels and seeds).	1 tangerine	86	87	40	1	Trace	—	—	—	10	108	1
317*	Tangerine juice, canned, sweetened.	1 cup	249	87	125	1	Trace	—	—	—	30	440	2
318*	Watermelon, raw, 4 by 8 in wedge with rind and seeds (1/16 of 32 2/3-lb melon, 10 by 16 in).	1 wedge with rind and seeds[37]	926	93	110	2	1	—	—	—	27	426	8
	GRAIN PRODUCTS												
	Bagel, 3-in diam.:												
319	Egg	1 bagel	55	32	165	6	2	0.5	0.9	0.8	28	41	—
320	Water	1 bagel	55	29	165	6	1	.2	.4	.6	30	42	—
321	Barley, pearled, light, uncooked	1 cup	200	11	700	16	2	.3	.2	.8	158	320	6
	Biscuits, baking powder, 2-in diam. (enriched flour, vegetable shortening):												
322	From home recipe	1 biscuit	28	27	105	2	5	1.2	2.0	1.2	13	33	175
323	From mix	1 biscuit	28	29	90	2	3	.6	1.1	.7	15	32	272
	Breadcrumbs (enriched):[38]												
324	●Dry, grated	1 cup	100	7	390	13	5	1.0	1.6	1.4	73	152	736
	Soft. See White bread (items 349-350).												
	Breads:												
325	Boston brown bread, canned, slice, 3 1/4 by 1/2 in.[38]	1 slice	45	45	95	2	1	.1	.2	.2	21	131	120
	Cracked-wheat bread (3/4 enriched wheat flour, 1/4 cracked wheat):[38]												
326	Loaf, 1 lb	1 loaf	454	35	1,195	39	10	2.2	3.0	3.9	236	608	2,664
327	Slice (18 per loaf)	1 slice	25	35	65	2	1	.1	.2	.2	13	34	148
	French or vienna bread, enriched:[38]												
328	Loaf, 1 lb	1 loaf	454	31	1,315	41	14	3.2	4.7	4.6	251	408	2,631
	Slice:												
329	French (5 by 2 1/2 by 1 in)	1 slice	35	31	100	3	1	.2	.4	.4	19	32	203
330	Vienna (4 3/4 by 4 by 1/2 in).	1 slice	25	31	75	2	1	.2	.3	.3	14	23	145

NUTRIENT TABLES OF COMMONLY USED FOODS FOR MODIFIED DIETARY PLANS

(Dashes (—) denote lack of reliable data for a constituent believed to be present in measurable amount)

Item No.	Foods, approximate measures, units, and weight (edible part unless footnotes indicate otherwise)			Water	Food energy	Protein	Fat	Fatty Acids: Saturated (total)	Fatty Acids: Unsaturated: Oleic	Fatty Acids: Unsaturated: Linoleic	Carbohydrate	Potassium	Sodium
	GRAIN PRODUCTS—Con.		Grams	Percent	Calories	Grams	Grams	Grams	Grams	Grams	Grams	Milligrams	Milligrams
	Italian bread, enriched:												
331	Loaf, 1 lb	1 loaf	454	32	1,250	41	4	.6	.3	1.5	256	336	2,654
332	Slice, 4 1/2 by 3 1/4 by 3/4 in.	1 slice	30	32	85	3	Trace	Trace	Trace	.1	17	22	176
	Raisin bread, enriched:[38]												
333	Loaf, 1 lb	1 loaf	454	35	1,190	30	13	3.0	4.7	3.9	243	1,057	1,656
334	Slice (18 per loaf)	1 slice	25	35	65	2	1	.2	.3	.2	13	58	91
	Rye Bread:												
	American, light (2/3 enriched wheat flour, 1/3 rye flour):												
335	Loaf, 1 lb	1 loaf	454	36	1,100	41	5	0.7	0.5	2.2	236	658	2,527
336	Slice (4 3/4 by 3 3/4 by 7/16 in).	1 slice	25	36	60	2	Trace	Trace	Trace	.1	13	36	139
	Pumpernickel (2/3 rye flour, 1/3 enriched wheat flour):												
337	Loaf, 1 lb	1 loaf	454	34	1,115	41	5	.7	.5	2.4	241	2,059	2,581
338	Slice (5 by 4 by 3/8 in)	1 slice	32	34	80	3	Trace	.1	Trace	.2	17	145	182
	White bread, enriched:[38]												
	Soft-crumb type:												
339	Loaf, 1 lb	1 loaf	454	36	1,225	39	15	3.4	5.3	4.6	229	476	2,300
340	Slice (18 per loaf)	1 slice	25	36	70	2	1	.2	.3	.3	13	26	127
341	Slice, toasted	1 slice	22	25	70	2	1	.2	.3	.3	13	26	127
342	Slice (22 per loaf)	1 slice	20	36	55	2	1	.2	.2	.2	10	21	101
343	Slice, toasted	1 slice	17	25	55	2	1	.2	.2	.2	10	21	101
344	Loaf, 1 1/2 lb	1 loaf	680	36	1,835	59	22	5.2	7.9	6.9	343	714	3,448
345	Slice (24 per loaf)	1 slice	28	36	75	2	1	.2	.3	.3	14	29	124
346	Slice, toasted	1 slice	24	25	75	2	1	.2	.3	.3	14	29	124
347	Slice (28 per loaf)	1 slice	24	36	65	2	1	.2	.3	.2	12	25	122
348	Slice, toasted	1 slice	21	25	65	2	1	.2	.3	.2	12	25	122
349	Cubes	1 cup	30	36	80	3	1	.2	.3	.3	15	32	152
350	Crumbs	1 cup	45	36	120	4	1	.3	.5	.5	23	47	228
	Firm-crumb type:												
351	Loaf, 1 lb	1 loaf	454	35	1,245	41	17	3.9	5.9	5.2	228	549	2,245
352	Slice (20 per loaf)	1 slice	23	35	65	2	1	.2	.3	.3	12	28	114
353	Slice, toasted	1 slice	20	24	65	2	1	.2	.3	.3	12	28	114
354	Loaf, 2 lb	1 loaf	907	35	2,495	82	34	7.7	11.8	10.4	455	1,097	4,490
355	Slice (34 per loaf)	1 slice	27	35	75	2	1	.2	.3	.3	14	33	134
356	Slice, toasted	1 slice	23	24	75	2	1	.2	.3	.3	14	33	134
	Whole-wheat bread:												
	Soft-crumb type:[38]												
357	Loaf, 1 lb	1 loaf	454	36	1,095	41	12	2.2	2.9	4.2	224	1,161	2,404
358	Slice (16 per loaf)	1 slice	28	36	65	3	1	.1	.2	.2	14	72	148
359	Slice, toasted	1 slice	24	24	65	3	1	.1	.2	.2	14	72	148
	Firm-crumb type:[38]												
360	Loaf, 1 lb	1 loaf	454	36	1,100	48	14	2.5	3.3	4.9	216	1,238	2,390
361	Slice (18 per loaf)	1 slice	25	36	60	3	1	.1	.2	.3	12	68	132
362	Slice, toasted	1 slice	21	24	60	3	1	.1	.2	.3	12	68	132
	Breakfast cereals:												
	Hot type, cooked:												
	Corn (hominy) grits, degermed:												
363	Enriched	1 cup	245	87	125	3	Trace	Trace	Trace	.1	27	27	1
364	Unenriched	1 cup	245	87	125	3	Trace	Trace	Trace	.1	27	27	1
365	Farina, quick-cooking, enriched.	1 cup	245	89	105	3	Trace	Trace	Trace	.1	22	25	1
366	Oatmeal or rolled oats	1 cup	240	87	130	5	2	.4	.8	.9	23	146	1
367	● Wheat, rolled	1 cup	240	80	180	5	1	—	—	—	41	202	708
368	● Wheat, whole-meal	1 cup	245	88	110	4	1	—	—	—	23	118	519
	Ready-to-eat:												
369	Bran flakes (40% bran), added sugar, salt, iron, vitamins.	1 cup	35	3	105	4	1	—	—	—	28	137	207
370	Bran flakes with raisins, added sugar, salt, iron, vitamins.	1 cup	50	7	145	4	1	—	—	—	40	154	212
	Breakfast cereals—Continued												
	Ready-to-eat—Continued												
	Corn flakes:												
371	Plain, added sugar, salt, iron, vitamins.	1 cup	25	4	95	2	Trace	—	—	—	21	30	251
372	● Sugar-coated, added salt, iron, vitamins.	1 cup	40	2	155	2	Trace	—	—	—	37	27	854

NUTRIENT TABLES OF COMMONLY USED FOODS FOR MODIFIED DIETARY PLANS

(Dashes (—) denote lack of reliable data for a constituent believed to be present in measurable amount)

Item No.	Foods, approximate measures, units, and weight (edible part unless footnotes indicate otherwise)		Grams	Water	Food energy	Protein	Fat	Fatty Acids: Saturated (total)	Fatty Acids: Unsaturated Oleic	Fatty Acids: Unsaturated Linoleic	Carbohydrate	Potassium	Sodium
			Grams	Percent	Calories	Grams	Grams	Grams	Grams	Grams	Grams	Milligrams	Milligrams
	GRAIN PRODUCTS—Con.												
373	Corn, oat flour, puffed, added sugar, salt, iron, vitamins.	1 cup	20	4	80	2	1	—	—	—	16	—	206
374	Corn, shredded, added sugar, salt, iron, thiamin, niacin.	1 cup	25	3	95	2	Trace	—	—	—	22	—	269
375 ●	Oats, puffed, added sugar, salt, minerals, vitamins.	1 cup	25	3	100	3	1	—	—	—	19	—	317
	Rice, puffed:												
376	Plain, added iron, thiamin, niacin.	1 cup	15	4	60	1	Trace	—	—	—	13	15	Trace
377 ●	Presweetened, added salt, iron, vitamins.	1 cup	28	3	115	1	0	—	—	—	26	43	318
378 ●	Wheat flakes, added sugar, salt, iron, vitamins.	1 cup	30	4	105	3	Trace	—	—	—	24	81	310
	Wheat, puffed:												
379	Plain, added iron, thiamin, niacin.	1 cup	15	3	55	2	Trace	—	—	—	12	51	1
380	Presweetened, added salt, iron, vitamins.	1 cup	38	3	140	3	Trace	—	—	—	33	63	56
381	Wheat, shredded, plain	1 oblong biscuit or 1/2 cup spoon-size biscuits.	25	7	90	2	1	—	—	—	20	87	1
382	Wheat germ, without salt and sugar, toasted.	1 tbsp	6	4	25	2	1	—	—	—	3	57	Trace
383	Buckwheat flour, light, sifted	1 cup	98	12	340	6	1	0.2	0.4	0.4	78	314	1
384 ●	Bulgur, canned, seasoned	1 cup	135	56	245	8	4	—	—	—	44	151	621
	Cake icings. See Sugars and Sweets (items 532-536).												
	Cakes made from cake mixes with enriched flour:[46]												
	Angelfood:												
385	Whole cake (9 3/4-in diam. tube cake).	1 cake	635	34	1,645	36	1	—	—	—	377	381	927
386	Piece, 1/12 of cake	1 piece	53	34	135	3	Trace	—	—	—	32	32	77
	Coffeecake:												
387	Whole cake (7 3/4 by 5 5/8 by 1 1/4 in).	1 cake	430	30	1,385	27	41	11.7	16.3	8.8	225	469	1,853
388	Piece, 1/6 of cake	1 piece	72	30	230	5	7	2.0	2.7	1.5	38	78	310
	Cupcakes, made with egg, milk, 2 1/2-in diam.:												
389	Without icing	1 cupcake	25	26	90	1	3	.8	1.2	.7	14	21	113
390	With chocolate icing	1 cupcake	36	22	130	2	5	2.0	1.6	.6	21	42	121
	Devil's food with chocolate icing:												
391	Whole, 2 layer cake (8- or 9-in diam.).	1 cake	1,107	24	3,755	49	136	50.0	44.9	17.0	645	1,439	2,900
392	Piece, 1/16 of cake	1 piece	69	24	235	3	8	3.1	2.8	1.1	40	90	181
393	Cupcake, 2 1/2-in diam	1 cupcake	35	24	120	2	4	1.6	1.4	.5	20	46	92
	Gingerbread:												
394	Whole cake (8-in square)	1 cake	570	37	1,575	18	39	9.7	16.6	10.0	291	1,562	1,733
395	Piece, 1/9 of cake	1 piece	63	37	175	2	4	1.1	1.8	1.1	32	173	192
	White, 2 layer with chocolate icing:												
396	Whole cake (8- or 9-in diam.)	1 cake	1,140	21	4,000	44	122	48.2	46.4	20.0	716	1,322	2,588
397	Piece, 1/16 of cake	1 piece	71	21	250	3	8	3.0	2.9	1.2	45	82	161
	Yellow, 2 layer with chocolate icing:												
398	Whole cake (8- or 9-in diam.)	1 cake	1,108	26	3,735	45	125	47.8	47.8	20.3	638	1,208	2,515
399	Piece, 1/16 of cake	1 piece	69	26	235	3	8	3.0	3.0	1.3	40	75	157
	Cakes made from home recipes using enriched flour:[47]												
	Boston cream pie with custard filling:												
400	Whole cake (8-in diam.)	1 cake	825	35	2,490	41	78	23.0	30.1	15.2	412	[48]734	1,535
401	Piece, 1/12 of cake	1 piece	69	35	210	3	6	1.9	2.5	1.3	34	[48]61	128
	Fruitcake, dark:												
402	Loaf, 1-lb (7 1/2 by 2 by 1 1/2 in).	1 loaf	454	18	1,720	22	69	14.4	33.5	14.8	271	2,250	717
403	Slice, 1/30 of loaf	1 slice	15	18	55	1	2	.5	1.1	.5	9	74	24
	Plain, sheet cake:												
	Without icing:												
404	Whole cake (9-in square)	1 cake	777	25	2,830	35	108	29.5	44.4	23.9	434	[48]614	2,331

NUTRIENT TABLES OF COMMONLY USED FOODS FOR MODIFIED DIETARY PLANS

(Dashes (—) denote lack of reliable data for a constituent believed to be present in measurable amount)

Item No.	Foods, approximate measures, units, and weight (edible part unless footnotes indicate otherwise)			Water	Food energy	Protein	Fat	Fatty Acids: Saturated (total)	Fatty Acids: Unsaturated: Oleic	Fatty Acids: Unsaturated: Linoleic	Carbohydrate	Potassium	Sodium
			Grams	Percent	Calories	Grams	Grams	Grams	Grams	Grams	Grams	Milligrams	Milligrams
	GRAIN PRODUCTS—Con.												
405	Piece, 1/9 of cake	1 piece	86	25	315	4	12	3.3	4.9	2.6	48	[48]68	258
	With uncooked white icing:												
406	Whole cake (9-in square)	1 cake	1,096	21	4,020	37	129	42.2	49.5	24.4	694	[48]669	2,488
407	Piece, 1/9 of cake	1 piece	121	21	445	4	14	4.7	5.5	2.7	77	[48]74	275
	Pound:[49]												
408	Loaf, 8 1/2 by 3 1/2 by 3 1/4 in.	1 loaf	565	16	2,725	31	170	42.9	73.1	39.6	273	345	1,006
409	Slice, 1/17 of loaf	1 slice	33	16	160	2	10	2.5	4.3	2.3	16	20	59
	Spongecake:												
410	Whole cake (9 3/4-in diam. tube cake).	1 cake	790	32	2,345	60	45	13.1	15.8	5.7	427	687	1,319
411	Piece, 1/12 of cake	1 piece	66	32	195	5	4	1.1	1.3	.5	36	57	110
	Cookies made with enriched flour:[50] [51]												
	Brownies with nuts:												
	Home-prepared, 1 3/4 by 1 3/4 by 7/8 in:												
412	From home recipe	1 brownie	20	10	95	1	6	1.5	3.0	1.2	10	38	50
413	From commercial recipe	1 brownie	20	11	85	1	4	.9	1.4	1.3	13	34	34
414	Frozen, with chocolate icing,[52] 1 1/2 by 1 3/4 by 7/8 in.	1 brownie	25	13	105	1	5	2.0	2.2	.7	15	44	40
	Chocolate chip:												
415	Commercial, 2 1/4-in diam., 3/8 in thick.	4 cookies	42	3	200	2	9	2.8	2.9	2.2	29	56	168
416	From home recipe, 2 1/3-in diam.	4 cookies	40	3	205	2	12	3.5	4.5	2.9	24	47	139
417	Fig bars, square (1 5/8 by 1 5/8 by 3/8 in) or rectangular (1 1/2 by 1 3/4 by 1/2 in).	4 cookies	56	14	200	2	3	.8	1.2	.7	42	111	141
418	Gingersnaps, 2-in diam., 1/4 in thick.	4 cookies	28	3	90	2	2	.7	1.0	.6	22	129	160
419	Macaroons, 2 3/4-in diam., 1/4 in thick.	2 cookies	38	4	180	2	9	—	—	—	25	176	13
420	Oatmeal with raisins, 2 5/8-in diam., 1/4 in thick.	4 cookies	52	3	235	3	8	2.0	3.3	2.0	38	192	84
	Cookies made with enriched flour[50] [51]—Continued												
421	Plain, prepared from commercial chilled dough, 2 1/2-in diam., 1/4 in thick.	4 cookies	48	5	240	2	12	3.0	5.2	2.9	31	23	166
422	Sandwich type (chocolate or vanilla), 1 3/4-in diam., 3/8 in thick.	4 cookies	40	2	200	2	9	2.2	3.9	2.2	28	15	193
423	Vanilla wafers, 1 3/4-in diam., 1/4 in thick.	10 cookies	40	3	185	2	6	—	—	—	30	29	101
	Cornmeal:												
424	Whole-ground, unbolted, dry form.	1 cup	122	12	435	11	5	.5	1.0	2.5	90	346	1
425	Bolted (nearly whole-grain), dry form.	1 cup	122	12	440	11	4	.5	.9	2.1	91	303	1
	Degermed, enriched:												
426	Dry form	1 cup	138	12	500	11	2	.2	.4	.9	108	166	1
427	Cooked	1 cup	240	88	120	3	Trace	Trace	.1	.2	26	38	264
	Degermed, unenriched:												
428	Dry form	1 cup	138	12	500	11	2	.2	.4	.9	108	166	1
429	Cooked	1 cup	240	88	120	3	Trace	Trace	.1	.2	26	38	264
	Crackers:[38]												
430	Graham, plain, 2 1/2-in square	2 crackers	14	6	55	1	1	.3	.5	.3	10	55	95
431	Rye wafers, whole-grain, 1 7/8 by 3 1/2 in.	2 wafers	13	6	45	2	Trace	—	—	—	10	78	140
432	Saltines, made with enriched flour.	4 crackers or 1 packet	11	4	50	1	1	.3	.5	.4	8	13	140
	Danish pastry (enriched flour), plain without fruit or nuts:[54]												
433	Packaged ring, 12 oz	1 ring	340	22	1,435	25	80	24.3	31.7	16.5	155	381	1,244
434	Round piece, about 4 1/4-in diam. by 1 in.	1 pastry	65	22	275	5	15	4.7	6.1	3.2	30	73	238
435	Ounce	1 oz	28	22	120	2	7	2.0	2.7	1.4	13	32	104
	Doughnuts, made with enriched flour:[38]												
436	Cake type, plain, 2 1/2-in diam., 1 in high.	1 doughnut	25	24	100	1	5	1.2	2.0	1.1	13	23	125

NUTRIENT TABLES OF COMMONLY USED FOODS FOR MODIFIED DIETARY PLANS

Item No.	Foods, approximate measures, units, and weight (edible part unless footnotes indicate otherwise)			Water	Food energy	Protein	Fat	Fatty Acids: Saturated (total)	Fatty Acids: Unsaturated: Oleic	Fatty Acids: Unsaturated: Linoleic	Carbohydrate	Potassium	Sodium
	(Dashes (—) denote lack of reliable data for a constituent believed to be present in measurable amount)												
	GRAIN PRODUCTS—Con.		Grams	Percent	Calories	Grams	Grams	Grams	Grams	Grams	Grams	Milligrams	Milligrams
437	Yeast-leavened, glazed, 3 3/4-in diam., 1 1/4 in high.	1 doughnut	50	26	205	3	11	3.3	5.8	3.3	22	34	118
	Macaroni, enriched, cooked (cut lengths, elbows, shells):												
438	Firm stage (hot)	1 cup	130	64	190	7	1	—	—	—	39	103	1
	Tender stage:												
439	Cold macaroni	1 cup	105	73	115	4	Trace	—	—	—	24	64	1
440	Hot macaroni	1 cup	140	73	155	5	1	—	—	—	32	85	1
	Macaroni (enriched) and cheese:												
441	●Canned[55]	1 cup	240	80	230	9	10	4.2	3.1	1.4	26	139	730
442	●From home recipe (served hot)[56]	1 cup	200	58	430	17	22	8.9	8.8	2.9	40	240	1,086
	Muffins made with enriched flour:[38]												
	From home recipe:												
443	Blueberry, 2 3/8-in diam., 1 1/2 in high.	1 muffin	40	39	110	3	4	1.1	1.4	.7	17	46	253
444	Bran	1 muffin	40	35	105	3	4	1.2	1.4	.8	17	172	179
445	Corn (enriched degermed cornmeal and flour), 2 3/8-in diam., 1 1/2 in high.	1 muffin	40	33	125	3	4	1.2	1.6	.9	19	54	192
446	Plain, 3-in diam., 1 1/2 in high.	1 muffin	40	38	120	3	4	1.0	1.7	1.0	17	50	176
	From mix, egg, milk:												
447	Corn, 2 3/8-in diam., 1 1/2 in high.[58]	1 muffin	40	30	130	3	4	1.2	1.7	.9	20	44	192
448	Noodles (egg noodles), enriched, cooked.	1 cup	160	71	200	7	2	—	—	—	37	70	3
449	Noodles, chow mein, canned	1 cup	45	1	220	6	11	—	—	—	26	—	—
	Pancakes, (4-in diam.):[38]												
450	Buckwheat, made from mix (with buckwheat and enriched flours), egg and milk added.	1 cake	27	58	55	2	2	.8	.9	.4	6	66	125
	Plain:												
451	Made from home recipe using enriched flour.	1 cake	27	50	60	2	2	.5	.8	.5	9	33	114
452	Made from mix with enriched flour, egg and milk added.	1 cake	27	51	60	2	2	.7	.7	.3	9	42	152
	Pies, piecrust made with enriched flour, vegetable shortening (9-in diam.):												
	Apple:												
453	Whole	1 pie	945	48	2,420	21	105	27.0	44.5	25.2	360	756	2,844
454	● Sector, 1/7 of pie	1 sector	135	48	345	3	15	3.9	6.4	3.6	51	108	406
	Banana cream:												
455	Whole	1 pie	910	54	2,010	41	85	26.7	33.2	16.2	279	1,847	1,765
456	Sector, 1/7 of pie	1 sector	130	54	285	6	12	3.8	4.7	2.3	40	264	252
	Blueberry:												
457	Whole	1 pie	945	51	2,285	23	102	24.8	43.7	25.1	330	614	2,533
458	● Sector, 1/7 of pie	1 sector	135	51	325	3	15	3.5	6.2	3.6	47	88	362
	Cherry:												
459	Whole	1 pie	945	47	2,465	25	107	28.2	45.0	25.3	363	992	2,873
460	● Sector, 1/7 of pie	1 sector	135	47	350	4	15	4.0	6.4	3.6	52	142	410
	Custard:												
461	Whole	1 pie	910	58	1,985	56	101	33.9	38.5	17.5	213	1,247	2,612
462	● Sector, 1/7 of pie	1 sector	130	58	285	8	14	4.8	5.5	2.5	30	178	373
	Lemon meringue:												
463	Whole	1 pie	840	47	2,140	31	86	26.1	33.8	16.4	317	420	2,369
464	● Sector, 1/7 of pie	1 sector	120	47	305	4	12	3.7	4.8	2.3	45	60	338
	Mince:												
465	Whole	1 pie	945	43	2,560	24	109	28.0	45.9	25.2	389	1,682	4,235
466	● Sector, 1/7 of pie	1 sector	135	43	365	3	16	4.0	6.6	3.6	56	240	605
	Peach:												
467	Whole	1 pie	945	48	2,410	24	101	24.8	43.7	25.1	361	1,408	2,533
468	● Sector, 1/7 of pie	1 sector	135	48	345	3	14	3.5	6.2	3.6	52	201	362
	Pecan:												
469	Whole	1 pie	825	20	3,450	42	189	27.8	101.0	44.2	423	1,015	1,823
470	Sector, 1/7 of pie	1 sector	118	20	495	6	27	4.0	14.4	6.3	61	145	260
	Pumpkin:												
471	Whole	1 pie	910	59	1,920	36	102	37.4	37.5	16.6	223	1,456	1,947
472	Sector, 1/7 of pie	1 sector	130	59	275	5	15	5.4	5.4	2.4	32	208	278
473	Piecrust (home recipe) made with enriched flour and vegetable shortening, baked.	1 pie shell, 9-in diam.	180	15	900	11	60	14.8	26.1	14.9	79	89	1,100

NUTRIENT TABLES OF COMMONLY USED FOODS FOR MODIFIED DIETARY PLANS

Item No.	Foods, approximate measures, units, and weight (edible part unless footnotes indicate otherwise)		Water	Water	Food energy	Protein	Fat	Fatty Acids: Saturated (total)	Fatty Acids: Unsaturated: Oleic	Fatty Acids: Unsaturated: Linoleic	Carbohydrate	Potassium	Sodium
	(Dashes (—) denote lack of reliable data for a constituent believed to be present in measurable amount)		Grams	Percent	Calories	Grams	Grams	Grams	Grams	Grams	Grams	Milligrams	Milligrams
	GRAIN PRODUCTS—Con.												
474	Piecrust mix with enriched flour and vegetable shortening, 10-oz pkg. prepared and baked.	Piecrust for 2-crust pie, 9-in diam.	320	19	1,485	20	93	22.7	39.7	23.4	141	179	2,602
475	●Pizza (cheese) baked, 4 3/4-in sector; 1/8 of 12-in diam. pie.[19]	1 sector	60	45	145	6	4	1.7	1.5	0.6	22	67	327
	Popcorn, popped:												
476	Plain, large kernel	1 cup	6	4	25	1	Trace	Trace	.1	.2	5	—	Trace
477	With oil (coconut) and salt added, large kernel.	1 cup	9	3	40	1	2	1.5	.2	.2	5	—	175
478	Sugar coated	1 cup	35	4	135	2	1	.5	.2	.4	30	—	Trace
	✱ Pretzels, made with enriched flour:												
479	Dutch, twisted, 2 3/4 by 2 5/8 in.	1 pretzel	16	5	60	2	1	—	—	—	12	21	269
480✱	Thin, twisted, 3 1/4 by 2 1/4 by 1/4 in.	10 pretzels	60	5	235	6	3	—	—	—	46	78	1,008
481	Stick, 2 1/4 in long	10 pretzels	3	5	10	Trace	Trace	—	—	—	2	4	50
	✱ Rice, white, enriched:												
482 ●	Instant, ready-to-serve, hot	1 cup	165	73	180	4	Trace	Trace	Trace	Trace	40	—	450
	Long grain:												
483	Raw	1 cup	185	12	670	12	1	.2	.2	.2	149	170	9
484 ●	Cooked, served hot	1 cup	205	73	225	4	Trace	.1	.1	.1	50	57	767
	Parboiled:												
485	Raw	1 cup	185	10	685	14	1	.2	.1	.2	150	278	17
486 ●	Cooked, served hot	1 cup	175	73	185	4	Trace	.1	.1	.1	41	75	627
	Rolls, enriched:[38]												
	Commercial:												
487	Brown-and-serve (12 per 12-oz pkg.), browned.	1 roll	26	27	85	2	2	.4	.7	.5	14	25	136
488	Cloverleaf or pan, 2 1/2-in diam., 2 in high.	1 roll	28	31	85	2	2	.4	.6	.4	15	27	136
489	Frankfurter and hamburger (8 per 11 1/2-oz pkg.).	1 roll	40	31	120	3	2	.5	.8	.6	21	38	202
490 ●	Hard, 3 3/4-in diam., 2 in high.	1 roll	50	25	155	5	2	.4	.6	.5	30	49	313
491 ●	Hoagie or submarine, 11 1/2 by 3 by 2 1/2 in.	1 roll	135	31	390	12	4	.9	1.4	1.4	75	122	783
	From home recipe:												
492	Cloverleaf, 2 1/2-in diam., 2 in high.	1 roll	35	26	120	3	3	.8	1.1	.7	20	41	98
	Spaghetti, enriched, cooked:												
493	Firm stage, "al dente," served hot.	1 cup	130	64	190	7	1	—	—	—	39	103	1
494	Tender stage, served hot	1 cup	140	73	155	5	1	—	—	—	32	85	1
	Spaghetti (enriched) in tomato sauce with cheese:												
495✱●	From home recipe	1 cup	250	77	260	9	9	2.0	5.4	.7	37	408	955
496 ●	Canned	1 cup	250	80	190	6	2	.5	.3	.4	39	303	955
	Spaghetti (enriched) with meat balls and tomato sauce:												
497✱●	From home recipe	1 cup	248	70	330	19	12	3.3	6.3	.9	39	665	1,009
498 ●	Canned	1 cup	250	78	260	12	10	2.2	3.3	3.9	29	245	1,220
499	Toaster pastries	1 pastry	50	12	200	3	6	—	—	—	36	[60]74	280
	Waffles, made with enriched flour, 7-in diam.:[38]												
500 ●	From home recipe	1 waffle	75	41	210	7	7	2.3	2.8	1.4	28	109	356
501 ●	From mix, egg and milk added	1 waffle	75	42	205	7	8	2.8	2.9	1.2	27	146	515
	Wheat flours:												
	All-purpose or family flour, enriched:												
502	Sifted, spooned	1 cup	115	12	420	12	1	0.2	0.1	0.5	88	109	2
503	Unsifted, spooned	1 cup	125	12	455	13	1	.2	.1	.5	95	119	3
504	Cake or pastry flour, enriched, sifted, spooned.	1 cup	96	12	350	7	1	.1	.1	.3	76	91	2
505	Self-rising, enriched, unsifted, spooned.	1 cup	125	12	440	12	1	.2	.1	.5	93	—	1,349
506	Whole-wheat, from hard wheats, stirred.	1 cup	120	12	400	16	2	.4	.2	1.0	85	444	4

NUTRIENT TABLES OF COMMONLY USED FOODS FOR MODIFIED DIETARY PLANS

Item No.	Foods, approximate measures, units, and weight (edible part unless footnotes indicate otherwise)			Water	Food energy	Protein	Fat	Fatty Acids: Saturated (total)	Fatty Acids: Unsaturated: Oleic	Fatty Acids: Unsaturated: Linoleic	Carbohydrate	Potassium	Sodium
			Grams	Percent	Calories	Grams	Grams	Grams	Grams	Grams	Grams	Milligrams	Milligrams
	LEGUMES (DRY), NUTS, SEEDS; RELATED PRODUCTS												
	Almonds, shelled:												
507*	Chopped (about 130 almonds)-----	1 cup--------------------	130	5	775	24	70	5.6	47.7	12.8	25	1,005	
508*	Slivered, not pressed down (about 115 almonds).	1 cup--------------------	115	5	690	21	62	5.0	42.2	11.3	22	889	
	Beans, dry:												
	Common varieties as Great Northern, navy, and others:												
	Cooked, drained:												
509*	Great Northern--------------	1 cup--------------------	180	69	210	14	1	—	—	—	38	749	1
510*	Pea (navy)------------------	1 cup--------------------	190	69	225	15	1	—	—	—	40	790	1
	Canned, solids and liquid:												
	White with—												
511* ●	Frankfurters (sliced)-----	1 cup--------------------	255	71	365	19	18	—	—	—	32	668	1,37
512* ●	Pork and tomato sauce-----	1 cup--------------------	255	71	310	16	7	2.4	2.8	.6	48	536	1,18
513*	Pork and sweet sauce------	1 cup--------------------	255	66	385	16	12	4.3	5.0	1.1	54	—	96
514*	Red kidney------------------	1 cup--------------------	255	76	230	15	1	—	—	—	42	673	[illegible]
515*	Lima, cooked, drained-----------	1 cup--------------------	190	64	260	16	1	—	—	—	49	1,163	
516*	Blackeye peas, dry, cooked (with residual cooking liquid).	1 cup--------------------	250	80	190	13	1	—	—	—	35	573	1
517	Brazil nuts, shelled (6-8 large kernels).	1 oz---------------------	28	5	185	4	19	4.8	6.2	7.1	3	203	Trac
518*	Cashew nuts, roasted in oil-------	1 cup--------------------	140	5	785	24	64	12.9	36.8	10.2	41	650	2
	Coconut meat, fresh:												
519	Piece, about 2 by 2 by 1/2 in---	1 piece------------------	45	51	155	2	16	14.0	.9	.3	4	115	1
520	Shredded or grated, not pressed down.	1 cup--------------------	80	51	275	3	28	24.8	1.6	.5	8	205	1
521*	Filberts (hazelnuts), chopped (about 80 kernels).	1 cup--------------------	115	6	730	14	72	5.1	55.2	7.3	19	810	[illegible]
522*	Lentils, whole, cooked-----------	1 cup--------------------	200	72	210	16	Trace	—	—	—	39	498	—
523 * ●	Peanuts, roasted in oil, salted (whole, halves, chopped).	1 cup--------------------	144	2	840	37	72	13.7	33.0	20.7	27	971	60
524	Peanut butter--------------------	1 tbsp-------------------	16	2	95	4	8	1.5	3.7	2.3	3	100	9
525*	Peas, split, dry, cooked---------	1 cup--------------------	200	70	230	16	1	—	—	—	42	592	2
526*	Pecans, chopped or pieces (about 120 large halves).	1 cup--------------------	118	3	810	11	84	7.2	50.5	20.0	17	712	Trace
527*	Pumpkin and squash kernels, dry, hulled.	1 cup--------------------	140	4	775	41	65	11.8	23.5	27.5	21	1,386	—
528*	Sunflower seeds, dry, hulled------	1 cup--------------------	145	5	810	35	69	8.2	13.7	43.2	29	1,334	4
	Walnuts:												
	Black:												
529*	Chopped or broken kernels-----	1 cup--------------------	125	3	785	26	74	6.3	13.3	45.7	19	575	[illegible]
530	Ground (finely)--------------	1 cup--------------------	80	3	500	16	47	4.0	8.5	29.2	12	368	[illegible]
531*	Persian or English, chopped (about 60 halves).	1 cup--------------------	120	4	780	18	77	8.4	11.8	42.2	19	540	[illegible]
	SUGARS AND SWEETS												
	Cake icings:												
	Boiled, white:												
532	Plain------------------------	1 cup--------------------	94	18	295	1	0	0	0	0	75	17	134
533	With coconut-----------------	1 cup--------------------	166	15	605	3	13	11.0	.9	Trace	124	277	196
	Uncooked:												
534	Chocolate made with milk and butter.	1 cup--------------------	275	14	1,035	9	38	23.4	11.7	1.0	185	536	168
535	Creamy fudge from mix and water.	1 cup--------------------	245	15	830	7	16	5.1	6.7	3.1	183	238	568
536	White------------------------	1 cup--------------------	319	11	1,200	2	21	12.7	5.1	.5	260	57	156
	Candy:												
537	Caramels, plain or chocolate----	1 oz---------------------	28	8	115	1	3	1.6	1.1	.1	22	54	64
	Chocolate:												
538	Milk, plain------------------	1 oz---------------------	28	1	145	2	9	5.5	3.0	.3	16	109	27
539	Semisweet, small pieces (60 per oz).	1 cup or 6-oz pkg--------	170	1	860	7	61	36.2	19.8	1.7	97	553	553
540	Chocolate-coated peanuts--------	1 oz---------------------	28	1	160	5	12	4.0	4.7	2.1	11	143	17
541	Fondant, uncoated (mints, candy corn, other).	1 oz---------------------	28	8	105	Trace	1	.1	.3	.1	25	1	60
542	Fudge, chocolate, plain---------	1 oz---------------------	28	8	115	1	3	1.3	1.4	.6	21	42	54
543	Gum drops-----------------------	1 oz---------------------	28	12	100	Trace	Trace	—	—	—	25	1	10
544	Hard----------------------------	1 oz---------------------	28	1	110	0	Trace	—	—	—	28	1	9
545	Marshmallows--------------------	1 oz---------------------	28	17	90	1	Trace	—	—	—	23	2	11

(Dashes (—) denote lack of reliable data for a constituent believed to be present in measurable amount)

(Dashes (—) denote lack of reliable data for a constituent believed to be present in measurable amount)

Item No.	Foods, approximate measures, units, and weight (edible part unless footnotes indicate otherwise)		Water	Food energy	Protein	Fat	Fatty Acids: Saturated (total)	Fatty Acids: Unsaturated: Oleic	Fatty Acids: Unsaturated: Linoleic	Carbohydrate	Potassium	Sodium
		Grams	Percent	Calories	Grams	Grams	Grams	Grams	Grams	Grams	Milligrams	Milligrams
	SUGARS AND SWEETS—Con.											
	Chocolate-flavored beverage powders (about 4 heaping tsp per oz):											
546	With nonfat dry milk------------ 1 oz----------------------	28	2	100	5	1	.5	.3	Trace	20	227	149
547	Without milk-------------------- 1 oz----------------------	28	1	100	1	1	.4	.2	Trace	25	142	76
548	Honey, strained or extracted------ 1 tbsp--------------------	21	17	65	Trace	0	0	0	0	17	11	1
549	Jams and preserves---------------- 1 tbsp--------------------	20	29	55	Trace	Trace	—	—	—	14	18	2
550	1 packet------------------	14	29	40	Trace	Trace	—	—	—	10	12	2
551	Jellies-------------------------- 1 tbsp--------------------	18	29	50	Trace	Trace	—	—	—	13	14	3
552	1 packet------------------	14	29	40	Trace	Trace	—	—	—	10	11	2
	Sirups:											
	Chocolate-flavored sirup or topping:											
553	Thin type-------------------- 1 fl oz or 2 tbsp----------	38	32	90	1	1	.5	.3	Trace	24	106	21
554	Fudge type------------------- 1 fl oz or 2 tbsp----------	38	25	125	2	5	3.1	1.6	.1	20	107	36
	Molasses, cane:											
555	Light (first extraction)------ 1 tbsp--------------------	20	24	50	—	—	—	—	—	13	183	3
556*	Blackstrap (third extraction)- 1 tbsp--------------------	20	24	45	—	—	—	—	—	11	585	19
557	Sorghum-------------------------- 1 tbsp--------------------	21	23	55	—	—	—	—	—	14	—	—
558	Table blends, chiefly corn, light and dark. 1 tbsp--------------------	21	24	60	0	0	0	0	0	15	1	14
	Sugars:											
559	Brown, pressed down------------ 1 cup---------------------	220	2	820	0	0	0	0	0	212	757	53
	White:											
560	Granulated------------------- 1 cup---------------------	200	1	770	0	0	0	0	0	199	6	1
561	1 tbsp--------------------	12	1	45	0	0	0	0	0	12	Trace	Trace
562	1 packet------------------	6	1	23	0	0	0	0	0	6	Trace	Trace
563	Powdered, sifted, spooned into cup. 1 cup---------------------	100	1	385	0	0	0	0	0	100	3	Trace
	VEGETABLE AND VEGETABLE PRODUCTS											
	Asparagus, green:											
	Cooked, drained:											
	Cuts and tips, 1 1/2- to 2-in lengths:											
564	From raw------------------- 1 cup--------------------	145	94	30	3	Trace	—	—	—	5	265	2
565	From frozen---------------- 1 cup--------------------	180	93	40	6	Trace	—	—	—	6	396	2
	Spears, 1/2-in diam. at base:											
566	From raw------------------- 4 spears-----------------	60	94	10	1	Trace	—	—	—	2	110	1
567	From frozen---------------- 4 spears-----------------	60	92	15	2	Trace	—	—	—	2	143	1
568	Canned, spears, 1/2-in diam. at base. 4 spears-----------------	80	93	15	2	Trace	—	—	—	3	133	189
	Beans:											
	Lima, immature seeds, frozen, cooked, drained:											
569*	Thick-seeded types (Fordhooks) 1 cup-------------------	170	74	170	10	Trace	—	—	—	32	724	172
570*	Thin-seeded types (baby limas) 1 cup-------------------	180	69	210	13	Trace	—	—	—	40	709	232
	Snap:											
	Green:											
	Cooked, drained:											
571	From raw (cuts and French style). 1 cup------------------	125	92	30	2	Trace	—	—	—	7	189	5
	From frozen:											
572	Cuts------------------- 1 cup------------------	135	92	35	2	Trace	—	—	—	8	205	1
573	French style----------- 1 cup------------------	130	92	35	2	Trace	—	—	—	8	177	3
574 ●	Canned, drained solids (cuts). 1 cup------------------	135	92	30	2	Trace	—	—	—	7	128	319
	Yellow or wax:											
	Cooked, drained:											
575	From raw (cuts and French style). 1 cup------------------	125	93	30	2	Trace	—	—	—	6	189	4
576	From frozen (cuts)-------- 1 cup------------------	135	92	35	2	Trace	—	—	—	8	221	1
577 ●	Canned, drained solids (cuts). 1 cup------------------	135	92	30	2	Trace	—	—	—	7	128	319
	Beans, mature. See Beans, dry (items 509-515) and Blackeye peas, dry (item 516).											
	Bean sprouts (mung):											
578	Raw---------------------------- 1 cup------------------	105	89	35	4	Trace	—	—	—	7	234	5
579	Cooked, drained---------------- 1 cup------------------	125	91	35	4	Trace	—	—	—	7	195	5
	Beets:											
	Cooked, drained, peeled:											
580	Whole beets, 2-in diam.------- 2 beets-----------------	100	91	30	1	Trace	—	—	—	7	208	43

NUTRIENT TABLES OF COMMONLY USED FOODS FOR MODIFIED DIETARY PLANS

Item No.	Foods, approximate measures, units, and weight (edible part unless footnotes indicate otherwise)			Water	Food energy	Protein	Fat	Fatty Acids: Saturated (total)	Fatty Acids: Unsaturated: Oleic	Fatty Acids: Unsaturated: Linoleic	Carbohydrate	Potassium	Sodium
			Grams	Percent	Calories	Grams	Grams	Grams	Grams	Grams	Grams	Milligrams	Milligrams
	VEGETABLE AND VEGETABLE PRODUCTS—Con.												
581	Diced or sliced---------------	1 cup-------------------	170	91	55	2	Trace	—	—	—	12	354	73
	Canned, drained solids:												
582	● Whole beets, small------------	1 cup-------------------	160	89	60	2	Trace	—	—	—	14	267	378
583	● Diced or sliced---------------	1 cup-------------------	170	89	65	2	Trace	—	—	—	15	284	401
584*	Beet greens, leaves and stems, cooked, drained.	1 cup-------------------	145	94	25	2	Trace	—	—	—	5	481	110
	Blackeye peas, immature seeds, cooked and drained:												
585*	From raw------------------------	1 cup-------------------	165	72	180	13	1	—	—	—	30	625	2
586*	From frozen---------------------	1 cup-------------------	170	66	220	15	1	—	—	—	40	573	66
	Broccoli, cooked, drained:												
	From raw:												
587*	Stalk, medium size------------	1 stalk-----------------	180	91	45	6	1	—	—	—	8	481	18
588*	Stalks cut into 1/2-in pieces-	1 cup-------------------	155	91	40	5	Trace	—	—	—	7	414	16
	From frozen:												
589	Stalk, 4 1/2 to 5 in long-----	1 stalk-----------------	30	91	10	1	Trace	—	—	—	1	66	4
590*	Chopped-----------------------	1 cup-------------------	185	92	50	5	1	—	—	—	9	392	28
	Brussels sprouts, cooked, drained:												
591*	From raw, 7-8 sprouts (1 1/4- to 1 1/2-in diam.).	1 cup-------------------	155	88	55	7	1	—	—	—	10	423	16
592*	From frozen---------------------	1 cup-------------------	155	89	50	5	Trace	—	—	—	10	457	22
	Cabbage:												
	Common varieties:												
	Raw:												
593	Coarsely shredded or sliced-	1 cup-------------------	70	92	15	1	Trace	—	—	—	4	163	14
594	Finely shredded or chopped--	1 cup-------------------	90	92	20	1	Trace	—	—	—	5	210	18
595	Cooked, drained---------------	1 cup-------------------	145	94	30	2	Trace	—	—	—	6	236	20
596	Red, raw, coarsely shredded or sliced.	1 cup-------------------	70	90	20	1	Trace	—	—	—	5	188	18
597	Savoy, raw, coarsely shredded or sliced.	1 cup-------------------	70	92	15	2	Trace	—	—	—	3	188	15
598	Cabbage, celery (also called pe-tsai or wongbok), raw, 1-in pieces.	1 cup-------------------	75	95	10	1	Trace	—	—	—	2	190	17
599	Cabbage, white mustard (also called bokchoy or pakchoy), cooked, drained.	1 cup-------------------	170	95	25	2	Trace	—	—	—	4	364	31
	Carrots:												
	Raw, without crowns and tips, scraped:												
600	Whole, 7 1/2 by 1 1/8 in, or strips, 2 1/2 to 3 in long.	1 carrot or 18 strips----	72	88	30	1	Trace	—	—	—	7	246	34
601	Grated--------------------------	1 cup-------------------	110	88	45	1	Trace	—	—	—	11	375	52
602	Cooked (crosswise cuts), drained	1 cup-------------------	155	91	50	1	Trace	—	—	—	11	344	51
	Canned:												
603	● Sliced, drained solids--------	1 cup-------------------	155	91	45	1	Trace	—	—	—	10	186	366
604	Strained or junior (baby food)	1 oz (1 3/4 to 2 tbsp)---	28	92	10	Trace	Trace	—	—	—	2	51	—
	Cauliflower:												
605	Raw, chopped--------------------	1 cup-------------------	115	91	31	3	Trace	—	—	—	6	339	15
	Cooked, drained:												
606	From raw (flower buds)--------	1 cup-------------------	125	93	30	3	Trace	—	—	—	5	258	11
607	From frozen (flowerets)-------	1 cup-------------------	180	94	30	3	Trace	—	—	—	6	373	18
	Celery, Pascal type, raw:												
608	Stalk, large outer, 8 by 1 1/2 in, at root end.	1 stalk-----------------	40	94	5	Trace	Trace	—	—	—	2	136	50
609*	Pieces, diced-------------------	1 cup-------------------	120	94	20	1	Trace	—	—	—	5	409	151
	Collards, cooked, drained:												
610*	From raw (leaves without stems)-	1 cup-------------------	190	90	65	7	1	—	—	—	10	498	24
611*	From frozen (chopped)-----------	1 cup-------------------	170	90	50	5	1	—	—	—	10	401	27
	Corn, sweet:												
	Cooked, drained:												
612	From raw, ear 5 by 1 3/4 in---	1 ear[61]----------------	140	74	70	2	1	—	—	—	16	151	Trace
	From frozen:												
613	Ear, 5 in long--------------	1 ear[61]----------------	229	73	120	4	1	—	—	—	27	291	1
614	Kernels---------------------	1 cup-------------------	165	77	130	5	1	—	—	—	31	304	2
	Canned:												
615	● Cream style-------------------	1 cup-------------------	256	76	210	5	2	—	—	—	51	248	604
	Whole kernel:												
616	● Vacuum pack-----------------	1 cup-------------------	210	76	175	5	1	—	—	—	43	204	496
617	● Wet pack, drained solids----	1 cup-------------------	165	76	140	4	1	—	—	—	33	160	604
	Cowpeas. See Blackeye peas. (Items 585-586).												

(Dashes (—) denote lack of reliable data for a constituent believed to be present in measurable amount)

NUTRIENT TABLES OF COMMONLY USED FOODS FOR MODIFIED DIETARY PLANS

Item No.	Foods, approximate measures, units, and weight (edible part unless footnotes indicate otherwise)			Water	Food energy	Protein	Fat	Fatty Acids: Saturated (total)	Fatty Acids: Unsaturated: Oleic	Fatty Acids: Unsaturated: Linoleic	Carbohydrate	Potassium	Sodium
			Grams	Percent	Calories	Grams	Grams	Grams	Grams	Grams	Grams	Milligrams	Milligrams
	VEGETABLE AND VEGETABLE PRODUCTS—Con.												
	Cucumber slices, 1/8 in thick (large, 2 1/8-in diam.; small, 1 3/4-in diam.):												
618	With peel----------------------	6 large or 8 small slices	28	95	5	Trace	Trace	—	—	—	1	45	2
619	Without peel--------------------	6 1/2 large or 9 small pieces.	28	96	5	Trace	Trace	—	—	—	1	45	2
620	Dandelion greens, cooked, drained-	1 cup-------------------	105	90	35	2	1	—	—	—	7	244	46
621	Endive, curly (including escarole), raw, small pieces.	1 cup-------------------	50	93	10	1	Trace	—	—	—	2	147	7
	Kale, cooked, drained:												
622	From raw (leaves without stems and midribs).	1 cup-------------------	110	88	45	5	1	—	—	—	7	243	47
623	From frozen (leaf style)--------	1 cup-------------------	130	91	40	4	1	—	—	—	7	251	27
	Lettuce, raw:												
	Butterhead, as Boston types:												
624	Head, 5-in diam---------------	1 head[63]---------------	220	95	25	2	Trace	—	—	—	4	430	15
625	Leaves------------------------	1 outer or 2 inner or 3 heart leaves.	15	95	Trace	Trace	Trace	—	—	—	Trace	40	1
	Crisphead, as Iceberg:												
626	Head, 6-in diam---------------	1 head[64]---------------	567	96	70	5	1	—	—	—	16	943	48
627	Wedge, 1/4 of head------------	1 wedge-----------------	135	96	20	1	Trace	—	—	—	4	236	12
628	Pieces, chopped or shredded---	1 cup-------------------	55	96	5	Trace	Trace	—	—	—	2	96	5
629	Looseleaf (bunching varieties including romaine or cos), chopped or shredded pieces.	1 cup-------------------	55	94	10	1	Trace	—	—	—	2	145	5
630	Mushrooms, raw, sliced or chopped-	1 cup-------------------	70	90	20	2	Trace	—	—	—	3	290	11
631	Mustard greens, without stems and midribs, cooked, drained.	1 cup-------------------	140	93	30	3	1	—	—	—	6	308	25
632	Okra pods, 3 by 5/8 in, cooked----	10 pods-----------------	106	91	30	2	Trace	—	—	—	6	184	2
	Onions:												
	Mature:												
	Raw:												
633	Chopped--------------------	1 cup-------------------	170	89	65	3	Trace	—	—	—	15	267	17
634	Sliced---------------------	1 cup-------------------	115	89	45	2	Trace	—	—	—	10	181	12
635	Cooked (whole or sliced), drained.	1 cup-------------------	210	92	60	3	Trace	—	—	—	14	231	15
636	Young green, bulb (3/8 in diam.) and white portion of top.	6 onions----------------	30	88	15	Trace	Trace	—	—	—	3	69	2
637	Parsley, raw, chopped-------------	1 tbsp------------------	4	85	Trace	Trace	Trace	—	—	—	Trace	25	2
638*	Parsnips, cooked (diced or 2-in lengths).	1 cup-------------------	155	82	100	2	1	—	—	—	23	587	12
	Peas, green:												
	Canned:												
639 ●	Whole, drained solids---------	1 cup-------------------	170	77	150	8	1	—	—	—	29	163	401
640	Strained (baby food)----------	1 oz (1 3/4 to 2 tbsp)--	28	86	15	1	Trace	—	—	—	3	28	—
641	Frozen, cooked, drained--------	1 cup-------------------	160	82	110	8	Trace	—	—	—	19	216	184
642	Peppers, hot, red, without seeds, dried (ground chili powder, added seasonings).	1 tsp-------------------	2	9	5	Trace	Trace	—	—	—	1	20	31
	Peppers, sweet (about 5 per lb, whole), stem and seeds removed:												
643	Raw----------------------------	1 pod-------------------	74	93	15	1	Trace	—	—	—	4	157	10
644	Cooked, boiled, drained--------	1 pod-------------------	73	95	15	1	Trace	—	—	—	3	109	7
	Potatoes, cooked:												
645*	Baked, peeled after baking (about 2 per lb, raw).	1 potato----------------	156	75	145	4	Trace	—	—	—	33	782	6
*	Boiled (about 3 per lb, raw):												
646*	Peeled after boiling----------	1 potato----------------	137	80	105	3	Trace	—	—	—	23	556	4
647	Peeled before boiling---------	1 potato----------------	135	83	90	3	Trace	—	—	—	20	385	3
	French-fried, strip, 2 to 3 1/2 in long:												
648*	Prepared from raw-------------	10 strips---------------	50	45	135	2	7	1.7	1.2	3.3	18	427	3
649	Frozen, oven heated-----------	10 strips---------------	50	53	110	2	4	1.1	.8	2.1	17	326	2
650* ●	Hashed brown, prepared from frozen.	1 cup-------------------	155	56	345	3	18	4.6	3.2	9.0	45	439	463
	Mashed, prepared from—												
	Raw:												
651* ●	Milk added----------------	1 cup-------------------	210	83	135	4	2	.7	.4	Trace	27	548	632
	Potatoes, cooked—Continued												
	Mashed, prepared from—Continued												
	Raw—Continued												
652* ●	Milk and butter added-------	1 cup-------------------	210	80	195	4	9	5 6	2.3	0.2	26	525	695

(Dashes (—) denote lack of reliable data for a constituent believed to be present in measurable amount)

NUTRIENT TABLES OF COMMONLY USED FOODS FOR MODIFIED DIETARY PLANS

(Dashes (—) denote lack of reliable data for a constituent believed to be present in measurable amount)

Item No.	Foods, approximate measures, units, and weight (edible part unless footnotes indicate otherwise)			Water	Food energy	Protein	Fat	Fatty Acids: Saturated (total)	Fatty Acids: Unsaturated: Oleic	Fatty Acids: Unsaturated: Linoleic	Carbohydrate	Potassium	Sodium
			Grams	Percent	Calories	Grams	Grams	Grams	Grams	Grams	Grams	Milligrams	Milligrams
	VEGETABLE AND VEGETABLE PRODUCTS—Con.												
653*●	Dehydrated flakes (without milk), water, milk, butter, and salt added.	1 cup	210	79	195	4	7	3.6	2.1	.2	30	601	485
*654●	Potato chips, 1 3/4 by 2 1/2 in oval cross section.	10 chips	20	2	115	1	8	2.1	1.4	4.0	10	226	200
*655●	Potato salad, made with cooked salad dressing.	1 cup	250	76	250	7	7	2.0	2.7	1.3	41	798	1,320
656*	Pumpkin, canned	1 cup	245	90	80	2	1	—	—	—	19	588	5
657	Radishes, raw (prepackaged) stem ends, rootlets cut off.	4 radishes	18	95	5	Trace	Trace	—	—	—	1	58	2
658●	Sauerkraut, canned, solids and liquid.	1 cup	235	93	40	2	Trace	—	—	—	9	329	1,554
	Southern peas. See Blackeye peas (items 585-586).												
	Spinach:												
659	Raw, chopped	1 cup	55	91	15	2	Trace	—	—	—	2	259	49
	Cooked, drained:												
660*	From raw	1 cup	180	92	40	5	1	—	—	—	6	583	94
	From frozen:												
661*	Chopped	1 cup	205	92	45	6	1	—	—	—	8	683	107
662*	Leaf	1 cup	190	92	45	6	1	—	—	—	7	688	93
663*●	Canned, drained solids	1 cup	205	91	50	6	1	—	—	—	7	513	910
	Squash, cooked:												
664	Summer (all varieties), diced, drained.	1 cup	210	96	30	2	Trace	—	—	—	7	296	2
665*	Winter (all varieties), baked, mashed.	1 cup	205	81	130	4	1	—	—	—	32	945	2
	Sweet potatoes:												
	Cooked (raw, 5 by 2 in; about 2 1/2 per lb):												
666	Baked in skin, peeled	1 potato	114	64	160	2	1	—	—	—	37	342	14
667	Boiled in skin, peeled	1 potato	151	71	170	3	1	—	—	—	40	367	15
668	Candied, 2 1/2 by 2-in piece	1 piece	105	60	175	1	3	2.0	.8	.1	36	200	44
	Canned:												
669*	Solid pack (mashed)	1 cup	255	72	275	5	1	—	—	—	63	510	122
670	Vacuum pack, piece 2 3/4 by 1 in.	1 piece	40	72	45	1	Trace	—	—	—	10	80	19
	Tomatoes:												
671	Raw, 2 3/5-in diam. (3 per 12 oz pkg.).	1 tomato[66]	135	94	25	1	Trace	—	—	—	6	300	4
672*	Canned, solids and liquid	1 cup	241	94	50	2	Trace	—	—	—	10	523	313
673●	Tomato catsup	1 cup	273	69	290	5	1	—	—	—	69	991	2,845
674		1 tbsp	15	69	15	Trace	Trace	—	—	—	4	54	156
	Tomato juice, canned:												
675*●	Cup	1 cup	243	94	45	2	Trace	—	—	—	10	552	486
676*●	Glass (6 fl oz)	1 glass	182	94	35	2	Trace	—	—	—	8	413	364
677	Turnips, cooked, diced	1 cup	155	94	35	1	Trace	—	—	—	8	291	53
	Turnip greens, cooked, drained:												
678	From raw (leaves and stems)	1 cup	145	94	30	3	Trace	—	—	—	5	—	17
679	From frozen (chopped)	1 cup	165	93	40	4	Trace	—	—	—	6	246	28
680	Vegetables, mixed, frozen, cooked	1 cup	182	83	115	6	1	—	—	—	24	348	96
	MISCELLANEOUS ITEMS												
	Baking powders for home use:												
	Sodium aluminum sulfate:												
681 ●	With monocalcium phosphate monohydrate.	1 tsp	3.0	2	5	Trace	Trace	0	0	0	1	5	329
682	With monocalcium phosphate monohydrate, calcium sulfate.	1 tsp	2.9	1	5	Trace	Trace	0	0	0	1	—	290
683 ●	Straight phosphate	1 tsp	3.8	2	5	Trace	Trace	0	0	0	1	6	312
684*	Low sodium	1 tsp	4.3	2	5	Trace	Trace	0	0	0	2	471	Trace
685	Barbecue sauce	1 cup	250	81	230	4	17	2.2	4.3	10.0	20	435	2,038
*●	Beverages, alcoholic:												
686*	Beer	12 fl oz	360	92	150	1	0	0	0	0	14	90	25
	Gin, rum, vodka, whisky:												
687	80-proof	1 1/2-fl oz jigger	42	67	95	—	—	0	0	0	Trace	1	Trace
688	86-proof	1 1/2-fl oz jigger	42	64	105	—	—	0	0	0	Trace	1	Trace
689	90-proof	1 1/2-fl oz jigger	42	62	110	—	—	0	0	0	Trace	1	Trace
	Wines:												
690	Dessert	3 1/2-fl oz glass	103	77	140	Trace	0	0	0	0	8	77	3

Item No.	Foods, approximate measures, units, and weight (edible part unless footnotes indicate otherwise)			Water	Food energy	Protein	Fat	Fatty Acids: Saturated (total)	Fatty Acids: Unsaturated: Oleic	Fatty Acids: Unsaturated: Linoleic	Carbohydrate	Potassium	Sodium
	(Dashes (—) denote lack of reliable data for a constituent believed to be present in measurable amount)												
			Grams	Percent	Calories	Grams	Grams	Grams	Grams	Grams	Grams	Milligrams	Milligrams
	MISCELLANEOUS ITEMS—Con.												
691	Table	3 1/2-fl oz glass	102	86	85	Trace	0	0	0	0	4	94	3
	Beverages, carbonated, sweetened, nonalcoholic:												
692	Carbonated water	12 fl oz	366	92	115	0	0	0	0	0	29	—	60
693	Cola type	12 fl oz	369	90	145	0	0	0	0	0	37	—	24
694	Fruit-flavored sodas and Tom Collins mixer.	12 fl oz	372	88	170	0	0	0	0	0	45	—	27
695	Ginger ale	12 fl oz	366	92	115	0	0	0	0	0	29	0	4
696	Root beer	12 fl oz	370	90	150	0	0	0	0	0	39	0	28
	Chili powder. See Peppers, hot, red (item 642).												
	Chocolate:												
697	Bitter or baking	1 oz	28	2	145	3	15	8.9	4.9	.4	8	235	1
	Semisweet, see Candy, chocolate (item 539).												
698	Gelatin, dry	1,7-g envelope	7	13	25	6	Trace	0	0	0	0	—	8
699	Gelatin dessert prepared with gelatin dessert powder and water.	1 cup	240	84	140	4	0	0	0	0	34	—	122
700	Mustard, prepared, yellow	1 tsp or individual serving pouch or cup.	5	80	5	Trace	Trace	—	—	—	Trace	7	65
	● Olives, pickled, canned:												
701	Green	4 medium or 3 extra large or 2 giant.[69]	16	78	15	Trace	2	.2	1.2	.1	Trace	7	323
702	Ripe, Mission	3 small or 2 large[69]	10	73	15	Trace	2	.2	1.2	.1	Trace	2	64
	Pickles, cucumber:												
703	● Dill, medium, whole, 3 3/4 in long, 1 1/4-in diam.	1 pickle	65	93	5	Trace	Trace	—	—	—	1	130	928
704	● Fresh-pack, slices 1 1/2-in diam., 1/4 in thick.	2 slices	15	79	10	Trace	Trace	—	—	—	3	—	101
705	● Sweet, gherkin, small, whole, about 2 1/2 in long, 3/4-in diam.	1 pickle	15	61	20	Trace	Trace	—	—	—	5	—	128
706	● Relish, finely chopped, sweet	1 tbsp	15	63	20	Trace	Trace	—	—	—	5	—	124
	Popcorn. See items 476-478.												
707	Popsicle, 3-fl oz size	1 popsicle	95	80	70	0	0	0	0	0	18	—	---
	Soups:												
	Canned, condensed:												
	Prepared with equal volume of milk:												
708 ●	Cream of chicken	1 cup	245	85	180	7	10	4.2	3.6	1.3	15	260	1,054
709 ●	Cream of mushroom	1 cup	245	83	215	7	14	5.4	2.9	4.6	16	279	1,039
710*●	Tomato	1 cup	250	84	175	7	7	3.4	1.7	1.0	23	418	1,055
	Prepared with equal volume of water:												
711 ●	Bean with pork	1 cup	250	84	170	8	6	1.2	1.8	2.4	22	395	1,008
712 ●	Beef broth, bouillon, consomme.	1 cup	240	96	30	5	0	0	0	0	3	130	782
713 ●	Beef noodle	1 cup	240	93	65	4	3	.6	.7	.8	7	77	917
714 ●	Clam chowder, Manhattan type (with tomatoes, without milk).	1 cup	245	92	80	2	3	.5	.4	1.3	12	184	938
715 ●	Cream of chicken	1 cup	240	92	95	3	6	1.6	2.3	1.1	8	79	970
716 ●	Cream of mushroom	1 cup	240	90	135	2	10	2.6	1.7	4.5	10	98	955
717 ●	Minestrone	1 cup	245	90	105	5	3	.7	.9	1.3	14	314	995
718 ●	Split pea	1 cup	245	85	145	9	3	1.1	1.2	.4	21	270	941
719 ●	Tomato	1 cup	245	91	90	2	3	.5	.5	1.0	16	230	970
720 ●	Vegetable beef	1 cup	245	92	80	5	2	—	—	—	10	162	1,046
721 ●	Vegetarian	1 cup	245	92	80	2	2	—	—	—	13	172	838
	Dehydrated:												
722 ●	Bouillon cube, 1/2 in	1 cube	4	4	5	1	Trace	—	—	—	Trace	4	960
	Mixes:												
	Unprepared:												
723 ●	Onion	1 1/2-oz pkg	43	3	150	6	5	1.1	2.3	1.0	23	238	2,871
	Prepared with water:												
724 ●	Chicken noodle	1 cup	240	95	55	2	1	—	—	—	8	19	578
725 ●	Onion	1 cup	240	96	35	1	1	—	—	—	6	58	689
726 ●	Tomato vegetable with noodles.	1 cup	240	93	65	1	1	—	—	—	12	29	1,025
727	Vinegar, cider	1 tbsp	15	94	Trace	Trace	0	0	0	0	1	15	Trace
728	White sauce, medium, with enriched flour.	1 cup	250	73	405	10	31	19.3	7.8	.8	22	348	948
	Yeast:												
	Baker's, dry, active	1 pkg	7	5	20	3	Trace	—	—	—	3	140	4
	Brewer's, dry	1 tbsp	8	5	25	3	Trace	—	—	—	3	152	10

NUTRIENT TABLES OF COMMONLY USED FOODS FOR MODIFIED DIETARY PLANS
FOOTNOTES

[1]Vitamin A value is largely from beta-carotene used for coloring. Riboflavin value for items 40-41 apply to products with added riboflavin.
[2]Applies to product without added vitamin A. With added vitamin A, value is 500 International Units (I.U.).
[3]Applies to product without vitamin A added.
[4]Applies to product with added vitamin A. Without added vitamin A, value is 20 International Units (I.U.).
[5]Yields 1 qt of fluid milk when reconstituted according to package directions.
[6]Applies to product with added vitamin A.
[7]Weight applies to product with label claim of 1 1/3 cups equal 3.2 oz.
[8]Applies to products made from thick shake mixes and that do not contain added ice cream. Products made from milk shake mixes are higher in fat and usually contain added ice cream.
[9]Content of fat, vitamin A, and carbohydrate varies. Consult the label when precise values are needed for special diets.
[10]Applies to product made with milk containing no added vitamin A.
[11]Based on year-round average.
[12]Based on average vitamin A content of fortified margarine. Federal specifications for fortified margarine require a minimum of 15,000 International Units (I.U.) of vitamin A per pound.
[13]Fatty acid values apply to product made with regular-type margarine.
[14]Dipped in egg, milk or water, and breadcrumbs; fried in vegetable shortening.
[15]If bones are discarded, value for calcium will be greatly reduced.
[16]Dipped in egg, breadcrumbs, and flour or batter.
[17]Prepared with tuna, celery, salad dressing (mayonnaise type), pickle, onion, and egg.
[18]Outer layer of fat on the cut was removed to within approximately 1/2 in of the lean. Deposits of fat within the cut were not removed.
[19]Crust made with vegetable shortening and enriched flour.
[20]Regular-type margarine used.
[21]Value varies widely.
[22]About one-fourth of the outer layer of fat on the cut was removed. Deposits of fat within the cut were not removed.
[23]Vegetable shortening used.
[24]Also applies to pasteurized apple cider.
[25]Applies to product without added ascorbic acid. For value of product with added ascorbic acid, refer to label.
[26]Based on product with label claim of 45% of U.S. RDA in 6 fl oz.
[27]Based on product with label claim of 100% of U.S. RDA in 6 fl oz.
[28]Weight includes peel and membranes between sections. Without these parts, the weight of the edible portion is 123g for item 246 and 118 g for item
[29]For white-fleshed varieties, value is about 20 International Units (I.U.) per cup; for red-fleshed varieties, 1,080 I.U.
[30]Weight includes seeds. Without seeds, weight of the edible portion is 57 g.
[31]Applies to product without added ascorbic acid. With added ascorbic acid, based on claim that 6 fl oz of reconstituted juice contain 45% or 50% o U.S. RDA, value in milligrams is 108 or 120 for a 6-fl oz can (item 258), 36 or 40 for 1 cup of diluted juice (item 259).
[32]For products with added thiamin and riboflavin but without added ascorbic acid, values in milligrams would be 0.60 for thiamin, 0.80 for riboflav and trace for ascorbic acid. For products with only ascorbic acid added, value varies with the brand. Consult the label.
[33]Weight includes rind. Without rind, the weight of the edible portion is 272 g for item 271 and 149 g for item 272.
[34]Represents yellow-fleshed varieties. For white-fleshed varieties, value is 50 International Units (I.U.) for 1 peach, 90 I.U. for 1 cup of slices.
[35]Value represents products with added ascorbic acid. For products without added ascorbic acid, value in milligrams is 116 for a 10-oz container, 103 for 1 cup.
[36]Weight includes pits. After removal of the pits, the weight of the edible portion is 258 g for item 302, 133 g for item 303, 43 g for item 304, and 213 g for item 305.
[37]Weight includes rind and seeds. Without rind and seeds, weight of the edible portion is 426 g.
[38]Made with vegetable shortening.
[39]Applies to product made with white cornmeal. With yellow cornmeal, value is 30 International Units (I.U.).
[40]Applies to white varieties. For yellow varieties, value is 150 International Units (I.U.).
[41]Applies to products that do not contain di-sodium phosphate. If di-sodium phosphate is an ingredient, value is 162 mg.
[42]Value may range from less than 1 mg to about 8 mg depending on the brand. Consult the label.
[43]Applies to product with added nutrient. Without added nutrient, value is trace.
[44]Value varies with the brand. Consult the label.
[45]Applies to product with added nutrient. Without added nutrient, value is trace.
[46]Excepting angelfood cake, cakes were made from mixes containing vegetable shortening; icings, with butter.
[47]Excepting spongecake, vegetable shortening used for cake portion; butter, for icing. If butter or margarine used for cake portion, vitamin A values would be higher.
[48]Applies to product made with a sodium aluminum-sulfate type baking powder. With a low-sodium type baking powder containing potassium, value would be about twice the amount shown.
[49]Equal weights of flour, sugar, eggs, and vegetable shortening.
[50]Products are commercial unless otherwise specified.
[51]Made with enriched flour and vegetable shortening except for macaroons which do not contain flour or shortening.
[52]Icing made with butter.
[53]Applies to yellow varieties; white varieties contain only a trace.
[54]Contains vegetable shortening and butter.
[55]Made with corn oil.
[56]Made with regular margarine.
[57]Applies to product made with yellow cornmeal.
[58]Made with enriched degermed cornmeal and enriched flour.
[59]Product may or may not be enriched with riboflavin. Consult the label.
[60]Value varies with the brand. Consult the label.
[61]Weight includes cob. Without cob, weight is 77 g for item 612, 126 g for item 613.
[62]Based on yellow varieties. For white varieties, value is trace.
[63]Weight includes refuse of outer leaves and core. Without these parts, weight is 163 g.
[64]Weight includes core. Without core, weight is 539 g.
[65]Value based on white-fleshed varieties. For yellow-fleshed varieties, value in International Units (I.U.) is 70 for item 633, 50 for item 634, and 80 for item 635.
[66]Weight includes cores and stem ends. Without these parts, weight is 123 g.
[67]Based on year-round average. For tomatoes marketed from November through May, value is about 12 mg; from June through October, 32 mg.
[68]Applies to product without calcium salts added. Value for products with calcium salts added may be as much as 63 mg for whole tomatoes, 241 mg for cut forms.
[69]Weight includes pits. Without pits, weight is 13 g for item 701, 9 g for item 702.
[70]Value may vary from 6 to 60 mg.

RECOMMENDED DAILY DIETARY ALLOWANCES (RDA)[1]

(Designed for the maintenance of good nutrition of practically all healthy persons in the United States.)

Sex-age category	Age: Years From	Age: Years To	Weight: Kilograms	Weight: Pounds	Height: Centimeters	Height: Inches	Food energy: Calories	Protein: Grams	Minerals: Calcium, Milligrams	Minerals: Phosphorus, Milligrams	Minerals: Iron, Milligrams	Vitamin A: International units	Thiamin: Milligrams	Riboflavin: Milligrams	Niacin: Milligrams	Ascorbic acid: Milligrams
Infants	0	0.5	6	13	60	24	kg × 115 lb × 52.3	kg × 2.2 lb × 1.0	360	240	10	1,400	0.3	0.4	6	35
	0.5	1	9	20	71	28	kg × 105 lb × 47.7	kg × 2.0 lb × 0.9	540	360	15	2,000	.5	.6	8	35
Children	1	3	13	29	90	35	1,300	23	800	800	15	2,000	.7	.8	9	45
	4	6	20	44	112	44	1,700	30	800	800	10	2,500	.9	1.0	11	45
	7	10	28	62	132	52	2,400	34	800	800	10	3,300	1.2	1.4	16	45
Males	11	14	45	99	157	62	2,700	45	1,200	1,200	18	5,000	1.4	1.6	18	50
	15	18	66	145	176	69	2,800	56	1,200	1,200	18	5,000	1.4	1.7	18	60
	19	22	70	154	177	70	2,900	56	800	800	10	5,000	1.5	1.7	19	60
	23	50	70	154	178	70	2,700	56	800	800	10	5,000	1.4	1.6	18	60
	51+		70	154	178	70	[2]2,400	56	800	800	10	5,000	1.2	1.4	16	60
Females	11	14	46	101	157	62	2,200	46	1,200	1,200	18	4,000	1.1	1.3	15	50
	15	18	55	120	163	64	2,100	46	1,200	1,200	18	4,000	1.1	1.3	14	60
	19	22	55	120	163	64	2,100	44	800	800	18	4,000	1.1	1.3	14	60
	23	50	55	120	163	64	2,000	44	800	800	18	4,000	1.0	1.2	13	60
	51+		55	120	163	64	[2]1,800	44	800	800	10	4,000	1.0	1.2	13	60
Pregnant							+ 300	+30	+400	+400	[3]18 +	+1,000	+.4	+.3	+2	+20
Lactating							+ 500	+20	+400	+400	18	+2,000	+.5	+.5	+5	+40

[1]Source: Adapted from Recommended Dietary Allowances, 9th ed., 1980, 185 pp. Washington, D.C. 20418. National Academy of Sciences—National Research Council. Also available in libraries. This publication tabulates the RDA for selected nutrients, discusses the basic for all the RDA, and reviews current knowledge of the dietary needs for other nutrients.

[2]After age 75 years, energy requirement is 2,050 calories for males and 1,600 calories for females.

[3]The increased requirement cannot be met by ordinary diets; therefore, the use of supplemental iron is recommended.

NOTE.—The Recommended Daily Dietary Allowances (RDA) should not be confused with the U.S. Recommended Daily Allowances (U.S. RDA). The RDA are amounts of nutrients recommended by the Food and Nutrition Board of the National Research Council and are considered adequate for maintenance of good nutrition in healthy persons in the United States. The allowances are revised from time to time in accordance with newer knowledge of nutritional needs.

The U.S. RDA are the amounts of proteins, vitamins, and minerals established by the Food and Drug Administration as standards for nutrition labeling. These allowances were derived from the RDA set by the Food and Nutrition Board. The U.S. RDA for most nutrients approximates the highest RDA of the sex-age categories in this table, excluding the allowances for pregnant and lactating females. Therefore, a diet that furnishes the U.S. RDA for a nutrient will furnish the RDA for most people and more than the RDA for many. U.S. RDA are protein, 45 grams (eggs, fish, meat, milk, poultry), 65 grams (other foods); vitamin A, 5,000 International Units; thiamin, 1.5 milligrams; riboflavin, 1.7 milligrams; niacin, 20 milligrams; ascorbic acid, 60 milligrams; calcium, 1 gram; phosphorus, 1 gram; iron, 18 milligrams. For additional information on U.S. RDA, see the "Federal Register," vol. 38, no. 49 (March 14, 1973), pp. 6959-6960, and Agriculture Information Bulletin 382, "Nutritional Labeling—Tools for Its Use."

Sodium Content of Selected Nonprescription Drugs*

Type of product	Trade name	Ingredients	Sodium content mg per dose	Sodium content mg per 100 ml
Analgesic	(Various)	Aspirin	49	—
Antacid analgesic	Bromo-Seltzer	Acetaminophen	717	—
		Sodium citrate		
	Alka-Seltzer (blue box)	Aspirin		
		Sodium citrate	521	—
Antacid laxative	Sal Hepatica	Sodium bicarbonate	1,000	—
		Sodium monohydrogen phosphate		
		Sodium citrate		
Antacids	Rolaids	Dihydroxy aluminum	53	—
		Sodium carbonate		
	Soda Mint	Sodium bicarbonate	89	—
	Alka-Seltzer Antacid (gold box)	Sodium bicarbonate	276	—
		Potassium bicarbonate		
		Citric acid		
	Brioschi	Sodium bicarbonate	710	—
		Tartaric acid		
		Sucrose		
Laxatives	Metamucil Instant Mix	Psyllium	250	—
		Sodium bicarbonate		
		Citric acid		
	Fleet's Enema	Sodium biphosphate	250-300	—
		Sodium phosphate	(absorbed)	
Sleep-aids	Miles Nervine Effervescent	Sodium citrate	544	—
Antacid suspensions	Milk of Magnesia	Magnesium hydroxide	—	10
	Amphogel	Aluminum hydroxide	—	14
	Basalgel	Aluminum carbonate	—	36
	Maalox	Magnesium hydroxide	—	50
		Aluminum carbonate		
	Riopan	Magnesium aluminum complex	—	14
	Mylanta I	Magnesium hydroxide	—	76
	Mylanta II	Aluminum hydroxide	—	160
	Digel	Simethicone	—	170
	Titralac	Calcium carbonate	—	220

*Reprinted by permission from table 4 of the American Medical Association's publication "Sodium and Potassium in Foods and Drugs " that was adapted from an article by D. R. Bennett, MD, PhD, entitled "Sodium Content of Prescription and Non-Prescription Drugs." Copyright (1979) to this information is held by the AMA.

Extra Recording Forms

The following 32 unnumbered pages contain sufficient Daily Food Records and Weekly Progress Records for nine weeks of daily recording.

WEEKLY PROGRESS RECORD

BASIC SKILLS:	SUN	MON	TUES	WED	THURS	FRI	SAT	*
Read Progress Record in morning								
Record food intake								
Stay within calorie/ exchange total								
SPECIFIC TECHNIQUES/EXERCISES:								
Daily Totals								

*This column is for the weekly totals for each specific technique or exercise.

DAILY FOOD RECORD

Food Item/ Beverage	Amount	Calories/Exchanges	Time of Day

Total Calories for day ______

Total Exchanges for day:

(1) Milk ______
(2) Vegetable ______
(3) Fruit ______
(4) Bread ______
(5) Meat ______
(6) Fat ______

Date ______

DAILY FOOD RECORD

Food Item/ Beverage	Amount	Calories/Exchanges	Time of Day

Total Calories for day ________

Date ________

Total Exchanges for day:
(1) Milk ____
(2) Vegetable ____
(3) Fruit ____
(4) Bread ____
(5) Meat ____
(6) Fat ____

DAILY FOOD RECORD

Food Item/ Beverage	Amount	Calories/Exchanges	Time of Day

Total Calories for day ________

Date ________

Total Exchanges for day:
(1) Milk ____
(2) Vegetable ____
(3) Fruit ____
(4) Bread ____
(5) Meat ____
(6) Fat ____

Copyright © Northwest Learning Associates, Inc., 1978. All rights reserved.

DAILY FOOD RECORD

Food Item/ Beverage	Amount	Calories/Exchanges	Time of Day

Total Calories for day ________

Date ________________

Total Exchanges for day:

(1) Milk ______
(2) Vegetable ______
(3) Fruit ______
(4) Bread ______
(5) Meat ______
(6) Fat ______

DAILY FOOD RECORD

Food Item/ Beverage	Amount	Calories/Exchanges	Time of Day

Total Calories for day ________

Date ________________

Total Exchanges for day:

(1) Milk ______
(2) Vegetable ______
(3) Fruit ______
(4) Bread ______
(5) Meat ______
(6) Fat ______

Copyright © Northwest Learning Associates, Inc., 1978. All rights reserved.

DAILY FOOD RECORD

Food Item/ Beverage	Amount	Calories/Exchanges	Time of Day

Total Calories for day ________

Date ____________________

Total Exchanges for day:

(1) Milk ______
(2) Vegetable ______
(3) Fruit ______
(4) Bread ______
(5) Meat ______
(6) Fat ______

DAILY FOOD RECORD

Food Item/ Beverage	Amount	Calories/Exchanges	Time of Day

Copyright © Northwest Learning Associates, Inc., 1978. All rights reserved.

Total Calories for day ________

Date ____________________

Total Exchanges for day:

(1) Milk ______
(2) Vegetable ______
(3) Fruit ______
(4) Bread ______
(5) Meat ______
(6) Fat ______

DAILY FOOD RECORD

Food Item/ Beverage	Amount	Calories/Exchanges	Time of Day

Total Calories for day ________

Date ________________

Total Exchanges for day:

(1) Milk ______
(2) Vegetable ______
(3) Fruit ______
(4) Bread ______
(5) Meat ______
(6) Fat ______

DAILY FOOD RECORD

Food Item/ Beverage	Amount	Calories/Exchanges	Time of Day

Total Calories for day ________

Date ________________

Total Exchanges for day:

(1) Milk ______
(2) Vegetable ______
(3) Fruit ______
(4) Bread ______
(5) Meat ______
(6) Fat ______

Copyright © Northwest Learning Associates, Inc., 1978. All rights reserved.

WEEKLY PROGRESS RECORD

BASIC SKILLS:	SUN	MON	TUES	WED	THURS	FRI	SAT	*
Read Progress Record in morning								
Record food intake								
Stay within calorie/ exchange total								
SPECIFIC TECHNIQUES/EXERCISES:								
Daily Totals								

*This column is for the weekly totals for each specific technique or exercise.

DAILY FOOD RECORD

Food Item/ Beverage	Amount	Calories/Exchanges	Time of Day

Total Calories for day ______

Total Exchanges for day:
(1) Milk ______
(2) Vegetable ______
(3) Fruit ______
(4) Bread ______
(5) Meat ______
(6) Fat ______

Date ______

DAILY FOOD RECORD

Food Item/ Beverage	Amount	Calories/Exchanges	Time of Day

Total Calories for day ______

Date ______

Total Exchanges for day:
(1) Milk ______
(2) Vegetable ______
(3) Fruit ______
(4) Bread ______
(5) Meat ______
(6) Fat ______

DAILY FOOD RECORD

Food Item/ Beverage	Amount	Calories/Exchanges	Time of Day

Total Calories for day ______

Date ______

Total Exchanges for day:
(1) Milk ______
(2) Vegetable ______
(3) Fruit ______
(4) Bread ______
(5) Meat ______
(6) Fat ______

Copyright © Northwest Learning Associates, Inc., 1978. All rights reserved.

DAILY FOOD RECORD

Food Item/ Beverage	Amount	Calories/Exchanges	Time of Day

Total Calories for day ________

Date ____________________

Total Exchanges for day:

(1) Milk ______
(2) Vegetable ______
(3) Fruit ______
(4) Bread ______
(5) Meat ______
(6) Fat ______

DAILY FOOD RECORD

Food Item/ Beverage	Amount	Calories/Exchanges	Time of Day

Copyright © Northwest Learning Associates, Inc., 1978. All rights reserved.

Total Calories for day ________

Date ____________________

Total Exchanges for day:

(1) Milk ______
(2) Vegetable ______
(3) Fruit ______
(4) Bread ______
(5) Meat ______
(6) Fat ______

WEEKLY PROGRESS RECORD

BASIC SKILLS:	SUN	MON	TUES	WED	THURS	FRI	SAT	*
Read Progress Record in morning								
Record food intake								
Stay within calorie/ exchange total								
SPECIFIC TECHNIQUES/EXERCISES:								
Daily Totals								

*This column is for the weekly totals for each specific technique or exercise.

DAILY FOOD RECORD

Food Item/ Beverage	Amount	Calories/Exchanges	Time of Day

Total Calories for day ________

Total Exchanges for day:
(1) Milk ____
(2) Vegetable ____
(3) Fruit ____
(4) Bread ____
(5) Meat ____
(6) Fat ____

Date ________

DAILY FOOD RECORD

Food Item/ Beverage	Amount	Calories/Exchanges	Time of Day

Total Calories for day ________

Date ________________

Total Exchanges for day:

(1) Milk ______
(2) Vegetable ______
(3) Fruit ______
(4) Bread ______
(5) Meat ______
(6) Fat ______

DAILY FOOD RECORD

Food Item/ Beverage	Amount	Calories/Exchanges	Time of Day

Total Calories for day ________

Date ________________

Total Exchanges for day:

(1) Milk ______
(2) Vegetable ______
(3) Fruit ______
(4) Bread ______
(5) Meat ______
(6) Fat ______

DAILY FOOD RECORD

Food Item/ Beverage	Amount	Calories/Exchanges	Time of Day

Total Calories for day ________

Date ____________________

Total Exchanges for day:

(1) Milk ______
(2) Vegetable ______
(3) Fruit ______
(4) Bread ______
(5) Meat ______
(6) Fat ______

DAILY FOOD RECORD

Food Item/ Beverage	Amount	Calories/Exchanges	Time of Day

Total Calories for day ________

Date ____________________

Total Exchanges for day:

(1) Milk ______
(2) Vegetable ______
(3) Fruit ______
(4) Bread ______
(5) Meat ______
(6) Fat ______

DAILY FOOD RECORD

Food Item/ Beverage	Amount	Calories/Exchanges	Time of Day

Total Calories for day ________

Date ________________

Total Exchanges for day:

(1) Milk ______
(2) Vegetable ______
(3) Fruit ______
(4) Bread ______
(5) Meat ______
(6) Fat ______

DAILY FOOD RECORD

Food Item/ Beverage	Amount	Calories/Exchanges	Time of Day

Copyright © Northwest Learning Associates, Inc., 1978. All rights reserved.

Total Calories for day ________

Date ________________

Total Exchanges for day:

(1) Milk ______
(2) Vegetable ______
(3) Fruit ______
(4) Bread ______
(5) Meat ______
(6) Fat ______

DAILY FOOD RECORD

Food Item/ Beverage	Amount	Calories/Exchanges	Time of Day

Total Calories for day ________

Date ____________________

Total Exchanges for day:

(1) Milk ______
(2) Vegetable ______
(3) Fruit ______
(4) Bread ______
(5) Meat ______
(6) Fat ______

DAILY FOOD RECORD

Food Item/ Beverage	Amount	Calories/Exchanges	Time of Day

Total Calories for day ________

Date ____________________

Total Exchanges for day:

(1) Milk ______
(2) Vegetable ______
(3) Fruit ______
(4) Bread ______
(5) Meat ______
(6) Fat ______

Copyright © Northwest Learning Associates, Inc., 1978. All rights reserved.

WEEKLY PROGRESS RECORD

BASIC SKILLS:	SUN	MON	TUES	WED	THURS	FRI	SAT	*
Read Progress Record in morning								
Record food intake								
Stay within calorie/ exchange total								
SPECIFIC TECHNIQUES/EXERCISES:								
Daily Totals								

*This column is for the weekly totals for each specific technique or exercise.

DAILY FOOD RECORD

Food Item/ Beverage	Amount	Calories/Exchanges	Time of Day

Total Calories for day ______

Date ______

Total Exchanges for day:

(1) Milk ______
(2) Vegetable ______
(3) Fruit ______
(4) Bread ______
(5) Meat ______
(6) Fat ______

Copyright © Northwest Learning Associates, Inc., 1978. All rights reserved.

DAILY FOOD RECORD

Food Item/ Beverage	Amount	Calories/Exchanges	Time of Day

Total Calories for day ______

Date ______________

Total Exchanges for day:
(1) Milk ______
(2) Vegetable ______
(3) Fruit ______
(4) Bread ______
(5) Meat ______
(6) Fat ______

DAILY FOOD RECORD

Food Item/ Beverage	Amount	Calories/Exchanges	Time of Day

Total Calories for day ______

Date ______________

Total Exchanges for day:
(1) Milk ______
(2) Vegetable ______
(3) Fruit ______
(4) Bread ______
(5) Meat ______
(6) Fat ______

Copyright © Northwest Learning Associates, Inc., 1978. All rights reserved.

DAILY FOOD RECORD

Food Item/ Beverage	Amount	Calories/Exchanges	Time of Day

Total Calories for day ________

Date ____________________

Total Exchanges for day:

(1) Milk ______
(2) Vegetable ______
(3) Fruit ______
(4) Bread ______
(5) Meat ______
(6) Fat ______

DAILY FOOD RECORD

Food Item/ Beverage	Amount	Calories/Exchanges	Time of Day

Copyright © Northwest Learning Associates, Inc., 1978. All rights reserved.

Total Calories for day ________

Date ____________________

Total Exchanges for day:

(1) Milk ______
(2) Vegetable ______
(3) Fruit ______
(4) Bread ______
(5) Meat ______
(6) Fat ______

WEEKLY PROGRESS RECORD

BASIC SKILLS:	SUN	MON	TUES	WED	THURS	FRI	SAT	*
Read Progress Record in morning								
Record food intake								
Stay within calorie/ exchange total								
SPECIFIC TECHNIQUES/EXERCISES:								
Daily Totals								

*This column is for the weekly totals for each specific technique or exercise.

DAILY FOOD RECORD

Food Item/ Beverage	Amount	Calories/Exchanges	Time of Day

Total Calories for day ______

Total Exchanges for day:
(1) Milk ______
(2) Vegetable ______
(3) Fruit ______
(4) Bread ______
(5) Meat ______
(6) Fat ______

Date ______

DAILY FOOD RECORD

Food Item/ Beverage	Amount	Calories/Exchanges	Time of Day

Total Calories for day ________

Date ________

Total Exchanges for day:
(1) Milk ________
(2) Vegetable ________
(3) Fruit ________
(4) Bread ________
(5) Meat ________
(6) Fat ________

DAILY FOOD RECORD

Food Item/ Beverage	Amount	Calories/Exchanges	Time of Day

Total Calories for day ________

Date ________

Total Exchanges for day:
(1) Milk ________
(2) Vegetable ________
(3) Fruit ________
(4) Bread ________
(5) Meat ________
(6) Fat ________

Copyright © Northwest Learning Associates, Inc., 1978. All rights reserved.

DAILY FOOD RECORD

Food Item/ Beverage	Amount	Calories/Exchanges	Time of Day

Total Calories for day ________

Date ________________

Total Exchanges for day:
(1) Milk ______
(2) Vegetable ______
(3) Fruit ______
(4) Bread ______
(5) Meat ______
(6) Fat ______

DAILY FOOD RECORD

Food Item/ Beverage	Amount	Calories/Exchanges	Time of Day

Total Calories for day ________

Date ________________

Total Exchanges for day:
(1) Milk ______
(2) Vegetable ______
(3) Fruit ______
(4) Bread ______
(5) Meat ______
(6) Fat ______

Copyright © Northwest Learning Associates, Inc., 1978. All rights reserved.

DAILY FOOD RECORD

Food Item/ Beverage	Amount	Calories/Exchanges	Time of Day

Total Calories for day ________

Date ________

Total Exchanges for day:
(1) Milk ____
(2) Vegetable ____
(3) Fruit ____
(4) Bread ____
(5) Meat ____
(6) Fat ____

DAILY FOOD RECORD

Food Item/ Beverage	Amount	Calories/Exchanges	Time of Day

Total Calories for day ________

Date ________

Total Exchanges for day:
(1) Milk ____
(2) Vegetable ____
(3) Fruit ____
(4) Bread ____
(5) Meat ____
(6) Fat ____

DAILY FOOD RECORD

Food Item/ Beverage	Amount	Calories/Exchanges	Time of Day

Total Calories for day ________

Date ____________________

Total Exchanges for day:

(1) Milk ______
(2) Vegetable ______
(3) Fruit ______
(4) Bread ______
(5) Meat ______
(6) Fat ______

DAILY FOOD RECORD

Food Item/ Beverage	Amount	Calories/Exchanges	Time of Day

Total Calories for day ________

Date ____________________

Total Exchanges for day:

(1) Milk ______
(2) Vegetable ______
(3) Fruit ______
(4) Bread ______
(5) Meat ______
(6) Fat ______

WEEKLY PROGRESS RECORD

BASIC SKILLS:	SUN	MON	TUES	WED	THURS	FRI	SAT	*
Read Progress Record in morning								
Record food intake								
Stay within calorie/ exchange total								
SPECIFIC TECHNIQUES/EXERCISES:								
Daily Totals								

*This column is for the weekly totals for each specific technique or exercise.

DAILY FOOD RECORD

Food Item/ Beverage	Amount	Calories/Exchanges	Time of Day

Total Calories for day ______

Date ______

Total Exchanges for day:
(1) Milk ______
(2) Vegetable ______
(3) Fruit ______
(4) Bread ______
(5) Meat ______
(6) Fat ______

DAILY FOOD RECORD

Food Item/ Beverage	Amount	Calories/Exchanges	Time of Day

Total Calories for day ________

Date ________________

Total Exchanges for day:

(1) Milk ______
(2) Vegetable ______
(3) Fruit ______
(4) Bread ______
(5) Meat ______
(6) Fat ______

DAILY FOOD RECORD

Food Item/ Beverage	Amount	Calories/Exchanges	Time of Day

Total Calories for day ________

Date ________________

Total Exchanges for day:

(1) Milk ______
(2) Vegetable ______
(3) Fruit ______
(4) Bread ______
(5) Meat ______
(6) Fat ______

Copyright © Northwest Learning Associates, Inc., 1978. All rights reserved.

DAILY FOOD RECORD

Food Item/ Beverage	Amount	Calories/Exchanges	Time of Day

Total Calories for day ________

Date ____________________

Total Exchanges for day:

(1) Milk ______
(2) Vegetable ______
(3) Fruit ______
(4) Bread ______
(5) Meat ______
(6) Fat ______

DAILY FOOD RECORD

Food Item/ Beverage	Amount	Calories/Exchanges	Time of Day

Total Calories for day ________

Date ____________________

Total Exchanges for day:

(1) Milk ______
(2) Vegetable ______
(3) Fruit ______
(4) Bread ______
(5) Meat ______
(6) Fat ______

Copyright © Northwest Learning Associates, Inc., 1978. All rights reserved.

WEEKLY PROGRESS RECORD

BASIC SKILLS:	SUN	MON	TUES	WED	THURS	FRI	SAT	*
Read Progress Record in morning								
Record food intake								
Stay within calorie/ exchange total								
SPECIFIC TECHNIQUES/EXERCISES:								
Daily Totals								

*This column is for the weekly totals for each specific technique or exercise.

DAILY FOOD RECORD

Time of Day	Food Item/ Beverage	Amount	Calories/Exchanges

Total Calories for day ______

Total Exchanges for day:
(1) Milk ______
(2) Vegetable ______
(3) Fruit ______
(4) Bread ______
(5) Meat ______
(6) Fat ______

Date ______

DAILY FOOD RECORD

Food Item/ Beverage	Amount	Calories/Exchanges	Time of Day

Total Calories for day ________

Date ____________________

Total Exchanges for day:

(1) Milk ______
(2) Vegetable ______
(3) Fruit ______
(4) Bread ______
(5) Meat ______
(6) Fat ______

DAILY FOOD RECORD

Food Item/ Beverage	Amount	Calories/Exchanges	Time of Day

Total Calories for day ________

Date ____________________

Total Exchanges for day:

(1) Milk ______
(2) Vegetable ______
(3) Fruit ______
(4) Bread ______
(5) Meat ______
(6) Fat ______

DAILY FOOD RECORD

Food Item/ Beverage	Amount	Calories/Exchanges	Time of Day

Total Calories for day ________

Date ________________

Total Exchanges for day:
(1) Milk ______
(2) Vegetable ______
(3) Fruit ______
(4) Bread ______
(5) Meat ______
(6) Fat ______

DAILY FOOD RECORD

Food Item/ Beverage	Amount	Calories/Exchanges	Time of Day

Copyright © Northwest Learning Associates, Inc., 1978. All rights reserved.

Total Calories for day ________

Date ________________

Total Exchanges for day:
(1) Milk ______
(2) Vegetable ______
(3) Fruit ______
(4) Bread ______
(5) Meat ______
(6) Fat ______

DAILY FOOD RECORD

Food Item/ Beverage	Amount	Calories/Exchanges	Time of Day

Total Calories for day ________

Date ________________

Total Exchanges for day:

(1) Milk ______
(2) Vegetable ______
(3) Fruit ______
(4) Bread ______
(5) Meat ______
(6) Fat ______

DAILY FOOD RECORD

Food Item/ Beverage	Amount	Calories/Exchanges	Time of Day

Total Calories for day ________

Date ________________

Total Exchanges for day:

(1) Milk ______
(2) Vegetable ______
(3) Fruit ______
(4) Bread ______
(5) Meat ______
(6) Fat ______

Copyright © Northwest Learning Associates, Inc., 1978. All rights reserved.

DAILY FOOD RECORD

Food Item/ Beverage	Amount	Calories/Exchanges	Time of Day

Total Calories for day ______

Date ______

Total Exchanges for day:

(1) Milk ______
(2) Vegetable ______
(3) Fruit ______
(4) Bread ______
(5) Meat ______
(6) Fat ______

DAILY FOOD RECORD

Food Item/ Beverage	Amount	Calories/Exchanges	Time of Day

Copyright © Northwest Learning Associates, Inc., 1978. All rights reserved.

Total Calories for day ______

Date ______

Total Exchanges for day:

(1) Milk ______
(2) Vegetable ______
(3) Fruit ______
(4) Bread ______
(5) Meat ______
(6) Fat ______

WEEKLY PROGRESS RECORD

BASIC SKILLS:	SUN	MON	TUES	WED	THURS	FRI	SAT	*
Read Progress Record in morning								
Record food intake								
Stay within calorie/ exchange total								
SPECIFIC TECHNIQUES/EXERCISES:								
Daily Totals								

*This column is for the weekly totals for each specific technique or exercise.

DAILY FOOD RECORD

Food Item/ Beverage	Amount	Calories/Exchanges	Time of Day

Total Calories for day ______

Date ______

Total Exchanges for day:
(1) Milk ______
(2) Vegetable ______
(3) Fruit ______
(4) Bread ______
(5) Meat ______
(6) Fat ______

DAILY FOOD RECORD

Food Item/ Beverage	Amount	Calories/Exchanges	Time of Day

Total Calories for day ______

Date ______

Total Exchanges for day:

(1) Milk ______
(2) Vegetable ______
(3) Fruit ______
(4) Bread ______
(5) Meat ______
(6) Fat ______

DAILY FOOD RECORD

Food Item/ Beverage	Amount	Calories/Exchanges	Time of Day

Total Calories for day ______

Date ______

Total Exchanges for day:

(1) Milk ______
(2) Vegetable ______
(3) Fruit ______
(4) Bread ______
(5) Meat ______
(6) Fat ______

DAILY FOOD RECORD

Food Item/ Beverage	Amount	Calories/Exchanges	Time of Day

Total Calories for day ________

Date ________________

Total Exchanges for day:

(1) Milk ______
(2) Vegetable ______
(3) Fruit ______
(4) Bread ______
(5) Meat ______
(6) Fat ______

DAILY FOOD RECORD

Food Item/ Beverage	Amount	Calories/Exchanges	Time of Day

Total Calories for day ________

Date ________________

Total Exchanges for day:

(1) Milk ______
(2) Vegetable ______
(3) Fruit ______
(4) Bread ______
(5) Meat ______
(6) Fat ______

Copyright © Northwest Learning Associates, Inc., 1978. All rights reserved.

WEEKLY PROGRESS RECORD

BASIC SKILLS:	SUN	MON	TUES	WED	THURS	FRI	SAT	*
Read Progress Record in morning								
Record food intake								
Stay within calorie/ exchange total								
SPECIFIC TECHNIQUES/EXERCISES:								
Daily Totals								

*This column is for the weekly totals for each specific technique or exercise.

DAILY FOOD RECORD

Food Item/ Beverage	Amount	Calories/Exchanges	Time of Day

Total Calories for day ______

Total Exchanges for day:

(1) Milk ____
(2) Vegetable ____
(3) Fruit ____
(4) Bread ____
(5) Meat ____
(6) Fat ____

Date ______

DAILY FOOD RECORD

Food Item/ Beverage	Amount	Calories/Exchanges	Time of Day

Total Calories for day ________

Date ____________________

Total Exchanges for day:
(1) Milk ______
(2) Vegetable ______
(3) Fruit ______
(4) Bread ______
(5) Meat ______
(6) Fat ______

DAILY FOOD RECORD

Food Item/ Beverage	Amount	Calories/Exchanges	Time of Day

Total Calories for day ________

Date ____________________

Total Exchanges for day:
(1) Milk ______
(2) Vegetable ______
(3) Fruit ______
(4) Bread ______
(5) Meat ______
(6) Fat ______

Copyright © Northwest Learning Associates, Inc., 1978. All rights reserved.

DAILY FOOD RECORD

Food Item/ Beverage	Amount	Calories/Exchanges	Time of Day

Total Calories for day ________

Date ____________________

Total Exchanges for day:

(1) Milk ______
(2) Vegetable ______
(3) Fruit ______
(4) Bread ______
(5) Meat ______
(6) Fat ______

DAILY FOOD RECORD

Food Item/ Beverage	Amount	Calories/Exchanges	Time of Day

Total Calories for day ________

Date ____________________

Total Exchanges for day:

(1) Milk ______
(2) Vegetable ______
(3) Fruit ______
(4) Bread ______
(5) Meat ______
(6) Fat ______

Copyright © Northwest Learning Associates, Inc., 1978. All rights reserved.

DAILY FOOD RECORD

Food Item/ Beverage	Amount	Calories/Exchanges	Time of Day

Total Calories for day ______

Date ______

Total Exchanges for day:

(1) Milk ______
(2) Vegetable ______
(3) Fruit ______
(4) Bread ______
(5) Meat ______
(6) Fat ______

DAILY FOOD RECORD

Food Item/ Beverage	Amount	Calories/Exchanges	Time of Day

Total Calories for day ______

Date ______

Total Exchanges for day:

(1) Milk ______
(2) Vegetable ______
(3) Fruit ______
(4) Bread ______
(5) Meat ______
(6) Fat ______

Copyright © Northwest Learning Associates, Inc., 1978. All rights reserved.

DAILY FOOD RECORD

Food Item/ Beverage	Amount	Calories/Exchanges	Time of Day

Total Calories for day ________

Date ______________

Total Exchanges for day:

(1) Milk ______
(2) Vegetable ______
(3) Fruit ______
(4) Bread ______
(5) Meat ______
(6) Fat ______

DAILY FOOD RECORD

Food Item/ Beverage	Amount	Calories/Exchanges	Time of Day

Copyright © Northwest Learning Associates, Inc., 1978. All rights reserved.

Total Calories for day ________

Date ______________

Total Exchanges for day:

(1) Milk ______
(2) Vegetable ______
(3) Fruit ______
(4) Bread ______
(5) Meat ______
(6) Fat ______

Bibliography

Behavior Modification and Weight Control

Jordan, Henry A., Levitz, Leonard S., and Kimbrell, Gordon M. *Eating is Okay!* New York: Signet Books, 1978.

Mahoney, Michael J. and Mahoney, K. *Permanent Weight Control.* New York: W.W. Norton, 1976.

Stuart, Richard B. and Davis, Barbara. *Slim Chance in a Fat World.* Champaign, Illinois: Research Press Co., 1972.

Nutrition

Deutsch, Ronald M. *The Family Guide to Better Food and Better Health.* New York: Bantam Books, 1973.

Mayer, Jean. *Diet for Living.* New York: Pocket Books, 1977.

Bray, George A. *The Obese Patient.* Philadelphia: W.B. Saunders, 1976.

Activity and Exercise

Anderson, Robert A. and Jean E. *Stretching.* Fullerton, CA: Andersons, 1975.

Cooper, Kenneth H. *The New Aerobics.* New York: Bantam Books, 1970.

Cooper, Mildred and Kenneth H. *Aerobics For Women.* New York: M. Evans Publishing Company, 1972.

Royal Canadian Air Force Exercise Plans for Physical Fitness. New York: Pocket Book, 1976.

Calorie and Nutritive Composition of Foods

Adams, Katherine F. *Nutritive Value of American Foods in Common Units.* Agriculture Handbook No. 456. Washington, D.C.: Government Printing Office, 1975.

Adams, Katherine F. and Richardson, M. *Nutritive Value of Foods,* Home and Garden Bulletin No. 72. Washington, D.C.: USDA, 1981.

Brownell, Kelly, with Copeland, Irene. *The Partnership Diet Program.* Rawson, Wade Publishers, 1980.

Carper, Jean and Krause, Patricia A. *The All-In-One Calorie Counter.* New York: Bantam Books, 1974.

Kraus, Barbara. *Calories and Carbohydrates.* New York: Signet Books, 1975.

Kraus, Barbara. *The Dictionary of Sodium, Fats and Cholesterol.* New York: Grosset and Dunlap, 1974.

Marsh, A.C., Klippstein R.N. and Kaplan, S.D. *The Sodium Content of Your Food.* Home and Garden Bulletin No. 233. Washington, D.C.: USDA, 1980.

Parfrey, P.S., et al. "Blood Pressure and Hormonal Changes Following Alteration in Dietary Sodium and Potassium in Mild Essential Hypertension." *Lancet,* 1:59-63, 1981.

Pennington, J.A.T. and Church, H.N. *Bowes and Church's Food Values of Portions Commonly Used.* Philadelphia: J.B. Lippincott Company, 1980.

Skrabal, F., et al. "Effect of Moderate Salt Restriction and High Potassium Intake in Pressor Hormones." *Clinical Science,* 59:157-160, 1980.

Stamler, J., et al. "Prevention and Control of Hypertension by Nutritional-Hygiene Means." *Journal American Medical Association,* 243:1819-1823, 1980.

Watt, Bernice K. and Merrill, Annabel L. *Composition of Foods.* Agriculture Handbook No. 8. Washington, D.C.: Government Printing Office, 1963.

About the Authors

Julie Waltz

Julie Waltz is the former Director of the Food Habit Management Program at University of Washington Hospital's Adult Development Program. As director, she designed and taught classes, and conducted training seminars for dietitians, physicians, nurses and social workers. She currently serves as a consultant to state and private health and educational agencies and has prepared materials for local industry. Julie holds Bachelor's and Master's degrees in Special Education from Wayne State University in Detroit, Michigan. Prior to coming to the Adult Development Program she designed and implemented a variety of specialized educational programs for people with learning problems. Julie now lives in Tucson, Arizona where she continues her work with food habit management.

Luanne Anderson

Luanne Anderson is a Registered Dietitian. She graduated from the University of Washington and completed a dietetic internship at New York Hospital, Cornell Medical Center. She has worked as a hospital therapeutic dietitian; taught basic foods, nutrition, and diet therapy at the University of Washington and served as a nutrition consultant for two visiting nurse services. Presently she is a nutrition consultant for several physicians; Chairperson of the Consulting Nutritionist Practice Group of the American Dietetic Association 1986-1987; and a busy wife and mother of three active children.

Denis Skog

Denis Skog owns and operates the Stillaquamish Athletic Club in Arlington, Washington. His goal is to provide a community facility which offers its citizens a daily opportunity to make fitness a meaningful and enjoyable part of their lives. Prior to construction of his athletic club Denis was the Metro Health and Fitness Director for the greater Seattle YMCA, and was the recipient of the Outstanding Physical Director Award for the Southwest in 1975. He was the Deputy Commissioner for physical fitness for the Pacific YMCA region from 1976-1980.

FOOD HABIT MANAGEMENT

STUDENT EDITION - FOOD HABIT MANAGEMENT

Number of Copies	Quantity Discount	Price (per copy)	Postage & Handling** (per copy)
One Copy	None	$15.95	+ $ 2.50 ea.
2 - 5	5%	$15.15	+ $ 1.75 ea.
6 - 13	15%	$13.55	+ $ 1.25 ea.
14* - 27	20%	$12.75	+ $ .85 ea.
28* - 55	25%	$11.95	+ $ .75 ea.
56* - 111	30%	$11.15	+ $ .65 ea.
112* - 293	35%	$10.35	**Freight: F.O.B. Tucson, AZ** shipping and handling will be prepaid and added to the invoice.
294* - or more	40%	$ 9.55	
***Student books are packaged 14 per case. For best prices order in multiples of 14.**			

INSTRUCTOR EDITION - FOOD HABIT MANAGEMENT

One Copy	None	$ 17.95	+ $ 2.50 ea.
Two or more	10%	$ 16.16	+ $ 1.75 ea.

***IN A HURRY?* Order by telephone! Call 1-(602) 299-8435** for a 24-hour 'record-a-message'. Just leave your name, telephone number, quantity of books and shipping address. We'll ship immediately and send an invoice.

**Unless other arrangements are specified, books will be shipped 4th Class Book Rate. Allow up to four weeks for delivery. Postage rates quoted above are current as of January, 1987. Fluctuations will be invoiced for the difference. First Class or UPS delivery, when specified, will be billed F.O.B. Tucson, Arizona.

BOOK ORDER FORM

NORTHWEST LEARNING ASSOCIATES, INC.
5728 N. Via Umbrosa
Tucson, AZ 85715

Please send the following:

(Quantity) (Price per book) (Total Amount)

______Instructors Edition(s) @ ________ = $________

______Student Edition(s) @ ________ = $________

Sub-total: $________

(AZ residents add applicable sales tax): + $________

Plus Shipping & Handling: ______ x ______ = + $________
(See Chart at left) (# books) (Rate)

TOTAL AMOUNT ENCLOSED*: $________

*(Including shipping and state tax if applicable.)

SHIP TO:

____
(Name) (Please Print)

____
(Street address)

____
(City, state, zip)

SPECIAL SHIPPING INSTRUCTIONS: ____________________

DATE NEEDED: ____________________

BOOK ORDER FORM

NORTHWEST LEARNING ASSOCIATES INC.
5728 N. Via Umbrosa
Tucson, AZ 85715

Please send the following:

(Quantity) (Price per book) (Total Amount)

______Instructors Edition(s) @ ________ = $________

______Student Edition(s) @ ________ = $________

Sub-total: $________

(AZ residents add applicable sales tax): + $________

Plus Shipping & Handling: ______ x ______ = + $________
(See Chart at left) (# books) (Rate)

TOTAL AMOUNT ENCLOSED*: $________

*(Including shipping and state tax if applicable.)

SHIP TO:

____
(Name) (Please Print)

____
(Street address)

____
(City, state, zip)

SPECIAL SHIPPING INSTRUCTIONS: ____________________

DATE NEEDED: ____________________

BOOK ORDER FORM

NORTHWEST LEARNING ASSOCIATES INC.
5728 N. Via Umbrosa
Tucson, AZ 85715

Please send the following:

(Quantity) (Price per book) (Total Amount)

______Instructors Edition(s) @ ________ = $________

______Student Edition(s) @ ________ = $________

Sub-total: $________

(AZ residents add applicable sales tax): + $________

Plus Shipping & Handling: ______ x ______ = + $________
(See Chart at left) (# books) (Rate)

TOTAL AMOUNT ENCLOSED*: $________

*(Including shipping and state tax if applicable.)

SHIP TO:

____
(Name) (Please Print)

____
(Street address)

____
(City, state, zip)

SPECIAL SHIPPING INSTRUCTIONS: ____________________

DATE NEEDED: ____________________